The three crowns

Structures of communal politics in early rabbinic Jewry

The three crowns

Structures of communal politics in early rabbinic Jewry

Stuart A. Cohen

The right of the University of Cambridge to print and sell all manner of books was granted by Henry VIII in 1534. The University has printed and published continuously since 1584.

CAMBRIDGE UNIVERSITY PRESS

Cambridge

New York   Port Chester   Melbourne   Sydney

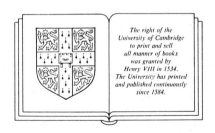

Published by the Press Syndicate of the University of Cambridge
The Pitt Building, Trumpington Street, Cambridge CB2 1RP
40 West 20th Street, New York, NY 10011, USA
10 Stamford Road, Oakleigh, Melbourne 3166, Australia

First published 1990

Printed in Great Britain at the University Press, Cambridge

British Library cataloguing in publication data
Cohen, Stuart A. (Stuart Alan), *1946–*
The three crowns: structures of communal politics in
early rabbinic Jewry.
1. Rabbis. Role, history
I. Title
296.6′1

Library of Congress cataloguing in publication data
Cohen, Stuart.
The three crowns: structures of communal politics in early
rabbinic Jewry / Stuart A. Cohen.
p. cm.
Bibliography
ISBN 0 521 37290 9
1. Judaism – History – Talmudic period, 10–425. 2. Rabbis – Office.
3. Jews – Politics and government. I. Title.
BM177.C64 1989
320.9′015′089924 – dc20 89–31423 CIP

ISBN 0-521-37290-9

WG

For

Amichai, Tzachi, Yonatan and Avner-Pinchas

Isaiah 54:13

CONTENTS

ACKNOWLEDGEMENTS

As will be apparent from references throughout the following pages, this work relies heavily on the learning of others. It does not claim to have uncovered new sources; rather it proposes merely a political re-interpretation of materials rigorously scrutinised for their theological and juridical meanings by several generations of scholars, the vast majority of whom approached the rabbinic corpus as sacred texts whose elucidation is a religious duty of supreme significance. To signify the contribution of their labours is not, of course, to burden them with responsibility for shortcomings which remain mine alone. I wish only to acknowledge the enormous part which they have played in guiding me to and through literature which, since I am not a trained talmudist in either the traditional or modern senses, would otherwise have remained largely inaccessible and impenetrable.

My professional interest in the academic analysis of Jewish political behaviour, past and present, was first aroused over a decade ago by Professor Daniel Elazar. Throughout the intervening period, he has proved a constant source of advice, inspiration and support; above all, he has been a true friend and colleague in every sense of those terms. It is therefore a pleasure as well as a duty to record my thanks both to him personally and to the Jerusalem Center for Public Affairs which, under his direction, has established itself in the very vanguard of this exciting field of intellectual endeavour.

I am similarly grateful to the other scholarly institutions which have honoured me by their association. Primary amongst these is the Department of Political Studies at Bar-Ilan University, Israel, which has been my academic home for many years and whose members have created an atmosphere singularly congenial to the civilised discussion of Jewish political affairs in their various manifestations. At a formative stage of research, it was also my good fortune to enjoy a sabbatical at the Center for Jewish Studies, Harvard University, where Professor Isadore Twersky profoundly influenced my thinking in ways both formal and otherwise. Indeed, it is impossible to quantify how much this work owes to his impeccable courtesy and learned counsel.

Although less directly relevant, equally informative were the small weekly study circles in Bible and Talmud privately conducted in our neighbourhood for several years by my close friends and esteemed colleagues, rabbis Professor Ranon Katzoff and the late Dr Elyakim Ellinson.

Thanks of a different order are also due to the Memorial Foundation for Jewish Culture for generous financial support during the academic year 1983–4, and to Dr Daniel Guttenmacher of Bar-Ilan University, who assisted me at various stages of research. Particularly welcome during the last tricky stages was the expertise of Alex Wright and Iain White, both of Cambridge University Press.

Amongst the several persons who provided me with occasional platforms for the ventilation of some of my ideas on the three crowns, particular thanks are due to: Dr David Patterson, of the Oxford Centre for Post-Graduate Hebrew Studies; to Rabbi Dr Jonathan Sachs, of Jews' College, London; to Professor Ernest Schwarz, Dean of General Studies at Queen's College, New York; to Professor Zvi Gitelman of the University of Michigan; and to Professor Moshe Davis, the Director of the International Center for the University Teaching of Jewish Civilization in Jerusalem.

My greatest debt, however, is to my wife and our family. The idea for this particular book came to me one sultry *shabbat* afternoon, when my sons insisted that I bestir myself and join them in reviewing the weekly portion of the 'Ethics of the Fathers'. For that pleasure, and for many more impossible to specify, I am deeply grateful. This book is dedicated to them with the prayer that they will continue to study – and thereby enrich – all of the great texts and traditions which are our most cherished heritage.

Bar-Ilan University, Israel
Tishrei 5749

A NOTE ON TRANSLITERATION AND TRANSLATION

In transliterating Hebrew words, citations and names (other than those for which a common English equivalent exists), I have adopted the phonetic guidelines suggested by Cambridge University Press as used, for instance, in: *Published Material from the Cambridge Genizah Collections: A Bibliography, 1896–1980* (ed. S.C. Reif; Cambridge, 1989).

Translation presents more daunting problems. As Rabbi Judah was long ago reported to have said: 'He who translates a verse like its form [i.e. literally] – lo, he is a liar; and he who adds [to clarify the context] – lo, he is a blasphemer' (*Tosefta', Megilah* 3:41). In an attempt to minimise both dangers, I have occasionally had recourse to the standard English-language editions of rabbinic works. Where these are not cited, the translations are my own.

ABBREVIATIONS

AJS	*Association for Jewish Studies*
ANRW	*Aufstieg und Niedergang der römischen Welt: Geschichte und Kultur Roms im Spiegel der Neueren Forschung.* Series 1, *Republic* Series 2, *Principate* (eds. H. Temporini & W. Haase; Berlin 1972 etc.).
BASOR	*Bulletin of the American School of Oriental Research*
CCAR	*Central Conference of American Rabbis*
HThR	*Harvard Theological Review*
HUCA	*Hebrew Union College Annual*
IEJ	*Israel Exploration Journal*
JBL	*Journal of Biblical Literature*
JJS	*Journal of Jewish Studies*
JQR	*Jewish Quarterly Review*
JSJ	*Journal for the Study of Judaism*
JTS	*Journal of Theological Studies*
PAAJR	*Proceedings of the American Academy for Jewish Research*
REJ	*Revue des Etudes Juifs*
SBL	*Society of Biblical Literature*
VT	*Vetus Testamentum*
WCJS	*World Congress of Jewish Studies*
ZAW	*Zeitschrift fuer die Alttestamentliche Wissenschaft*

Introduction

Unlike ancient and modern products of the western tradition of political thought, the classic texts of formative Judaism offer no explicitly architectured statements of political philosophy in which a monolithic corpus of constitutional doctrine is systematically extrapolated, step by theoretical step, from fundamental postulates concerning the nature of man and the purposes of human society. Nowhere do the Bible or early rabbinic writings formally summarise the wealth of political concepts which they contain. Characteristically elliptical where such matters are concerned, they seem deliberately to eschew discussions of political theory and to prefer cameo portraits of political behaviour. Jewish political teachings, it is thus suggested, are inherently dynamic in form. If they are not conveniently distilled in a written canon, it is because they can better be inferred from an empirical study of the behavioural dimensions of Jewish public life. Retrospective analyses must perforce accommodate themselves to that style. Specifically, the content of Jewish political traditions can best be identified by an examination of the constitutional structures and arrangements which have periodically regulated relationships within and between the component segments of the polity referred to in the Pentateuch as the 'congregation of the children of Israel' (*'adat benei yisra'el*). Indeed, only through the examination of those arrangements do the ultimate implications of Jewry's early political experience become fully manifest.

The present study is designed as a contribution to that enquiry. Its chronological focus is the first five centuries of the common era, and thus that epoch of formative Judaism which – for want of a better term – is conventionally referred to as the 'early rabbinic' age of Jewish history. Although the designation begs several important questions (how 'early'? or, for that matter, how 'rabbinic'?), for the purposes of political analysis it nevertheless remains serviceable. At the very least, it expresses the transformation in Jewish administrative priorities and perspectives consequent upon the destruction of the second Commonwealth in 70 C.E. and the defeat of the Bar Kokhba' rebellion 65 years later. From a polity centred on Temple and state, Jewry was on the way to becoming a conglomeration of communities unified by their shared fidelity to the rabbinic definitions of law (*halakhah*). Equally seismic was the parallel shift in the identity of the nation's authoritative agents of indigeneous government. Gone (until the coming of the Messiah) were the days when Israel was ruled by kings, priests, or prophets. Instead, if their own testimony is to be believed, by the sixth century C.E. it was the early rabbis and their disciples who had propelled themselves to positions of – in some cases undivided – communal authority throughout the Jewish world.

Central to the thesis presented here is the argument that the eventual hegemony of rabbinic Judaism, as thus portrayed, was not inevitable. Neither was there anything haphazard about the process whereby it occurred. In the political arena, as in others, the rabbis had to struggle for the realisation of their ambitions – often from positions of intrinsic constitutional inferiority. If the enormity of their achievement is to be properly assessed, appropriate note must be taken of the persistence with which they pursued an essentially political campaign. Their avowed purpose was to confound the contrary aspirations of rival contestants, some sacerdotal, others civil, for whatever communal authority native Jewish agencies could still claim to command.

Ensuing chapters will attempt to explore and illustrate the various facets of that enterprise. It must be stressed, however, that they do not purport to reconstruct all aspects of early rabbinic political philosophy. Still less will they claim to compose a conventional history of every branch of Jewish political activity throughout the period spanned by the composition and transcription of tanna'itic and amora'ic literature. Jewry's relations with its gentile neighbours and suzerains, for instance, are discussed only intermittently. Instead, attention is concentrated on the domestic concerns of Jewish society and, even more so, on what the rabbis themselves chose to record about the structure of government within that introspective world. In part, the latter limitation is unavoidable.

As has often been pointed out, early rabbinic writings constitute altogether slippery chronicles of their own times; as sources for the writing of political history, they are especially recalcitrant. For one thing, the available texts bristle with technical difficulties, only some of which can be overcome by form-critical attempts to determine their temporal provenance and root out their anachronisms. For another, they were not designed to be read as straightforward narratives. Composed and edited by men who were jurists and mystics (sometimes both), they comprise internally consistent repositories of belief systems, not sequential statements of fact. Even when they do claim to recount historical events, the materials tend to deploy their data in a way more likely to create rabbinic myths and/or confirm rabbinic dogma than to transmit verifiable and objective information.[1]

Thus to acknowledge that the information contained in early rabbinic literature is typically a-historical is not altogether to deny its historiographical utility. On the contrary, and precisely because of their prejudices, the texts do articulate identifiable perspectives on what rabbinic tradents considered to be the vectorial trajectory of Israel's past. Still more emphatically do they mirror their authors' views on the procedures which had confirmed their own God-given right to play a significant role in Jewry's present government. Even if all are not exact records of events as they occurred (and some might be), their retrospective significance therefore remains almost unimpaired. They incorporate the conceptual images formed in order to explain and interpret how the rabbinic apotheosis was thought to have been attained.

On matters of constitutional relevance, it will here be argued, those images were largely shaped in a mould already set in pre-Destruction times. Specifically, early rabbinic perspectives on the distribution and exercise of Jewish political authority were informed by the notional existence of three ordained clusters of Jewish governmental instrumentalities, each endowed with its own Divine mandate to participate in national rulership. Eventually designated the three *ketarim* (literally translated as 'crowns'), those domains were together understood to comprise an administrative matrix; within the framework laid down by the *ketarim* Jewish polities shared and distributed whatever autonomous powers they were permitted – under God – to command. From a polemical point of view, not the least of early rabbinic accomplishments was to re-interpret that concept in a manner suited to the rabbis' own purposes. In pursuit of their corporate communal purposes, 'the sages' progressively modified what appear to have been the normative premises of the paradigm, transforming it from a model of quasi-federal government into a symbol which projected the notion of unitary rabbinic rule. It was partly by so doing that they generated and monitored a revolution in the structure of Jewish organisational life.

The concept of the three *ketarim* does not stride imposingly from page to page of the available texts. Explicit references are intermittent, surfacing in random snatches of exegesis and homiletics. Far more resonant (and frequent) are its implicit appearances in the structure of early rabbinic discussions on matters of political import, where it insinuates itself through the tri-functional arrangement of what is otherwise an often disjointed accumulation of anecdotes and statutes. It is that category of source which testifies to the resilience of the notion and its employment as a referent over a lengthy period of time. In the term coined by Kadushin, the triple configuration of the *ketarim* in effect constitutes an 'organic' concept, less a systematised philosophy than a coherent – and consistent – mode of classification, itself saturated with elements plucked from the national memory.[2] To put matters another way: as embedded in early rabbinic literature, the notion rests upon a set of collective rabbinic assumptions about the ordained parameters of Jewish political society and its authorised agencies of rule.

Conceived as an extended essay in political anthropology, this book seeks to uncover those assumptions and explore their influences on early rabbinic communal thought and action. To that end, it will employ the theme of the three *ketarim* as an organisational device, with whose help seemingly disparate elements of domestic Jewish behaviour might retrospectively be illuminated and understood. As far as I am aware, no previous work has thus attempted to utilise the concept. In early modern scholarship, the resonance of this particular model of power-sharing in formative Jewish thought was obliquely acknowledged in Bruell's introduction to *Mishnah*, in Tchernowitz's history of early *halakhah* and in Hoenig's study of the second Commonwealth Sanhedrin.[3] More recently, it has been fleetingly noted by Flusser.[4] Otherwise, however, only Sonne seems to have noted the paradigmatic potential inherent in the concept of the three *ketarim* – and even he largely restricted his enquiries to the mysteries of synagogal art during the period of late antiquity.[5] Although explicitly building on those foundations, the present book contends that the concept of the three *ketarim* is amenable to more sustained and synoptic analysis. Reflecting what seems to have been an indigenous view of Israelite society and government, the notion of the *ketarim* and their hierarchy informed and defined the very structure of domestic Jewish political discourse in the early rabbinic world.

NOTES

1. If any scholar is single-handedly responsible for the current elucidation of these difficulties, it is Professor Jacob Neusner, an author whose massive output makes him almost as impossible to read as to overlook. To date, the most trenchant re-statement of his arguments is presented in his *Wrong Ways and Right Ways in the Study of Formative Judaism* (Brown Judaic Studies no. 145; Atlanta, 1988), esp. pp. 36–46 and 75–90. Neusner's analyses of the 'systematic' character of early rabbinic texts are compared with alternative assumptions about their 'fundamental synchronicity' in P. Schaefer, 'Research into Rabbinic Literature: An Attempt to Define the Status Quaestionis', *JJS*, 37 (1986), esp. pp. 140–2, 149–52.
2. First posited in *Organic Thinking* (New York, 1938), the thesis was expanded in M. Kadushin, *The Rabbinic Mind* (first edition 1952, 3rd edtn., New York, 1972). A summary is contained on p. 70 of the latter work:

   > First, Rabbinic thought as a whole does possess coherence, an organismic [sic], conceptual coherence which can be traced and demonstrated. Second, that because of this kind of conceptual coherence each statement is an integrated, independent entity. The independent character of the [...] statement is not an indication that rabbinic thought is chaotic or haphazard. On the contrary, it is the result of a conceptual organisation far more subtle than is to be found in any 'system', one that is inherent in value-concepts and in them alive.

   Similar influences, albeit in an entirely different context, are discerned in G. Duby, *The Three Orders: Feudal Society Imagined* (trans. A. Goldhammer; Chicago, 1980), esp. p. 63.
3. J. Bruell, *Mavo 'ha-Mishnah*, vol. 1 (Frankfurt-am-Main, 1876), pp. 1–2; Ḥ. Tchernowitz (Rav-Ṣair), *Toledot ha-Halakhah*, vol. 2 (New York, 1945) – where separate sections are devoted to: *'amud ha-melukhah* ('the pillar of kingship', pp. 11–55); *'amud ha-kehunah* ('the pillar of priesthood', pp. 56–82); and *'amud ha-nevu'ah* ('the pillar of prophecy', pp. 83–107); and S. B. Hoenig, 'The Tripartite System of Government', *The Great Sanhedrin* (Phila., 1953), pp. 165–8.
4. D. Flusser, 'Hishtaqfutan Shel 'Emunot Meshiḥiyot Yehudiyot ba-Naṣrut ha-Qedumah', *Meshiḥiyut we-'Esqatologiah* (ed. Z. Baras; Jerusalem, 1984), pp. 119–20.

5. I. Sonne, 'The Paintings of the Dura Synagogue', *HUCA*, 20 (1947), pp. 255–362 and (less convincingly) 'The Zodiac Theme in Ancient Synagogues and in Hebrew Printed Books', *Studies in Bibliography and Booklore*, 1 (1953), pp. 3–13. I am indebted to Mrs S. Weingarten for calling both articles to my attention.

1

The concept of the three *ketarim*

While the full span of political teachings contained in Biblical and early rabbinic literature still awaits comprehensive analysis, the bases of Judaism's earliest constitutional heritage are sufficiently clear to permit a preliminary synoptic review. Three notions – all formulated in the Old Testament and all enlarged upon to one degree or another in subsequent Jewish writings – are identifiably prominent amongst ancient Israel's formative political traditions.[1] The first, thus placed in recognition of both its axiomatic status and its enduring influence, is the principle of theocratic government; the second, the ideal of covenantal partnership between independent units of the polity; the third, the normative distribution of human rulership amongst specifically accredited jurisdictional domains. Admittedly, formative Jewish texts do not deploy these three great themes in sequential progression. Still less do they severely compartmentalise their respective inferences and implications. Rather, each is portrayed as a necessary complement to the others, with which it interacts. Nevertheless, for the purposes of analysis, the following paragraphs will differentiate between theocracy, covenant and power-diffusion, and discuss them separately. Their aim is not to compress a survey of Biblical and early rabbinic political thought into the space of a few pages, but to direct attention to those earlier traditions which arguably exerted the greatest manifest influence on the rabbinic concept of three *ketarim*.

Theocracy, covenant and power-sharing

The theocratic principle implies that Jewish government is, in every sense of the term, government by God. Even in its most basic renditions, there is more to this teaching than the notion that the Creator of the world – by virtue of the omnipotence illustrated in Psalm 97 – exercises proprietary rights over what is indubitably His domain. As the Decalogue's very first commandment makes explicit, God is considered to be actively and continuously involved in the direct governance of His people; indeed, having taken the Children of Israel out of Egypt, He is recognised to be an intrinsic segment of that government. He persistently assumes and fulfils the roles of law-giver, judge, administrator, warrior and – ultimately – Redeemer.

Early rabbinic literature articulated the principle of theocracy in the term *malkhut shamayim* (lit. 'the kingdom of heaven'), a phrase which – although not explicitly found in the Old Testament – aptly conveys the Biblical notion that the appropriate yardstick for the measurement of all human endeavours (public and private) is God's purpose, not man's desires.[2] From this it follows that neither the polity nor its human institutions are regarded as ends in themselves. They exist solely as means to a Divine purpose. Whatever their precise form, regimes are regarded as little more than instruments, useful only for fostering and maintaining the good society and for facilitating mankind's attainment of the highest possible moral goals. Human rulers of such entities, even if they do appropriate God's own title of *melekh* [lit. 'king'], are denied anything other than mortal status.[3]

One consequence of that position is articulated in Deuteronomy 17:14–20. From the moment of their accession, that text prescribes, Israel's native kings must affirm the contingent nature of their constitutional status; they, too, are subject to God's laws and judged by the standards of His will. A second consequence is implicit in the narrative portions of Scripture, several of which comprise an extended commentary on the degenerative tendencies to which, they suggest, human agents of monarchic government are inherently prone. Gideon's refusal to arrogate to himself a position of hereditary rulership (Judges 8:22–3), together with Samuel's initial resistance to the popular demand for the establishment of a monarchy (I Sam. 8:11–19), thus articulate what might be designated the normative Biblical viewpoint. As the next chapter will argue, early rabbinic commentators on matters of constitutional import considered it to have been confirmed by later developments. Even the emergence of the Davidic kingship, they taught, represented a regrettable – albeit Divinely sanctioned – regression from the scriptural ideal of God's unique rule.

Nevertheless, theocracy was never considered equivalent to a blatant Divine dictatorship. On the contrary, the very notion that it might thus be portrayed was explicitly refuted by the second of ancient Israel's great political themes – that relationships between God and mankind, and especially between God and Israel, are founded on their having come together in covenant (*berit*).[4] Although necessarily compacts between unequal entities, covenants nevertheless preserve the respective integrities of the parties and provide bases for their co-operation in order to attain mutually agreed ends. Such was the *berit* between God and mankind – as represented by Noah – after the flood (Genesis 9:8–17); such was the *berit* between God and Abraham (then Abram; Genesis, chap. 17); and such – most relevant of all – was the *berit* between God and the entire house of Israel at Sinai (Exodus, chaps. 19 and 20). In each case, according to the Biblical account and its subsequent rabbinic reconstructions, God limited Himself drastically by recognising the freedom of humans to contract obligations with Him and to maintain their own integrity whilst doing so, not simply to obey Him but to hearken to His words as covenantal partners.

Of the several political implications of this crucial concept perhaps the most significant is that which is most straightforward. Through the process of covenant, God recognises humans to be His partners in the perfection of His own creation. This is a breathtakingly radical notion, whose clear thrust is the declaration that all sovereignty – whatever its expression – must normatively be based upon the principle of reciprocity between rulers and ruled. Even when initiating (perhaps even imposing) His covenants with Israel, God acknowledges as much. Indeed, He transcends His own covenantal stipulations when undertaking to implement them with *ḥesed* ('covenant love'), the relationship between parties whose actions express their mutual feelings and are not merely prescribed by the formal terms of their agreement.[5] Human sovereigns, whose scope for unilateral action is in any case more confined, must necessarily follow that example. This theme resonates throughout the string of post-Sinaitic covenantal reaffirmations recounted in the Old Testament, and especially those concluded under the human aegis of Joshua, David, Josiah and Ezra. Each reiterates the consensual foundation of Israelite political association; similarly, each stresses that the partnerships thus created (and to which God is Himself witness, guarantor and sometimes partner) are based upon an agreed recognition of the mutually binding force of the *berit*-as-constitution. It is from covenants, as periodically renewed and mediated, that contracting parties derive their respective mandates for legitimate political action.

Modern critics have occasionally been tempted to extend the consensual thrust of the Bible's covenant conception in a representative direction. Indeed, some have hypothesised its translation into a doctrine of public responsibility, thus invoking Scriptural sanction for an almost avowedly democratic structure of government. Arguably, individual passages can be said to substantiate the thesis that the Israelite polity is – to use classical terminology – a *res publica*, owned in common by all the on-going parties to the original covenant by which it was first called into being.[6] But since most of the Biblical texts have little to say on Israelite government at its grass roots, suppositions of a general nature must be deemed speculative. Invariably, the Old Testament restricts its horizons to the apex of the governmental pyramid, portraying relationships within and amongst ruling elites rather than between the governors and the masses of the governed.

At the hierarchical level of analysis, however, the literary evidence – although less populist in tone – is perhaps even more striking in implication. What emerges from the texts as a constitutional corollary of the covenantal principle is not democracy throughout the political system, but a distinct notion of power-sharing at its highest levels. Neither Scripture nor early rabbinic writings express any sympathy whatsoever for a system of government in which a single body or group possesses a monopoly of political authority. Instead they mandate that the concentration of its prerogatives and privileges is – in principle – to be avoided and denigrated. Only the diffusion of power among various legitimate, sometimes legitimated, franchises can prevent its arbitrary exercise and thus preserve the covenantal spirit with which all Jewish political behaviour should be infused. Untrammelled freedom of action, consequently, is occasionally and implicitly refused to God (whence the appeals to jurisprudential principles to which He too must submit in Genesis 18:25 and Numbers 16:22); it is permanently and explicitly denied to man. Even Moses, notwithstanding his extraordinary status in Jewish history – and especially in Jewish constitutional history – was subject to those restraints. That is why, according to later rabbinic legend preserved in Exodus *Rabbah* 2:7, he was denied the preponderance of political authority which he had at one stage craved. His immediate successor was bound by restrictions which were still more formal and precise. 'Joshua had need of Elazar [the priest] and Elazar of Joshua', is the fourth-century *Sifrei* comment on the mode of induction narrated in Numbers 27:15–23.[7] Their joint presence at that particular ceremony of power transference enunciated Israel's commitment to the principle of power-sharing at an embryonic stage of the nation's constitutional progession.

If the record preserved in Scriptural and rabbinic historiography is to be believed, subsequent Jewish constitutional doctrines had re-affirmed that axiom. Accordingly, examples of deviation from the norm could be stringently castigated. Particularly was this so whenever the most powerful rulers of either the first or second Commonwealths were thought to have violated constitutional propriety by attempting simultaneously to function as both priests and kings. Whether the specific point of departure was sacerdotal or secular was immaterial: at issue was the preservation of the principle of power-diffusion and the prevention of unauthorised intrusions into a sphere of public activity constitutionally considered out of bounds to any but an ordained circle. To take just one example of each case: II Chronicles 26:16–21 is altogether explicit in attributing king Uzziah's attack of leprosy to his insistence on performing a sacerdotal function properly reserved to the priesthood (see also the discussion on the constitutional consequences of that royal sin in Babylonian Talmud [hereafter TB; tractate] *Horayot* [folios] 10a and 12b); talmudic chroniclers were equally forthcoming in their explanations for the string of tragedies which sullied their memories of the royal experiment initiated by the Hasmoneans during the second Commonwealth. R. Ḥiyya' bar ['Ab]Ba' (*'amora'*; 3rd–4th centuries) must certainly have regarded members of that dynasty, all of whom were genetic priests, as monarchical interlopers. The juxtaposition of Deuteronomy 17:20 and 18:1, he argued, constituted a standing prohibition against anointing any priest as king.[8]

The paradigm of three domains

It would not be difficult to adduce further examples of Scriptural and early rabbinic admonitions pertaining to constitutional power-sharing in Jewish public life. The exercise would undoubtedly be instructive, since each case possesses intrinsic contextual interest. But for present purposes such repetition would probably be superfluous. Unless subjected to further analysis, a mere catalogue of literary comments on the desiderata of Jewish governmental arrangements would add little to a proper understanding of the ordinances whereby such teachings were sustained and nothing at all to an identification of the procedures whereby they were put into effect. If those facets of the subject are to be clarified, attention ought to be directed elsewhere. Specifically, an examination must be made of the forms and structures of the separation of powers which early versions of the Jewish political tradition seem most consistently to have favoured and to which (as far as the evidence allows) they might most faithfully have adhered.

The history of western political ideas suggests several arrangements which might be adopted as appropriate referents in the search for early Jewish structures of power-sharing. Of the most familiar, one is the doctrine of two governmental 'swords' which, although only fully developed in medieval Christendom by Gelasius, Aquinas and John of Salisbury, traces its roots to Jesus' reported injunction: 'Render therefore unto Caesar the things which are Caesar's; and unto God the things which are God's' (Matthew 22:21). Another is the theory of the 'separation of powers', first mooted in several of the seminal works of Greek political science, which was eventually (and most famously) transmuted by Montesquieu into the division of government into the three 'branches' labelled the legislature, the executive and the judiciary.[9]

The attested antiquity of both formulas certainly denies the possibility that the principle of constitutional power-sharing was an early rabbinic invention. However, the evidence to hand also precludes the hypothesis that, singly or jointly, they might retrospectively be accommodated within the mainstream of political traditions which the early rabbis inherited and embellished. Occasional passages of the Old Testament do, superficially, lend themselves to one or another of such non-rabbinic paradigms. Premonitions of the Gelasian binary, for example, might be identified in Jehoshafat's designation of the agents of his reforms (II Chron. 19:11) and in

Zechariah's vision of two Messiahs (Zech. 4:12–14). Montesquieu's triptych, similarly, could possibly be strait-jacketed into Isaiah 33:22 ('For the Lord is our judge; the Lord is our law-giver; the Lord is our king; He will save us.'). But for present purposes all such texts must be considered red herrings. Neither complements the fundamental thrust of Biblical and early rabbinic attitudes towards government and its exercise; if anything, each is basically alien to classic Jewish purposes and designs.

The medieval Christian division into the two 'swords' of government, for instance, is most blatantly contradicted by the unitarian concept of the polity which is characteristic of all early Jewish political thought. Neither the Old Testament nor early rabbinic writings abide the binary demarcation between Church and State to which the Gelasian paradigm must logically lend itself and to which, indeed, it has ultimately led in the western world. The framework of three 'branches', as eventually formulated by Montesquieu, is similarly at odds with early expositions of Jewish political teachings, albeit for different reasons. Methodologically, it would have been deemed to place the cart before the horse. Essentially focussing on definitions of the major functions of government – which agency is to be responsible for which actions – Montesquieu (and, in this respect, Polybius before him) portrayed a separation of powers to be a virtually mechanistic guarantee of constitutional freedom. As such, 'balance' became an end in itself. In one summary of his thesis:

> Liberty does not flourish because men have natural rights or because they revolt if their rulers push them too far; it flourishes because power is so distributed and so organised that whoever is tempted to abuse it finds legal restraints in his way.[10]

Early Jewish teachings on the science of politics, however, suggested a different order of priorities. For them, *how* instruments of government ought to exercise power was a secondary consideration; *whence* such instruments derive the authority to do so was a subject of prior importance. To put matters another way, Biblical and rabbinic political thought tends to examine the precise *source* of constitutional authority before analysing possibly appropriate *functions* of available constitutional institutions.[11] For that reason, it also addresses itself to an entire range of questions which Montesquieu, in particular, would doubtless have considered antecedent to his own concerns: what is the nature of Israel's Divinely-inspired framework of national partnership? which agencies are normatively authorised to instrumentalise that relationship and thus retain its sanctity? whence do they derive the discretionary powers of exegesis and jurisdiction which might enable them to do so?

Early rabbinic answers to these questions both reflected and enhanced the covenantal traditions of Judaism's Biblical heritage. When identifying the just system of government, sources dating from the tanna'itic and amora'ic periods posit a framework which is both federal in arrangement and consensual in tone. More precisely, they depict the distribution of political power amongst three distinct clusters of governmental authority: the domain of the *torah*; that of the *kehunah* (priesthood); and that of the *malkhut* (kingship). Each of these spheres possess a unique public franchise, with exclusive prerogatives enunciated in various sets of Biblical pronouncements. As thus ordained, the domain of the *torah* constitutes the vehicle whereby God's teachings to Israel are interpreted, specified and transmitted; the *kehunah*, the conduit whereby God and His people are brought into constant contact and close proximity; the *malkhut*, the legitimately empowered means whereby civic relationships are structured and regulated in accordance with the requirements of Mosaic law. While each of these Divinely-mandated combinations does possess its own area of activity, their basic demarcations are thus of focus rather than of function. Their distinctions lie less in the needs they serve than in the perspectives which they bring to bear on Jewish political activity. In its own way, every one of the domains possesses its own range of interests, an attribute which is reflected in their generic behaviour as separate mediating devices between the Children of Israel and their God. Each thus acts as a particular prism on the constitution of the Jewish polity. Accordingly, each possesses a mandate to exercise a check on the others.

Text and context

To judge from the literary evidence now available, the tripartite division of Jewish political authority here described was most comprehensively articulated some time during the two centuries which immediately followed the Destruction of the second Temple in 70 C.E. Only in rabbinic texts attributed to that period is the framework explicitly portrayed as an axiomatic characteristic of Jewish public life. Most obviously (and, for that matter, most succinctly) is this so in *Mishnah, 'Avot* 4:13, where R. [Rabbi] Simeon (Shim'on bar Yoḥ'ai; *tana'*, mid-second century C.E.) is reported to have declared:

> There are three crowns [*ketarim*]: the crown of *torah*, the crown of *kehunah*, and the crown of *malkhut*; but the crown of a good name excels them all.[12]

The attribution of the epigram is significant; so too is the timing of its appearance. Together with his teacher R. 'Aqiva', R. Simeon bar Yoḥ'ai emerges from the talmudic texts as one of the most politically sensitive sages of his generation. Soon after the failure of Bar Kokhba's abortive revolt in 135 C.E., we are informed (TB *Shabbat* 33b), the Roman authorities convicted Simeon for his incautious criticisms of their regime and its achievements; *in absentia* he was condemned to death. For twelve years thereafter he lived the life of a fugitive. But, if subsequent rabbinic traditions are to be believed, not even that enforced isolation from communal life dulled either Simeon's interest in political affairs or what appears to have been his almost congenital itch for political activity. On his emergence from the underground, we are told, he participated in at least two of the most pivotal events of his time: the convocation of a *sanhedrin* at 'Usha' (Songs *Rabbah* 2:5) and the intercalation of the month in the valley of Rimmon (TJ *Ḥagigah* 3:1); he was also short-listed for the deputation to Rome which requested abolition of the administrative injunctions against Jewish observances (TB *Me'ilah* 17a–b). It was these activities, in addition to his reputed scholastic skills and reported mystical attainments, which ensured Simeon's lasting prominence in both talmudic traditions and medieval legend.

As is evident from many of the statements which early rabbinic literature attributes to Simeon, he ought not to be numbered amongst Jewry's political revolutionaries. Much though he insisted on the need to reform national behaviour and thus repent for the sins which had brought about the destruction of the Temple and the imposition of Roman rule, he did not transpose his feelings into doctrines which demanded the complete overhaul of every aspect of Jewish thought and action. On the contrary, precisely because he was so conscious of the political uncertainties produced by the contemporary liquefaction of his society and its focal institutions, he is reported to have advocated a policy of national retrenchment – sacerdotal, scholastic and territorial. *Ipsissima verba* or not, the thrust of his recorded teachings is manifest: notwithstanding the destruction of the Temple, Israel was not to abandon the memory of its cultic heritage; neither, despite Bar Kokhba's abject failure to withstand the might of Rome, was the nation to modify the traditional character of its messianic aspirations.[13] Recent calamities, in other words, invited a rigorous measure of spiritual stock-taking not a complete re-structuring of the historically sanctified touchstones of Jewish life, public or private. In both spheres, re-appraisals were therefore to be essentially conservative in style. Earlier modes were not to be totally abandoned; rather, they were to be more comprehensively articulated, and thereby preserved for future enhancement.

Simeon's depiction of the *torah*, the *kehunah* and the *malkhut* as three domains was of a piece with that outlook. The only feature of the statement to bear the stamp of originality is its use of the term *keter* as a generic emblem of Jewish authority. On the evidence provided by the Old Testament canon, ancient Israel had attached relatively minor importance to the crown as a symbol of rulership, and Biblical Hebrew had reserved no single term to connote that artefact. *Keter* appears only in the book of Esther (1:11; 2:17; 6:8), where – in gentile surroundings – 'the crown of kingship' adorns just two women and one horse.[14] The Hasmoneans, probably influenced by hellenistic practice, had admittedly endowed some form of royal headdress with greater prominence,[15] a development which underscores the intended irony in the Roman soldiers' emplacement of 'a *stephanos* of thorns' on the head of Jesus (Matthew 27:19; Mark 5:17; John 19:2,5). Nevertheless, it demanded a manifest exercise of literary licence for R. Simeon bar Yoḥ'ai to transfer that mark of rank to the *torah* and the *kehunah* and thus confer on those domains the same presence and identities commonly observed in civil forms of rulership. No less remarkable was his use of the term *keter* in order to convey his meaning.

But that linguistic peculiarity apart, the statement reported in *'Avot* makes no claims to inventiveness. Specifically, it does not purport to contain political allusions which might in any way be described as novel. If anything, the epigram explicitly assumes that the demarcation into the three separate franchises of government which it names had, by tanna'itic times at the very latest, been incorporated into conventional constitutional parlance. Only by assuming extensive familiarity with that framework could the author hope to make the point that the accepted categories of popular status should be considered inferior to the virtue of good behaviour. Had the statement adumbrated an entirely original political formulary, it would probably have lost much of the intended impact. Its effectiveness largely depended on the graphic invocation of a trinary structure of authority already deeply embedded in the Jewish political consciousness. It is therefore appropriate that *'Avot de Rabi Natan*, whose two versions contain our earliest (probably tanna'itic) 'Talmud' on Simeon bar Yoḥ'ai's epigram, refrains from comment on 'the crown of a good name' altogether.[16]

The evidence suggests that the concept of the three *ketarim* – albeit without its attendant terminological apparatus – was indeed rooted in Israel's earlier traditions, practical as well as literary. Biblical references to such a division, although characteristically oblique, are quite recognisable. One precedent for the tripartite structure so pithily summarised by Simeon bar Yoḥ'ai was long ago discerned in the outline of governmental provisions sketched in Deuteronomy chapters 17 and 18.[17] There, after a general prologue (17:8–13), separate paragraphs are allotted to the rights and duties of public officials designated the *melekh* ('king'; 17:14–20), the *kohanim* and *lewi'im* ('priests and levites'; 18:1–8), and the *navi'* ('prophet'; 18:9–22). Far more obtrusive is the evidence provided by narrative disquisitions located in books of the Old Testament which purport to describe political realia at a later stage of the Israelite chronicle. When studied synoptically, several of the relevant accounts clearly underscore the existence of resonant linkages between the ideal of power-sharing and its practical implementation through a triad of governmental instrumentalities. Particularly relevant, in this context, is the Biblical record of recurrent tensions between individual kings, priests and prophets. Their adversarial relationships, the texts suggest, cannot be attributed solely to the personal ambitions of the *dramatis personae* immediately involved. At a deeper level such struggles also reflected the constitutional positions adopted by legitimate embodiments of Israel's three ordained franchises, each in rightful possession of its own sphere of independent jurisdiction.[18]

Precisely how the Biblical notion of tripartite government might have been adapted to the convulsive ambience of Jewish political life during the second Commonwealth cannot easily be ascertained. In this sphere, as in so many others, the surviving evidence appertaining to much of the inter-testamental period of Jewish history is far too sparse to permit viable consecutive summaries of contemporary political theory and practice. What can be conjectured with reasonable confidence, however, is that the notion of a tripartite division of government does seem to have persisted. Notwithstanding occasional modifications, the motif remained common coinage, recurring in diverse literary genres of the pre-Destruction period. Scattered references to a triad of prerogatives and authorised agencies can be distilled from Philo (*Legum Allegoria* 3:79–83; where Melchizedek is portrayed as 'the great combination' of king, priest and logos); the Testament of Levi (8:11–16: 'Levi, thy seed shall be divided into three offices ...'); and Josephus (*The Jewish War* [hereafter BJ] 1:68 cf. *Antiquities of the Jews* [AJ] 13:299–300: John Hyrcanus combined 'three of the highest privileges: supreme command of the nation, the high priesthood and the gift of prophecy'). As Flusser has shown, elements of the same structure also permeate Christian depictions of the powers inherited by Jesus.[19]

Early rabbinic comments on the diffusion of political authority seem explicitly to have built on those foundations. *Mishnah* and Scripture did certainly possess significantly different perspectives on matters appertaining to government;[20] but the distinctions were of emphasis rather than structural. The concept of the three *ketarim*, too, was an evolutionary phenomenon; the early rabbinic contribution was to refine an intellectual theme which already lay to hand. Delving back into Jewish history for earlier manifestations of the tripartite structure of *torah*, *malkhut* and *kehunah*, *tana'im* and *'amora'im* defined the rights and prerogatives of each franchise and its respective instruments with greater cogency than any of their known literary predecessors. By utilising their many analytical skills, they also explored the ramified constitutional implications of the tripartite form as a unified entity. In so doing, they imposed upon the particular notion of power-sharing the stamp of their own communal purposes and designs. In their writings, the concept of the three *ketarim* was transposed into a political slogan supplying a standard by which they could evaluate the authenticity of all Jewish regimes.

Operation and implications

When thus deploying the ketaric framework as a mental presentation of Jewish political structures, early rabbinic authorities were to emphasise two of its dominant features. One was the normative autonomy of each of the triad's constituent domains; the other the interdependence of the tripartite system as a whole. The first finds expression in those texts which emphasise the intrinsic sovereignty of each *keter* (a concept itself neatly conveyed by their common adornment with the generic artefact of the 'crown'). They depict each as wielding – under God – independent authority within its own sphere of independent jurisdiction. Briefly summarised (see also chapter 2, below), this is the theme underlying early rabbinic reconstructions of the ordained differences in the internal structures of each domain. From their inception, each is reputed to have possessed its own network of officers; each, furthermore, instituted its own procedures in order to determine the manner of their appointment and succession. Moreover, the demarcations thus regulated were said to have been further hallowed by the imposition of a ternary division on the most important aspects of Jewish public life. The priceless privilege of sacerdotal office is reserved exclusively to genetic members of the *keter kehunah* and none but the High Priest (*kohen gadol*), the principal instrument of that domain, may enter the innermost precincts of Israel's sacred shrine. Similarly, only the chief officer of the *keter malkhut* is entitled to enjoy the powers which Scripture bestows on the nation's civil leaders. Finally, human interpretations of God's ordinances are not valid unless and until they are sanctioned by 'sages' (*ḥakhamim*), who described themselves as the accredited embodiments of the *keter torah*. No *keter*, is the clear implication, possesses a constitutional right to impinge upon the domain of the others, far less to deprive them of their ordained constitutional franchises.

Interdependence – the second characteristic of the arrangement – is no less marked a feature of the framework here outlined. Indeed, the necessity for co-operation amongst the domains constituted a logical corollary of their co-ordinate status as equivalent agencies of God's will. Hence the intimation that no Jewish polity is constitutionally complete unless it contains representatives of all three *ketarim* in one form or another. *Torah*, *kehunah* and *malkhut* are, indeed, the governmental extensions of the three pillars of *torah*, temple service (*'avodah*) and correct civil behaviour (*gemilut ḥasadim*) upon which 'the world' had long been said to rest;[21] remove any one and the entire social edifice is bound to collapse. They are not, therefore, portrayed as severely compartmentalised spheres of jurisdiction, with one (or more) being responsible for matters civil and the other (or others) for matters ecclesiastical. On the contrary, what characterises the system in its entirety – indeed, what transposes it into a system – is the insistence that they must be seen jointly to participate in the most crucial areas of Jewish public affairs: judicial as well as legislative, military as well as sacerdotal. That is why authorised officers of the three *ketarim* must come together in order to give constitutional effect to all acts of political significance.

The Bible can be understood to have made that point when portraying the combined presence of priest, prophet and king at ceremonies of crucial public importance (the installation of a new monarch, as in the first chapter of I Kings; or the initiation of constitutional reforms, II Kings 22:3–20). Early rabbinic texts add other instances. *Mishnah, Shevu'ot* 2:2 ordains that no extensions can be made to the city limits of Jerusalem, or to the boundaries of the Temple, unless sanctioned by the senior representatives of all three domains. In its exegesis on Numbers 27:21, TB *Sanhedrin* 16a mandates a similarly composed forum for the ratification of a decision to embark on an 'optional' war (*milkhemet reshut*; cf., however, TJ *Sanhedrin* 2:5). Elsewhere, the same sources record the presence of the high priest (and, at least on one famous occasion, *ḥakhamim* too; *Mishnah, Soṭah* 7:8) when Israel's monarch ceremoniously re-confirmed the national commitment to the *torah*-as-constitution on the septenniel *yom ha-qahal* ('day of the assembly'). The proper Jewish polity, is the implication of all such texts, contains fully articulated and functioning institutions in all three *ketarim*.[22] The good Jewish polity is that in which, furthermore, the balance between the constituents of the triad is both buttressed and respected.

From theory to practice

As the rabbis were fully aware, in practice Jewish history had rarely obliged by conforming to such neat categorisation. Looking back over the chronicles of Israel's past, they could identify only brief moments of what by their own gauge could be described as perfect constitutional equilibrium. Predominantly, they knew, the Jewish experience of self-government had been characterised by constitutional turbulence; over long stretches of time its major concern had been the attempt (usually forlorn) to resolve tensions continuously breaking out between accredited representatives of the three *ketarim*.

Admittedly, the struggles which punctuate Jewish constitutional history during the Biblical and post-Biblical periods had never been taken to extremes; invariably, the weapons employed were those of usurpation rather than destruction. Not even the royal despots who stalk the pages of early rabbinic demonologies (Jeroboam, Ahab and Menasseh; *Mishnah*, *Sanhedrin* 10:2) were accused of advocating the disenfranchisement of the *torah* and the *kehunah*, or of attempting their utter elimination. What could be discerned, however, were numerous instances of a process of co-option. Principal instruments of the *keter malkhut* had often attempted – sometimes, and for limited periods, successfully so – to attain commanding national authority by posing as the repositories of two domains. Overstepping the bounds of their own prescribed franchise, they were reported to have arrogated to themselves prerogatives which belonged to a second branch of the triad. By thus wearing, as it were, two crowns, they had contrived to assert the pre-eminence of the monarchical facet of Jewish constitutional interpretation and to eclipse that of any other. Such was the policy of royal aggrandisement apparently typified by Jeroboam's appointment of priests who were devoid of the necessary genetic criteria;[23] such – more recently and more blatantly, according to the rabbinic account – was the constitutional anomaly created when the Hasmoneans added monarchical titles to the priestly distinctions which were their birthright. In subsequently playing fast and loose with the traditional rules governing appointments to the high priesthood,[24] Herod had merely illustrated the extent to which *kohanim* had already been relegated to an honorific constitutional status. In all but name, they had long been servants of the royal crown.

From the constitutional perspective, the significance of all such episodes lay as much in the responses to which they gave rise as in the circumstances from which they evolved. On occasion, members of the caste whom R. Simeon bar Yoḥ'ai designated the *keter kehunah* had apparently managed to re-assert their rightful autonomy by skilfully exploiting fissures in the cohesiveness of royal authority. According to the Biblical account, at least two such opportunities arose in the southern kingdom of Judah. Jehoida the priest had led popular opposition to the bloody rule of queen Athalia; Hilkiah, the first individual to whom the Bible explicitly appends the title of *kohen gadol* (cf., e.g., II Kings 22:4–8 and 23:4 with the anonymous use of that terminological adornment in Numbers 35:25, Joshua 20:6 and even II Kings 12:11) had played an equally crucial role during the halcyon days of Josiah's far-reaching reforms. Josephus indicates that matters took a similar course half a millennium later. On the very eve of the destruction of the second Commonwealth, he reports, priests had been prominent members of the rebel groupings who sought to restore Jewish administration to its pristine form.[25]

Rabbinic tradents expressed far more interest in the reaction of the *keter torah* to all attested infringements of the tripartite alignment. Placed in a position of dangerous isolation by the putative institutional amalgamation of the *malkhut* and the *kehunah*, instruments of the *torah* (they reported) had necessarily sought to redress the balance by reminding the nation that the separation of powers was a Divine command. During the monarchical periods described in the Bible, that principle was most effectively stressed by such prophets as Elijah, Elisha, Amos, Isaiah, Hosea and Micah. All had posed as the guardians of Israel's constitutional heritage, not least by their constant critiques of the behaviour of the nation's kings and priests and by their atavistic invocation of the standards originally set in the *torat mosheh* (Mosaic law; see, e.g., Malachi 3:22 and the confrontation recorded in Amos 7:10–12). During the second Commonwealth, precisely the same stand was said to have been taken against the Hasmonean kingship by the Pharisaic sages who, so early rabbinic traditions were to claim (see below, chapter 3), had by then inherited the constitutional mantle of the prophets. According to the relevant talmudic text (TB *Qidushin* 66a), it was Alexander Yannai's combination of the two crowns of royalty and priesthood which aroused their ire, quite as much as his rude infringements of the niceties of sacerdotal protocol or the allegedly murky circumstances of his mother's past. Whatever the veracity of the verbal exchange which ensued between the parties, the use of the term *keter* in its literary reconstruction can hardly have been arbitrary. Carrying an unmistakable whiff of the manifesto, that source seems designed as much to repeat constitutional dogma as to describe a specific event. 'Suffice yourself with the *keter malkhut*', the *ḥakhamim* are reported to have exhorted their ruler in a classic exposition of the power-sharing thesis, 'and leave the *keter kehunah* to the descendants of Aaron.'[26]

Much though they thus championed the maintenance of an ordained equilibrium between the three *ketarim* in theory, the rabbis of the tanna'itic and amora'ic ages did not hesitate to infringe that balance when they considered it in their own corporate interest to do so. It is the thesis of this book that between the first and fifth centuries of the common era they deliberately predicated the inherent superiority of the *keter torah* to both of the other franchises. Committing themselves to a campaign of communal conquest, they sought to implement strategies of constitutional displacement broadly similar to those which they otherwise so strenuously denigrated. Israel, they taught, had to come to institutional terms with the diminution in the powers of civil administration which had once sustained the agencies of the *keter malkhut* as well as the destruction of the Temple which had provided a cultic focus for the *keter kehunah*. Neither of those national disasters (for such they were admitted to be) could be repaired by clinging with gritty determination to modes of rulership which, at least temporarily, had so obviously been overtaken by the march of Divinely-ordained events. Their damage could only be contained by a recognition of the need to fashion new patterns of constitutional articulation in tandem with the exploration of new forms of religious expression.

It was with those ends in view that early rabbinic Judaism generated a reinterpretation of the traditional model of tripartite administration. Proponents of the primacy of rabbinic perspectives on every aspect of Jewish expression used the model in order to justify their own claims to communal hegemony. What they advocated was a re-arrangement of the triad in such a way that it might be portrayed as a triangle, with the domain of the *torah* situated at its apex. They thus sought to give expression to their belief in the normative majesty and constitutional supremacy of their own society of scholarship. The *keter torah*, they declared, was not to be regarded as a co-equal branch of the Jewish polity, but its base and circumference.

One method of asserting that position was to point out that the number of 'virtues' (*ma'alot*) required in order to attain the *torah* (48 according to *'Avot* 6:5) was greater than those needed in order to attain either the *malkhut* or the *kehunah* (30 and 24 respectively). More far-reaching, however, was the proposition that – as a consequence of that hierarchy – proficiency in the *torah* constitutes the path to the attainment of whatever authority the *malkhut* and *kehunah* themselves possessed. *'Avot de Rabi Natan* (Version 'B', chap. 48) recalled that Aaron and David had merited their individual *ketarim* 'by virtue of the *torah*'. *Tanḥuma', Tisa'* (28: see also TB *Giṭin* 62a) goes even further, transposing the example thus set into a general norm ('Whoever occupies himself with the *torah* becomes king and head [*melekh we-r'osh*]'.) Most forceful of all, however, is the extended commentary recorded in *Sifrei* on Numbers (*pisqa'* [section] 119 [ed. Horovitz], p. 144), which explicitly contrasts the relative merits of the three *ketarim* and regulates their standing within Jewish society:

We have found it to be said: there are three *ketarim* – *keter torah*, *keter kehunah* and *keter malkhut*. Aaron merited the *keter kehunah* and took it; David merited the *keter malkhut* and took it; but behold the *keter torah* is not apportioned. This is in order not to give people an excuse to say: 'Were the *keter kehunah* and *keter malkhut* still available, I would have merited them and taken them.' Behold the *keter torah*, it is an admonition to everybody. For anyone who merits it is considered by God as though he had merited all three. Conversely, anyone who does not merit it, is considered by God as though all three *ketarim* were available and he had forfeited them all. And should you say: 'Which is the greater?' R. Simeon b. Elazar used to say: 'Who is the greater, he who appoints the ruler, or he who rules [*ha-mamlikh o' ha-molekh*]? Obviously the former [...] The entire force of the other two *ketarim* derives solely from the strength of the *keter torah*; as Scripture says: 'By me kings reign [...] by me princes rule' [Proverbs 8:15–16].

In several respects, it will be here argued, much of Jewry's domestic history during the period of late antiquity can be read as an attempt to establish the veracity of that claim and to implement its premises.

NOTES

1. Some of the ideas developed here have been sketched in D. J. Elazar & S. A. Cohen, *The Jewish Polity: Jewish Political Organisation from Biblical Times to the Present* (Bloomington, Indiana, 1985).
2. E.g., ''Abba' Saul said: ''Israel is the suite of the King [God] whence it is incumbent upon them to imitate the King''' *Sifra'* to Leviticus 19:2 and Babylonian Talmud (hereafter TB) [tractate] *Shabbat* [folio] 133b. In general, S. Schechter, *Some Aspects of Rabbinic Theology* (N.Y., 1923) pp. 65–101; and E. E. Urbach, *The Sages: Their Concepts and Beliefs* (translated by I. Abrahams; Jerusalem, 1979), pp. 80–96, 400–19. The Old Testament bases of the theocratic principle are collated in *'Enṣiqlopedia' Miqra'it*, vol. 4 (Jerusalem, 1962), clmns. 1118–28, and analysed with greater panache in M. Buber, *The Kingship of God* (N.Y., 1967).
3. A. R. Johnson, *Sacral Kingship in Ancient Israel* (2nd. ed., Cardiff, 1967) itemises and analyses the scholarly debate.
4. For analyses of this seminal concept in its widest Jewish setting, see D. J. Elazar, 'Covenant as the Basis of the Jewish Political Tradition',

Kinship and Consent: The Jewish Political Tradition and its Contemporary Uses (ed. Elazar; Ramat Gan, 1981), pp. 21–56. Rabbinic materials are discussed in G. Freeman, *The Heavenly Kingdom: Aspects of Political Thought in the Talmud and Midrash* (London, 1986), esp. pp. 43–128; on the Biblical origins: D. J. McCarthy, *Treaty and Covenant* (rev. ed., Rome, 1977).

5. Elazar, 'Covenant', p. 27; cf. K. D. Sakenfeld, *The Meaning of Hesed in the Hebrew Bible* (Harvard Semitic Monographs, 17; Missoula, 1978). Whether or not the Sinaitic covenant could have been foisted upon an unwilling and virgin Israel is discussed in *Mekhilta' de R. Yishma'el*, the tanna'itic Midrash on Exodus probably compiled in the fourth century C. E., tractate *Ba-Ḥodesh* (ed. J. Z. Lauterbach; Phila. 1933, II, pp. 219ff) and in TB *'Avodah Zarah* 2b and *Shabbat* 88a (see also the appended medieval comments, generically known as *tosafot*, s.v. *kafah*). These sources are analysed in Y. Blidstein, '"Kafah 'Aleihem Har ka-Gigit": Midrash u-Metaḥim', *Bar-Ilan Workshop in the Covenant Idea*, working paper no. 28 (1988).
6. Notably, R. Gordis, 'Democratic Origins in Ancient Israel – The Biblical Edah', *Alexander Marx Jubilee Volume* (ed. S. Lieberman; N.Y., 1950), pp. 369–88; and R. de Vaux, 'Le sens de l'expression "peuple du pays" dans l'Ancien testament et le rôle politique du peuple en Israël', *Revue d'Assyriologie*, 58 (1964), pp. 167–72.

   Rabbinic intimations of similar themes can be discerned in midrashic reconstructions of the exchanges which are said to have preceded the appointment of Bezalel (Exodus 35:30) in TB *Berakhot* 55a, and of the elders (Numbers, 11:16) in *Sifrei* Numbers [*piska'*] 92 [ed. Horovitz], p. 93).
7. *Sifrei* Numbers 141 (p. 186). See also TB *Sanhedrin* 105b and Numbers *Rabbah* 12:9. Compare Thomas Hobbes, *Leviathan*, pt. III, chap. 40.

   The fullest analysis of the rabbinic materials which discuss Moses' extraordinary range of powers remains R. Bloch, 'Quelques aspects de la figure de Moïse dans la tradition rabbinique', *Cahiers Sioniens*, 8 (1954), pp. 211–85.
8. Jerusalem Talmud (hereafter TJ) *Soṭah* [chapter] 8: [*halakhah*] 3 and parallels, especially as cited in the medieval commentary to Genesis 49:10 by Moses b. Naḥam (*Ramban*: 1194–1270). The political context of this passage (together with the teaching attributed to R. Yosie in TB *'Avodah Zarah* 8b) has recently been analysed in D. R. Schwartz, 'Lishe'eilat Hitnagdut ha-Perushim la-Malkhut ha-Ḥashmona'im', *'Umah we-Toldotehah*, Vol. 1 (ed. M. Stern; Jerusalem, 1983), pp. 45–7.

   For rabbinic comments on Uzziah's actions see: TB *Soṭah* 9b and sources cited in L. Ginzberg, *Legends of the Jews*, Vol. 3 (Phila. 1942), p. 303.
9. Of the numerous discussions of these themes, particularly helpful are:

C.H. McIlwain, *Constitutionalism: Ancient and Modern* (N.Y., 1947); F.D. Wormuth, *The Origins of Modern Constitutionalism* (N.Y., 1949); K. von Fritz, *The Theory of the Mixed Constitution in Antiquity* (N.Y., 1954); M.J.C. Vile, *Constitutionalism and the Separation of Powers* (Oxford, 1967); and H.A. Myers, *Medieval Kingship* (Chicago, 1982).

10. J. Plamenatz, *Man and Society*, Vol. 1 (London, 1963), p. 194.

11. Hence:

    The division of powers, in its technical details at any rate, is a legal not a political theory. It does not provide an answer to the question who should be the holder of sovereignty, but only to the question of how power should be organised in order to achieve certain aims, whoever is the ultimate holder of sovereignty.

    A.P. D'Entreves, *The Notion of the State* (Oxford, 1967), p. 121. See also F.W. Walbank, *Polybius* (Berkeley, Cali., 1972), pp. 135, 149–56 and my 'The Concept of the Three *Ketarim*: Its Place in Jewish Constitutional Thought and its Implications for a Study of Jewish Constitutional History', *AJS review*, 9 (1984), pp. 33–5.

12. For an exhaustive list of parallels and derivatives see M.M. Kasher, *Torah Shelemah*, Vol. 20 (Jerusalem, 1961), pp. 27 (no. 105*), 29 (no. 110) and 46–49 (nos. 160–8).

    Of the several variations, one of the most interesting (attributed to R. Yoḥanan [3rd century *tana'*] in TB *Yoma'* 72b) designates precisely the same clusters as *zeirin* ('wreaths'; a play on Exodus 25:11; 25:24 and 30:3). Significantly, however, in his remarks on the passage, the most prominent of all medieval commentators (*Rashi*; R. Solomon ben Isaac; 1040–1105) reverts to the term *ketarim*.

13. M. Beer illustrates these teachings in 'Har ha-Bayit u-Veit ha-Miqdash be-Mishnato Shel Rashbi'i', *Peraqim be-Toledot Yerushalayim Bimei Bayit Sheini* (ed. A. Oppenheimer, et al.; Jerusalem, 1981), pp. 361–85. Sayings attributed to R. Simeon bar Yoḥ'ai are collated, and thematically arranged, in Y. Kanowitz, *R. Shim'on bar Yoḥ'ai. 'Osef Shalem Shel Devaraw u-Ma'amaraw ba-Sifrut ha-Talmudit we-ha-Midrashit* (Jerusalem, 1965).

    On the possible ambivalence in Simeon bar Yoḥ'ai's attitude towards Roman rule see the sources cited in L.I. Levine, 'R. Simeon b. Yoḥai and the Purification of Tiberias: History and Tradition', *HUCA*, 49 (1978), pp. 180–1 fn. 152.

14. The OT contains seven other 'crown' synonyms, of which by far the most common (22 occurrences) is *'aṭarah*. Nevertheless, and as the terminological multiplicity itself underscores, the crown was a comparatively minor symbol of royal distinction and certainly inferior, for instance, to the throne [*kisei'*]. See, T. Ishida, *The Royal Dynasties in Ancient Israel* (N.Y., 1977), pp. 104–6.

15. Although, one suspects, not nearly as much as is suggested by E.E. Goodenough, 'Victory and Her Crown', *Jewish Symbols in the Greco-Roman Period* (Vol. 7; N.Y., 1958), pp. 135–71. Nevertheless, note must

be taken of the significance which Josephus attaches to the emplacement of the *diadema* in, e.g., *The Jewish War* [BJ] 1:70; 2:57 and *Antiquities of the Jews* [AJ] 18:237; 20:244. Compare the absence of a royal headdress amongst the insignia of office granted to Alexander Balas at a crucial stage in Seleucid-Jewish relationships in 145 B.C.E. (I Maccs. 10:89, 14:44). See the seminal discussion in L. Loew, 'Kranz und Krone', *Gesamelte Schriften*, Vol. 3 (Szegedin, 1893), esp. pp. 430–35.

16. Compare *'Avot de Rabi Natan* [ARN] version 'A', chap. 41 and version 'B', chap. 48; ed. Schechter, pp. 130–1 and J. Goldin, *The Fathers According to Rabbi Nathan* (New Haven, CT, 1955), p. 169. For the view that this commentary is not subsequent to and built around *Mishnah 'Avot*, but that both texts developed within a common tradition 'to reach different and parallel forms', see A. J. Saldarini, *Scholastic Rabbinism: A Literary Study of the Fathers According to Rabi Nathan* (Chico, Cali., 1982).
17. Moses Alshekh of Safed (16th cent.), commences his commentary to Deut. 18:1 with the statement: 'Here are the three *ketarim* ...', *Torat Mosheh*, parag. 6.
18. A detailed review of the Biblical materials is attempted in my article: 'Kings, Priests and Prophets: Patterns of Constitutional Discourse and of Constitutional Conflict in Ancient Israel', *The Quest for Utopia* (ed. Z. Gitelman; Michigan University Press; forthcoming).
19. D. Flusser, 'Hishtaqfutan Shel'Emunot Meshiḥiyot Yehudiyot ba-Naṣrut ha-Qedumah', *Meshiḥiyut we-'Esqatologiah* (ed. Z. Baras; Jerusalem, 1984), pp. 119–20.
20. As is argued by J. Neusner, 'Scriptural, Essenic and Mishnaic approaches to civil law and government; some comparative remarks', *HThR*, 73 (1980), pp. 419–34.
21. *'Avot* 1:1; a text whose subsequent interpretation is traced in J. Goldin, 'The Three Pillars of Simon the Righteous', *PAAJR*, 27 (1958), pp. 43–58 and N. Goldstein, *Meḥqarim be-Hagutam Shel Ḥazal 'Al ha-'Avodah be-Veit ha-Miqdash we-Hashpa'atam 'Al 'Iṣuvah* (unpub. Ph.D. thesis; The Hebrew University, Jerusalem, 1977), pp. 144–7.
22. Possible anomalies, therefore, could not be ignored. One possible example is provided by *Tosefta*'s ruling (*Sanhedrin* 2:15) that neither a high priest nor a king is permitted to participate in the determination of a leap year. TB *Sanhedrin* 18b resorts to manifestly forced explanations in order to explain this prohibition.
23. I Kings 12:31. Nevertheless, as the rabbis were prepared to concede, that incident merely highlighted a process in progress. Solomon's own blunt deposition of Abiathar (I Kings 2:26) was also a cause of embarrassment (TB *Soṭah* 48b), not least because it had already indicated the direction in which the wind was likely to blow. A possible apotheosis is described in II Kings 16:15–17; see comments in TB *Sanhedrin* 103b.

24. Rabbinic recollections are discussed below, chap. 2; Josephus' summary in AJ 20:247–51.
25. The sources are collated and analysed in M. Stern, 'Ha-Manhigut Bi-qvuṣot Loḥamei ha-Ḥerut be-Sof Yemei Bayit Sheini', reprinted in *Ha-Mered ha-Gadol: Ha-Sibot we-ha-Nesibot li-Periṣato* (ed. A. Kasher; Jerusalem, 1983), pp. 299–308. It has been calculated that priests comprised at least half of the persons appointed to administrative office by the popular assembly in the Temple court after the outbreak of the revolt. C. Roth, 'The Constitution of the Jewish Republic of 66–70', *Jewish Social Studies*, 9 (1964), p. 300.
26. Earlier analyses of the text and context of the confrontation which it describes (dated either to the reigns of Hyrcanus I or Alexander Yannai) are superseded by Y. Efron, 'Shim'on ben Sheṭaḥ we-Yann'ai ha-Melekh', *Ḥiqerei ha-Tequfah ha-Ḥashmona'it* (Tel Aviv, 1980), pp. 131–94.

    The linguistic antiquity of the passage was noted (albeit without specific reference to the use of *keter*) by M. H. Segal, *A Grammar of Mishnaic Hebrew* (Oxford, 1927), p. 27.

SECTION A

Versions of the past: visions of the future

2

Institutions and their instruments

As described in early rabbinic literature, the three *ketarim* constitute abiding features of organised Jewish society. In part, this is because they are consistently called upon to service needs considered indispensable to the preservation of Israel's unique identity. More essentially, however, their permanence is the consequence of the extraordinary manner of their inception. In the rabbinic reconstruction, each of the three domains had been called into individual being at God's express command; none was represented as an evolutionary response to human interests or concerns. Governmental authority within Israel had been expressly delegated complete and from on high, thus assigning for ever more the powers and privileges to be possessed by organs of national adjudication, administration and legislation.

Most obviously was this so in the case of the *torah*, the most beloved of all God's creations and hence the very first in their order of appearance. The *torah* had not merely witnessed the events described in the first chapters of Genesis; it had been the architectural plan in accordance with which the cosmos was designed and history unfolded. (The Almighty, in the words of one account, had 'looked into the *torah* and created the world').[1] Thus, it reflected the very essence of all that was sublime, providing man's only key to an understanding of the Divine purpose. Alone among all the nations of the world, Israel had appreciated the value of that gift and at Sinai had covenanted to cherish and obey the *torah*. Ever since, its status as the very basis of all national behaviour had been immutable; its authority was absolute. Commanded 'to a thousand generations', the *torah* – in keeping with God's original covenants with the Patriarchs – was to be remembered 'for ever' (*le-'olam*; I Chron. 16:15; cf. Deut. 7:9).

Neither the *kehunah* nor the *malkhut* could possibly match such credentials. Nevertheless, those franchises too had always been intrinsic components of Israel's government and would enduringly remain so. Again, as much was guaranteed by the exceptional circumstances of their instrumentalisation. Like the *torah*, both the *kehunah* and *malkhut* traced their authority to a set of unique compacts between God and His selected partners. Their foundation, too, had been the starting-point of a historical development, not its outgrowth. The everlasting deposition of the *keter kehunah* had been formalised by the Almighty's covenant with Phineas, the grandson of Aaron; similarly, it had been a parallel covenant with David which had ensured his dynasty's perpetual possession of the *keter malkhut*. Irrespective of occasional human weaknesses, the charters thus granted would never be revoked. Although individual priests and kings would be punished for their own failures to live up to the standards required by their respective franchises, the Aaronide clergy and the Davidic monarchy – as corporate entities – would remain abiding agencies of the two *ketarim* to which they alone were entitled. According to *'Avot de Rabi Natan*, Scripture had itself made that promise. Therein lies the significance of the verses which version 'B' selects in order to authenticate the origins and emergence of the two domains. Numbers 25:13, in the case of the *kehunah*, and Ezekiel 37:24–5, in that of the *malkhut*, were chosen because both contain the key word *'olam*.[2]

Since the competence and composition of the three *ketarim* had thus been pre-ordained at the moment of their inception, human and political action could have played no part in the subsequent determination of their respective prerogatives and obligations. In that sense, the entire system of which they formed a part had been abstracted from the conventional historical process. Nevertheless, the three *ketarim*, individually and collectively, did possess a recorded past which had extended beyond their inception and the story repaid careful analysis. The virtual rabbinic fixation on the origins of these domains of government did not induce the suspension of all intellectual enquiry into their later – and especially Biblical – development over time. What it generated, rather, was a modification in historiographical perspectives and a bias in historical priorities. Israel's past attained a didactic role. It contained models of regimes both ideal and flawed, and hence standards by which the accomplishments and ambitions of contemporary society could be assessed. Moreover, if rightly understood, events and situations in earlier periods (however cursory and ill-preserved their records) could be applied to supposedly analogous ones in the present. Consequently, while it is true that some items of information appertaining to the received chronologies of the three *ketarim* were indeed ignored or consigned to oblivion, others were selected as subjects of detailed scrutiny and, where necessary, of inventive elaboration.[3]

Within the former category came broadly defined sociological influences on the relative standings of the three *ketarim* within the Jewish polity as a whole. The early rabbinic version of the 'mixed constitution' (unlike, for instance, its Aristotelian counterpart) was nowhere made contingent upon a particular social setting. Its proponents, although undoubtedly aware of the linkages between politics and economics, did not therefore posit a correlation between any of the three *ketarim* and defined strata in Jewish society. If anything, they denied the very possibility that the transient motion of class alignments could ever have determined the discharge of the public duties which Revelation had originally ordained. Ideal government, they stressed, was an exercise in preservation not accommodation; and what had to be preserved, notwithstanding the ebb and flow of societal pressures, was the structure of the regime dictated by God's express command. Perhaps that is why the model here surveyed seems so detached from other interpretations, rabbinic and non-rabbinic, of the social iniquities and civil strife which were known to have accompanied the nemesis of the second Commonwealth. The lines of enquiry are parallel rather than convergent.[4]

The institutional articulation of the three *ketarim* was, however, an entirely different matter. This was an area of the national past upon which early rabbinic analysts of the triadic model did lavish considerable attention – indeed, on which they had to do so if they were to explain and illustrate the durability of the power-sharing arrangement which they described. In none of the three franchises, they stressed, had the founding covenants of the matrix been allowed to atrophy. Instead, throughout every generation of Israel's recorded history its fibre had been toughened by the maintenance of appropriate bureaucratic frameworks, each of which was recognised to embody the values of the *keter* which it served. Institutionalisation, then, had transposed administrative abstractions into vibrant organisms. Institutions, moreover, had joined Israel and God in a partnership which fleshed out the structure of the *ketarim* and operationalised their combined commitment to its on-going impact on their mutual relationship. It followed that the competence of the infrastructure was reflected in the health of its separate systemic components; their resilience testified to its capacity for unending survival.

The *keter kehunah*

Institutional resilience could most convincingly be demonstrated in the case of the *keter kehunah*, the domain which God had Himself charged with responsibility for the maintenance of His unique ritual association with Israel. According to early rabbinic sources, perpetuity was in fact embedded in each of the rituals and devices which articulated that relationship. From its very foundation, they teach, the *keter kehunah* had operated through a sacred synthesis of cult, shrine and clergy. Almost without interruption, the same holy triad had ever since made manifest the promise of Divine salvation to which its own existence largely contributed.

Unlike Josephus, whose *Antiquities* incorporates several chronologies of both the priesthood and its ministrations in Biblical and post-Biblical times, early rabbinic texts do not reconstruct a consecutive history of the *keter kehunah*. Where the cult itself was concerned, they could perceive no reason to do so. Quite simply, no item in the service had ever been altered. Each of the elaborate ceremonies whose every particular *Mishnah* describes in precise detail (sometimes on the basis of testimony submitted by *tana'im* who had themselves witnessed their performance)[5] is said to have conformed unremittingly to Sinaitic regulations. The entire network of cultic offerings and ministrations – public and private, daily and festive, voluntary and obligatory – is traced to explicit Biblical ordinances; so, too, are the attendant stipulations for their precise timing and cyclic sequence. Cultic practice during the second Commonwealth had thus replicated that instigated during the first. Throughout both periods, Israel had achieved atonement by means of the High Priest's annual re-enactment of the rites prescribed in Leviticus chapter 16. Day in day out, Israel's association with its God had been affirmed through the *tamid* (lit. 'the perpetual'; i.e. the burnt-offering of a lamb made every morning and every afternoon on behalf of the entire people) stipulated in Numbers chapters 28 and 29. Such had been the importance attributed to consistency in this last rite that its occasional interruption (*biṭul ha-tamid*) was understood to have been a sure omen of impending calamity (TB *Soṭah* 49b). Even during the last Roman siege of Jerusalem, it had not been discontinued until almost the very last (*Mishnah, Ta'anit* 4:6).

Equally impressive had been the continuity maintained in the site of cultic activity. According to rabbinic legend, the establishment of the Temple (*beit ha-miqdash*) in Jerusalem had been part of God's very first design; until realised, the entire universe had been deficient and its existence provisional. Solomon, therefore, had not in fact built the shrine with which his name is associated; his contribution had been to orchestrate the descent to earth of a structure already extant in heaven, where it had been prepared prior to Creation. Once *in situ* at the very navel of the world, it was inconceivable that the Temple might have any other home.[6] Jerusalem was now the acknowledged centrepiece of religious life – the only permissible locality of sacrificial worship (*Mishnah, Zevaḥim* 14:8) and the place to which every Jew (other than the categories exempted in *Ḥagigah* 1:1) was expected to strive to make three annual pilgrimages.[7]

Thereafter, the Temple had also provided physical evidence of God's protective residence in Israel's midst. Popular recognition of that quality had brought about the failure of Jeroboam's sinful attempt to erect a murderous 'iron curtain' between his own citizenry and the national shrine when emplacing two golden calves at Dan and Bethel (I Kings 12: 25–33; see also *Tosefta', Ta'anit* 4:7, TB *Sanhedrin* 101b; even his son had publicly disobeyed the prohibition on pilgrimage to Jerusalem; TB *Mo'ed Qaṭan* 28b). It also accounted for the fact that – after the tragedy of the first Destruction – the reconstruction of the sanctuary had played so prominent a role in Ezekiel's vision of a renewed Jewish polity (Ezek. chaps. 40–8). Ultimately, permission to rebuild God's house in Jerusalem had constituted the most crucial clause in the historic proclamation with which Cyrus inaugurated the period of the Return to Zion and the second Commonwealth (cf. II Chron. 36:23 and Ezra 1:2–4).

As recalled by rabbinic memories, the Divine gift thus miraculously regained was not thereafter lightly relinquished. Whatever its other failings, second commonwealth Jewry had certainly not treated its reconstructed shrine with the disdain which might otherwise have been generated by the initial shabbiness of its outward appearance. The alternative sanctuary established in Egypt by Onias was always considered intrinsically inferior (*Mishnah, Menaḥot* 13:10 and TB ibid. 109b) – even, apparently, by its own votaries.[8] Although it no longer housed the original ark of the covenant,[9] the *miqdash* in Jerusalem was the only one truly worthy of its designation. The building and its inner recesses had continued to be endowed with the very highest grades of sanctity (*Mishnah, Kelim* 1:6–9). Consequently, *Mishnah* recalls, it had been to that shrine that the faithful had flocked (especially during the early hours of the Day of Atonement; *Yoma'* 1:8); that the first-fruits had been brought (*Bikurim* 3:1–9); that the half-*sheqel* taxes had been paid (*Sheqalim* 2:1); and that prospective proselytes had come in order to offer their required sacrifices (*Keritut* 2:1). In time, it was also in the direction of that Temple that Jews prayed from afar (*Berakhot* 4:5 and TB ibid. 30a), and – even prior to the Destruction – in accordance with its ritual that they arranged the liturgy of their local synagogues.[10]

The precision with which rabbinic texts record the voluntary gifts made to the second Temple complements their portrait of its popular affection and esteem. Jews in both Judea and the Diaspora, they recount, had contributed regularly, and substantially, to the upkeep of the shrine and the preservation of the cult. Their donations had throughout filled the thirteen trumpet-shaped coffers (*shofarot*) strategically placed at various points in the Temple courtyards (*Mishnah, Sheqalim* 4:1–2,6; 5:4), and their gifts had enabled the Temple treasury to support various charitable enterprises (Ibid. 5:6). Some signs of devotion were remembered to have been more ostentatious – and less anonymous. Certain individuals, often specified, had bought immortality by the provision of lavish artefacts for the decoration of the Temple (*Mishnah, Yoma'* 3:10 and *Midot* 3:8). Entire families had reportedly undertaken to donate wood for the altar's fire on specific dates each year (*Mishnah, Ta'anit* 4:5 and TB idem. 28a).

To record such manifestations of piety was not to indulge in name dropping. It was to point out, rather, that anyone who had contributed to the beautification of the Temple and the preservation of its service deserved a share of its reflected renown. So much was this so, that even persons otherwise castigated were treated with retrospective rabbinic respect. Mindful of the later failings of the Hasmonean progeny, talmudic tradents may (perhaps) have shuffled their feet in embarrassment when recounting the deeds of martial valour to which the family owed its original prominence. Nevertheless, the same sources did preserve those traditions which recorded how the first Maccabees had purified the shrine and restored the cult previously interrupted by Seleucid decree.[11] Even Herod, so often the butt of early rabbinic acrimony and disdain, could not be denied his due. After all, and whatever his precise motives, it had been thanks to his initiative and energy that the Temple had become an object of aesthetic wonder as well as religous awe (TB *Bava' Batra'* 3b–4a).

But the principal contributors to the resilience of the *keter kehunah* had been the priests themselves. They had been the only persons authorised to officiate in the Temple, enter its innermost precincts and bless the congregation. Their other public functions, such as adjudicating, teaching or healing, were in early rabbinic *halakhah* (as in the Bible) considered subordinate to their sacerdotal activities. Normatively, priesthood was a full-time occupation whose practitioners were entitled to suitable reimbursement for the labours imposed by the ritual station to which they had been called. The Bible itself grants priests a unique right to partake of certain classes of produce (whilst also denying the entire tribe of Levi a share in the territorial allotments to be apportioned in the land of Canaan). Early rabbinic *halakhah* is even more generous. *Tosefta', Ḥalah* 2:7–9 calculates there to have been no less than 24 exclusively priestly tithes and emoluments during the second Temple period – some of them transferred from levites to priests as recently as the time of Ezra.[12]

Participation in priestly duties (together, for the most part, with the enjoyment of the concomitant privileges) was absolutely dependent upon patrimony and restricted entirely to male descendants of Aaron. In fact, the boundaries of the domain were irrevocably laid down by natural descent. No person biologically entitled to membership of the *kehunah* could ever be excluded. Conversely, no person who lacked the necessary qualification of legitimate genealogy could ever be admitted. Both postulates, although plain enough from the Biblical texts, receive enhanced attention in early rabbinic teachings. The first was emphasised in the ruling that high priests, even when defrocked because they had been remiss in their duties, retained the indelible dignity and sanctity which was their birthright (TJ *Sanhedrin* 2:1 and *Horayot* 3:1). The second was more graphically illustrated by commentaries on the Scriptural references to the rebellion of Korach. As Beer has shown, several aggadic elaborations on the episode described in Numbers 16 deliberately shift its dramatic emphasis. Korach, they relate, had not only challenged the national leadership of Moses (in some reconstructions, this aspect of the Biblical tale is in fact altogether underplayed); more germane to his purposes had been his indictments against the propriety of the high priesthood of Aaron.[13] The cataclysmic failure of his enterprise thus constituted a standing warning against its repetition. Whatever the shortcomings of individual instruments of the *keter kehunah* (and, as the episode of the Golden Calf showed, surely none had been more delinquent than Aaron himself), they could never be deposed and replaced.

Any system of public administration which permits a particular caste to monopolise a defined sphere of communal activity, especially one so central to national well-being as the cult, necessarily runs the risk of fragmentation. In the specific case of the *keter kehunah*, the danger was particularly acute. The priesthood might have developed into a secluded coterie. That such had never been the case could in part be attributed to the Biblical stipulations which had themselves underscored the public responsibilities attendant upon sacerdotal office.[14] No less instrumental, however, had been the division of the *keter kehunah* as a whole into 24 contingents (*mishmarot* and *ma'amadot*; lit. 'circuits') which followed a weekly rota of Temple service.

Said to have originally been established by Moses and expanded by Samuel and David (*Tosefta', Ta'anit* 4:2), the system of *mishmarot* and *ma'amadot* may originally have been designed to ensure an equitable distribution of the ecclesiastical work-load. Its true significance, however, lay elsewhere. All Levites and Israelites, it was noted, had been likewise allotted to one circuit or another, rotating such subsidiary – but essential – duties as the preparation of the sacrifices and the provision of musical accompaniment to the ritual. *Mishmarot* and *ma'amadot*, thus constituted, had provided the organisational frameworks within which the entire community had been able to participate in the cult. (Without the attendance of non-priests, asked *Mishnah*, how could public sacrifices ever be truly public? *Ta'anit* 4:2.) They had also made manifest Israel's nation-wide commitment to the fulfilment of those responsibilities with which the *keter kehunah* was most closely associated. During their week of service, *Mishnah* relates, even lay affiliates of the serving *mishmar* were subjected to stringent rules of behaviour (idem., 2:7; 4:2–3); and members of the *ma'amad* unable to come to Jerusalem were expected to pray for the welfare of persons considered in particular danger. In effect, the arrangement had been a vital attribute of organic existence; without the *ma'amadot*, runs one saying, heaven and earth could themselves not have survived (TB *Ta'anit* 27b).

Although not a completely self-contained entity, the priesthood nevertheless remained an almost entirely self-regulating body. Indeed, its most outstanding institutional characteristic was its ancient and rigid hierarchy. Biblical sources (e.g. II Kings 23:4; 25:18) themselves provide some indication of the pyramidal structure of the order, suggesting that a regimented bureaucracy had always been one of the *kehunah*'s principal features. In this case too, however, rabbinic portraits were still more explicit. *Mishnah, Sheqalim* chapter five and the second chapter of the same *Tosefta'* tractate, for instance, depict a framework staffed by ascending grades of Temple functionaries and sacerdotal specialists. Each is said to have possessed a rank whose responsibilities were carefully designated; some are remembered to have been entrusted with duties whose technical secrets were jealously guarded (even from other priests; TJ *Sheqalim* 5:2). Altogether, we are informed, differentials within the *keter kehunah* were not limited to the broadest categories of the High Priest and his 'ordinary' colleagues (*hedyoṭot*). They also pervaded the very highest echelons of the domain, all of which were uniformly subject to rules of seniority predicated upon the sanctity of a particular office and prescribing precedence in the performance of clerical duties (*Mishnah, Horayot* 3:6). Thus, careful distinctions were preserved between the High Priest proper (*meshamesh*) and such finely shaded grades as the High Priest prospective (*segan*); the High Priest emeritus (*she'avar*) and the High Priest in locus (*merubeh begadim*).[15]

As all such indications testify, the High Priest himself stood at the undisputed apex of the sacerdotal structure. Known throughout rabbinic literature as the *kohen gadol*, the incumbent of that office was endowed with a status denied even to other members of his own caste. In a general sense, he alone possessed the intercessionary power which might cause God to extend human life or, in another view, bring His Divine presence to rest upon man on earth (*Sifrei* Numbers 160 [p. 220], exegesis on Numbers 35:25). More specifically, only the *kohen gadol* possessed the sanctity required for the performance of the prescribed salvific rituals in the Holy of Holies on the Day of Atonement (Leviticus 16:16–17 and *Mishnah, Yoma'* 5:3) and the public authority to consult the oracles known as the *'urim* and *tumim* (Numbers 27:21 and *Mishnah, Yoma'* 7:5). True, such distinctions had become most apparent at occasional moments of high cultic drama. But, the texts stress, they had also been given more regular expression. Once appointed, high priests had for the remainder of their lives been subject to a discriminatory range of purity restrictions, circumscribing both the mourning rites which they could observe and the category of woman whom they might marry (Lev. 21:10–14; Ezek, 44:22–5 and *Mishnah, Nazir* 7:1). The other side of the coin was that, throughout the year, they had also retained certain privileges entirely unique to their office. Some were sartorial; whereas ordinary priests wore four holy vestments when performing their Temple duties, the *kohen gadol* did so in eight (enumerated in Exodus chaps. 28–9 and 39; and in *Mishnah, Yoma'* 7:5); others were more obviously tangible: only high priests might jump the circuit queue when wishing to participate in the daily ritual; and they alone could elbow aside colleagues whenever seeking first choice in the distribution of the 'holy things of the Temple'.[16]

Concentrating on the sacral character of such privileges, early rabbinic texts tend to downplay – and at some junctures ignore – the temporal powers of patronage and of rulership which, as we know from other sources, further added to the material value of the high priesthood during the second Commonwealth. Nevertheless, talmudic traditions do stress that for much of that period competition for the office amongst rival contestants had been particularly fierce – and decidedly unseemly. The generations immediately prior to the Destruction, they recalled, had witnessed especially frequent cycles of appointments and dismissals. Still worse, the sequence of such changes had been virtually unaffected by the traditional rules of hereditary succession and their velocity equally unrelated to the mortality of the incumbents. Under the Herodians, in fact, the office had been altogether politicised and/or commercialised; appointment and possession more often reflected the erratic chance of court intrigue and the purse of the office-holder than the standing interests of moral and cultic fitness.[17]

That chronology undoubtedly tarnished the reputation of second commonwealth high priests, whose individual length of service early rabbinic literature compared unfavourably with that said to have been enjoyed by their predecessors during the period of the first Temple.[18] Together with the absence of the *'urim* and *tumim*, the ecclesiastically controlled oracles reported to have been in use for much of the Biblical epoch (perhaps throughout; cf. *Mishnah, Soṭah* 9:12 and *Tosefta'*, idem. 13:2), it contributed to a feeling that the high priests of the second Temple had been in every respect an inferior genus of the breed. Even so, the office itself remained sacrosanct. Once appointed to their august positions, all high priests – including second Temple high priests – had assumed the dignities and honours which God had conferred upon the very first of their line. Their holiness had remained intrinsic. Every priest (and *a fortiori*, we are given to understand, every High Priest), had been invested at birth with a *kedushah* ('sanctity') which always had been – and always would be – eternal (and, again, the word used is *'olam*; *Mishnah, Nazir* 7:1). By the same token, the public authority invested in the *keter kehunah* itself could never be eroded.

The *keter malkhut*

Like the *keter kehunah*, the *keter malkhut* could also boast a stirring pedigree stretching back to the Biblical past. Nevertheless, from the early rabbinic perspective, the constitutional status of Israel's monarchy was always somewhat less august than was that of its priesthood. In part, the reasons stemmed from the contrasting chronologies of the two domains. Ever since its inception, the *keter kehunah* had apparently preserved its integrity and unity. Peripheral exceptions apart, it had throughout been focussed around one sacred cult, one legitimate temple, and one acknowledged high priest. By comparison, the historical record of the *keter malkhut* exhibited numerous examples of discontinuities and dissensions. David himself, the very first recipient of the monarchic covenant and its most illustrious expression, had been a usurper whose reign was punctuated with frequent rebellions. Under his successors, too, the domain had staggered from one constitutional crisis to another – invariably downhill. Ultimately, the Davidic dynasty had proved incapable of retaining its original station at the operational pinnacle of the franchise with which its founder had been entrusted. Shortly after the return from the first Exile, all remnants of the line had abruptly dropped from active view. Such monarchical prerogatives as the Jewish polity had subsequently possessed were assumed by a string of alternative claimants, the most prominent of whom (the Hasmoneans) had also been priests.

In their eagerness to emphasise the moral thrust of the scriptural narrative, early rabbinic traditions frequently attributed those developments to the personal failings of Israel's individual monarchs – southern as well as northern.[19] In conglomerate sketches, however, they were often portrayed as fitting reflections on an institution whose very existence was in some degree theologically suspect. This was hardly surprising. After all, and as the dialogue preserved in chapter 8 of I Samuel makes absolutely plain, God had Himself discredited the spasm of monarchic fervour which had first fuelled the popular clamour for a native king. At the very least, that demand had disavowed the theocratic principle which had been enunciated at the Red Sea (Exodus 15:18) and reconfirmed by Gideon (Judges 8:23).

For all the messianic properties with which it was subsequently to be endowed, even the Davidic monarchy therefore constituted a flawed concession to human frailty, legitimated only retrospectively and belatedly. Strictly speaking, the very nomenclature employed by instruments of the *keter malkhut* was still tainted with blasphemy. The Almighty alone was Israel's true king; indeed, only He deserved that designation. Saul, significantly, had originally been invested with the alternative title of *nagid* (I Sam. 9:16; lit. 'prince', perhaps more accurately 'syndic' or 'chief executive'); Ezekiel, similarly, had employed the noun *nasi'* ('prince'; Ezek. 34:23–4) to describe the lay instrument of Israel's restored polity. Although *Mishnah* did occasionally fudge some of these terminological distinctions,[20] the general tenor of tanna'itic and amora'ic texts nevertheless acknowledged the implication that the supreme royal title of *melekh* ought normatively to be reserved for God alone. As much is illustrated by their use of that root as a generic connotation for the 'holy commonwealth' of Jewish aspirations. As generally portrayed in early rabbinic literature, the authentic *malkhut* is that of heaven – the *malkhut shamayim*.

Notwithstanding the materials which thus lay to hand for a denigration of the *keter malkhut*, very few early rabbinic tradents went to the lengths of portraying that domain as an altogether superfluous accretion to Israel's ordained political culture. Faithful to the concept of a triadic complement of functioning franchises, most projected the *keter malkhut* as one of its imperative components. Even before the formal inception of the domain, they taught, its prerogatives had been exercised by Moses.[21] More explicitly, they had been foreshadowed in Deuteronomy chapter 17. Admittedly, the latter prooftext was uncomfortably enigmatic. It could be read as an optional provision, rather than a categorical obligation, and thus itself be nicely harmonised with the critical and anti-monarchical thrust of I Samuel chapter 8. Such, indeed, is one of the arguments enunciated in *Sifrei*'s record (Deut. 156 [p. 208; trans. Hammer, p. 191]) of a second century tanna'itic debate:

And you shall say, I will set a king over me: (Deut. 17:14). R. Nehor'ai says: This is in disparagement of Israel, as it is said: 'For they have not rejected thee but they have rejected Me that I should not be a king over them.' (I Sam. 8:7).

But, as *Sifrei* itself immediately points out, that was not the only point of view. R. Judah, for one, is reported to have advocated that Deuteronomy 17:15, where the Children of Israel are explicitly enjoined to 'surely place [*som tasim*] a king over you', be understood in an imperative sense. Cognate evidence seemingly confirmed his position. The command to appoint a king had been one of the three communal obligations imposed on the Children of Israel when they entered the Holy Land (the others were to erect the sanctuary and to eradicate the Amalakites; *Sifrei* Deut. 67 [p. 132] and parallels).

Thus presented, the legitimacy of the monarchy was not open to question. All that needed to be elucidated were two chronological issues, substantive but nevertheless subsidiary. First, when precisely was the obligation specified in Deuteronomy 17 to become operative (even R. Judah was prepared to concede that it had been implemented with unseemly haste: 'Why then were they punished [...] in the days of Samuel? Because they initiated it prematurely on their own'); second, should it have been carried out before, between, or after, the construction of the Temple and the eradication of the Amalakites. After much huffing and puffing over the relevant sources, some *tana'im* were to maintain that the proper sequence ought to have been Temple–King–Amalake. R. Judah was prepared to concede that the Temple precede Amalake. But, true to what appear to have been steadfast monarchic convictions, he nevertheless insisted that the appointment of a king had been the primary requirement, and hence should have come first.

Blidstein's recent analysis of this and allied exegetical activity has drawn attention to its temporal provenance. Noting that the majority of the relevant dicta are attributed to scholars active around the middle of the second century C.E., he has suggested that at least some of their perspectives on the monarchy might have been stimulated by the conflicting passions aroused during and immediately after the Bar Kokhba' revolt of 132–5 C.E. True, we do not possess the historical data necessary to prove a direct correlation between a particular Biblical commentary and the political orientation of its proponent. But early rabbinic discussions on the propriety of Israel's early monarchy are unlikely to have been entirely abstract. Like so many other contemporary debates on concerns of political relevance, they were probably stimulated – and certainly influenced – by the tumultuous upheavals recently experienced in Judea. Even those *tana'im* whose attitude towards the revolt was throughout circumspect could hardly have avoided addressing the questions which it posed.[22] Whatever the extent of his own monarchic pretensions, Bar Kokhba' had certainly aroused messianic expectations in some quarters. Simply by assuming the ancient rank of '*nasi*", he might also have fostered a belief that a restoration of the *keter malkhut* constituted an overture to the revival of Jewry's national and religious fortunes.

If such was indeed the case, an appropriate theological explanation had to be found for the bitter failure of Bar Kokhba's enterprise and the retributions which had thereafter ensued. One possible lesson to be learnt from the trauma was quietistic: Israel had altogether sinned in attempting to rush its own Redemption. But the debates on the monarchic imperative indicate that other interpretations might also have come to mind. It was not the act of rebellion which had been illegitimate, still less – according to the pro-monarchic camp – its instrument. The sin, for such it must have been, had lain with Bar Kokhba's apparent priorities. Had he and his supporters acted with less haste (hence R. Judah's retrospective lament on the dangers of impetuosity) or set out to rebuild the Temple before proclaiming Israel's renewed political autonomy (an alternative perhaps encoded in the Temple–King sequence) then the Amalakites (= Romans) would surely have been expelled from the land.

Be that as it may, the institutional inference remained unmistakable. The majoritarian weight of early rabbinic opinion could discern no exegetical justification for entirely detaching Israel's promised messianic future from the constitutional framework established in Israel's Biblical past, and thus visualising a spiritualistic (alternatively, an apocalyptic) moment which might dispense with the model of human royalty as an expression of the effluence of Divine grace. By the same token nor was it thought possible, or even desirable, to erase the *keter malkhut* from statutory depictions of the ordained political spectrum. On the contrary, the senior instrument of that domain, generally referred to as *melekh*, features prominently in each of the early rabbinic outlines of Jewish government at the national level. The second chapter of *Mishnah Sanhedrin* does emphasise the immutable constitutional limitations on monarchs' powers of unilateral action in their personal and public lives. Nevertheless, within the bounds set by Deuteronomic law, their prerogatives remain *sui generis*.[23] Kings are there granted exceptional privileges in times of war (2:4) and all incumbents of the office deemed worthy of extraordinary marks of respect (2:5; cf. *Tosefta', Sanhedrin* 4:2). Likewise, *Sifrei* Deut. 161 (p. 212) insisted that, other than in matters of *torah* itself, the king could have no equal; TB *Sanhedrin (20b)*, furthermore, was to proclaim all *melakhim* at liberty to exercise each of the royal proprietary rights which the prophet Samuel had initially decried. Only where ceremonial and ritual precedence are concerned are kings considered inferior to high priests; even so, were both officeholders ever to be held captive at one and the same time, it was the King who would have to be ransomed first.[24]

Significantly, few of the standing prerogatives which tanna'itic and amora'ic ordinances would thus entrust to the *melekh* are restricted to authentic possessors of specifically Davidic lineage. For the most part, the texts make no distinctions between Davidic kings and all others; and even where they do, the delineations are invariably limited to matters of ceremonial.[25] In some passages, moreover, consideration of the dynastic properties upon which so much of the *malkhut*'s authority might otherwise have been thought to depend is almost abruptly shunted aside. Legitimacy, they insist, is a consequence of the effective (although not arbitrary) exercise of power. According to *'agadah*, David himself had been reminded of the impropriety of acting against Saul at a time when his own coinage was not yet commonly accepted currency (TB *Megilah* 14a–b). Doubtless all subsequent pretenders to the throne would similarly have to earn their rank. In the phraseology ultimately adopted by TJ *Horayot* 1:2: 'a king of Israel [*melekh yisra'el*] and a [Davidic] king of Judah are both equal'.

Thus to equate the two categories of monarchs was not, of course, to deny the uniqueness of the Davidides' ultimate messianic mission and status. It was, however, to legitimise the titles of all other claimants to whatever authorities the *keter malkhut* would in the interim bestow. Indeed, in none of their references to Israel's post-Biblical past do rabbinic traditions suggest that the political submersion of David's direct descendants soon after the initiation of the second Commonwealth had resulted in the absolute decomposition of the franchise which the family had originally been authorised to embody. Even when dynastically deficient, the institutional framework of the monarchy had continued to survive.

Under the aegis of Simon the Maccabee and his successors, it had even been granted a lease of vigorous life. As the researches of Alon and Efron have demonstrated, the suggestion that *tana'im* and *'amora'im* might have resorted to 'internal censorship' where that period was concerned needs to be drastically revised. Detailed investigation refutes the allegation that the tradents of *'Eres Yisra'el* (in particular) might have sought deliberately to expunge the entire Hasmonean interlude from Israel's history. They did not suppress existing copies of I Maccabees or *Megilat Ta'anit*, the chronicles which record and calendar the heroic exploits which had first earned the family its fame; neither did they foster a neglect in the observation of *Ḥannukah*, the annual festival which commemorates the Maccabean contribution to the purification of the Temple during the war against Seleucid oppression.[26]

Equally unfounded is the alternative charge that the sources uniformly and indiscriminately blacken the Hasmoneans' name on genetic grounds. Rabbinic criticism concentrates on the improper style of their kingship, not – as is the case in the *Psalms of Solomon* (below, chap. 4) – on the illegitimacy of its very existence. Although the public policies of John Hyrcanus and Alexander Yannai are roundly condemned, sometimes interchangeably so, neither is depicted as a usurper, constitutionally disqualified to rule solely because he lacked the required Davidic pedigree. If anything, that consideration seems to have been considered entirely irrelevant. How else, asks Alon, are we to account for the favourable rabbinic portrait of the non-Davidic reign of Queen Salome Alexandra (reigned 76–67 B.C.E.) who, her gender apart, emerges from the texts as almost the prototype of an ideal monarch? How else, too, are we to explain the absence of specifically Davidic references from tanna'itic allusions to the questionable legitimacy of King Agrippa I (ruler of Judea between 41 and 43/44C.E.; in whose case the issue was the possibly dubious nature of his ethnic Jewish identity, not his lack of the traditional blood royal)?[27]

Thus placed in context, the various rabbinic references to the operational attributes of the *keter malkhut* are at several significant points incongruous with the rather rudimentary intimation that appropriate Davidic genealogy be considered the exclusive criterion of legitimate monarchical competence. The spirit which animates several of the relevant discussions suggests, rather, that dynasty and rulership be treated as separate categories and not as sequential attributes linked by an umbilical cord which renders royal majesty altogether dependent upon appropriate genealogy. Equally pertinent is their inclination to regard some form of civil rulership, whatever its dynastic hue, as an instrument of government whose existence was vital for the retention of social stability and the avoidance of anarchy. According to *Tosefta', Sanhedrin* 4:8, what distinguished all kings of Israel (again, not Davidic kings alone), was their devotion to public service. The *keter malkhut*, in other words, was a public necessity almost as much as it was a sacred framework. That, according to the *beraitah* quoted in the name of R. Eliezer ben Jacob (TB *Sanhedrin* 14b; exegesis on Deut. 21:2), was why the King had to join the High Priest and the *sanhedrin* in determining urban responsibility for unsolved cases of homicide.

Hence, even those *melakhim* who lacked the messianic charisma of the Davidides could be – and should be – empowered to carry out the executive tasks most closely associated with the domain whose crown they wore. Indeed, it was their capacity to enlist other agents in their service which gave their franchise its bureaucratic depth. The regulations specified in Deuteronomy chapter 17 were not therefore restricted only to the very apex of monarchic government. In some measure, posited *Midrash Tana'im* on verse 14, they equally applied to the entire gamut of its subsidiary functionaries: constables (*shoṭerim*), charity wardens (*gabai'ei ṣedaqah*), clerks of the court (*soferei dayanim*) and the administrator of judicial punishments (*makeh be-reṣuah*). Together, all comprised institutional expressions of a domain without which organised Jewish society could not function.

The *keter torah*

As far as the *tana'im* and *'amora'im* were themselves concerned, the institutional vertebrae which most obviously articulated the administrative capacity of the *keter torah* were the *batei din*. Literally 'courts of law', the competence of such bodies was for the most part arbitrational.[28] Adjudicating civil cases either singly or in sessions of three, the persons by whom they were manned resorted more to moral suasion than to coercion. Nevertheless, tribunals of that name constituted far more than judicial assemblies. Following the pattern first articulated in Numbers 11:16 and Deuteronomy 17:8ff, and thereafter reportedly revived by both Jehoshafat and Ezra (II Chron. 19:8 and Ezra 7:25), *batei din* – according to early rabbinic accounts – in effect mediated the entire body of precepts and practices embodied in the *torah*-as-constitution. Especially was this so since, at some levels, they also functioned as academies of learning. Thus constituted, they rendered intelligible the dictates of God's laws, enabling the nation to move closer to its religious and social ideals and thereby itself become holy.

Vast portions of the Jerusalem and Babylonian talmuds are devoted to what purport to be factual reconstructions of the deliberations and workings of local and national *batei din* in their various capacities. Admittedly, the relevant texts are not altogether straightforward. In quintessentially rabbinic style, they are often riddled with legal oddities and complexities, all of which have been well raked over by subsequent generations of litigious scholars in their resoundingly erudite marginalia. Even stripped of such encrustations, however, the prominence of the materials which deal with the *batei din* as the functional instruments of the *keter torah* is pronounced. Neither before nor after the destruction of the second Temple in 70 C.E., is the impression, were such agencies merely peripheral cogs in the machinery of Jewish government; wherever Jews lived, they were its most pervasive and sublime expression. At their highest levels, especially, they had wielded regulatory, managerial and even representative powers. Staffed by scholars renowned for their exegetical skills, they had been empowered to discover and unravel the entire meaning of the timeless *torah*, and not merely to pronounce and record immediately relevant *halakhah*. Hence, their jurisdiction had encompassed administrative matters nominally associated with the *keter malkhut* and ritual concerns formally appertaining to the *keter kehunah*. In sum, they had regulated, ratified and/or supervised every conceivable facet of Jewish life, in the public domain as well as the private.

Supreme amongst the *batei din* of early rabbinic depiction is the *sanhedrin*, also known to *Mishnah* as the *beit din ha-gadol* ('great tribunal'). Although no such institution is explicitly referred to in the Biblical texts, rabbinic tradents emphatically assigned its origins to the very earliest period of Jewish political articulation. The *sanhedrin*, they reported, was first established in the wilderness of Sinai, with the Divine command that Moses appoint a consultative council of 70 elders (*Mishnah*, *Sanhedrin* 1:6 on Numbers 11:16). Subsequently, it had become one of the standing institutions of Israelite self-government, functioning in both pre-monarchic and monarchic regimes.[29] Even after the Destruction, when a forum thus designated apparently migrated between various centres of

Jewish settlement in Judea and Galilee (TB *Ro'sh ha-Shanah* 31a–b), it had continued to play a pivotal role in national life. In each of its locations, it is reported to have constituted an essential adjunct to the administrative apparatus associated with the *nasi'* (here meaning 'Patriarch'; see below chap. 7). Within its framework, indeed, the latter was only *primus inter pares*. Especially where questions based upon exegetical understanding were involved, the *nasi'* was – or ought to have been – subject to precisely the same norm of majority rule applied to all other members of the *sanhedrin* over which he presided. (At least, such was the view taken by R. 'Aqiva' in one of his exchanges with the *nasi'* Rabban Gamli'el II; *Tosefta', Berakhot*, 4:12). The intercalation of the calendar, the enactment of *taqanot* and the pronouncement of bans of excommunication (although all admitted to be Patriarchal prerogatives) are said to have been properly effective only when duly sanctioned by the *sanhedrin* and/or its accredited representatives.[30]

For all the eminence which they attributed to the post-Destruction *sanhedrin*, early rabbinic tradents admitted that it had not then been truly worthy of its designation (*Mishnah, Soṭah* 9:11, for instance, speaks of the curtailments on festivities once the [classic] *sanhedrin* had been abolished). To be fully competent, the institution required conditions of complete Jewish self-government. Specifically, ultimate civil authority ought to be in native hands. That had not been the case, it was remembered, during the last generation of the second Commonwealth. Forty years prior to the Destruction, recalls TB *'Avodah Zarah* 8b, the *sanhedrin* had been deprived of the right to try capital cases and ignominiously forced to remove its sessions to '*ḥanuyot*' (lit. 'bazaars').

Thereto, however, the *sanhedrin* had enjoyed much of the glory reflected by the universal centrality of the Sanctuary itself (TB *Sanhedrin* 37a). Its sessions had been timed to coincide with the cycle of cultic ritual; it had occupied a permanent seat in or alongside the Temple precincts (specifically, the *lishkat ha-gazit*, 'the chamber of hewn stone', e.g. *Mishnah, Sanhedrin* 11:2). Above all, it had made, declared and – where necessary – modified law. As codified in the mishna'ic tractate most closely concerned with the subject (*Sanhedrin*; especially 1:5), 'the court of seventy-one' is said to have stood at the undisputed apex of a carefully regulated system of halakhic jurisprudence. Only the King (but not the High Priest) had been independent of its jurisdiction. Otherwise, on cultic affairs, on major criminal cases, on critical political issues and on matters affecting religious law its decisions were nationally binding. 'From there', it was remembered, 'Law [*torah*] had gone forth to all Israel' (*Mishnah, Sanhedrin* 11:2; *Tosefta', Sanhedrin* 7:1).

Strung together, early rabbinic accounts of the *sanhedrin*'s competence enumerate an obviously impressive range of powers.[31] But how they might have been exercised remains shrouded in mystery; tanna'itic references to the operational workings of the *sanhedrin* during second Temple times are especially lacking in realistic detail. Almost sterile in tone, the stark portraits are for the most part entirely detached from a clearly defined historical context. *Mishnah* records just two concrete cases (one concerned with agricultural law [*Pe'ah* 2:6], the other with a detail of purity regulations [*'Eduyot* 7:4]) on which the *lishkat ha-gazit* was asked for an opinion. Otherwise, that source restricts itself to generalities. It provides not one instance of the procedures whereby the *sanhedrin* might have tried one of its own offending members (a *zaqen mamrei*; lit. 'rebellious elder') – let alone 'a tribe, a false prophet, or a High Priest'. Neither does it supply even one substantive depiction of that body's active participation in Hasmonean decisions to go to war[32] or to extend the geographical boundaries of Jerusalem and the Temple.

For over a century now, critical scholarship has wrestled with the difficulties thus posed, attempting – sometimes ingeniously so – to harmonise the early rabbinic portraits of a second Commonwealth *sanhedrin* with those which might be distilled from the Gospels and Josephus. It has recently been suggested, however, that the entire effusion of academic energy has largely been wasted. In Efron's words, the rabbinic sources are patently anachronistic, perhaps blatantly so; they reflect nothing more than 'the pious visions of the tanna'itic masters'. As reconstructions of circumstances as they existed in late second Temple times, they are worthless.[33] Whatever their precise nature, the judicial tribunals and/or political senates referred to in the latter sources functioned at different levels and for different purposes than did the quasi-governmental academies to which the Pharisees of the age might have simultaneously delegated ultimate authority in the regulation of their own personal lives. The two (or three) institutions – if they ever existed – were not related, and certainly not synonymous. The term *sanhedrin* meant separate things to separate people; indeed, it continued to do so until all institutions of that name were finally disbanded by Roman decree in the fifth century.[34]

Early rabbinic authors were of course blissfully ignorant of the academic minefield which their own traditions were thus to lay. But even had that not been the case, it is doubtful whether they would have taken much trouble to substantiate their portrait of the workings and functions of the *sanhedrin* during what they considered to be its second Temple heyday. As much is evident from the monotone which characterises their depictions of its personnel. In their references to the pre-Destruction *sanhedrin*, the rabbinic texts provide no item of sociological and geographical information which might permit a Namierian analysis of its composition. All we are told is that members of the body were *ipso facto* considered to descended from irreproachable stock (*Mishnah, Qidushin* 4:4), that they were supposed to include among their number at least a sprinkling of priests and levites (*Sifrei* Deut. 153 [p. 206]), and that their appointed leaders (the Pharisaic 'pairs' of officials named in *Mishnah, Ḥagigah* 2:2 and *'Avot* 1:4–12) were all scholars of repute. Individual pen-portraits, however, are consistently eschewed.

So, too, are any allusions which might be interpreted as overtures to the intra-institutional factionalism and rivalry which the same sources acknowledge to have affected the *sanhedrin* at various stages of its post-Destruction history. Only the tanna'itic debate on the precise complement of the assembly (seventy or seventy one; *Mishnah, Sanhedrin* 1:6) allows for the possibility that jurisdictional friction between the rank and file of the members and their president might always have been one of its intrinsic characteristics. Similarly, only the famous '*semikhah* controversy' admits the possible influence of rival parties on its deliberations.[35] Otherwise, however, tanna'itic recollections go out of their way to emphasise the fact that sessions of the second Commonwealth *sanhedrin* had – initially at least – been a byword for cordiality, unanimity and conformity. R. Josei ben Ḥalafta's account of the procedures whereby the 'court of 71' then functioned as the final court of jurisdiction for all uncertainties presents a model chain-of-command. Moreover, his attached description of the manner whereby prospective candidates to that body were screened, selected and progressively raised in station through a series of district tribunals contains not a whisper of the jockeying for position which conventionally intrudes upon the conduct of such matters.[36] Equally bland is *Mishnah*'s stylised depiction of the seating arrangements which, once a meeting of the (lesser) *sanhedrin* was under way, is said to have carefully demarcated the rank and precedence of its participants (*Sanhedrin* 4:2).

Clearly, documents of that sort were not framed in order to satisfy antiquarian curiosity or the criteria of accurate historical presentation. If they had any practical purpose, it was to serve the contemporary and partisan need of their authors, who deployed them in order to capture the high constitutional ground and claim it as their own. Therein, indeed, lies the intrinsic *political* value of the sources to hand. The *sanhedrin* of rabbinic depiction is, perhaps at root, a vehicle for the transmission of at least two distinctly polemical messages. First, by providing a graphic demonstration of the principle of power-sharing, it emphasises the accountability of the *keter malkhut* and the *keter kehunah* to the dictates of constitutional law. Since the statutory jurisdiction of the *sanhedrin* is said to have embraced both the civic responsibilities of the former and the cultic practices of the latter, neither can be an altogether independent domain, entirely free of external (human) authority. They do not even exercise exclusive influence over the spheres of activity with which each is most closely concerned.

Far more substantially, however, the same portrait also emphasises the corporate identity of the *keter torah*. This branch of government, it shows, had never been an ephemeral and unorganised entity. The very anonymity of the Pharisaic sages appointed to the *sanhedrin*'s membership testifies to the fact that they too had constituted a fully articulated franchise of rulership. What is more, because the basis for the *sanhedrin*'s supreme powers of appeal and regulation is the supreme word of God, the eminence of its majority (the scholars who interpreted that word and clarified its intent) necessarily transcends that of the most aristocratic of its earthly members.

On what grounds, however, could those 'sages' themselves claim to represent the authority thus vested in the *keter torah*? Which were the qualities of the Jewish spirit which they were said to embody and what their qualifications to be considered its authentic – indeed sovereign – representatives? Through what procedures, and at what stages, had they assumed the powers with which they were said to be endowed? The following chapter will argue that early rabbinic answers to those questions further refined the concept of the three crowns of Jewish government. Over the long haul, they also generated a complete reformulation of Israel's constitutional history and priorities.

NOTES

1. Exegesis on Proverbs 8:22–30 in Genesis *Rabbah* 1:1; see also *Sifrei* Deut. 37 (p. 70): 'Since *torah* is more beloved than anything else, it was created before all else.' Possible Platonic influences, and parallels, are discussed in Urbach, *Sages*, pp. 198–202. The nuances are analysed in A. J. Heschel, *Torah Min ha-Shamayim be-'Aspaklariyah Shel ha-Dorot*, Vol. 2 (Jerusalem, 1965), pp. 8–12.
2. Chap. 48; ed. Schechter, pp. 130–1. Compare, however, the alternative citations provided in version 'A': Malachi 3:22 (for the *keter torah*); Numbers 18:19 (*kehunah*); and II Chron. 13:5 (*malkhut*).
3. The absence of tanna'itic historiography, and the 'abnegation of [political] history' to which it gave rise, was first analysed in modern scholarship by N. N. Glazer, *Untersuchungen zur Geschichtslehre der Tannaiten* (Berlin, 1933). For recent surveys: M. D. Herr, 'Tefisat ha-Hisṭoriyah 'Eṣel Ḥazal', *WCJS*, 6 (3), 1977, pp. 129–42 and Y. H. Yerushalmi, *Zakhor: Jewish History and Jewish Memory* (London, 1982), pp. 5–26.
4. Compare, for instance, the disjointed rabbinic depictions of the various conflicts (e.g. *Tosefta' Menaḥot* 13:21; TB *Pesaḥim* 57a and *Yoma'* 9b), with Josephus' intimation that they were integral to the breakdown of order during the Commonwealth's last years. On the latter see T. Rajak, *Josephus: The Historian and His Society* (Phila., 1984), pp. 78–103 and M. Goodman, *The Ruling Class of Judaea: The Origins of the Jewish Revolt Against Rome A.D. 66–70* (Cambridge, 1987).
5. Specific instances are cited in A. Büchler, *Ha-Kohanim we-'Avodatam be-Miqdash Yerushalayim be-'Esor ha-Shanim she-Lifnei Ḥurban Bayit Sheini* (translated N. Ginton; Jerusalem, 1966), pp. 15–36; see also D. Hoffmann's suggestion that several such passages constituted *Mishnah*'s earliest layer in *The First Mishna* (translated P. Forchheimer; New York, 1977), pp. 36–7. Rabbinic sources on the cultic services as practised in second Temple times are summarised in E. Schürer, *The History of the Jewish People in the Age of Jesus Christ: A New English Version Revised and Edited*, Vol. 2 (eds. G. Vermes & F. Millar; Edinburgh, 1979 [hereafter *History* (Revised)]), pp. 275–308.
6. *Tanḥuma', Naso'* 19 and parallels cited in N. Goldstein, *Meḥqarim be-Hagutam Shel Ḥazal 'Al ha-'Avodah be-Veit ha-Miqdash we-Hashpa'atam 'Al 'Iṣuvah* (unpub., Ph.D., the Hebrew University, Jerusalem, 1977) pp. 151–6. For the location of Jerusalem at the navel of the world see *Tanḥuma', Qedoshim* 10; and – on the *'even shetiyah* as the stone around which the world was woven – S. Lieberman, *Ha-Yerushalmi Kifshuto* (Jerusalem, 1974), p. 431.
7. That pilgrimage to Jerusalem was considered a non-obligatory act rather than a binding duty in second Temple times, is argued in S. Safrai,

'Miṣwat ha-'Aliyah le-Regel we-Qiyumah Bimei ha-Bayit ha-Sheini', *Zion*, 25 (1960), pp. 67–84.

8. V. Tcherikover, *Hellenistic Civilization and the Jews* (Phila., 1959), pp. 276–81, 392–4 and M. Delcor, 'Le Temple d'Onias en Egypte', *Revue Biblique*, 75 (1968), pp. 188–203.
9. *Mishnah, Yoma'* 5:2; according to one later opinion the Ark had been carried away into captivity by Nebuchanezer; alternatively, it was said to have been 'hidden' (together with various other artefacts) by Josiah. TB *Yoma'* 53b–54a and the discussion in S. Lieberman, *Tosefta' Kifshutah* [hereafter TK], vol. 8 (*Nashim*; N.Y., 1973), pp. 733–5.
10. Although the origins and development of the synagogue (in Hebrew *beit ha-keneset*, sometimes also designated in the Greek sources as *proseuche*) remain shrouded in mystery, it has been conjectured that some such institution may even have existed before the first Exile (a circumstance possibly reflected in the enigmatic lament of Psalms 74:8). That it functioned in various forms and styles during the second Commonwealth seems undeniable. The subject has most recently been treated in L. I. Levine, 'The Second Temple Synagogue: The Formative Years', *The Synagogue in Late Antiquity* (ed. L. I. Levine; N.Y., 1987), pp. 7–32.
11. G. Alon, 'Did the Jewish People and its Sages Cause the Hasmoneans to be Forgotten?', *Jews, Judaism, and the Classical World* (trans. I. Abrahams; Jerusalem, 1977), pp. 1–17. See also below n. 26.
12. The priestly dues are enumerated and described in Schürer, op. cit., pp. 257–70. Ibid., p. 259 fn. 5 cites the sources which explain that Ezra had transferred certain tithes from the priests to the levites because so few of the latter had participated in the Return. See also TB *Soṭah* 47b–48a. On priestly duties as described in the Bible: M. Haran, 'Ha-Kohen, ha-Miqdash we-ha-'Avodah', *Tarbitz*, 48 (1979), p. 176.
13. E.g. *Sifrei* Numbers 116 and 117 (pp. 132, 134–5). These and other sources are analysed in M. Beer, 'Meridat Qoraḥ u-Meni'ehah be-'Agadot Ḥazal', *Meḥqarim ... le-Zekher Yosef Heinemann* (eds. E. Fleischer, S. J. Petuchowsky; Jerusalem, 1981), pp. 9–33.
14. See, e.g., the depiction of the sacrificial punishment imposed upon the High Priest for judicial error in Leviticus 4:3 and *Mishnah, Horayot* 2:1–3, and the analysis in Z. Steinfeld, 'Hora'at ha-Kohen ha-Mashiaḥ', *Sinai*, 95 (1984), pp. 135–56.
15. Z. Steinfeld, 'Mashiaḥ, Merubeh Begadim, Kohen Meshamesh we-Kohen she'Avar', *Tarbitz*, 52 (1983), pp. 411–34.
16. J. Jeremias, *Jerusalem in the Time of Jesus* (trans. F. H. & C. H. Cave; Phila., 1969), pp. 149–54. On restrictions in marriage partners: Lev. 21:13–15 and *Mishnah, Yevamot* 6:4.
17. *Tosefta', Yoma'* 1:7 (and Lieberman, TK, vol. 4 [*Mo'ed*; N.Y., 1962], p. 729); *Sifrei* Numbers 131 and TB *Yoma'* 9a; the historical accuracy

and legal inferences of such sources are discussed in Alon, *Jews, Judaism* etc., pp. 58–65, 82–3.

18. For reconstructed lists of the high priests of the second Commonwealth see Jeremias, *Jerusalem*, pp. 377–8 (after 200 B.C.E.); Schürer, op. cit., pp. 229–232 (after 37 B.C.E.) and Y. Greenwald, *Toledot ha-Kohanim ha-Gedolim* (N.Y., 1933).

    For the Biblical record, H. J. Katzenstein, 'Some Remarks on the Lists of the Chief Priests of the Temple of Solomon', *JBL*, 81 (1962), pp. 371–84 and J. R. Bartlett, 'Zadok and his Successors at Jerusalem', *JTS*, 19 (1968), pp. 1–18.
19. Thus, according to Rav (TB *Shabbat* 56b), David's improper behaviour towards Mephiboshet had itself been partly to blame for Jeroboam's secession. See, in general, E. E. Urbach, 'Ha-Melukhah ha-Miqra'it be-'Einei Ḥakhamim', *Sefer Seligman*, pp. 439–51.
20. E.g., *Horayot* 3:3: 'Who is the *nasi'*? This is the *melekh*.' Cf., however, Rav' Ashi's delineation of the contrasting honour due to the offices of *melekh* and *nasi'* by their incumbents in TB *Qidushin* 32b.
21. The relevant rabbinic sources are collated in Kasher, *Torah Shelemah*, Vol. 15 (N.Y., 1953), Appendix 2, pp. 124–7; for an examination of the Biblical materials which intimate the same notion, see J. R. Porter, *Moses and Monarchy*, pp. 27–8.
22. It is difficult to imagine anyone talking in 150 C.E. about Israel's search for a king in the distant past who was not painfully aware of the more recent attempt and did not realize that his discussion implied an attitude towards this attempt or toward the public policy that his people ought to attempt in the future.

    G. Blidstein, 'The Monarchic Imperative in Rabbinical Perspective', *AJS review*, 7–8 (1983), p. 31. See also, with particular reference to the view of R. Simeon bar Yoḥ'ai on the issue, M. Beer, 'Har ha-Bayit u-Veit ha-Miqdash', op. cit. Tanna'itic attitudes towards the Bar Kokhba' revolt are further discussed below, chap. 6, pp. 161–3.
23. For the most part, the relevant limitations (on the numbers of the King's permitted wives and horses) adhere to the tone and structure of Deuteronomy chapter 17. One of the very few innovations (2:1) is the provision that the King may neither participate in the judicial proceedings of the *sanhedrin*, nor be judged by that body. For later explanations see TB *Sanhedrin* 18b, commentary on Exodus 23:2; and TJ *Sanhedrin* 2:1. *Tosefta' Sanhedrin* 4:5 and TB *Sanhedrin* 20b are analysed in A. Halevi, 'Mishpaṭ ha-Melekh', *Tarbitz*, 38 (1969), pp. 225–30.
24. Compare *Sifrei Zuṭa'* on Numbers 27:21 and *Tosefta'*, *Horayot* 2:8–9; TB idem 13b and TJ idem 3:7.
25. Specific instances are detailed below, chap. 9, pp. 238–9.
26. Alon, above n. 11 and Y. Efron, 'Shim'on ben Sheṭaḥ we-Yann'ai ha-Melekh', *Ḥiqerei ha-Tequfah ha-Ḥashmona'it* (Tel Aviv, 1980), pp. 131–94. Compare L. Ginzberg's earlier statement that: 'the older haggadah never alludes to the Hasmoneans [...] The latter haggadah

[...] hardly knew of [them]. *Legends of the Jews*, Vol. 6 , p. 156 n. 925.

27. *Mishnah, Soṭah* 7:8; *Tosefta'*, ibid. 7:16 and TJ idem 7:7. The sources and their meanings are discussed in D. Schwartz, *'Agripas ha-R'ishon: Melekh Yehudah ha-'Aḥaron* (Jerusalem, 1987), pp. 172–6, who points out, however, that Agrippa was not necessarily the darling of the Pharisees, still less one of them. Ibid., pp. 228–30 analyses Agrippa's possible ethnic disqualifications.
28. A characteristic thrashed out in TB *Bava' Batra'* 27b–28a and forcefully developed in S. Albeck, *Batei ha-Din Bimei ha-Talmud* (Ramat Gan, 1980).
29. Hoenig, *The Great Sanhedrin*, pp. 143–4. Also noteworthy is the teaching that the *sanhedrin* – like the priesthood, the monarchy and various other subjects which God claimed as His own – was endowed with eternity. Moreover, here too, the term used is *'olam*; *Sifrei*, Numbers 92.
30. H. Mantel, *Studies in the History of the Sanhedrin* (Cambridge, MA., 1965), pp. 175–252. The functions and powers of the *nasi'*, and the tensions between incumbents of that office and other rabbis, are discussed in greater detail below, chapter 8.
31. See, e.g., D. Hoffmann's *The Highest Court*; Tchernowitz, *Toledot ha-Halakhah*, vol. 4, pp. 215–61 and G. Alon, *The Jews in Their Land in the Talmudic Age* (trans. G. Levi; Jerusalem, 1980), Vol. 1, pp. 185–205.
32. Contrast the ratification procedure said to have been adopted by King David in TB *Berakhot* 3b.
33. All the evidence points to one certain conclusion: from the age of the Return [under Ezra] until the Destruction, there appear and then vanish various representative, administrative and public bodies: – *gerousiyot*, *sanhedriyot* and *mo'eṣot*. But not one of them equals or incorporates the sublime image of the *sanhedrin* standing at the apex of the judicial system, pronouncing law and spreading God's *torah* throughout Israel.

    Y. Efron, 'Ha-Sanhedrin ba-Ḥazon u-va-Meṣiut Shel ha-Bayit ha-Sheini', *Ḥiqerei ha-Tequfah ha-Ḥashmona'it*, p. 268. See also E. Rivkin, 'Beth Din, Boulé, Sanhedrin: A Tragedy of Errors', *HUCA*, 46 (1975), pp. 181–99.

    The theories earlier put forward to accommodate the various sources are summarised in Hoenig, *Great Sanhedrin*, pp. 121–2, 160–3; H.D. Mantel, *Sanhedrin*, pp. 54–70; and Schürer, op. cit., pp. 200–8.
34. Indeed, it has further been suggested that even the post-Destruction Galilean *sanhedrin* of rabbinic description is a fiction of talmudic imagination (although a pre-Destruction forum of that name did exist); Y.L. Levine, *Ma'amad ha-Ḥakhamim be-'Ereṣ Yisra'el Bitkufat ha-Talmud* (Jerusalem, 1986), pp. 47–52.

35. Hoenig, *Great Sanhedrin*, pp. 44–52.
36. *Ḥagigah* 2:9; but other sources do allow for the possibility of regional influences on the presentation of candidates, and imply that local lobbies might have been formed. S. Lieberman, *Tosefta' Kifshutah*, Vol. 5 (*Mo'ed*; N.Y., 1962), pp. 1297–9.

3

History as propaganda: the rabbinic version

To read the summary records which early rabbinic Judaism composed of its own historical antecedents is to gain an impression of strictly sequential transmission. The *torah* expounded by the sages, they suggest, is not the outgrowth of a momentary cultural oscillation; still less might the rabbinic interpretation of the Bible's teachings be considered the contingent product of recent political revolutions. Notwithstanding the turbulence of Jewry's recent and distant past, the integrity of the original Law had always been preserved, principally because the links of continuity in the chain of its transmission had never been broken.

In its blandest and most condensed form, rabbinic Judaism's own version of its parentage is encapsulated in the very first paragraphs of *Mishnah 'Avot*:

> Moses received *torah* from Sinai and handed it down to Joshua; and Joshua to the elders [*zeqeinim*]; and the elders to the prophets; and the prophets handed it down to the men of the great assembly [*'anshei keneset ha-gedolah*].

Having thus reached a point roughly midway into the chronology of the second Commonwealth, the tractate then goes on to record a handful of the traditions transmitted by Simon the Just ('one of the last survivors of the men of the great assembly'). Others, it relates, were thereafter 'received' from him by a string of personalities, beginning with a certain 'Antigonus of Socho' and culminating with the twin titans of Pharisaic memory, Hillel and Shamm'ai. By concluding with a selection of sayings attributed to Rabban Gamli'el and his son, Simeon, the chapter ultimately arrives at the generation which witnessed the Destruction of the Temple and the emergence of Judaism in its early rabbinic form.[1]

Trenchantly political in its refusal of any overt political content or allusion, *'Avot* 1 is a stunningly audacious piece of propaganda. Like most examples of its genre, it is also tendentious. Compressing over a millennium of Jewish history into just half a dozen lines, it is characteristically 'whiggish' in depicting an unabashedly slanted view of Israel's constitutional chronology. Paying attention only to evidence which points to a supposedly inevitable consummation of events, the authors of the passage bequeathed to posterity a polemical tract on their past rather than accurate reconstructions of its evolution. As proponents of a distinct aspect of Jewish constitutional interpretation, their avowed intention was to justify and (as far as possible) to authenticate their own perspective on its antecedents and development.

Subsequent rabbinic tradents followed that model. Unlike later scholars (medieval as well as modern), they did not fret too much over the blank areas in their records or attempt to reconcile any but the most blatant of its contradictions.[2] Intent only upon fleshing out the chain of *torah* transmission outlined in *'Avot* 1:1, *tana'im* and *'amora'im* were quite content to ignore large parts of their own claimed genealogy. What mattered to them was the depiction of selected phases and personalities of the past in a way which confirmed the dogmas of the present and thus ensured the rabbis themselves of the constitutional primacy which they believed to be their due. They did not need to tell the 'whole truth'; they were required only to accompany its kernel safely through the political and sectarian squabbles of the second Commonwealth period and thus show it to have arrived intact in their own time. Rabbinism, they sought to demonstrate, was an authentic genus of the species Pharisaism,[3] whose *torah* was itself directly derived from that entrusted to Israel at Sinai.

Characterisation and content in *'Avot*

If the thrust of the case presented in *'Avot* is to be fully understood, a distinction might be drawn between two of its component foci: one appertains to the identity of Israel's constitutional authorities; the other addresses the nature of their inherited constitutional referent. The first finds expression in the text's specification of the method whereby the current of *torah* instruction was conducted along Jewry's chain of constitutional transmission. Each teacher is said to have 'received' (*qibeil*) his traditions from predecessors with whom he had no attested genetic relationship. With the singular exceptions of such Hillelites as Rabban Gamli'el and his son (to whom, significantly, the term *qibeil* is not applied), none of *'Avot*'s named authorities are reported to have inherited their teachings from their fathers. Rather, and very much in the manner of the relationship between Joshua and Moses (or, for that matter amongst ancient Greek philosophers),[4] their links were solely those of disciples to their masters.

Taking that argument one stage further, Neusner has recently emphasised its corollary. In his view, what is most distinctive about *'Avot* 1:1 (indeed, about the entire tractate which it introduces) is the manner in which its presentation legitimises and sanctifies all contemporary exponents of rabbinic Judaism. The latter, conventionally designated throughout the tractate as *ḥakhamim* ('sages'), are portrayed as the true heirs of the original architects of Israel's constitutional corpus; they trace their spiritual ancestry directly to Moses. Consequently, they have inherited his attested plenitude of constitutional authority. Like Moses, the *ḥakhamim* are considered the authentic agents of the *torah*'s transmission, interpretation and specification.[5] Moreover, since no other group can boast intellectual patrimony of such distinction, none are qualified to possess the constitutional primacy which that asset bestows.

Perhaps because *'Avot* sought to minimise the influence of non- and anti-rabbinic elements in post-Destruction society, it nowhere specifies their identity. Of the several candidates mooted by critical speculation, particularly prominent have been Gnostic and Christian anti-nomists whose denial of the doctrine of a single revelation to Moses presented early rabbinic Jewry with a particularly serious challenge.[6] The paradigm of the three *ketarim*, however, indicates an entirely different set of possible targets. Specifically, it suggests that *'Avot* 1:1 might have complemented a more circumscribed domestic strategy, whose purpose was to stress the hegemony of the *keter torah* over the Jewish world and the supremacy within it of the early rabbinic facet of constitutional interpretation. Integral to that purpose was the denial of any parallel status to instruments of either the *keter malkhut* or the *keter kehunah*.

Although *'Avot* 1:1 makes no direct reference to the concept of the three *ketarim*, the text is manifestly cast in a literary mould which invokes the underlying resonance of that particular structure. As much becomes apparent, albeit in a negative sense, once its own catalogue of Israel's constitutional architects is contrasted with that which might reasonably be compiled from the Bible. Only in its reference to the fact that Moses was succeeded by Joshua does *'Avot* adhere to the scriptural history of *torah* transmission; otherwise, the two records are strikingly asymmetrical. Even in comparison to some other early rabbinic passages, *'Avot* 1:1 seems deliberately to inflate the overall constitutional prominence of those whom it generically designates 'prophets', depicting them as the principal teachers and interpreters of the Law in ancient Israel, and hence as the functional precursors of the rabbinic *keter torah*.[7] On the other hand, the text makes no acknowledgement whatsoever of the several scriptural indications that constitutional mediation during the first Commonwealth had frequently been the preserve of those public officials who had then embodied the domains of the *malkhut* and the *kehunah*. Totally unrecognised in *'Avot*'s reconstruction, for instance, are the Biblical suggestions that individual judges (*shofeṭim*) or kings (*melakhim*) had played a role which was often dominant and (as in II Chronicles 30) sometimes decisive in regulating the terms of the *torah*. Even more crucial, as Herr has recently emphasised, is *'Avot*'s blatant silence with regard to the constitutional role and functions of the Biblical priesthood. Of the several scriptural passages – some attributed to men who were themselves prophets – which specify the generic rights of *kohanim* to be considered the *torah*'s most authoritative exponents (Leviticus 10:11–12; II Chronicles 15:3; Jeremiah 18:18; Ezekiel 44:23–4), *'Avot* contains not a single echo.[8]

In fairness to subsequent tanna'itic chroniclers, it must be pointed out that some of them did criticise the way in which their predecessors had thus apparently doctored Scripture's constitutional record. *Mekhilta' de-Rabi Yishma'el* (a halakhic Midrash on Exodus, probably compiled towards the end of the 4th century C.E.), for instance, was explicitly to point out that the omission of Aaron from the chain of *torah* transmission was at best questionable; not only does the Pentateuch often couple his name with that of Moses when recording the enunciation of Divine commands; in three of the instances when the ordinances were of specifically priestly concern (Lev. 10:8; Numb. 18:1 and 8), Aaron is depicted as their *sole* recipient.[9] Later aggadic materials, likewise, were to make more generous acknowledgement of the constitutional initiatives which Scripture attributes to certain kings. In their embellishments on the lives of David and Solomon, for instance, they were to attribute to those personages the enactment of certain landmark constitutional amendments (*taqanot*).[10]

But retractions such as these, quite apart from being comparatively belated, were also singular. Far more dominant in early rabbinic literature was the tendency to reinforce the tendencious thrust of constitutional historiography articulated in *'Avot* 1:1 (often by resorting to forced explanations of the peculiar circumstances which necessitated Pentateuchal references to Aaron's own receipt of Divine instruction).[11] On the whole, Biblical sources were presented in a way which left no doubt that, in matters appertaining to the *torah*-as-constitution, representatives and descendants of the other two franchises occupied what was only a tolerated and secondary position. Ever since Sinai, it had been the *keter torah* – in which domain the sages had now inherited the prerogatives of the prophets – which had functioned as Israel's authentic repository of God's own law.

An essential complement to *'Avot*'s characterisation of the sages as the authentic descendants of Israel's earliest constitutional authorities is its portrait of the nature of their inheritance. This, the second layer of the text, finds expression in its extended use of the term *torah* (the absence of the definite article is explicit;[12] the need for a capital letter is obscure) as a generic term for the entirety of Israel's Divinely mandated ordinances. That corpus, is the premise, constitutes a seamless web of revelation. Still more radically, it also encompasses the framework of beliefs and practices transmitted by the sages. Indeed, the *torah* of the rabbis is to all intents and purposes one and the same as that of the scriptural canon itself. Although composed in different literary styles, *Mishnah* and Bible thus constitute a single exegetical unit. As theological and constitutional referents, they are together absolutely sufficient and (almost) entirely self-contained.[13]

Thus presented, there could exist no contradiction between the Biblical – especially Pentateuchal – texts and what was to become known as the rabbinic *halakhah*. Both constituted component segments of the same Divinely-inspired totality, a single arch of teachings which spanned the entire national experience. Admittedly, and as *Mishnah, Ḥagigah* 1:8 itself conceded, only limited portions of the code of conduct prescribed in early rabbinic literature could be shown to possess 'Scriptures on which they may lean' (civil law; the rules of the Temple service; the laws of purity; and those of incest). By contrast, there remained vast areas of rabbinic legislative activity in which – not to put too fine a point on matters – the *halakhot* of the sages were admitted to 'hover in the air'; lacking all but the flimsiest of Scriptural supports they could only be compared to 'mountains hanging on a hair'. Nevertheless, it remained axiomatic that even the latter categories of teachings were to be designated 'essentials of [*gufei*] *torah*.'[14] Not even the distinction – always carefully preserved – between those *halakhot* which were explicit in the Biblical text (*mi-d'oraita'*) and those which were the product of rabbinic exegesis (*mi-de-rabanan*; e.g. TB *Shabbat* 4a and 128b), could in the early rabbinic view ever vitiate the inherent validity of the latter. On the contrary, they too possessed Divine sanction.

While various elements of that doctrine are reflected in a number of scattered obiter dicta, several of its principal lineaments are conveniently consolidated in Jerusalem Talmud *Pe'ah* 2:6 (ed. Steinzaltz [1987], pp. 69–72). Comprising a sustained, albeit still occasionally rambling, enquiry into the phenomenon of received tradition, the point of departure for the passage is the Mishnaic report by Naḥum the 'libellarius' that he had received (and here, too, the root verb is *qbl*) a certain ruling on agricultural law

From R. Meya'sha', who had received it from his father, and he from the *zugot* ['pairs' of Pharisaic sages], and they from the prophets as a *halakhah* [transmitted] to Moses at Sinai. (*Mishnah, Pe'ah* 2:6; cf. the different version, and slightly different subject, in TB *Nazir* 56b.)

Notwithstanding the specific nature of the particular matter under discussion, the choice of prooftext was clearly not arbitrary. Even as it stands, Naḥum's report is insistent in its inference that the chain of *torah* transmission had never been broken and that rabbinic law was therefore an extension of the Sinaitic revelation. In keeping with other tanna'itic uses of the phrase *halakhah le-Mosheh mi-Sinai*, it is thus designed to score theological and polemic points rather than to advance a historical argument.[15] From the first, it intimates, the Word had consisted of layer upon layer of intentions and instructions, all of which had been communicated to those who had been empowered to reveal their meanings. Our passage of TJ *Pe'ah*, however, pushes that case several stages further. Indeed, in its very first comment on the relevant *Mishnah*, it posits that text and its exegesis, quite apart from being entirely contemporaneous and congruent, are also one and the same. Hence:

R. Z'eira' said in the name of R. Yoḥanan: If you come across a *halakhah* and you do not know its meaning, do not disregard it. For many laws were dictated to Moses [independently of Scripture] and all of them have been embedded in *Mishnah*.

The force of that argument is considerably augmented a few lines later, when the same text expands upon a notion which modern scholarship has termed the doctrine of 'the dual *torah*'. Briefly referring to a thesis more comprehensively established and developed elsewhere in early rabbinic literature, the passage argues that what made Israel's corpus of Divine laws unique was the bifurcate method of their communication: as originally transcribed by Moses at God's dictation, some were handed down in writing (*bikhtav*); others – the majority – were transmitted orally (*ba-peh*).[16] Both of these integrated segments of *torah* emanated from the same Divine source and both had originally been revealed at the same time. Even more to the point, both were equivalent in status (indeed, if anything, the oral law was even more 'beloved' of God than the written commandments, since the observance of the latter assumes the acceptance of the former). Consequently, when the sages expound *halakhah* they are not modifying or adding to the original Divine utterance. More accurately, they are validating the holy text by exposing to view an immanent radiance which has hitherto been covered up. Therein lies the strength of the contention which TJ *Pe'ah* goes on to attribute to the renowned third-century aggadist and mystic, R. Joshua b. Levi:

Scripture, *Mishnah*, *halakhot*, *tosefta'* [oral laws not included in the *Mishnah*], *'agadah* [homiletical expositions] and even the decision to be hereafter given before his master by a *talmid watiq* [trustworthy, perhaps also experienced, student] was already communicated to Moses at Sinai.

Of the several advantages of that position from the early rabbinic perspective, perhaps the most significant was the legislative authority which it assigned to the sages themselves. Admittedly, the latter were not altogether free agents. Since the grant of the unalterable Law had long anticipated their own birth, its students could not possibly claim to be participants in its creation. In the main, their task was to preserve its supernatural authenticity, primarily through the relentless (and, as Gerhardsson has shown, the carefully regulated)[17] safekeeping of the original texts. Nevertheless, the *torah* was not to be approached as a primitive heirogram. Conservation had to be accompanied by commentary, and the latter could only be accomplished by equally painstaking efforts directed at the continuous re-discovery of the Law's limitless meanings. Deuteronomy 17:11, after all, had explicitly acknowledged humans to be partners in revelation when enjoining Israel to observe the *torah* as taught by those who has mastered its secrets. *Sifrei* Deut. 154 (p. 207; trans. Hammer, p. 190) was still more graphic:

Even if they point out to you that right is left and left is right, obey them.[18]

Provided that the formalities of due exegetical process were observed, it thus mattered little that many of the rabbinic interpretations and amplifications of the Holy Writ would have been unintelligible to Moses himself.[19] The *torah* was not a mummified entity. Precisely because the original Word was inexhaustible, it could only fulfil itself through the disclosures of those to whom it had been entrusted. Interpretation had never to cease; for unless given repeated application and definition by successive generations of exegetes, the Bible would become bereft of all meaning. Summarising that attitude, Judah Goldin has concluded that:

The permanent and the fluid [...] are not two opposing features, or even sharply distinguished from each other. [...] the once-upon-a-time revealed Word and the subsequent words which are its outgrowth continue with unceasing life and liveliness to release successive truths which are not novel, but only newly recognisable permanent elements of the original content.[20]

TB *Qidushin* 49b put the matter more succinctly: 'What is *torah*? It is the interpretation [*midrash*] of *torah*.'

From prophecy to scholarship

But through what processes and by which mechanisms was the process of revelation to be constantly refreshed and sustained? In their numerous descriptions of the phenomenon of prophecy, the Biblical texts seemed to provide an answer as straightforward as it was extraordinary. In his very last address to the Children of Israel, Moses had foretold that 'a prophet will the Lord your God raise up to you, from your midst, of your brothers, like myself; you shall hearken to him' (Deuteronomy 18:15). All subsequent books of the Bible, according to early rabbinic traditions, constituted an enduring testament to the fulfilment of that promise. True, no subsequent prophet had ever managed to equal the proximity to the Divine attained by Moses himself.[21] Nevertheless, the phenomenon of which he had been the master had itself never ceased. In every phase of its history, Israel had been privileged to receive the counsel of numerous men and women (some specified, others not)[22] who, because they had received direct intimations of the Divine word, were set apart from ordinary folk. Selected and dispatched by God, prophets had followed in the pedagogic footsteps of Moses by transmitting a long series of inspired pronouncements, thus vigorously – even vociferously – imparting the constantly renewed dictates of Divine revelation.

Modern critics stress that it is only the 'latter' (alternatively 'classical') prophets who explicitly emerge from their writings as teachers of Law. Early rabbinic traditions, although aware of that impression, tended to minimise its significance. Instead, they preferred to emphasise that 'early' ('pre-classical') prophets too are in the Bible designated by the generic term *navi'* (lit. 'one who has been called', a title first applied in the Bible to Abraham; Genesis 20:7). What distinguished and united all members of that class, they taught, was that each had spoken in the name of the God of Israel and had articulated messages whose content, because rooted in the original Sinaitic Covenant, would forever form part of Jewry's single religious faith. Their sublime messages were, therefore, not only a source of comfort and inspiration; they also contained intrinsic (albeit, as we shall see, secondary) keys to the meaning of the *torah* itself. Therein lay the generic constitutional importance of all prophets and their collective prominence in the chain of *torah* transmission which *'Avot* 1:1 so pithily traced.

Post-Mishnaic rabbinic authors enlarged upon that theme. Scrutinising the books of the Bible, *'amora'im* found its prophetic portions to be subjects for the application of what in another intellectual environment might have been called 'scientific' methodology. The Babylonian Talmud, especially, contains several discussions concerning the context of the prophetical writings and their chronological orders of composition and canonisation. References also abound to the *curricula vitae* of individual prophetic personalities; the forms of prophetic activity; and the differences in the style and mode of prophetic expression.[23] Exceptional in a work usually indifferent to precise chronology and strict historicity, such passages articulate more than conventional respect for the content of prophetic teachings. They also indicate the extent to which early rabbinic authors sought to come to terms with the nature of the prophetic phenomenon. Prophecy engaged their interest because they considered it to have been God's unique way of revealing to humans new facets of His Law throughout the Biblical period. As such, it had then constituted – in addition to all else – a method and process of jurisprudential transmission.

No members of early rabbinic society ever claimed to be prophets nor even sons of prophets (in fact, according to the tale recounted in TB *Berakhot* 34b that pedigree was explicitly denied by the first century pietist, Ḥanina' b. Dosa'). On the contrary, they insisted that the entire phenomenon of prophecy had, some time during the course of the second Commonwealth, come to an irrevocable end.[24] What complexion one put upon that fact – did it underscore Israel's unworthiness to receive prophetic pronouncements or was it to be understood as a sign that improvements in the national character had made prophets redundant? – apparently remained, and remains, a matter of some dispute. But the issue was really only of secondary significance. Far more important was the crystallisation of the view that Israel had entered upon an entirely new stage in its history subsequent to the deaths of Haggai, Zechariah and Malachi. Thenceforth, it was taught, the 'holy spirit' (*ruaḥ ha-qodesh*) had ceased to play a direct role in national life (e.g. *Tosefta', Soṭah* 13:2 and parallels in S. Lieberman, *Tosefta' Kifshutah*, vol. 8 [*Nashim*: N.Y., 1973], p. 736).

Such pronouncements did not imply that, with the cessation of classical prophecy, God had altogether stopped communicating His wishes to man *viva voce*. On the contrary, according to reports preserved in early rabbinic traditions themselves, He had continued to do so – after as well as before the destruction of the second Temple. In both periods, several persons had been privileged to hear a 'heavenly voice' (*bat qol*) and thus to become intimately acquainted with God's wishes, His future course of action and, in some cases, even His opinion on certain legal issues. But, however frequent those occurrences, they were never granted an authority to match that of Biblical prophecy. Instead, such revelations are in the early rabbinic sources treated with a noticeable degree of ambivalence. Miracle workers and mystics, claiming the ability to communicate directly with God and thereby influence the Divine will, are criticised – not least so when (as was reported to be the case with Ḥoni 'the circle-maker') they were successful.[25] Heavenly interventions in legislative deliberations – even when authenticated by miraculous signs and wonders – were by the same token deliberately rejected. Once entrusted to man, *halakhah* had become a matter for human deliberation and affirmation, not heavenly decree.[26] Hence, never again would it be legitimate for any individual to claim a manifest mission borne of direct Divine revelation and, solely by virtue of that fact, to transmit *torah* to the House of Israel. In the words of *Sifra'*, the late fourth-century tanna'itic commentary on Leviticus (section 13, and parallels):

'These are the commandments' [Lev. 27:34] – henceforth a prophet may no longer make any [even technical] innovation.

The chronology of most of the sources which articulate rabbinic views on the cessation of prophecy has led to the suggestion that they were impressed into polemic service against third- and fourth-century Christianity. Following that view, they can be read as implicit (but no more) rejections of the doctrine that Scriptural law had still to be given a spiritual interpretation. More directly, they can be said to articulate a view at variance with the early Christian message that Jesus represents the true extension of the line which stretches back to the classical prophets of the Biblical era, whose writings had foretold his advent and whose teachings on the Suffering Servant had already proclaimed the dawn of a new faith. Undoubtedly, the challenge of early Christianity did lend particular urgency to the early rabbis' opposition to the authority of ongoing prophecy in their own days. Nevertheless, the attitude of mind which cultivated the rabbinic view need not necessarily have been originally dependent upon that context.[27] Extemporaneous prophecy, tracing its mandate to a source quite beyond human jurisdiction, altogether jars with the concept of organised religion. (Pauline history itself demonstrated that such was the case in the early Church too.) Whatever the magnetism of their personal appeal, visionaries who claim to receive their revelation directly from God necessarily present intractable problems of recognition and are therefore invariably distrusted by proponents of more conventional lines of established authority. How, indeed, are charismatics to be identified? Charlatans, after all, are not easily distinguished from men inspired – and even if they are so inspired, is it by God?

In the Jewish context, these were not new questions. Said to have been first raised in the wilderness of Sinai by the ecstatic prophecies of Eldad and Medad (Numbers 11: 26–9; see especially TB *Sanhedrin* 17a on verse 28), they had thereafter recurred with noticeable frequency. Particularly was this so during the period of the second Commonwealth. According to the Biblical account, Ezra had demonstrated his own feelings on the matter at the very inception of the restored polity, when establishing regularised agencies of constitutional review which appeared deliberately to dispense with prophecy and its instruments. Admittedly, if we are to trust the accounts preserved in I Maccabees, the hope that 'a true prophet' would once again arise in Israel did persist for some considerable time. But mainstream Pharisees (amongst whom, for this purpose, one might include Josephus) thereafter appear to have been far more circumspect in its articulation. In their eyes, the emergence of what seems to have been an ecstatic and apocalyptic 'frenzy' during the Destruction (BJ 6:285–6) perhaps even encouraged a tendency to remove the entire aspiration from recent Jewish history.[28] Certainly, unilateral 'prophecies' had to be more carefully monitored and self-proclaimed 'prophets' to be tightly controlled.

The critical rabbinic reaction to the emergent portrait of Jesus and his disciples during the first centuries of the Christian era thus seems to have followed a pattern which had long before struck deep roots. It cannot be attributed entirely to disapproval of the early Christian refusal to conform with the rabbinic Jewish standards of their times in matters of behaviour and/or religious observance. More fundamental was the threat which Jesus, like some other '*ḥasidim*', posed to the very notion of established constitutional order.[29] Experience had already shown that sudden outbreaks of prophetic spirit and apocalyptic vision had an alarming tendency to trample on due processes and on conventional mechanisms of jurisprudence. Because inherently unrestrained by authority, they had challenged and subverted the very fabric on which the continued existence of society had to depend. Considering themselves to be the only authentic interpreters of God's word, the early rabbis were bound to regard as suspect any person who claimed spontaneous access to God independent of the rabbinic structure which they were attempting to establish. Indeed, even to state that claim was, according to R. 'El'azar of Modi'im (first century), tantamount to apostasy. Hence his inclusion of 'one who gives an interpretation [*megaleh panim*] to the *torah* (which is not according to the *halakhah*)' in the list of miscreants who – whatever their good works – forfeit their place in the world to come.[30]

The pronouncement that 'From the day the [first] Temple was destroyed, prophecy was taken from the prophets and given to the sages [*ḥakhamim*]', (attributed to 'Avdimi of Ḥaifa, a fifth-century *'amora'*, in TB *Bava' Batra'* 12a) accurately summarised the political philosophy which underlay that conception. Positing far more than a statement of fact, it embraced an entire perspective on what the early rabbis considered to be legitimate modes of constitutional transmission. Revelation, it announced, was no longer to be regarded as a spontaneous and pneumatic experience, entirely unrelated to either the desire of the privileged individual or even his attested piety (several of the Biblical prophets, after all, had initially resisted their selection; few emerge from the Scriptural account as men of outstanding spiritual virtue prior to their calls to service). Instead, it was to be replaced by solicited revelation – consciously aspired to and conscientiously acquired, principally through the medium of relentless study. In effect, the true understanding of *torah* depended not upon irrational inspiration, but upon man's exercise of his critical faculties as manifest in sound philology and diligent exegesis. It was thus that prophecy and scholarship came to be presented as incompatible alternatives rather than equal imperatives. The term *torah* itself now meant a concern and preoccupation – even obsession – with study. In Glatzer's words:

> In the Talmudic literature, the resting of the holy spirit upon a man means no sudden experience of revelation, overwhelming him by its newness and immediateness [...] It becomes the result of preparation achieved by study and good deeds, in contradistinction to Scriptural prophecy, where God's call to the prophet marked the beginning of a process.[31]

Subsequent chapters (6 and 7 below) will trace the manner in which, by emphasising the inherent sanctity of *torah* study, early rabbinic texts were also able to assert the constitutional primacy of the *keter torah* and its superiority to the domains of the *kehunah* and the *malkhut*. In the present context, more immediately relevant is their employment of that theme in order to establish what was logically (although not necessarily chronologically) a prior position. In an effort to substantiate their claims to be the true instruments of the *keter torah*, the authors of those texts moved beyond *'Avot*'s original and straightforward statement that the sages had succeeded to the constitutional mantles once worn by the Biblical prophets. They even modified the more extended variant that, at some past watershed in Jewish constitutional history, scholarship had replaced prophecy as the authentic mode of understanding God's *torah* and therefore as the legitimate vehicle of halakhic pronouncement. Instead, by modifying some of the distinctions between the two categories of revelation, they suggested that sages were intrinsically superior to prophets – indeed perhaps had always been so.

Of the several formulations of that argument, one primary variant was essentially – albeit not intentionally – negative in form. Accumulating a series of otherwise disjointed legends and anecdotes, early rabbinic portraits tended to deprive classical prophecy of much of its uniqueness. Some texts gave expression to that theme by depicting the entire prophetic phenomenon as one which could be generalised. The spirit of prophecy, they indicated, had not been granted exclusively to the individuals cited in the Bible. In the world of the ancient Hebrews, inspiration of that sort (sometimes referred to as *ruaḥ ha-qodesh*; 'the holy spirit') had been a nationwide experience. In its own day, direct Divine revelation had been almost commonplace; even the most sublime of prophetic sayings had merely articulated what each individual member of the House of Israel had personally perceived. At moments of high drama, especially, God had revealed His glory to the entire people. ('A maid-servant at the [Red] Sea', R. 'Eli'ezer ben Hyrcanus is reported to have said, 'saw more than Isaiah, Ezekiel and all the other prophets.' [*Mekhilta' Shirata'* [ed. Lauterbach, II, p. 24].) There was every reason to believe that, with the advent of the Messianic age, such miracles would again occur.

An allied but nevertheless alternative theme was to overlay the classical experience of prophecy with the contemporary nuance of scholarship. Designed to flatten rather than wound, this view did not deny to prophets the status of authentic interpreters of God's *torah*. It did, however, deflate and thereby 'de-mystify' the procedures whereby major Biblical exponents of the prophetic calling were retrospectively perceived to have performed their task. Prophecy, instead of being a phenomenon which defied conventional categorisation, became incorporated into the modes standardised by the various frameworks of the mishnaic and talmudic interpretative apparatus. In this version too, therefore, the classical figures of scriptural fame could be deprived of their exclusivity. Not only 'did all the prophets receive their prophecy from Sinai, but also the sages that have arisen in every generation received their respective teaching from Sinai' (*Tanḥuma'*, *Yitro* 11, see also Exodus *Rabbah* 28:6).

In an article devoted to early rabbinic perceptions of the relationship between prophecy and *halakhah*, Urbach has charted the various nuances of that position.[32] As interpreted by the authors of several talmudic texts, he shows, the prophetic pronouncements recorded in the Bible – especially when they affected matters perceived to be of halakhic concern – were effectively re-modelled. Quite apart from being denied the legislative status accorded to the Pentateuchal code,[33] they were also wrenched from their obvious scriptural contexts. In effect, they were approached as a kind of literary laboratory, in which the early rabbis could experiment with their own methodology of textual reconciliation and test its ramifications. In some cases, *halakhot* otherwise thought to be of prophetic origin were represented as Divinely sanctioned rediscoveries of matters which had unfortunately been 'forgotten' at Moses' death. More often – and more significantly – they were transmuted into exegetical statements which, by and large, employed precisely the same procedures of deduction and reasoning which were recognised to be the stock in trade of the early rabbinic enterprise itself.

Conceptually, the result was to 'rabbinise' the prophets. Samuel, thus, could be depicted as a *poseq* when reasoning that King David possessed the right of admission to the Jewish fold (TB *Yevamot* 76b–77a; cf. Ruth *Rabbah* 2:5) and Haggai is portrayed as a legal authority capable of pronouncing on equally intricate points of law (TB *Yevamot* 16a). Ultimately, even Moses could be designated 'our rabbi'.[34] It followed that prophetic *taqanot* were just that. Their instigators had uniformly been required to justify their actions before the bar of the pentateuchal referent of Israel's Divine code. Prophetic authority, such as it was, had amounted to the power to suspend *torah*, not abrogate it entirely. According to later gloss, even Elijah must have satisfied that norm; had he not done so, he would never have received Divine sanction for his decision to take the sacrilegious – albeit urgently necessary – step of offering up sacrifices on Mount Carmel.[35]

Thus to state that prophets of old were subject to precisely the same groundrules of constitutional mediation as were the sages of the present was implicitly to invite comparisons between the performances of two classes. Since the rabbis were themselves umpires as well as players, it is hardly surprising to find that they tended to adjudicate in their own favour. Whereas the Oral Law, as transmitted by *ḥakhamim*, was indispensable (according to R. Yoḥanan, the Sinaitic covenant itself would have been unthinkable without it [TB *Giṭin* 60b]), the teachings of the prophets – in an otherwise perfect world – would have been superfluous.[36] It therefore followed that, 'the words of elders [*zeqenim*] were more stringent than were those of the prophets' (TJ *Berakhot* 1:4, contrasting Deut. 13:2 with Deut. 17:11). Each of the latter had been enjoined to prove his credentials through 'signs' and 'wonders'; in short, they had been forced to resort to paraphernalia which – precisely because they were supernatural – merely emphasised the prophet's absolute dependence on forces which were quite beyond even his own understanding. Sages, however, needed no such media; by mastering the *torah* they had become its unquestioned possessors. Hence their interpretations of its meanings could, and should, be taken on the trust inspired by their own scholarship.

The development of the *keter torah*: from Ezra to Hillel

Looking back over time, early rabbinic tradents of the post-Destruction generations identified an entire pantheon of worthies who had deserved that accolade. As the era of the second Commonwealth receded inexorably into history, its sages increasingly came to be regarded as folk heroes, and hence to be encrusted with almost as much hagiography as was lavished on the giants of Biblical fame. Unlike the latter, however, the distinction of the sages was not thought to reside (at least, not principally) in the intimacy of their association with their Maker. It was founded upon what was believed to have been their strict fulfilment of the Biblical commandment to study (lit. 'ponder') the *torah* and its contents day and night (Deut. 6:7 and Josh 1:8; see TB *Yoma'* 35b and *Menaḥot* 99b). Notwithstanding the succession of upheavals, dilemmas and delusions which had characterised the history of their times, each had reportedly managed to steer a vertiginous course in pursuit of that end. Combining meticulous scholarship, literary sensibility and profound respect for their received traditions, they had thereby made an immortal contribution to the development and vitality of the *keter torah*, shaping for eternity its themes, its genres and its procedures. In so doing, they had also ensured the status of the Oral Law as one of the very linchpins of Jewry's distinctive culture. That was why, next only to Israel's earliest forefathers, the sages of the second Commonwealth came to constitute rabbinic paradigms of human perfection. That, too, is why they – rather than the prophets – were projected as the most important precursors of the post-Destruction rabbis themselves. In sum, they were the nation's *'avot ha-'olam* (lit. 'fathers of the world', i.e. pillars of society; *Mishnah, 'Eduyot* 1:4).

First amongst such second Commonwealth dignitaries, both chronologically and in order of importance, was Ezra, the only man in Jewish history, says *Tosefta'*, *Sanhedrin* 4:7, who would have himself deserved to receive the *torah* 'had Moses not anticipated him'. That distinction was not the consequence of either Ezra's priestly genealogy or his prophetic status. Although he possessed both (Nehemiah 8:9 refers to him as *ha-kohen*; in TB *Megilah* 15a he is identified with the prophet Malachi), he had recourse to neither. Instead, it was in his capacity as *sofer* (lit. 'scribe') that he took it upon himself 'to expound (*lidrosh*) God's *torah* [...] and to teach in Israel statute and judgement' (Ezra 7:10 and TB *Sanhedrin* 21b). From the early rabbinic perspective, the designation proclaimed the nature of the mission. Ezra's distinctive title magnified the singularity of his own constitutional position and role. Single-handedly, or so it is made to appear,[37] he re-established a *torah* which had almost completely been forgotten (TB *Sukah* 20a). Compared to that accomplishment, even his religious ordinances ('the ten *taqanot* of Ezra'; TJ *Megilah* 4:1), pale in importance. Of far greater intrinsic significance were those of his reforms which were retrospectively perceived to have provided the *keter torah* with an embryonic institutional form: regular and frequent public readings of the *torah* (TB *Megilah* 31b; *Bava' Qama'* 82a–b); the inscription of the Bible in a more accessible form (TB *Sanhedrin* 21b) and – possibly most crucial of all – the establishment of a formalised educational system perhaps designed to encourage scholastic rivalry among schools and pupils (TB *Bava' Batra'* 21b–22a and *tosafot* s.v. *qin'at soferim*).

Early rabbinic statements which purport to relate the sequel to Ezra's activities are notoriously sketchy. Until they reach the time of Hillel (a gap of almost 350 years) they name very few names and supply only random notes about both the topics of scholastic research and the methodology of its application. Instead, what they provide are patent idealisations, most of which are clearly designed to convey an impression of infrequently interrupted consensus. At its apex, the sources suggest, the *keter torah* was throughout the first centuries of the second Commonwealth characterised by broad agreement about the *halakhah*. Prior to the age of the five *zugot* ('pairs' of [Pharisaic] leaders, reputed to have officiated during the second century B.C.E.) the *torah* was taught with a single voice, 'in the manner of Moses our teacher' (TB *Temurah* 15b); not until the confrontations between the disciples of Hillel and Shamm'ai during the first century C.E. were there any halakhic 'disputes in Israel' (*Tosefta'*, *Ḥagigah* 2:8). Scholastic debate, although plentiful,[38] was thus all very civilised. Conducted within an intellectual milieu which unquestioningly accepted the authority of the Oral Law, it avoided the pitfall of sectarian dissension and disarray. Despite all the fissures in the world around them, the sages of the period – we are invited to understand – had cultivated continuity and fostered stability. Within the framework of a *keneset gedolah* ('Great Assembly'), they had discovered the institutional means of ensuring both.

Although the *keneset gedolah* is nowhere mentioned in the Bible (or in any other non-rabbinic source, for that matter), rabbinic texts obstinately preserved and transmitted a tradition which associated its founding with Ezra.[39] Whatever that attribution might have lacked in historical accuracy, it certainly possessed the virtue of coherence with the thrust of the Biblical account. Dedicated though Ezra was to putting down several roots, the book which bears his name testifies that he assiduously pulled up many others. Specifically, he had challenged much of the religious hegemony of the high priesthood, especially when exploiting to the full the opportunities which his Persian mandate afforded to absorb the *kehunah*'s instructional roles.[40] The precedent thus established, rabbinic literature implies, survived even the political power subsequently wielded by the high priests of the Persian and Greek periods. It was not they, but 'the men of the Great Assembly' who were credited with having 'restored the crown [*'aṭarah*] of the *torah* to its former greatness' (TB *Yoma'* 69b). 'Simon the Just', traditionally identified with the fourth-century-B.C.E. High Priest of the same name, is the only member of that council explicitly named in *'Avot* 1:1. But from that source alone we would never have known that he was also Israel's supreme sacerdotal official.

'Avot 1:1 reveals its own estimate of the contribution which the men of the Great Assembly made to the stabilisation of an independent and non-priestly *keter torah* when reporting three of their maxims: 'Be slow in giving judgement' (which has been interpreted as an advocacy of lay judicial expertise – such as the Pharisees claimed to possess); 'set up many disciples' (i.e. establish a class of scholars whose selection and advancement would be independent of genetic criteria); 'and make a barrier about the *torah*' (i.e. utilise the constitutional mechanisms provided by the Oral Law).[41] Much later, *'amora'im* were to claim that the authors of those sayings had

been as good as their word. Following in Ezra's footsteps, they had canonised certain Biblical books (lit. 'they wrote' Ezekiel, the works of the twelve minor prophets, Daniel and Esther; TB *Bava' Batra'* 15a); issued various *taqanot* on extra-Temple liturgies and prayers (TB *Berakhot* 33a); and established the tripartite division of the Oral Law into *midrash*, *halakhah* and *'agadah* (TJ *Sheqalim* 5:1).

Precisely if and when the Great Assembly had ceased to function is not at all clear from the early rabbinic chronologies. (Was it absorbed by the '*sanhedrin*' or were the two assemblies one and the same, operating only in different capacities?) What is emphasised, however, is that the traditions and procedures which rabbinic Judaism owed to that body did not lapse. They were, rather, sustained by the class of scholars designated *soferim* (lit. 'scribes').[42] True, the gentlemen thus entitled are nowhere referred to, let alone specified, in *'Avot*. Elsewhere in early rabbinic writings, however, they are invested with critical importance in the chain of *torah* transmission between Ezra and Hillel. *Mishnah* designates several early *halakhot* affecting purity regulations as 'the ordinances of *soferim*' (*diverei soferim*: e.g. *Tohorot* 4:11; *Ṭevul Yom* 4:6). TB speaks of others whose 'main [elements] are in Scriptures but the interpretation of which comes from the works of the *soferim*' (*Sanhedrin* 88b). Even more significant is the admonition that a *zaqen mamrei* ('rebellious elder') who 'teaches against the ordinances of the *soferim* is more culpable than [one who teaches] against the words of the *torah*' (*Mishnah, Sanhedrin* 11:3).

Prominence of that order cannot be attributed exclusively to either the quality of the *soferim*'s scholarship nor to the magnitude of their substantive legal innovations. If anything, both are somewhat downplayed in the texts to hand. Although credited with the enactment of some *taqanot*, *soferim* were not retrospectively regarded as academic experts of the very first rank: on the contrary, they were subsequently considered to have been superseded in both authority and knowledge by the *ḥakhamim* of the post-Destruction period (which is one possible interpretation of the enigmatic threnody attributed to R. 'Eli'ezer [b. Hyrcanus] in *Mishnah, Soṭah* 9:15). Moreover, their accomplishments, whilst not insubstantial, were predominantly technical: enumerating the letters of the *torah* (TJ *Sheqalim* 5:1 and TB *Qidushin* 30a) and determining, sometimes slightly emending, its text (TB *Nedarim* 37b).[43]

Data such as this suggest that the *soferim* were measured by yardsticks quite different to those employed when gauging the historical importance of other instruments of the *keter torah*. From the early rabbinic perspective, indeed, their true significance seems to lie less in their academic attainments than in their methodological initiatives. *Soferim*, it appears, had applied to the study of the sacred texts philological tools recognisably distinct from those conventionally used thereto. In so doing, not only had they paved the way for a revolution in the study of the *torah*. Far more significantly, they had also shown how the priestly monopoly on the scribal calling might be broken and had thereby substantiated the independence of the *keter torah* from the *keter kehunah*.

As various studies have pointed out, the generic title conferred on those whom rabbinic literature refers to as *soferim* was not exclusively their own. Throughout several generations prior to the destruction of the second Temple, the term *sofer* was probably applied to any person whose profession afforded him the opportunity for intimate familiarity with sacred texts and who, especially when employed in public service, could be expected to explain their meaning. Ezra, we recall, was himself designated a *sofer*; and the appearance of the term in both Ecclesiasticus (where it is applied to Wisdom teachers; 38:24 [ed. Segal, pp. 251, 253]) and in the First Book of Enoch (12:3–4; 15:1; in the sense of 'scholar') would seem conclusively to deprive it of any uniquely Pharisaic connotations.[44] What that evidence also reflects, however, is the equal degree to which the designation was gradually becoming divorced from its strictly priestly connotations. Although perhaps originally priests of a secondary rank,[45] some time before the Maccabean revolt *soferim* had ceased to be Temple copyists in the strict sense, either priests themselves or working directly under priestly tutelage. Instead, they had already come to occupy instructional roles essentially independent of both the shrine and its management. Hengel has observed that even writings as early as those of Ben Sira 'demonstrate how the position of the teacher is breaking away from its association with the temple'.[46]

Discerning in this development 'a sign that the individualism of the Hellenistic period was also gaining significance among the Jewish people', Hengel posited three of its principal consequences. One was the establishment of new institutions of learning not tied to the Temple; a second was the democratisation of educational opportunities ('anyone who belonged to the people of God – even the proselyte – was now invited to study wisdom [...] and provided that he had the application and the aptitude, he had the possibility of being a great teacher of the law'); the third was the emergence of named teachers as personalities in their own right. Early rabbinic masters were certainly sensitive to the importance of these developments, whose pace they were themselves to quicken (see below, chapter 8). Nevertheless, when addressing the novelty of the *soferim*, their interest focused on a somewhat tangential matter. From their point of view, it was not sufficient to show that the elucidation and transmission of the *torah* had at some unspecified period become public property rather than a priestly preserve (a process which – notwithstanding the Pharisaic insistence on the importance of oral teachings – probably owed much to the spread of literacy in second Commonwealth times).[47] What they also wished to demonstrate was how, in the process, the methodologies of *torah* scholarship had also undergone radical revision.

Urbach's study of the emergence of *derash* ('exegesis') as the basis of *halakhah* is in this context of particular value.[48] Without asserting that early rabbinic philological techniques were either entirely novel or uniquely Pharisaic (probably neither),[49] he indicates how the sages of the late second Commonwealth appropriated the exegetical approach to Pharisaic purposes, making it distinctively their own. By refining its techniques to an unprecedented extent, they invested the Biblical term *derash* with new meaning. At the same time, they also threw into sharp relief the novel resonances of the title *sofer*.

That development, Urbach suggests, probably commenced during the reigns of either John Hyrcanus (135–104 B.C.E.), or Alexander Yannai (103–76), when it was stimulated by essentially political circumstances. Anti-Sadducean elements of the literate population, a category which included both proto-Pharisees and those purists who were subsequently to constitute the nucleus of the communities at Qumran, then went into voluntary exile and sought refuge in 'Syria'. Thus physically distanced from the Temple and its associated centres of textual activity, they necessarily fell back on their own intellectual and scholastic resources. Not all became intransigent sectarians. Only the groups whom Josephus defines as Essenes subsequently refused to return to Jerusalem, thereby demonstrating their intellectual dissociation from the cultural and cultic ambience of the capital (see below, chapter 4). But even those of the original dissidents who opposed such extremism, and whose point of view might have been summarised in Hillel's injunction not 'to withdraw from the community' (*'Avot* 2:4), did concur in at least one common principle. Pharisaic *soferim*, quite as much as Essenes, took a conscious decision to institutionalise their independence from the scriptural interpretations currently being promulgated by their Sadducean protagonists. The technique of *derash*, although pursued quite independently – even antagonistically – by the two groups,[50] provided them with the means of doing so. Therein, apparently, lies the significance of the similarities in the designations with which both groups honoured their masters. In the Damascus Code (6:7), the *meḥoqeq*, the Essenes' supreme legislative instrument, is defined as *'doresh ha-torah'*. TB (*Pesaḥim* 70b) preserves a tradition that Shema'yah and 'Avṭalyon, scholars whom the great Hillel was honoured to call his own teachers, were the first of the 'great *darshanim*' (cf. Josephus' reference to the otherwise shadowy figures of Judas and Mathias as 'unrivalled *exegetae* of the ancestral laws'; AJ 17: 149).

Rabbinic traditions which purport to describe the subsequent development of the pre-Destruction *halakhah* are replete with illustrations of the extended use of the exegetical techniques by those men and their successors. Admittedly, the distinctions between rulings regarded as received traditions and those which could be justified only as the result of exegetical analysis (*diverei soferim*) were never forgotten. But they did become blurred. Largely as a result, the *keter torah* attained a scholastic independence and presence which became hallmarks of the juridical identity of its devotees. Relying on their own powers of interpretation, Pharisaic scholars of the first century B.C.E. (some of whom were remembered to have been 'grapeclusters', *'eshkolot*, an ultimate accolade),[51] exercised increasing freedom in the legislation and publication of decisions which they had reached solely on the basis of their own distinctive methodologies. At the same time, they also felt sufficiently confident to proceed from individual glossations on the *torah* to the formulation of principles whereby it was to be interpreted. Thus seen, the attainments of the *soferim* certainly amounted to far more than mere letter-counting. Ultimately, they were considered to have bequeathed to posterity both the very first collections of post-Biblical *halakhot* and a wholly new jurisprudential form, with its own techniques and methodologies.

By far their most outstanding exponent was remembered to have been Hillel 'the Elder' who, according to subsequent legend, brought off the exceptional feat of starting out in academic life as a rather mature *wunderkind* and ending up a grand old man. Like most of his contemporaries, Hillel is a difficult man to date with any accuracy, especially since his exact origins were obscured in the subsequent Patriarchal scramble to claim descent from both his reported Davidic lineage and his supposed incumbency of the *nesi'ut*.[52] Perhaps the only reliable reports are the two briefest: first, he was amongst the last of the *zugot* (*Mishnah*, *Ḥagigah* 2:2, and therefore probably reached the height of his powers between 10 B.C.E. and 10 C.E.); second, like Ezra, he originated from *Bavel*. Even if we resist Mantel's invitation to extend the general implications of the latter scrap of information,[53] it must certainly be considered of more than passing interest; later rabbinic literature certainly judged Hillel's influence on the development of the *keter torah* to have been quite as considerable as that of his illustrious countryman (TB *Sukah* 20a, see also the coupling of Hillel with Ezra in TB *Sanhedrin* 11a). In part, his contribution to that domain was reflected in the quality of his students (TB *Sukah* 28a; who, together with those of Shamm'ai, are also designated *soferim*; TJ *Berakhot* 1:7). In part, it consisted of his success in extending its popular appeal. In stories which lose nothing in the telling, Hillel is said to have substantially influenced the public image of the *keter torah* by insisting on the intrinsic virtues of *torah* study and by setting legendary standards of personal humility and humanity. In both instances, the contrast with the *keter kehunah* was pointed. Only he who studies without cessation, runs one report of his teachings, can truly be said to be serving God (TB *Ḥagigah* 9b on Malachi 3:18); those who were 'disciples of [*talmidei*]' Aaron (*'Avot* 1:12) were implicitly superior to the High Priest's genetic offspring.

As Neusner has demonstrated, several of the tanna'itic 'fables' concerning Hillel have to be treated with caution. Sometimes embellishments on earlier materials, they may have been compiled with a view to their contemporary relevance rather than their historical accuracy. But that observation seems only to reinforce their value for our understanding of later rabbinic purposes, as well as Patriarchal designs. Particularly is this so when attention is turned to those traditions which purport to describe Hillel's legislative attainments and exegetical formularies. The former, and especially those of his landmark *taqanot* which regulated economic affairs, articulate the burgeoning independence of the *halakhah* from its strict dependence on the Written Law.[54] The latter demonstrate the extent to which – in the hands of a truly great master – the ground was being prepared for further developments of a similar import.

Hillel himself may, indeed, not have been the first sage to enunciate the seven hermeneutical 'rules' (*midot*) of exegesis, nor did he necessarily apply them with consistency when determining practical *halakhah*.[55] Nevertheless their association with his name in early rabbinic tradition remains significant. Thereafter, they were to remain the basis for all formularies which listed the distinctive norms whereby accredited masters could disect the sacred texts and so discover their meanings.

Even within the Pharisaic camp the prominence thus attributed to *derash* as a basis of halakhic decision-making did meet with some early resistance, much of which seems to have been pretty stiff. TJ *Pesaḥim* 6:1 reports that Hillel was himself challenged on this very account.[56] That circumstance did not necessarily reflect irreconcilable scholastic opposition to *derash* per se. It was more probably the result of an appreciation of the fissiparous consequences to which, unless carefully watched, the technique was likely to give rise. Exegesis, after all, is necessarily a tenuous jurisprudential practice. By nature open-ended, it can hardly have been conducive to unanimity: what one sage characterised as *derash* (sometimes 'professional' *derash*),[57] might to another very easily appear far-fetched or fantastic, and hence unwarranted. Moreover, the quantity of variant interpretations offered on any single text was likely to multiply in direct relation to the number of its practitioners. With the increase in the student population attending Pharisaic schools during the first century B.C.E. (otherwise, of course, a highly gratifying phenomenon), that particular danger seems to have become very real indeed. One dispute between Hillel and Shamm'ai, it was recalled, caused 'a sword to be embedded in the academy' (TB *Shabbat* 17a). No less ominously, as a result of the differences between their schools, the composite body of Israel's laws teetered on the brink of disarray, becoming 'like two *torot*' (*Tosefta', Ḥagigah* 2:9).[58]

One method of arresting that dangerous development was to place severe restrictions on the application of rabbinic exegetical techniques; R. 'Abba' bar Memel's later admonishments which specifically proscribed the free-wheeling use of *gezeirah shawah* (the inference of law from a similarity of Biblical phrases; TJ *Pesaḥim* 6:1) provide a case in point. Another was to institute binding rules of procedure for the resolution of academic differences and to ensure that they were conformed to (e.g. *Mishnah, 'Eduyot* 5:6 discussing the case of 'Aqavya' Mehalal'el). Admittedly, most of our data on these matters is of relatively late provenance; but the instances described in the available sources seem to have been not entirely unprecedented. Even prior to the Destruction, it had apparently been agreed that *taqanot* would generally only be regarded as valid if agreed to by the majority of scholars present when they were discussed; in other cases, conventional standards of precedence had been established.[59] The principle that the decisions of the school of (*beit*) Hillel were to be preferred to those of the school of Shamm'ai (although not formulated until the Yavnean period, and even then sometimes disregarded; TJ *Berakhot* 1:7), is likely to have been a rule of thumb some time before 70 C.E.

Whichever the case, the flow of exegetical continuity had not been interrupted. In its rabbinic guise, the *keter torah* was not breaking new constitutional ground; on the contrary, it was embellishing a tradition of scholarship which stretched back to the dawn of national history. *'Avot* 1:1 and its various elaborations illustrated the degree to which that was so. Neither the *keter kehunah* nor the *keter malkhut*, it argued, had ever played a direct and independent role in the transmission of *torah*. That privilege had been reserved for Moses' designated successors – the prophets and, more substantially still, the sages. The status of the latter was assured, notwithstanding their tendency towards academic dispute. The ordained competence of the *torah* had always guaranteed the supremacy of its teachers; and since the rabbis were manifestly qualified to fulfil that role, their claims to communal authority were inherently respectable. *Ḥakhamim* had protected the purity and integrity of the *torah* throughout all the upheavals of the first and second Commonwealths; their rabbinic successors, similarly, would ensure the survival of Israel's unique heritage throughout whatever tribulations were still to come.

NOTES

1. This source has generated a particularly large corpus of commentary. For a summary of the literature, and an elucidation of the text, with particular regard to its historical utility, see: B. Dinur, 'Le-Mashma'utah Shel Masekhet 'Avot ke-Maqor Hisṭorie', *Zion*, 35 (1970), pp. 1–18.
2. For one exception: TB *Nazir* 56b and Rashi, s.v. *we-'amru*.
3. Although the connection is not stressed until early medieval times,

it is often assumed in tanna'itic and amora'ic passages. The talmudic texts are subjected to critical analysis in: J. Neusner, 'Pharisaism and Rabbinic Judaism: A Clarification', *History of Religions*, 12 (1973), pp. 250–70; see also (with specific reference to the Josephus texts) A. I. Baumgarten, 'The Pharisaic *Paradosis*', *HThR*, 50 (1987), pp. 63–77.

4. A point made in E. Bickerman, 'La Chaine de la tradition Pharisienne', *Revue Biblique*, 59 (1952), p. 53.
5. J. Neusner, 'From Scroll to Symbol: The Meaning of the Word Torah', *Formative Judaism*, III, p. 41. The argument is further developed in idem., *Torah: From Scroll to Symbol in Formative Judaism* (Philadelphia, 1985).
6. B. J. Bamberger, 'Revelations of Torah after Sinai', *HUCA*, 16 (1941), pp. 102–4.
7. Cf., e.g., *'Avot* 1:1 and *ARN* (ed. Schechter, p. 2; which also inserts Haggai, Zechariah and Malachi) with the omission of all prophets in *Mishnah, Pe'ah* 2:6 and *'Eduyot* 8:7.
8. M. D. Herr, 'Ha-Reṣef she-ba-Shalshelet Mesiratah Shel ha-Torah', *Zion*, 44 (1979), pp. 46–7. See also the earlier discussions in I. Loeb, 'Notes sur le Chapitre 1er des Pirke Abot', *REJ*, 19 (1899), esp. pp. 191–2.
9. *Mekhilta', Pisḥa'* 1 (ed. Lauterbach, I, pp. 1–2). Cf. the forced explanation in *Sifrei* Numbers 117 (p. 134). Later materials in Kasher, *Torah Shelemah*, Vol. 20 (N.Y., 1961), p. 43, no. 148 and Vol. 36 (Jerusalem, 1982), p. 79, no. 140.
10. Thus David, quite apart from having composed several prayers and setting the number of priestly divisions at 24 (TB *Ta'anit* 27a), is also reported to have initiated some significant *halakhot* in inter-personal relations (TB *Sanhedrin* 21b and *Shabbat* 56a). He is also depicted as being an halakhic authority, and even an *'av beit din* in TB *Berakhot* 4a. On the *taqanot* of Solomon see: TB *'Eruvin* 21b.

    Additional sources are cited, and compared to Qumran texts, in Y. Yadin, *Megilat ha-Miqdash*, Vol. 1 (Jerusalem, 1977), p. 308.
11. *Sifra'* to Lev. 10.3 and TB *Zevaḥim* 115b (*tosafot* s.v. *'we-qibeil'*). Further sources in Kasher, *Torah Shelemah*, Vol. 36, pp. 88–9, no. 1 and Bamberger, *Revelations*, pp. 97–113.
12. J. Goldin, 'The Three Pillars of Simon the Righteous', *PAAJR*, 27 (1958), pp. 48–9.
13. As has often been pointed out, early rabbinic authors rarely cite any of the numerous writings produced by Jews between the canonisation of Scripture and their own works. Their own teachings, they thus proclaim, are the only traditions which deserve to be treated in tandem with the Bible itself. For the exceptions see: M. H. Segal's introduction to his edition of Ecclesiasticus: *Ben Sira'*, pp. 37–42 and, on the reference to *Megilat Ta'anit* in *Mishnah, Ta'anit* 2:8, H. D. Mantel, *'Anshei Keneset ha-Gedolah* (Tel Aviv, 1983), pp. 213–23.

14. The same phrase, with even greater force, is attributed to Reish Laqish in TB *Ḥullin* 60b (see Rashi s.v. *harbei* and *wehen*). The Mishnaic text has recently been discussed in J. Neusner, 'The Description of Formative Judaism: The Social Perspective of Mishnah's System of Civil Law and Government', *AJS review*, 5 (1980), pp. 77–8 and M. I. Gruber, 'The Mishnah as Oral Torah: A Reconsideration', *JSJ*, 15 (1984), pp. 114–16.
15. Prominent amongst other sources are: *Mishnah*, *'Eduyot* 8:7 (R. Joshua); *Mishnah*, *Yadayim* 4:3 and *Tosefta'*, *Yadayim* 2:2 (R. Eliezer). A recent study of these and other occurrences demonstrates that the term was not applied in a specific category of cases, but was used in a general sense. S. Safrai, 'Halakhah le-Mosheh Mi-Sinai – Hisṭoriah 'O Te'ologiah?', *WCJS*, 9 (3), 1986, pp. 23–30. Indeed, R. 'Aqiva' maintained that 'the entire *torah* was "*halakhah le-Mosheh mi-Sinai*"', TB *Nidah* 45b.
16. The origins of the term, and its transmutation into *torah she-be-'Al peh*, are traced in Y. (G.) Blidstein, 'Le-Qorot ha-Munaḥ Torah she-be-'Al Peh', *Tarbitz*, 42 (1973), pp. 496–8. Earlier expressions of the doctrine of the 'dual *torah*' are recorded in *ARN* ('A') 15:61; *Sifrei* Deut. 351 (p. 408); and *Sifra'* to Lev. 24:46. The extent to which such sources reflect possible differences between the rabbinic schools of 'Aqiva' and Yishma'el are discussed in A. J. Heschel, *Torah Min ha-Shamayim be-'Aspaklariyah Shel ha-Dorot*, Vol. 1 (Jerusalem, 1962), pp. 5–9. On the supposed technique of transmission by Moses himself, see TB *'Eruvin* 54b, and Lieberman's comment in *Hellenism*, p. 93.
17. B. Gerhardsson, *Memory and Manuscript: Oral Tradition and Written Transmission in Rabbinic Judaism and Early Christianity* (Uppsala, 1961), esp. pp. 123–70.
18. Cf. the version in TJ *Horayot* 1:1. For analysis: Hoffmann, *Highest Court*, pp. 110–16 and Gerhardsson, pp. 93–112.
19. That seems to be the thrust of Rav's remarkable legitimisation of the exegetical work of R. 'Aqiva and his disciples (TB *Menaḥot* 29b). Granted a glimpse into the future (so the story goes), Moses was upset to find that he did not understand what R. 'Aqiva' was sitting and expounding. 'His mind was set at ease' when he heard that, in reply to the question, 'Master, how do you know this?', R. 'Aqiva' told his disciples: 'It is a *halakhah* of Moses given at Sinai.'
20. J. Goldin, 'Of Change and Adaptation in Judaism', *History of Religions*, 4 (1965), pp. 277–8. Also Gerhardsson, pp. 93–112.
21. Numbers 12:6–8; TB *Yevamot* 49b expressed the same thought somewhat more graphically: whereas Moses beheld the Divine as through a clear mirror, the other prophets did so through a distorted mirror (lit. 'a mirror which does not shine', cf. I Corinthians 13:12: 'speculum in aenigmate'). Only Isaiah came anywhere near to the same degree of sanctity (TB *Ḥagigah* 13b). On earlier applications of the Deuteronomic text, in non-rabbinic as well as rabbinic literature:

B. Jackson, 'Jésus et Moïse: le statut du prophet a l'égard de la Loi', *Revue Historique de Droit Français et l'Etranger*, 59 (1981), pp. 341–60.

22. Ancient prophets and prophetesses were 'double the number of the Children of Israel who went forth from Egypt' (TB *Megilah* 14a). Every tribe produced them (TB *Sukah* 27b).
23. See, especially, TB *Megilah* 14a and *Bava' Batra'* 14b–15a, and the analysis in Heschel, *Torah Min ha-Shamayim*, Vol. 2 (Jerusalem, 1965), pp. 290–3.
24. The variant rabbinic datings are discussed in E. E. Urbach, 'Matai Paskah ha-Nevu'ah?', *Tarbitz*, 17 (1946), pp. 1–11.
25. See, e.g., Simeon ben Sheṭaḥ's reported message: 'Were it not that you are Ḥoni, I would decree a ban against you.' On the development of this tale in the sources (*Mishnah, Ta'anit* 3:8; *Tosefta'*, ibid. 3:1; TJ *Ta'anit* 3:11), see W. S. Green,. 'Palestinian Holy Men: Charismatic Leadership and Rabbinic Tradition', *ANRW* II, 19.2 (1979), pp. 619–47.
26. For which the locus classicus is TB *Bava' Meṣ'ia* 59b. The implications and context are discussed in B. Jackson, 'Ha-Hakarah ha-'Enoshit we-ha-Yediah ha-'Eloqit ba-Mishpaṭ ha-Miqra'i we-ha-Tana'i', *Shenaṭon ha-Mishpaṭ ha-'Ivri*, 6–7 (1980), pp. 61–70. The progress of traditional rabbinic commentaries on the tale is traced in Y. Englard, 'Tanur Shel 'Akhn'ai: Peirushehah Shel 'Agadah', *Shenaṭon ha-Mishpaṭ ha-'Ivri*, 1 (1975), pp. 45–56.
27. E. E. Urbach, *The Sages: Their Concepts and Beliefs* (2 vols., trans. I. Abrahams; Jersualem, 1979), Vol. 1, pp. 300–8.
28. Certainly on the part of Josephus himself. For an analysis of his treatment of I Maccs 4:44–7 in AJ 12:318 and of I Maccs 9:27 in AJ 13:5, see Y. Gafni, 'Le-Darkhei Shimusho Shel Yusefus be-Sefer Maqabim I', *Zion*, 45 (1980), pp. 84–5. Cf. Goldstein, *I Maccabees*, pp. 12–13.
29. G. Vermes, *Jesus the Jew: A Historian's Reading of the Gospels* (Phila., 1975), pp. 58–82 and M. Hengel, *The Charismatic Leader and His Followers* (Edinburgh, 1981), pp. 45–9. The strength of the non Pharisaic 'school' which placed deeds above learning, is also discussed in L. Jacobs, 'The Concept of the Hasid', *JJS*, 8 (1957) and S. Safrai, 'Ḥasidim we-'Anshei Ma'aseh', *Zion*, 50 (1985), pp. 133–54.
30. *Mishnah, 'Avot* 3:11; textual variants in: L. Finkelstein, *Mavo' le-Masekhtot 'Avot we-'Avot de-Rabi Natan* (N.Y., 1950), pp. 74, 160–1 and Urbach, *Sages*, Vol. 2, p. 818, notes 33–5.
31. N.N. Glatzer, 'A Study of the Talmudic Interpretation of Prophecy', *Review of Religion*, 10 (1946), pp. 123–4. See also the sources cited in J.W. Bowman, 'Prophets and Prophecy in Talmud and Midrash', *Evangelical Quarterly*, 22 (1950), esp. pp. 255–75. Pithier than both was Naḥmanides (1194–1270), who distinguished between 'the prophecy of prophets, which is that of vision, and the prophecy of sages through the medium of wisdom', *Ḥidushei ha-Ramban* on TB *Bava' Batra'* 12a.

32. 'Halakhah U-Nevu'ah', *Tarbitz*, 18 (1947), pp. 1–27. See also *Sages*, pp. 302–4.
33. As Urbach has shown (op. cit.), TB's pronouncement that 'we do not derive *divrei torah* from the words of the prophets [*qabalah*]' (*Ḥagigah* 10b; *Nidah* 23a and *Bava' Qama'* 2b), although never slavishly followed – and, indeed, entirely absent from TJ – remained a rule of thumb.
    Commenting on *Mishnah, Ta'anit* 2:1, Hoffmann (*First Mishna*, p. 7) suggests that the teachings of the prophets were designated *qabalah* 'because they did not teach anything new'.
34. Although, it must be noted, nowhere in *Mishnah*. For TB references, see G. Vermes, *Scripture and Tradition* (2nd ed.; Leiden, 1973), pp. 51–2; and J. Neusner, 'The Myth of the Two Torahs: A Prolegomenon', *Formative Judaism*, III, p. 8.
35. Talmudic attitudes to the incident are thrashed out in the medieval commentaries by the tosafists and Samuel Eliezer Edels (*Maharshah*; 1555–1631) to TB *Yevamot* 90b and *Sanhedrin* 89b. For a more recent, and comparative, analysis: Jackson, 'Jésus et Moïse', esp. pp. 350–7.
36. According to R. 'Ada' b. R. Ḥunya', had not Israel sinned, they would have been given only the Pentateuch and the Book of Joshua: TB *Nedarim* 22b exegesis on Eccles, 1:18.
37. Compared to the Biblical account, early rabbinic histories of the early second Commonwealth period tend to stress Ezra's contribution to the age and to obfuscate that of Nehemiah. Even the canonical book which bears the latter's name is called 'the second part of Ezra' (TB *Sanhedrin* 93b).
38. As Hoffmann notes (*First Mishna*, p. 86): 'It is more than likely that many differences which our Mishna (i.e. in its redacted form) relates in the names of later Tannaim have already been part of the old (i.e. pre-Destruction) Mishna.' For an analysis of the authenticity of the debates between the schools of Shamm'ai and Hillel see M. Weiss, 'Ha-'Autenti'ut Shel ha-Shaqla' we-Ṭarya' be-Makhloqot Beit Shamm'ai u-Veit Hillel', *Sidra*, 4 (1988), pp. 53–66.
39. E.g., TB *Berakhot* 33b; *Yoma'* 69b; TJ *Berakhot* 1:9; *Megilah* 2:8. For discussions of the authenticity of these and other sources, and the possible identity and activities of the body, see H. D. Mantel, *'Anshei Keneset ha-Gedolah* (Tel Aviv, 1983), pp. 63–133, some of which repeats the same author's 'The Nature of the Great Synagogue', *HThR*, 60 (1967), pp. 69–91. Compare, I. J. Schiffer, 'The Men of the Great Assembly' in W. S. Green (ed.), *Persons and Institutions in Early Rabbinic Judaism* (Missoula, 1977), pp. 237–76.
40. E.g. Nehemiah 8:6–8. The fact that none of the thirteen assemblies reported in Ezra-Nehemiah were held within the Temple precincts proper may itself have underscored Ezra's declaration of independence from the authority of the high priesthood.

41. L. Finkelstein, 'The Maxims of the Men of the Great Synagogue', *JBL*, 59 (1940), pp. 455–69.
42. Lieberman, *Hellenism*, p. 47 suggests that the designation may approximate to 'grammarius'.
43. On the *tiqunei soferim*, idem, pp. 28–37, and on the 'degeneration' of the term *soferim* in rabbinic literature, Gerhardsson, pp. 45–55.
44. Neusner, 'Formation of Rabbinic Judaism', pp. 39–41. See also R. T. Beckwith, 'The Pre-History and Relationships of the Pharisees, Sadducees and Essenes', *Revue de Qûmran*, 41 (1982), pp. 18–20.

    It has recently been argued that the 'scribes' of the synoptic gospels are also not necessarily Pharisees. Usually appearing as either subordinate judicial and clerical associates of the High Priest, or as teachers and spiritual authorities (in which capacity they may have been aligned with the Pharisees), they were probably Levites. D. Schwartz, 'Soferim u-Perushim Ḥanfanim: Mi Heim ha-Soferim bi-Vrit ha-Ḥadashah', *Zion*, 50 (1985), pp. 121–32.
45. E. E. Urbach, *Ha-Halakhah: Meqorotehah we-Hitpatḥutah* (Jerusalem, 1984), p. 72; on the basis of TJ *Sheqalim* 4:3, Urbach also argues that – even subsequently – *soferim* probably continued to draw salaries from Temple funds. See also the same author's *Sages*, p. 576, where he speaks of the class of *soferim* being 'penetrated' by the sages. Compare, however, Mantel, *'Anshei Keneset ha-Gedolah*, pp. 146–66.
46. M. Hengel, *Judaism and Hellenism* (Eng. trans.; Phila., 1974), Vol. 1, p. 79.
47. M. Bar-Ilan, *Ha-Pulmus Bein ha-Ḥakhamim la-Kohanim be-Shelhei Yemei Bayit Sheini* (unpub. Ph.D. thesis, Bar-Ilan University, 1982), pp. 102–7 and 234–6.
48, 'Ha-Derashah ke-Yesod Ha-Halakhah u-Va'ayat ha-Soferim', *Tarbitz*, 27 (1958), pp. 166–82; and *Ha-Halakhah*, pp. 69–78.
49. As has independently been argued, Deuteronomy too provides several examples:

    > The talmudic rabbis did not invent the idea that legislation must somehow be linked with a biblical text. They were but following a pattern of thought and practice which modern literary critics attribute to the work of the so-called Deuteronomist.

    J. Widengreen, *From Bible to Mishnah* (Manchester, 1976), p. 22.
50. H.D. Mantel, *'Anshei Keneset ha-Gedolah*, pp. 186–95 cites 34 instances of similarity between Qumran and Pharisaic *halakhah*. Nevertheless, the differences between their *derash* always remained. Note, thus, the Essenes' disparaging references to the Pharisees as *dorshei ḥalaqlaqot* ('seekers of smooth things'; alternatively '*halakhot*') in *The Thanksgiving Scroll*, 2:15 and 32 (ed. M. Mansoor; Leiden, 1961), pp. 106 and 110 fn. 6. For a definition of *midrash* see: G. Vermes, *Scripture and Tradition in Judaism* (Leiden, 1961), p. 7.
51. Hoenig, *Great Sanhedrin*, pp. 28–9 and 171–3 and J. Neusner, *From*

Politics to Piety: The Emergence of Pharisaic Judaism (Hoboken, N.J., 1973), pp. 127–9.

52. TB *Shabbat* 15a, *Pesaḥim* 66a and TJ ibid. 6:1, all state that he was – improbably – a *nasi'*. On these sources, see J. Liver, *Toledot Beit David* (Jerusalem, 1959), pp. 28–32.
53. Mantel, *'Anshei Keneset ha-Gedolah*, pp. 116–27, elaborates on the possible Babylonian influence on early Pharisaic *halakhah*, arguing that Hillel's activity only confirmed that feature of second Commonwealth life.
54. However, commenting on *Mishnah*'s account of Hillel's decision to introduce the *prozbul* as a means of circumventing the Biblical command to cancel all debts with the advent of the sabbatical year, J. Neusner remarks:

    Judah the Patriarch preferred for the Mishnah the story that traces the *prozbul* to historical necessity. It provided a precedent for two important propositions. First, Judah's ancestor had exercised enormous power. Second, the *nasi* does not have to rely upon exegesis, but can do pretty much whatever he wants in response to historical conditions.

    'From Exegesis to Fable in Rabbinic Traditions About the Pharisees', *JJS*, 25 (1974), pp. 263–9.
55. Hillel's rules are mentioned in *Tosefta'*, *Sanhedrin* 7:11; *ARN* ,'A' 37, 110; and *Sifra'*, intro. 1:7. On their indigenous character, and origins: Lieberman, *Hellenism*, pp. 53–68.
56. See the analysis in Urbach, *Ha-Halakhah*, pp. 73–4 and p. 260 fn. 25. Opposition emanated from the *benei betaira'* whom Hoenig, *The Great Sanhedrin*, designates 'an opposition group in matters of law' (p. 199). Cf. Mantel, *Sanhedrin*, p. 219, fn. 274.
57. As did Hillel who *'darash leshon hedyoṭ'*, see *Tosefta'*, *Ketubot* 4:9 and Lieberman's note in *Tosefta' Kifshutah* [hereafter, TK, vol.] 6 (*Nashim*; N.Y., 1967), p. 246.
58. For contrasting interpretations of this passage and its parallels compare Lieberman in both *Hellenism*, p. 92 and TK 5 (*Mo'ed*; N.Y., 1962), pp. 1297–9 with L. Ginzberg, *On Jewish Lore and Law* (Phila., 1955), pp. 94–5.
59. Note, especially, the '18 measures' said to have been decided in favour of *beit Shamm'ai* (*Mishnah*, *Shabbat* 1:4 and TJ ibid. 1:7 [3c]) and the resolution of the long-running dispute concerning *semikhah* ('laying of hands' [on sacrifices]); *Mishnah*, *Ḥagigah* 2:3 and *Tosefta'*, idem, 2:10–12 [Lieberman, TK, idem.].

4

Other positions, other priorities

As epitomised by *'Avot* 1:1, early rabbinic historiography eventually became entrenched as the normative version of the Jewish constitutional record. All others, even when acknowledged to have once existed, had by the fifth century been banished to the sectarian margins of the national ethos.

Only if we restrict our reading solely to avowedly rabbinic texts of the post-Destruction era do matters always seem to have been thus. Quite the contrary impression is conveyed by what has survived of earlier writings, pre-rabbinic and non-Pharisaic. For all their own divergences, none substantiate the rabbinic claim that the *keter torah* had throughout the second Commonwealth been universally considered superior to the other two clusters of Jewish government. If anything, the rabbinic formulation might have seemed less coherent and creditable than the rival doctrines already formulated on behalf of the *keter malkhut* and (with even greater force) the *keter kehunah*.

The purpose of the present chapter is to review those various projections and, by reconstructing their own hierarchy of the three *ketarim*, to demonstrate the adversarial backcloth to the rabbinic version of Israel's past and vision of Jewry's future.

The *keter malkhut*: from Davidic to Herodian polemic

Literary comparisons which measure the polemical output of what are here referred to as the domains of the *kehunah* and *malkhut* are inherently disadvantageous to the latter. Principally, this is because pronouncements which explicitly proclaim the constitutional primacy of the *keter malkhut* are a remarkably late feature of second

Commonwealth literature. For the vast majority of the period, even the memory of the House of David seems to have been submerged and largely devoid of immediate political relevance. Recent research has rejected the simplistic explanation that biological mortality was largely responsible for that condition. Liver, especially, has offered a more politically slanted solution.[1] The Return from Babylon, he argues, was inherently unlikely to have been accompanied by the full rehabilitation of the monarchy's ancient prestige. Admittedly, some (although not all) of post-Exilic Biblical literature did propagate the eschatological hope of a Davidic restoration. Admittedly, too, remnants of the Davidic house had probably managed to retain much (but, again, not all) of their traditional leadership during the Babylonian exile. However, neither of those circumstances could have entirely erased the unhappy memories of earlier failures of royal leadership immediately prior to Nebuchanezer's final onslaught. Davidides could in any case claim no particular credit for instrumentalising the eventual Return; their share in that process was certainly less than that of Cyrus – which is why a messianic adornment was now appended to his name.[2] To all intents and purposes, in fact, Davidic pretensions to a quotidian share in Jewish public authority affected only the ancient past or the distant future; they were not a matter of immediate practical concern.

In large part, Liver argues, that is why Jewish sentiments seemed hardly affected by the manner in which post-Exilic Davidides were unceremoniously deprived of their formal offices (Zerubbabel, notably, simply dropping into obscurity during the very first decade of Darius' reign almost as suddenly as he had previously shot into prominence); on the evidence of Chronicles, neither did Jewish history show more than cursory interest in their precise physical fate. Although *Mishnah* (*Ta'anit* 4:5) does contain one tantalising reference to the existence of some *benei dawid ben yehudah* during the last years of the second Temple, it is not clear that the gentlemen referred to were direct offspring of Israel's greatest king. Far more eloquent is the earlier absence of any explicit and/or fully substantiated individual claims to Davidic ancestry and the silence of all contemporary sources on the prospect of an immediate Davidic restoration. Prior to its literary disinterment by postbellum *nesi'im* and *r'ashei ha-golah*, the entire family was presumed to be physically incapable of furnishing a pretender to the throne.

But if the Davidides were thus incapacitated, then so too was the *keter malkhut* as a whole. Even were other dynasties to attain quasi-monarchical powers, it was unthinkable that they could thereby aspire to the full plenitude of traditional royal authority. Still less might they propagate acceptable doctrines of monarchical supremacy. Formally, the reasons were genetic. As depicted in the Biblical sources, possession of the *keter malkhut* was unconditionally reserved for David and his seed. Whatever their faults, theirs was an exclusive patrimony rooted in Divine covenant; all other occupants of the throne would necessarily be suspect – temporary replacements at best, and usurpers at worst. Certainly, their assumption of a royal designation would contradict the eschatological prophecies attributed to Deutero-Isaiah, which associate at least some part of messianic redemption with the ultimate restoration of a Davidic king.[3] To claim otherwise was to defy what was universally recognised to be a central tenet of the faith.

Hasmonean pretensions to royal status, especially as articulated by Alexander Yannai (103–76 B.C.E.), obviously breached the bounds of that convention. Moreover, they did so in a manner which – because forthright as well as tyrannical – clearly demanded the formulation of a doctrine sufficiently powerful to deter all possible insurgents. The First Book of Maccabees was designed to serve that end. Over a century ago, A. Geiger posited that the chronicle of that name must have been written by 'the state historian of the Maccabean dynasty'. In his more recent edition of the work, J. Goldstein has gone still further. Noting that I Maccabees was deliberately framed as 'propaganda for the Hasmoneans', he suggests that its aim permeates its very style. 'So eager was our author to prove the divinely ordained legitimacy of the Hasmonaean dynasty that he cast his book in the impressive Hebrew diction of the books of Samuel. Just as the books of Samuel proved the legitimacy of the Davidic dynasty and became scripture, so our author hoped First Maccabees would serve to prove Hasmonaean legitimacy.' Moreover, although 'our author never claims openly that the achievements of his heroes fulfilled the words of the prophets', he was 'audacious enough [...] to describe those achievements in words obviously taken from the famous prophecies, so as to lead his readers to think that the Hasmonaeans fulfilled them'.[4]

For all its literary merits ('both a presumptuous work and a stylistic tour de force' are Goldstein's accolades), as a work of political polemic I Maccabees cannot be considered a complete success. However strenuously its author strove to legitimise the rule of his protagonists, not even he could formulate a convincing doctrine of *keter malkhut* supremacy. Perhaps it was because he appreciated the difficulties entailed that he did not even try to do so. Nowhere does the work explicitly refer to any of the Hasmoneans as a *melekh*. Most pointedly, that title is even absent from the list of honours reportedly heaped upon Simon during the halcyon days of 135 B.C.E. The public charter which conferred (or confirmed) Simon's military, sacerdotal and civil rulership, (I Macc. 14:41–5), did permit him to 'wear purple robes and gold ornaments'. But, quite apart from making Simon's 'perpetual' chieftainship and high priesthood conditional upon the eventual rise 'of a true prophet', the document contains no royal designation. At the very most, the founder of the dynasty might have assumed the title of ''*asar'am'el*',[5] and some of his later successors posed as the reincarnations of Melchizedek, the Biblical king described in Genesis 14:18 as 'the High Priest of the Most High God' (AJ 16:163 on Hyrcanus II; cf. TB *R'osh ha-Shanah* 18b). Notwithstanding those pretensions, however, not even Yannai dared consistently to append a monarchical rank to the high priestly title on the Hebrew inscriptions of his coins. He did so, the numismatic evidence suggests, only when he considered his throne absolutely secure.[6] Such caution (otherwise surely uncharacteristic in Yannai's case) is itself indicative of the Hasmoneans' awareness that their assumed royalty smacked of heresy and would almost certainly be denounced as such.

In large part, that was precisely the accusation spread abroad in the collection of pseudoepigraphical poems conventionally designated 'The Psalms of Solomon'. Generally believed to have been composed about a generation after I Maccabees,[7] the political allusions in the Psalms are thought to refer to the circumstances which preceded and accompanied Pompey's entry into Jerusalem in 63 B.C.E. (just a dozen years after Yannai's death), when Hyrcanus II and Aristobulus II were squabbling over the disposition of their late father's twin offices of King and High Priest. Evidently the author(s) of the Psalms considered the subsequent Roman domination of Judea to be nothing but a recent variation on the punishment which God had earlier visited on the sinners of the first Commonwealth. More specifically, it indicated the extent of His wrath with the transgressions of Judea's Hasmonean rulers and – in particular – with their unauthorised occupancy of the throne traditionally reserved for the house of David.

Thou, O Lord [reads the most abrasive passage (17:5–11)] did choose David to be king over Israel and swore to him concerning his seed that never should his kingdom fail before Thee. But for our sins sinners rose up against us; they assailed us and thrust us out; what You did not promise to them, they took away [from us] with violence. They in no way glorified Thy honourable name; they set up a monarchy in place of [that which was] their excellency. They laid waste the throne of David in tumultuous arrogance. But Thou, O Lord, did cast them down and remove their seed from the earth, in that there rose up against them a man that was alien to our race [...].

It is now generally accepted that these were outspokenly anti-Hasmonean sentiments.[8] They did not, however, necessarily mirror opposition to the reconstitution of the *keter malkhut* per se. On the contrary, in several respects the *Psalms* seem to share the enthusiasm of I Maccabees for the revival of a kingship in Israel – disputing only the propriety of its present auspices. Opinions differ as to whether monarchical tendencies of that sort might have been (or, for that matter, needed to have been) fostered by the influence of 'Hellenism' – and specifically of the Hellenistic royal ideology sometimes thought to have been foisted upon the classical Middle East by Alexander the Great and his successors.[9] What remains certain, nevertheless, is that during the course of the first century B.C.E. the polemical fortunes of the *keter malkhut* were enjoying a remarkable recovery, enabling that domain to recapture much of the ground lost during previous generations of ineptitude and disesteem.

In this respect, as in so many others, the tempo of developments undoubtedly increased with the advent to power of Herod 'the Great'. Indeed, it was during his sulphurous reign (37–4 B.C.E.) that most of the postulates of a revived *keter malkhut* ideology first implicit in I Maccabees were given full rein. In part, that situation must be attributed to the absence of any viable alternative. Herod's gentile antecedents necessarily ruled out the possibility that he might lay claim to the same priestly foundations of communal authority upon which his Hasmonean predecessors had, if all else failed, ultimately been able to depend.[10] Accordingly, re-assertions of the innate supremacy of the *keter kehunah* were in his case clearly inappropriate. It was equally inconceivable, however, that Herod might accept Pharisaic domination of Judea's internal and external affairs (as apparently, had Yannai's widow and immediate successor, Salome Alexandra, between 76 and 67 B.C.E.), and thereby accept the domination of the polity by those or any other claimants to the *keter torah*. Admittedly, in 28/27 B.C.E. Herod did release some Pharisees and – for different reasons – the Essenes from the obligatory royal oath (AJ 15:370–2). But, given the probability that membership of both sects was at the time very limited, that action can hardly be invested with serious political consequences.[11] Still less can it be regarded as an ideological concession, reflecting Herod's readiness to accept any view of the royal prerogative which did not unquestionably acknowledge the principle of monarchical absolutism. On the contrary, what has to be noted is that he seems to have had recourse precisely to that form of political propaganda which explicitly proclaimed the constitutional hegemony of the *keter malkhut*.

As Schalit argued at some length,[12] Herod was not (or, at least, not always) the despotic megalomaniac and somewhat pathetic philistine of subsequent caricature. Despite his possibly demonic disposition towards violence, Herod emerges from the few available sources as a sophisticated administrator and a realistic politician. Moreover, he appreciated the subtleties of both Jewish and Roman thought and was adroit in his manipulation of the symbols and motifs of both cultures when he considered that they might serve his ends. His success in navigating a remarkably successful course through a series of domestic and foreign upheavals cannot therefore be attributed merely to occasional moments of good fortune or the uninhibited use of ruthless force. Neither need the case for his greatness rest entirely on either the duration of his survival or the magnificence of his cities. In fact, his most remarkable achievement may have been polemical rather than material. It consisted in the extent to which – against almost all the odds – he gradually managed to transcend the probational status originally granted to him by both his Imperial masters and his Jewish citizenry, and establish himself as both a true Roman subject and (for much of his reign) a legitimate Jewish king.

The precise circumstances which brought about Herod's recognition by Augustus as 'rex socius et amicus populi Romani' need not concern us here. More relevant is the manner in which he exploited that status for domestic purposes within Judea itself. As presented by Schalit, the evidence indicates that Herod orchestrated his propaganda in a manner which suggested the existence of an intimate connection between his standing at Rome and his position in Jerusalem. Both were effluences of Divine grace and expressions of a Divine will. Both, accordingly, possessed an inherently metaphysical dimension. His efforts to win Jewish affections were not therefore restricted to matters material. Flamboyant displays of his military prowess, diplomatic flair and architectural talent were undoubtedly essential props to power. So, too, was the establishment of a new social foundation for Herodian rule by the removal of traditional Jewish aristocrats from positions of executive influence and their replacement by hand-picked Idumeans, Galileans, Samaritans and – most interesting of all – Babylonians.[13] But all such revolutions – for such they were – remained subsidiary to Herod's primary contention. His various attainments, he attempted to demonstrate, had to be placed within a cosmic context. His geographical reconstitution of Israel's ancient Empire and his physical restoration of the Temple to its former glory had to be recognised as providential indications that the Messianic age of Biblical prophecy was imminent – and may even have arrived.[14]

This position necessarily represented a reformulation of previous Jewish messianic doctrines. Most conspicuously, it articulated (even if it did not itself forge) a new conceptual relationship between gentile rule and the fulfilment of Israel's eschatological hopes. The former, it posited, was not an obstacle to the latter. On the contrary, it made the advent of the Messiah dependent on the establishment of the universal dominion exemplified in the Augustinian *orbis terrarum*. Only under the conditions of hegemony, stability and prosperity which Destiny was manifestly allowing the Romans to enjoy could the nation's millenarian aspirations attain full expression. Consequently, Jews everywhere – and especially in Judea – had to abjure their former isolationism and participate, culturally as well as economically, in Roman life.[15]

Quite apart from its possibly genuine ideological impulse, Herodian royal propaganda (as thus described) was clearly designed to serve an immediate political and personal purpose. At the very least, it suggested a mutual dependence between the communal attainment of messianic perfection and the individual standing of the King. By extension, it also served to underscore the corporate hegemony of the monarchical domain of government and its right to be considered superior to all other bases of authority in Jewish life (even that represented by the Temple itself).[16] What emerged, in fact, was a statement of *keter malkhut* supremacy which adopted most of the forms today associated with personality cults. To insist on the vital importance of Jewry's accommodation with Rome, it argued, was also to accept the equal necessity for the polity's retention of Herodian rule. Judea's position in the integrated Roman empire was dependent upon Herod's own activities; he constituted, in effect, the buckle which bound those two Divinely-protected entities. That being so, however, his status too could not be reduced to something mundane. He had to be perceived, if not as a demi-God,[17] then certainly as God's chosen instrument. His attainments undoubtedly entitled him to the rank of Redeemer. Would it be stretching matters to regard him as the Messiah?

Ultimately, arguments such as these failed to carry conviction. Pharisees and Essenes especially, but not necessarily exclusively, were obdurately opposed to relinquishing the notion of Israel's unique holiness. Josephus suggests, although he cannot prove, that those and other circles were also disgusted by the goings-on within the palace (AJ 16:373–6). For whatever reason, Herod was denied the affection and respect for which he unquestionably craved, as well as the messianic status to which (in this reading) he possibly aspired. Nevertheless, not even Herod's own death in 4 B.C.E. caused the immediate suspension of the claims to *keter malkhut* supremacy which he had adumbrated. If anything, those claims were implicitly revived by Herod's grandson Agrippa I (10/11 B.C.E.–43/44 C.E.), who ruled Judea during the last three years of his life. As Schwartz has recently shown, Agrippa in no way deserves his reputation as the darling of the Pharisees and the pliant instrument of their will. Portraits which depict him as an uncritical devotee of *keter torah* supremacy are especially questionable. If Agrippa was inclined to any native Jewish party, it was probably to the Sadducees; more consistently close to his heart, however, was the defence of precisely the same monarchical interests which Herod had so assiduously pursued. Even more estranged from native Jewish culture than his grandfather, Agrippa was equally high-handed in his treatment of native sentiment. Like Herod, he followed an avowedly pro-Roman orientation in foreign and domestic affairs; he also employed the same techniques when imposing his own will on the high priesthood.[18] Only Agrippa's sudden death (perhaps murder), is the impression, prevented the emergence of a fully articulated doctrine of *keter malkhut* hegemony over the other two domains. Even so, the notion of a distinct royal franchise lived on. According to Josephus, the symbolism of its sartorial artefacts was to be deliberately – and fatally – exploited by Menaḥem, the leader of the dagger-toting zealots (*'Sicarii'*), who ostentatiously donned royal robes when entering the Temple (BJ 2:443–4). In entirely different circumstances, many of the pretensions of the *keter malkhuṭ* were to be still later resurrected in the atmosphere which in the third century surrounded Judah *ha-nasi'* and his quasi-monarchical court.

The *keter kehunah*

(a) From rulership to authority

Pharisaic advocates of the supremacy of the *keter torah* were not, it must be stressed, the most obvious beneficieries of Hasmonean and Herodian failures to revive the polemic fortunes of the *keter malkhut*. Whatever advantages became available accrued, rather, to second Commonwealth advocates of the primacy of the *keter kehunah*. In several respects, the latter were in any case inherently better placed to command whatever native authority Judea's Roman overlords were prepared to allow. For one thing, they could cite incontrovertible scriptural support for exclusive priestly control over Israel's most sacred shrine; in addition, they could also parade a lengthy record of administrative experience at the very helm of the nation's secular affairs. Consequently, according to Josephus, the 'aristocracy' established after the deaths of Herod and his son Archelaus specifically entrusted the priests 'with the leadership of the nation' (AJ 20:251). That situation did not necessarily ensure permanent priestly domination over the *sanhedrin* (if, again, a council thus named then existed). But it certainly augmented clerical influence over the nation's affairs. Even during the final period of turmoil which preceded the outbreak of rebellion in 66 C.E., priests played a role which was often dominant and sometimes crucial in the formulation of policy in both the pro- and anti-Roman sections of Jerusalem's body politic.[19]

In time, early rabbinic chroniclers were to look back on those periods of priestly supremacy with undisguised disdain. But such indications as we now possess of Jewish political thought towards the end of the second Commonwealth impart a somewhat different impression of contemporary moods. The political power then wielded by priests, they suggest, was not disputed on strictly constitutional grounds. Rather, instruments of the *keter kehunah* – provided that they were true to their calling – were thought to possess inherent political legitimacy, born of their dynastic right to interpret Israel's constitution and therefore to determine its implementation. Thus armed, they could resist the recent Hasmonean programme of massive monarchical agitation on behalf of the *keter malkhut* as authoritatively as they could dismiss (where they even acknowledged) the existence of a rival Pharisaic contention in favour of the *keter torah*.

Members of the Sadducean party were undoubtedly the most forceful and effective exponents of what was eventually to become the 'establishment' version of *keter kehunah* supremacy; the sectarians gathered at Qumran were the most articulate advocates of its 'anti-establishment' expression. But for all the prominence which both groups deservedly command (they are here discussed below, pp. 104–11 and chapter 5, respectively) their writings are not the only testimonies to the resilient appeal of the political doctrines which they preached. Josephus, often despite his own protestations, was also an ardent hierocrat (albeit *avant la lettre*);[20] so too, and far less reservedly, were men otherwise as far apart as the anonymous author(s) of the *Testament of Judah* and Philo of Alexandria. Notwithstanding their different conceptions of religious orthodoxy, both of the latter shared remarkably similar political prejudices. Both, moreover, couched them in a similar literary style. In order to substantiate the contention that priestly predominance is a normative crux of a pre-ordained Divine plan, the *Testament of Judah* invokes the charters which (according to its own account) God had personally granted to the precursors of the *keter malkhut* and the *keter kehunah* ('To me [i.e. Judah]', reads 21:2–5 [ed. Charles, p. 322], 'the Lord gave the kingdom, and to him [Levi] the priesthood; and He set the kingdom beneath the priesthood.').[21] Philo, particularly as interpreted by Goodenough, posited the same order of priorities. Citing the precedent of Israel's earliest constitutions, he claimed:

> That there is nothing more delightful or pleasant or seemly or noble than to be a servant to God, which surpasses the greatest kingship. And it seems to me that the early kings were at the same time high priests, who by their acts showed that those who rule over others should for themselves dutifully worship God. (*Quaestiones et solutiones in Exodum* 2:105).[22]

Moses himself had signified the proper order of government when 'setting a turban on the priest's head instead of a diadem', thus signifying that 'he who is consecrated to God is superior – when he acts as a priest – to all others, not only the ordinary layman, but even kings' (*De Vita Mosis* 2:131).[23] Subsequent Jewish behaviour had necessarily to follow that example.

These were not entirely novel formulations of Jewish constitutional theory. Insofar as they wished to compose commentaries on the ideal structure of Jewish government (which was not, of course, their only purpose), both Philo and the *Testaments* had ample earlier sources on which to draw. Indeed, the force of their contentions is probably best appreciated when it is noted that their sacerdotal prejudices had long been anticipated. Some considerable time before the Hasmonean interlude, spokesmen for priestly supervision over the Jewish governmental structure had already exploited the benefits inherent the *keter kehunah*'s prestige, formulating statements of sacerdotal primacy which were as extensive as they were forthright. In so doing, they had at the same time effectively extended the arc of the priesthood's corporate claims far beyond the limits assigned by the Biblical authority to which they invariably referred. Priestly government, they had asserted, need not be restricted to the site of the Temple. Because the priesthood was concerned with so crucially important a nexus of Israel's life, its influence had inevitably to permeate the complete fabric of the polity's affairs. Specifically, instruments of the *keter kehunah* deserved to be considered the nation's accredited constitutional practitioners and its authentic constitutional guides. The other two franchises were in every respect subordinate: *kehunah*, in effect, encompassed the *malkhut* and incorporated the *torah*.

Far from being transmitted as a unified whole, that position probably evolved in several sequential stages. In its simplest, and possibly most primitive, version it perhaps amounted to little more than a slightly modified reiteration of late Biblical projections. Post-Exilic representatives of the *keter kehunah*, was the claim, had inherited the entire range of powers possessed by their predecessors; with the Return, that domain (more precisely its Zadokite branch)[24] had thereby assumed all earlier priestly rights to wield civil as well as sacerdotal power. Constitutional practice during the following three centuries could only have substantiated the doctine. Indeed, if thus presented, it would merely have re-formulated what several contemporary observers (Gentile and Jewish) repeatedly reported as fact: during large periods of the second Commonwealth senior priests conventionally functioned as princes. Thus seen, there is no call to postdate the conjunction of the *keter malkhut* with the *keter kehunah* until the formal assumption of both crowns during the first generations of the Hasmonean dynasty. Aristobulus I (104–103 B.C.E.) may indeed have been the first High Priest ever to provide physical evidence of that circumstance, notably by sporting a royal diadem (according to AJ 13:301 he 'saw fit to transform the government into a kingdom, which he judged the best form, and he was the first to put a *diadema* on his head'). But his was a symbolic innovation, not a constitutional revolution. His pre-Maccabean predecessors in Jewry's most exalted sacerdotal office had in any case long been regarded as '*prostates tou laou*', persons in possession of an office which was as much civil as sacerdotal.[25]

Tanna'itic silence on that development is doubtless an eloquent testimony to early rabbinic disapproval of both its historical course and constitutional implications. Drawing a discreet veil over the structure of Jewish government throughout the entire 'Persian' period, Pharisees and their literary successors effectively erased the era of High Priestly rule from their record of Israel's constitutional past; in its place (as we have seen) they projected an uninterrupted progression from Ezra's stewardship of the nation to their own. Prior to the advent of the Hasmoneans, however, the literary view of Israel's ecclesiastical traditions seems to have been more benign. Not until the reproofs apparently composed by scattered purists during the time of Antiochus IV[26] do we possess written attacks on priestly behaviour and persons. Otherwise, the general tenor of such literature as has survived is anything but critical. In the more interesting versions, acclaim could even verge on the panegyric. Not content to justify priestly involvement in the civil government of Judea, hierocrats also posited the existence of a priestly prerogative to shape the direction of the polity's constitutional law.

Undoubtedly the most outstanding exposition of that doctrine is to be found in 'The Words of Simeon ben Jeshua' (*Ben Sira'*), the apocryphal work better known by the title of its Greek translation as Ecclesiasticus. Composed (probably by a priest)[27] in Judea some time during the second century B.C.E., most of the work is taken up with a long litany of various aphorisms directing man towards right conduct and good deeds. Generally classified as an ethical tract, its author's principal purpose was to warn the faithful of the dangers which awaited all who succumbed to the ungodly enticements of Hellenism.[28] But by identifying the priests as the group most suited to preserve Israel's ancient traditions, he also injected a political doctrine into some portions of his work. Thereby, he composed what deserves to be considered a landmark in the evolution of a hierocratic brand of political polemic. In addition to all else, Ecclesiasticus can be read as a tract on the priesthood's hereditary right to act as authorities in Israel's law and hence as a proclamation of priestly hegemony. That station in Jewish public life, is its message, cannot be attributed solely to the clerical attributes of the instruments of the *keter kehunah*. It is also the consequence of their Divine mandate to act as the guardians of the canonical text and – in the final analysis – its most competent exegetes.

In part, the polemical stratum of Ecclesiasticus is evident in some of its aphorisms, particularly those which identify Wisdom (which in the book of Proverbs, for instance, is spoken of as a primordial fascinating entity), with the *torah* given to Israel. It is especially prevalent, however, in the author's eulogies on the great figures of the Bible. Chapters 45–50 of the Hebrew version (together entitled 'In Praise of the Fathers' and comprising an historical excursus into the transmission of national traditions and teachings) are in this context of particular interest. They focus, not on the content of Wisdom-as-*torah* but on its provenance. Identifying the links in the chain of Israel's constitutional tradition, they thus address precisely the same issue which was later to be of concern to *'Avot* 1:1. Like *'Avot*, Ecclesiasticus traces the progression of that chain from its Sinaitic source until its contemporary manifestations. In so doing, the work also concurs with some of *Mishnah*'s subsequent prejudices. Specifically, it assigns to the prophets a teaching authority somewhat more explicit than that articulated by Scripture. Likewise, it makes only passing reference to the roles which might once have been played in the constitutional process by incumbents of the Biblical office of *melekh*.[29]

From that point onwards, however, the two texts diverge. *'Avot* (as we have seen), was to designate the prophets as the sole literary antecedents of the sages of its own day and thus to emphasise the normative supremacy of an independent *keter torah*. Ecclesiasticus is either ignorant of any such tradition or determined to forestall its development. Indeed, its author studiously avoids any acknowledgement of the putative autonomy of a sphere concerned exclusively with the *torah*. Nowhere does the text recognise the possible existence of a *ḥakham*. Even its references to the *sofer* are guarded and limiting. The latter is portrayed as little more than a student of the sacred texts; his tasks, as laid out in 39:1–11, are in effect technical (which is why their description immediately succeeds those of the farmer, artisan, smith and potter). Boiled down, they amount to the preservation of Wisdom through intensive contemplation. If successfully carried out, these duties will undoubtedly endow the *sofer* with a significant aura of sanctity and invest him with the authority of a secondary channel of God's wisdom. But those attributes will not themselves entitle 'scribes' to wield independent executive power in the interpretation and transmission of the *torah*. That is a function reserved primarily, and permanently, for the priests. It is their forefather, Aaron, whom Ecclesiasticus considers to have been the most important of all links in the historic chain of constitutional transmission. As a focus of attention (as in 45:6–22), he rivals even Moses.

Commenting on this bias, Rivkin has suggested that Ecclesiasticus 'filters the Pentateuch through Aaronide eyes'.[30] In effect, it does even more. By depicting priests as the legitimate interpreters of the Pentateuch and its teachings, the author of the work invested their domain with irrefutable constitutional primacy. Especially was this so in what has come down to us as his final chapters. Consisting of a eulogy to one 'Simeon ben Johanan the priest' (identified by scholars as the fourth-century B.C.E. *kohen gadol* known to rabbinic traditions as 'Simon the Just'), not only does that section of the text describe the High Priest as an ideal civil-cum-ecclesiastical leader of his people. More significantly, it also places a polemical con struction on the original everlasting covenant bestowed upon Aaron and his descendants when anointed by Moses. Thus, only one portion of the priestly mandate was reserved for conventional sacerdotal duties: 'to minister [to the Lord], to execute the priestly office and to bless His people in His name [...] to make atonement for the Children of Israel'. In addition, says Ecclesiasticus 45:15, the principal instrument of the domain was also entrusted with precisely those duties which the early rabbis were subsequently to entrust to the principal instruments of the *keter torah*:

And He gave him His commandments [*miṣwotaw*]
And invested him with authority over statute and judgement [*ḥoq u-mishpaṭ*]
That he might teach His people statute and judgement [...].[31]

In the absence of adequate supplementary evidence, it is impossible to gauge the precise extent to which Ecclesiasticus mirrored the shift in Jewish cultural tastes which its author abhorred.[32] That at least some portion of his hierocratic prejudices were consonant with current political attitudes would, however, seem to be indicated by what is known of Judea's subsequent history. Not even the unseemly character of events immediately prior to the outbreak of the Maccabean revolt, it has been noted, threatened to remove the high priesthood from its standing at the very pinnacle of Jewry's internal government. Notwithstanding the manner whereby the rival claimants to the office played fast and loose with the genealogical tables of their clans between 175 and 168, its institutional prestige remained remarkably untarnished. Once the dust raised in those years by the various squabbles had been allowed to settle, all that had changed was the identity of the incumbents of the position. Its attendant authority, as M. A. Cohen has noted, suffered no diminution at all.

> There was certainly no revolution against the priests between 175 and 168 B. C. E. In fact, the sources record no antihierocratic agitation in these years of turmoil and rebellion, though judging from their blanket condemnation of priests, there is every reason to believe that neither I nor II Maccabees would have failed to record such events had they occurred.[33]

Martial success during the Maccabean revolt, accompanied by the purification of the Temple and the renewal of its various services, notably enhanced the normative religious importance attached to the shrine and the observance of its ritual.[34] Equally relevant is the extent to which those events simultaneously promised to augment the governmental status of priests within the reconstituted polity. Until they succumbed to the mirage of royal grandeur, Simon the Maccabee's immediate successors manifestly acknowledged the potential advantages of their geneaology. Once they had legitimised their high priestly status, they set about exploiting it for all its political worth. John Hyrcanus (135–104 B. C. E.) was a particularly adept exponent of the strategy. Even if he did harbour monarchical ambitions, Hyrcanus never publicised the fact. Indeed, he insisted that it was by virtue of his high priesthood that he had been endowed with whatever was left of the Divine gift of prophecy[35] and, consequently, with the power to enact legislation on all aspects of public and religious affairs. Such was the success of the claim that Hyrcanus came to regarded as the very model of priestly rule. Even rabbinic records, which never forgave him for eventually becoming a Sadducee (TB *Berakhot* 29a; cf. AJ 13:288), preserve fond memories of his occupancy of the office; they are particularly appreciative of his enactment of several landmark *taqanot* which affected the Temple and priestly portions.[36]

Possibly because he was dazzled by the prospect of establishing a style of kingship more in keeping with current Hellenistic tastes, Yannai altogether failed to emulate Hyrcanus' example. Instead of exploiting to the full the power inherent in his inherited position as *kohen gadol*, he bid for a radically new brand of monarchical legitimacy. But that gambit, notwithstanding the additional literary support provided by I Maccabees, ultimately failed. Even Sadducees might have found it offensive, which is possibly why (as will be seen) they preferred to stress that their political preferences were more deeply ingrained within Israel's Biblical culture. Josephus, who admits to having once flirted with Sadduceanism and was certainly sensitive to its teachings, made the same point by recourse to history. Particularly interesting, in this context, is his description of the decline of Hasmonean fortunes soon after Yannai's death, when Hyrcanus II and Aristobulus II had disputed his widow's disposal of their father's royal and priestly offices. As Josephus tells it, this example of internecine conflict within the *keter malkhut* generated a public movement deliberately designed to foster the reinstatement of the former hegemony of the *keter kehunah*. In 63 B.C.E., he records (AJ 14:41), Pompey was specifically asked to ensure that the nation would:

> Not be ruled by a King, saying that it was the custom of their country to obey the priests of the God who was venerated by them, but that these two, who were descended from the priests, were seeking to change their form of government in order that they might become a nation of slaves.

(b) The sectarian version

On the basis of a fragment of the Qumran text known as the Nahum Commentary (4Q Nahum), Dupont-Sommer suggested that the petitioners of Josephus' description were Essenes. Although perhaps questionable,[37] the identification is highly suggestive. Not least, it highlights the importance of distinguishing between two of the major political choices available to late second Commonwealth supporters of the *keter kehunah*. One, most cohesively adopted by the Sadducean party (although not exclusively so) was to regard the Temple as an integral facet of Jerusalem's ruling establishment. Indeed, given Roman intrusions into every other aspect of Jewish public life, that was the only area which native aspirants to government could reasonably hope to control. Incumbent officers of the shrine had to be encouraged to utilise that base, thereby extending their authority throughout the polity and ensuring the primacy of the constitutional interpretations which they and their supporters considered essential to the preservation of Israel's unique association with its God. An alternative option was to invert the process. True faith demanded an attack on the existing establishment, including its present high-priestly component, rather than its infiltration. In that reading, the supremacy of the *keter kehunah* was not to be fostered from within the metropolis; instead, it was to be imposed from without. Neither were the incumbent priests in Jerusalem in any way qualified to fulfil that mission. Because they had forsaken the teachings of their caste and disdained the enlightenment bestowed by God's law, they and their Temple were *ipso facto* 'impure'. Ultimately, therefore, the battle would have to be fought and won by the remnant which had preserved true sacerdotal traditions in the wilderness of Judea, rigidly quarantined from the contaminations of the age.[38]

The sectarians whom Josephus referred to as Essenes (AJ 13:171, 18:18–22; BJ 2:120–61) undoubtedly identified themselves as that remnant. Although their true origins remain clouded in mystery, the various documents fortuitously discovered in the vicinity of the Dead Sea (generically known to modern scholarship as the Qumran Scrolls) do provide what must have been the sect's own chronicle of its past. Particularly instructive is the Habbakuk Commentary (1Qp Hab. 8:12ff and 11:5ff) which speaks of an episode – generally dated to the early decades of the second century B.C.E. – during which the 'Sons of Zadok' were unlawfully displaced from the high priesthood by 'the wicked priest'. The Damascus Rule (CD, the only Qumran Essene compilation known prior to 1947), also tells of a small band of refugees ('the root' – numbering, in one version, no more than 3 priests and 12 laymen), who, after existing 'for 20 years like blind men groping for the way', eventually accepted the leadership of 'the teacher of righteousness' (*moreh ṣedeq* [CD 1:4–12]; referred to in CD manuscript 'B' 20:14 as *moreh ha-yaḥid* – 'the unique teacher'), himself a priestly fugitive from Jerusalem. Since the Scrolls do not otherwise name this charismatic figure, his precise identity has generated considerable speculation, and it has recently been suggested that the title denoted an office rather than a historical personality.[39] No such doubts arise, however, regarding either the veneration in which the memory of the first person thus designated was held by his followers or the impact which he and his successors are said to have had on the sects' communal life. Each functioned, in effect, as administrator, counsel and, in the term used by 1Qp Hab. 2:1–2, inspired 'interpreter' of the prophetic scriptures. In all three guises the *moreh ṣedeq* shaped for the sectarians their entire outlook on the world which they set out to create. Under his instruction, the *yaḥad* ('Union', as the members of the sects designated themselves) compacted a 'new covenant', by whose terms they came to constitute the nucleus of a perfect and sacred community.

As laid down by the *moreh ṣedeq*, members of the sect possessed a mission which was virtually apocalyptic. They were to lead the Sons of Light into battle against the Sons of Darkness. Ultimately, victory in that struggle would purge the Land of Israel from the defilement caused by the iniquitous dominance exercised by the sons of Belial over the Temple and its service. However, in order meanwhile to preserve the country for their own future occupation after the destruction of the wicked, members of the sect had in the interim to provide a substitute for the Jerusalem Temple and a replacement for its definition as the seat of the Law.[40] That imperative did not demand that they construct an alternative shrine in their desert hideouts. But it did require them to constitute themselves into a living sanctuary, made holy by its organisation, discipline and meticulous attention to the Biblical purity-regulations. Thus, the entire community itself became the true temple, with its inner council (the 15 founding-members and their successors) comprising the holy of holies. Until such time as they could replace the wicked priests, prayer and 'perfection of the way' were to take the place of sacrifices. The cult would not be restored until the seventh year of the eschatological war. Thereto, atonement was to be achieved by the 'offering of the lips' and the acceptance of suffering.[41]

With the *yaḥad* thus acting as a surrogate sanctuary, there could be no question about the identity of its supreme governmental authorities – prospective as well as contemporary. Josephus, for whatever reason, seems to have been reticent about the personal and political connections between Essenes and priests.[42] The Scrolls themselves are not. Whatever the exact provenance and dating of individual texts, all those which have hitherto been published (a caution necessitated by the fact that several of the discoveries still await that stage) proclaim the same message. As laid down by the *moreh ṣedeq*, the government of the sect was to be priestly government. Moreover, since the administration of the *yaḥad* was to provide a paradigm of all Jewish rulership, it followed that the domain which rabbinic texts subsequently referred to as the *keter kehunah* is entitled to overall communal superiority in every ideal Jewish polity – as much in the realm of the *torah* as in that of civil government.[43]

At the level of future aspirations, the hierocratic emphasis of the Qumran sectarians is illustrated in the two bodies of texts which Yadin designated 'The War Rule' (1QM) and 'The Temple Scroll' (11Q Temple). The first (15:4 [ed. Yadin, pp. 330–1]) stresses the prominent part to be allotted to the '*kohen ha-r'osh*' in the preparations for the ultimate battle against the sons of darkness. The second contains detailed prescriptions for the ordinances, sacrifices, procedures, courts and architecture to be adopted once the Jerusalem Temple would be restored to legitimate hands. Quite apart from thus supplying (perhaps deliberately) the 'missing' *torah* on these matters reportedly given to David by God,[44] the Temple Scroll also prescribes a distinct order of rank. Particularly interesting, in this context, is its subordination of the *melekh* to the *kohen gadol*, in its depictions of both the installation of the former and the rights of the latter when leading the community into battle.[45]

Priestly dominance is equally pronounced, moreover, in those passages of other Scrolls which provide – not for the future welfare of Jewry at large – but for the immediate government of the faithful in their current exile. From their very foundations, according to their own accounts, the sects had been led by the descendants of Zadok: 'the chosen of Israel, men of renown'. The ordinances set down in the Scrolls were designed to ensure that matters remained that way. Priests figure prominently, sometimes exclusively, in the assemblies and courts (duodecimal and otherwise) of Qumran descriptions.[46] Similarly, 'the sons of Zadok and the Priests who keep the Covenant' are singled out as prospective candidates for senior office in the contemporary management of the sect and accorded dominant positions in the determination of its rules. It is they who had been chosen by God 'to confirm His covenant for ever, and to enquire into all His precepts in the midst of His people, and to instruct them as He commanded'. According to the Manual of Discipline (1QS) they were 'to command in matters of justice and property'; every rule concerning 'the multitude of the men of the Community who hold fast to the Covenant' was to be determined in accordance with their instruction.[47]

As is commonly observed, the Essenes – for all their striking originality – did not break entirely with every other stream of contemporary Jewish thought and practice, and particularly not in matters of self-government. It is open to question whether we might therefore follow Jeremias and 'draw from the strict life of the Essene community inferences about the communal character of the

Pharisees'.[48] What can be attempted, however, is a more limited exercise in comparison. The depictions of Essene administrative ordinances contained in the Qumran texts do bear particularly marked resemblances to those which seem simultaneously to have been conventional amongst their coreligionists elsewhere. Especially intriguing are indications that they might have been framed with particular regard for the division of communal government into the three domains of jurisdiction which rabbinic literature was later to refer to as *ketarim*. Thus observed, the singularity of the Scrolls lies in the ordering of those clusters; not in the portrait of the basic structure upon which their hierarchy was based. As much is indicated by the care which they apparently take to attribute quite separate functions to the public officials there designated, respectively, as the '*kohen*'; the '*doresh ha-torah*'; and the '*mevaqer 'al melekhet ha-rabim*'.

In *The Dead Sea Scrolls in English* (first published in 1962, revised in 1965 and 1968), Vermes presented a particularly lucid analysis of these three offices. In so doing, he also summarised their functional distinctions. As Vermes himself points out, the differences between the roles performed by these officiants are sometimes blurred in the normative descriptions provided in the Scrolls (and probably were so in practice, especially in the smaller communes where one individual might have performed several functions). Nevertheless, what remains remarkable is the lengths to which some of the Scrolls – and especially the Damascus Rule and the Manual of Discipline – went in order to accentuate their theoretical differentiations. According to the account there presented, and as reconstructed by Vermes, three distinct spheres of activity were delineated. The *kohen* served as priest proper; he was enjoined to perform those sacerdotal functions which strictly appertained to his official nomenclature: pronouncing the blessing over the meals; presiding over assemblies; and exercising the functions specifically reserved to his own caste (1QS 6:5–6). The practical administration of the community and its finances, on the other hand, were matters entrusted to the *mevaqer 'al melekhet ha-rabim* (lit. 'inspector of the work of the congregation', rendered by Vermes as 'Bursar'). It was he who performed what might be termed the conventional roles of an instrument of the *keter malkhut*: 'to take charge of the finances of the Community and provide for its material interests and needs'.[49]

Both of these officials, however, performed roles quite distinct from that of the *doresh ha-torah* (sometimes rendered *paqid* or, rather confusingly, also as *mevaqer*). However these titles are translated, Vermes suggests the generic 'Guardian', they all convey the notion that the authority assigned to the official concerned clearly fell within the purview of what rabbinic literature was later to designate the instruments of the *keter torah*. Indeed, his chief duties lay in the field of instruction. 'He was to interview all who sought admission to the sect and teach the Rule of the Community to the people he judged worthy to enter [...] for the "professed" also he was to act as final arbiter in all matters concerned with orthodoxy and right conduct. In the words of the Damascus Rule [13:7–8], he was to "instruct the congregation [the many] in the works of God."'

Nowhere do the Scrolls themselves mandate that genetic priests occupy this particular office.[50] What they do stress, however, is the primacy of a priestly interpretation of the duties inherent in the proper performance of its functions. Early rabbinic writings, as we have already noted, were to posit the possible divorce of the didactic from the sacerdotal demesnes in Jewish life (or at least to resist the idea that the two were necessarily connected). To that end, they were to interpose the prophets as an independent line of the *torah*'s transmission and elucidation. The Qumran Scrolls, although clearly conscious of the importance of the prophetic stage of Israel's history,[51] stubbornly resisted this notion. In constitutional terms, they maintained, prophecy represented a dead-end; having revealed Divine teachings once and for all, the prophets had completed their mission. For its preservation, transmission and application the *torah* would have to rely on other agencies.

Those tasks could not be left exclusively to laymen – even if they be laymen inspired. They had to remain the preserve of the true priests. The latter were not merely students of the prophets; on the contrary, under the guidance of the *moreh ṣedeq*, they had reached a stage at which they understood the scriptural writings – and especially the scriptural prophetic writings – 'more than the prophets themselves'.[52] Altogether, the prophetic function had been absorbed by the priestly clan (and perhaps particularly in this instance by its levitical section); in its members was therefore vested the ultimate right and duty to determine its future development. To quote Vermes:

Since the sect expressly intended to model its organisation as a microcosmic Israel, it followed that, as in Judaism generally, the prime religious duties of worship and instruction were divided between priests and levites.[53]

The inferences of this structure were self-declaratory. The doctrines propounded in the Qumran Scrolls implied far more than the mere subordination of the *keter malkhut* to the *keter kehunah*. Quite inadequate, therefore, is the observation that their priorities reflected 'a significant and potentially subversive claim for the superiority of the religious over the worldly arm'.[54] At issue was not the relative rank of the arms of the triad, but their collective incorporation into an overarching priestly framework to which they all belonged. In the person of the *'ish doresh ha-torah*, the sacerdotal branch of the triad had become the embodiment of both the *keter torah* and the *keter malkhut*. In Vermes' rendering of 1QS 5:7–9:

Whoever approaches the Council of the Community [...] shall undertake by a binding oath to return [...] to every commandment of the Law of Moses in accordance with all that has been revealed of it to the sons of Zadok, the keepers of the Covenant and the Seekers of His will, and to the multitude of the men of the Covenant.[55]

This structure was not to be limited to the here-and-now. If the sectarians were to keep faith with the eschatological thrust of their teachings and beliefs, there had to exist a clear correlation between the present position of the priests and their roles in messianic times. Admittedly, this is a region of speculation in which the message of the Scrolls is even more obscure than is usually the case. Confusion has been generated by, amongst other things, a matter of arithmetic. Some Scrolls, possibly reflecting a particular stage of Essenic messianic aspirations, speak only of a single Messiah ('the Messiah of Aaron and Israel'). Others, however, conform more faithfully to the traditional patterns set in the Moses–Aaron and Zerubabel–Joshua models, and refer to two messianic figures (often, but not always, designated 'the annointed ones of Aaron and Israel'). A minority of texts suggest yet another possibility, adding to this dyarchy the mysterious personage of 'a Prophet' (e.g. IQS 9:11; elsewhere simply referred to as *gever* – 'man') and thus completing the trio who were to be positioned at the apex of the three rabbinic *ketarim*.[56]

Less problematic appears to be the prescribed division of functions amongst these personalities. Those of the sources which do speak of a single figure, suggest the absorption into the concept of the

Priest-Messiah of the prerogatives of his priestly partner. Others, however preserve a strict delineation in the functions attributed to these figures and clearly posit their hierarchy. Most texts portray the King-Messiah as a Davidic prince, entrusted with a role of paradigmatic *keter malkhut* proportions. His future mission would be to lead the people to triumph, defeat the Gentiles, and bring into being the Kingdom of God. Crucially important though these tasks undoubtedly were, their fulfilment was not left to chance. In matters of doctrine, the King-Messiah was to obey the Priest-Messiah. Indeed, to the latter was assigned not only the conduct of the liturgy during the battle against the ultimate foe, but also – and more importantly – the final interpretation of the Law and the ultimate revelation of the significance and relevance of the Scriptures. It was in that guise that the Priest-Messiah would continue to wear two crowns, serving as both the High Priest of the ultimate Kingdom [*keter kehunah*] and the final Interpreter of the Law [*keter torah*] (IQSa 2:1ff; cf. Ezek. 44:3ff).[57] In sum:

> The Priest Messiah [...] was to be the supreme authority in all matters of interpretation of the Torah, as also the guide and instructor in Torah of his lay partner.[58]

Jewish literature dating from the period of late antiquity records no direct confrontation between the doctrine of *keter kehunah* supremacy thus enunciated at Qumran and the notion of *keter torah* primacy upon which the early rabbinic sages were subsequently to put so much stress. Indeed, the strict sectarianism of the Essene communities probably precluded the social and political intercourse which could alone have generated a dialogue between their own point of view and any of its rivals. But other groupings in Jewish society, because more actively involved in national and communal life, exerted a far more immediate effect on its course. Not content merely to proclaim the ordained predominance of their own inherited or adopted *ketarim*, they also took active steps to deny that position of primacy to self-styled representatives of the *keter torah*. As the next section will argue, the early rabbinic bid for communal hegemony did not, therefore, succeed by default. Rather, both before and after the Destruction it gave rise to a series of tussles for power amongst adversaries who were equally concerned to translate their own doctrinal assertions into effective authority. It is to the course of those struggles that attention must now be turned.

NOTES

1. J. Liver, *Toledot Beit David* (Jerusalem, 1959), pp. 32–102.
2. Is. 45:1; see E.E. Urbach, 'Koresh ve-Hakhrazato be-'Einei Ḥazal', *Molad*, 19 (1961), pp. 368–74.
3. On the origins of the concept of a Davidic Messiah see Liver, pp. 104–16 and J. Klausner, *Ha-Ra'ayon ha-Meshiḥi be-Yisra'el* (Jerusalem, 1926), pp. 159–64. Later developments, and transformations, in *Judaisms and their Messiahs at the Turn of the Christian Era* (eds. J. Neusner, et al.; Cambridge, 1988).
4. J.A. Goldstein, *I Maccabees* (The Anchor Bible, Vol. 41; New York, 1976), pp. 13, 77; cf. A. Geiger, *Urschrift und Uebersetzungen der Bibel* (Berlin, 1857), p. 206.
5. I Maccs. 14.27; a difficult term which may or may not be translated as 'ethnarch'. See Goldstein, pp. 507–9 and Y. Yadin, *The Scroll of the War of the Sons of Light Against the Sons of Darkness* (Oxford, 1962), p. 44 n. 6; compare the longer note in the Hebrew edition of Yadin's work: *Megilat Milkhemet Benei ha-'Or Bivnei ha-Ḥosheh* (Jerusalem, 1955), pp. 41–2 fn. 16. Prior to Aristobulus I the official title seems to have been *strategos*; after Hyrcanus II – *ethnarch*.
6. Y. Meshorer, *Maṭbe'ot ha-Yehudim Bimei Bayit Sheini* (Tel Aviv, 1966), pp. 32 and 83–4, no. 17 suggests that (in at least one case) the inscription 'Yonatan ha-Melekh' was probably erased; cf. A. Adler, 'Une Image Controversée d'Alexandre Jannée', *REJ*, 138 (1979), pp. 337–49.
7. The editors of Schürer's *History* (revised), Vol. 3 (i) (Edinburgh, 1986), pp. 192–5, reject the Christian authorship posited in Y. Efron, '"Mizmorei Shelomoh", ha-Sheqi'ah ha-Ḥashmona'it we-ha-Naṣrut', *Zion*, 30 (1964–5), pp. 1–46 (= *Ḥiqerei ha-Tequfah ha-Ḥashmona'it*, pp. 195–249). On the dating of I Maccs., cf. Goldstein (not later than 90 B.C.E.) and Schürer, op. cit., p. 181 (1st decade of 1st century B.C.E.).
8. E.P. Sanders, *Paul and Palestinian Judaism: A Comparison of Patterns of Religion* (Phila., 1977), pp. 403–4. The first person plural (verse 6) suggests that the author may have claimed descent from the Davidic line. A. Büchler, *Types of Jewish-Palestinian Piety 70 B.C.E. to 70 C.E.* (London, 1922), pp. 171–2.
9. Much of the discussion of the precise extent (if any) of Hellenistic influences on pre-Destruction Judea winds about like a talmudic argument, and is equally inconclusive. For presentations which touch specifically on the issue to hand, see: E.R. Goodenough, 'Hellenistic Kingship', *Yale Classical Studies*, 1 (1928), pp. 55–102; S.K. Eddy, *The King is Dead: Studies in Near Eastern Resistance to Hellenism, 334–31 B.C.E.* (Lincoln, Nebraska, 1961), esp. pp. 196–7, 239–40; M. Avi-Yonah, *Hellenism and the East: Contacts*

and Interrelations from Alexander to the Roman Conquest (Ann Arbor, 1978), esp. pp. 50–81.

10. Note, however, the ingenious interpretation of Herodian coin finds (based on the royal and priestly insignia specified in TB *Keritut* 5b) in Y. Meshorer, *Ancient Jewish Coins*, Vol. 2 (N.Y., 1982), pp. 25–6.
11. Y.L. Levin, ''Al ha-Me'oravut ha-Poliṭit Shel ha-Perushim Bitqufat Hordus u-Vimei ha-Neṣivim', *Kathedra*, 8 (1978), p. 21.
12. A. Schalit, *Hordus ha-Melekh: ha-'Ish u-Fo'alo* (Jerusalem: 1960), pp. 240–73. For an alternative perspective, see, e.g., S. Zeitlin, 'Herod: A Malevolent Maniac', *JQR*, 54 (1964), pp. 26–7.
13. M. Stern, 'Social and Political Realignments in Herodian Judea', *The Jerusalem Cathedra*, Vol. 2 (1982), pp. 40–62.
14. Schalit, *Hordus*, p. 272. See his statement when announcing his plan to rebuild the Temple: AJ 15:380–7.
15. See, e.g., Nicolas' speech (AJ 16:29–58) as analysed in Schalit, pp. 217–19. Cf. Klausner, op. cit., pp. 233–4.
16. That, at least, is one possible explanation for Herod's placement of the image of an eagle over the gates of the Temple. The symbol might have suggested, amongst other things, the need of that shrine for some form of royal protection. See, however, Schalit, p. 227.
17. Schalit (idem.), collates Josephus' references to the traditions which were designed to demonstrate Divine protection over Herod and his own miraculous attributes (e.g. AJ 14:462–3 and 15:425). He also notes (p. 226, fn 929) the archeological evidence that Herod was indeed regarded as a demi-God by his gentile subjects.
18. D.R. Schwartz, *'Agripas ha-R'ishon: Melekh Yehudah ha-'Aḥaron* (Jerusalem, 1987), esp. pp. 80–1 and 129–30 (for his appointment, and dismissal, of high priests); pp. 130–43 (for his pro-Sadducean leanings); pp. 147–58 (for his pro-Roman orientation); and pp. 171–84 (for an analysis of the rabbinic traditions).

    The 'persistent' appearance of a royal diadem on his coins is noted in Meshorer, op. cit., p. 53. Similar conclusions are independently posited in D. Goodblatt, 'Agrippa I and Palestinian Judaism in the First Century', *Jewish History*, 2 (1987), pp. 7–32.
19. See, e.g., M. Stern, 'Ha-Manhigut Bikvuṣot Loḥamei ha-Ḥerut be-Sof Yemei Bayit Sheini', *Ha-Mered ha-Gadol* (ed. A. Kasher; Jerusalem, 1983), pp. 302–4; E. M. Smallwood, 'High Priests and Politics in Roman Palestine', *Journal of Theological Studies*, 13 (1962), pp. 14–34 and C. Roth, 'The Constitution of the Jewish Republic of 66–70', *Jewish Social Studies*, 9 (1964), p. 300.
20. D.R. Schwartz, 'Josephus on the Jewish Constitutions and Community', *Scripta Classica Israelica*, 7 (1984), pp. 32–49.
21. Flusser has noted that this contentious passage was also used and developed in the medieval polemic between the papacy and the Emperors.

Dante, an adherent of the monarchy, composed a reply in *De Monarchia* 3:4–5. 'Patriarchs, Testaments of the Twelve', *Encyclopedia Judaica* (Jerusalem, 1971), 13:186. The origins, background and precise dating of the *Testaments* is a matter of much academic debate. See the summary of the present status of such questions in Schürer, *History* (revised), Vol. 3 (ii) (Edinburgh, 1987), pp. 767–81.

22. Translated by R. Marcus in the Loeb edition, Supplement Vol. 2 (London, 1961), p. 153; cf. the slightly different version in E. Goodenough, *The Politics of Philo Judaeus: Practice and Theory* (New Haven, CT., 1938) p. 97. It has also been noted that 'in Philo's political theory, the role of the monarch in Judea in his own time and in the period immediately before him plays no role whatsoever'. Moreover, his writings contain no allusions to the Davidic kingship. S. Sandmel, *Philo of Alexandria: An Introduction* (Oxford, 1979), p. 103. In fact, his only reference to David ('the Psalmist') is in *De Confusione Linguarum* 149.

23. Translated by F. H. Colson in the Loeb edition, Vol. 6 (London, 1935), p. 513. See also the analysis in Goodenough, op. cit., pp. 95–120 and more expansively in the same author's *By Light, Light: The Mystic Gospel of Hellenistic Judaism* (New Haven, CT., 1935). More cautious in every respect is H. A. Wolfson, *Philo: Religious Foundations of Religious Philosophy in Judaism, Christianity and Islam* (revised edtn., Cambridge, Mass., 1962), esp. Vol. 2, pp. 322–437.

    Philo's priestly prejudices (perhaps reflecting the fact that he was a closet Sadducee) have also been discerned in *De Specialibus Legibus*, and especially in his conception of the sinless high priest and his claim that Israel's chief judges are priests. D. R. Schwartz, 'Philo's Priestly Descent', *Nourished With Peace: Studies in Hellenistic Judaism in Memory of Samuel Sandmel* (ed. F. E. Greenspahn, et. al; Chico, California, 1984), pp. 155–71. Cf., however, R. Barraclough, 'Philo's Politics. Roman Rule and Hellenistic Judaism', *ANRW* 4:21 (1984), pp. 417–553.

24. See, e.g., the analysis of Ezekiel chapter 44 in N. Allan, 'The identity of the Jerusalem Priesthood during the Exile', *Heythrop Journal*, 23 (1982), pp. 254–69.

25. AJ 12:161 and the Loeb edition, Vol. 7 (trans. R. Marcus; London, 1957), p. 84, fn. 'd'. Cf. Lieberman, *Greek in Jewish Palestine*, p. 65, and Schwartz, 'Josephus on Constitutions', pp. 35–6.

    For the extent to which Josephus' description of the powers of the High Priest is substantiated by several gentile observers in late antiquity, see Schürer, *History* (revised), Vol. 2, pp. 202, 215–17, 227.

26. On the 'ḥasidic' diatribes composed in that period: Liver, *Toledot Bet David*, pp. 130–1.

27. The issue is discussed in J. F. A. Sawyer, 'Was Jeshua ben Sira a Priest?', *WCJS*, 8 (i) (1982), pp. 65–71.

28. 'It was the time of the invasion of Hellenism. The writer belonged to the old, faithful core and [...] complained bitterly that "ungodly men have forsaken the law of the Most High God" (41:8).' Schürer, Vol. 3(i), pp. 200–1.
29. See, especially, the analysis in Liver, op. cit., pp. 108–9.
30. E. Rivkin, 'Ben Sira', *Eretz Israel*, 12 (1975), English section, p.98:
   All other systems of authority recorded in the Pentateuch – be they prophetical, Levitical, priestly or monarchical – are subordinated to the overarching authority of Aaron and his sons.
31. Ed. Segal, pp. 311, 315; ed. Charles, p. 488. For Biblical intimations of the same notion see, e.g., Malachi 2:7. Note the commentaries by *Rashi* and David Qimḥi (*Radaq*; 1160–1235) to the latter verse, both of whom refer back to Deut. 33:10 '[Levi] shall teach Jacob thy judgements and Israel thy law [*torah*].'
32. On 'Ben Sira's controversy with Hellenistic liberalism', see Hengel, *Hellenism and Judaism*, Vol. 1, pp. 131–52.
33. 'The Hasmonean Revolt Politically Considered', *Salo Wittmayer Baron Jubilee Volume* (eds. S. Lieberman, et al.; Vol. 2, Jerusalem, 1974), p. 267.
34. B. Renaud, 'La Loi et les Lois dans les Livres de Maccabees', *Revue Biblique*, 78 (1961), p. 49, contends that the heavy emphasis on the Temple and its observance in I Maccabees indicates that the fulfilment of the priestly code was now regarded as equivalent to the fulfilment of the entire law.
35. Even though the conviction that true prophecy belonged only to a Biblical past or a messianic future remained firm (see above chapter 3), the early Hasmoneans – and particularly Hyrcanus – nevertheless certainly claimed to have been endowed with some of the residual elements of that gift. See the note to AJ 13:300 in the Loeb edition (Vol. 7, pp. 377–8) and TB *Soṭah* 33a (where Hyrcanus is said to have heard a *bat qol*). In general, J. Blenkinskopp, 'Prophecy and Priesthood in Josephus', *JJS*, 25 (1974), esp. pp. 252–5.
36. *Mishnah, Soṭah* 9:10. See the analyses in Lieberman, *Hellenism*, pp. 139–43; S. Zeitlin, 'Johanan the High Priest's Abrogations and Decrees', *Studies and Essays in Honor of A. Neuman* (N.Y., 1962), pp. 569ff; and Y. Efron, 'Shim'on ben Sheṭaḥ we-Yann'ai ha-Melekh', *Sefer* [...] *Alon*, p. 86. That this and allied material echoes earlier pro-Hasmonean propaganda is argued in A. Aptovitzer, 'Poliṭiqah Ḥashmon'it we-Neged-Ḥashmona'it ba-Halakhah u-ve-'Agadah', *Sefer Zikaron* [...] *Poznanski* (reprinted; Jerusalem, 1969), pp. 145–69. For the suggestion (implied in BJ 1:68) that Hyrcanus had straddled all three *ketarim*, see above chap. 1, p. 18.
37. A. Dupont-Sommer, 'Observations sur le Commentaire de Nahum découvert près de la Mer Morte', *Journal des Savants*, Oct.–Dec. 1963, pp. 201–27. Cf., however, Alon, *Jews, Judaism and the Classical World*, pp. 29–30; and Y. Efron, *Ḥiqerei he-Tequfah ha-Ḥashmona'it*, pp. 201–5.

38. The intricate pervasiveness of the 'Temple vs Wilderness' motif in Jewish thought of the time is fully investigated in D.R. Schwartz, 'Midbar u-Miqdash', *Kehunah u-Melukhah: Yaḥasei Dat u-Medinah be-Yisra'el u-ve-'Amim* (eds. Y. Gafni and G. Motzkin; Jerusalem, 1987), see esp. his table on p. 77.
39. Some candidates are placed very early in the second Commonwealth (Ezra and Nehemiah), others at its end (the leaders of the revolt against Rome). All are summarised in B. Thiering, *Redating the Teacher of Righteousness* (Sydney, 1979), who argues for an intermediate point during 'the second phase of the Roman occupation'.

    For the view that the *moreh ṣedeq* does not always denote a single individual, 'but any priest who was believed by the sect (and there were several) to be qualified to function as a legitimate High Priest', see G. W. Buchanan, 'The Priestly Teacher of Righteousness', *Revue de Qûmran*, 6 (1969), pp. 553–8.
40. Sanders, *Paul and Palestinian Judaism*, p. 303; P.R. Davies, 'The Ideology of the Temple in the Damascus Document', *JJS*, 33 (1982), pp. 300–1.
41. 'The Community did not consider itself to have broken with the temple and the cultus in all its forms; instead, they transferred the whole complex of ideas from the Jerusalem Temple to the community.' B. Gartner, *The Temple and the Community in Qumran and the New Testament* (Cambridge, 1965), pp. 18–21. The same thesis is developed in Schürer (revised), Vol. 2, pp. 575–85, which also analyses the government of the sects. Cf., however, the possibility that 'in the subsequent stage of Qumran history [...] the sectarians now found it possible to send sacrifices to the Jerusalem Temple', see J. M. Baumgarten, 'The Essenes and the Temple: A Re-appraisal', *Studies in Qumran Law* (Leiden, 1978), p. 68.
42. He mentions only three Essenes by name: Judah, Jonathan and Simon, and it is not clear whether any were priests. D. Ben-Ḥayim Trifon, *Ha-Kohanim mi-Ḥurban ha-Bayit we-'Ad 'Aliyat ha-Naṣrut* (unpub. Ph.D.; Tel Aviv, 1985), p. 29, fn. 139.
43. G. Vermes, 'The Essenes and History', *JJS*, 32 (1981), pp. 18–31; in the same article Vermes also summarises the reasons for identifying Essenes with the Qumran sectarians.
44. I Chron. 28:11ff and Y. Yadin's citations of rabbinic texts in *Megilat ha-Miqdash*, Vol. 1 (Jerusalem, 1977), p. 308.
45. The manner in which the Temple scroll consistently 'strips' the King of his Biblical authority is analysed in M. Hengel, J. H. Charlesworth and D. Mendels, 'The Polemical Character of ''On Kingship'' in the Temple Scroll: An Attempt at dating 11Q Temple', *JJS*, 37 (1986), pp. 28–38. Note, especially, 56:21 (Yadin, vol. 2, p. 178; reading '*we-kotvu lo*' for '*we-kotav lo*' on the scroll to be written by the King;

cf. Deut. 17:18 and Mishnah, *Sanhedrin* 2:4); 57:14 (Yadin, Vol. 2, p. 181; on the position of the King *vis-à-vis* a council of priests); and 58:18–21 (Vol. 2, p. 186; on going to war).

46. J. M. Baumgarten, 'The Duodecimal Courts of Qumran, Revelation and the Sanhedrin', *JBL*, 95 (1976), pp. 63–4. In sum, there seems to be little reason to accept the 'democratic' models discerned for some periods of Qumran history by C. Rabin, *Qumran Studies* (Oxford, 1957). Still less-acceptable is his conclusion (p. 105) that: 'The priests are [...] only an executive body.' Cf. B. Sharvit, 'Ha-Hanhagah Shel Kat Midbar Yehudah', *Beit Miqra'*, 78 (1979), pp. 295–304.
47. IQS 5:1–6; translated in A. Dupont-Sommer, *The Essene Writings from Qumran* (Oxford, 1961), pp. 82–3 and (as 'The Blessings of the Priests') in Vermes, *Scrolls in English*, p. 207. In general, A. R. C. Leaney, *The Rule of Qumran and its Meaning* (London, 1966), esp. pp. 91–5, 164–6.
48. J. Jeremias, *Jerusalem in the Time of Jesus* (Eng. edn.; Phila., 1969), p. 247. See also the earlier remarks in on the possible affinities of the groups of *ḥaverim* to the Essenes in S. Lieberman, 'The Discipline in the So-Called Dead Sea Manual of Discipline', *JBL*, 71 (1952), pp. 199–206.
49. Vermes, *Scrolls in English*, pp. 18–20. The relevant texts are translated in Dupont-Sommer, pp. 84–5 and Leaney, pp. 189, 196, and analysed in B. Sharvit, 'Ha-Kohen be-Kat Midbar Yehudah', *Beit Miqra'*, 70 (1977), pp. 313–20.
50. Sharvit, 'Ha-Kohen', p. 316. But cf. F. M. Cross jnr, *The Ancient Library of Qumran* (N.Y., 1961), pp. 227–30.
51. Indeed, the declared object of all initiates was to 'do what is good and right before Him in accordance with the commands which He gave through Moses and through all His servants the prophets' (1QS 1:2–4; in Leaney p. 117 and Vermes, p. 72).
52. M. Smith, 'Palestinian Judaism from Alexander to Pompey', *Hellenism and the Rise of Rome* (ed. P. Grimal; London, 1965), p. 256.
53. Vermes, *Scrolls in English*, p. 25 and Sharvit, 'Ha-Kohen', p. 317. For further remarks on the position of the Levite (and especially the levitical *maskil*) *vis-à-vis* the priest see: the commentary in Leaney, op. cit., pp. 229–30 and M. Gertner, 'The Masorah and the Levites', *VT*, 10 (1960), pp. 241–72.
54. M. Grant, *The Jews in the Roman World* (N.Y., 1973), p. 44.
55. Vermes, *Scrolls in English* p. 79. Compare Dupont-Sommer, op. cit., p. 85.
56. Vermes, *Scrolls in English*, pp. 247–8. The problems and sources are further discussed in Liver, 'The Doctrine of the Two Messiahs in Sectarian Literature in the Time of the Second Commonwealth', *HThR*, 52 (1959), pp. 149–85 and G.L. Brooke, *Exegesis at Qumran: 4Q Florilegium in its Jewish Context* (Sheffield, 1985), pp. 197–205.

On the possible stages of Essene messianism see: J. Starcky, 'Les Quartre Étapes du Messianisme à Qûmran', *Revue Biblique*, 70 (1963), pp. 481–505.

57. See, in this connection, Y. Liver's interpretation of the phrase *'beit malkhut kehunata' raba' min malkhut'* in the fragment found in Qumran cave 1: 'Ha-Mashiaḥ mi-Beit Dawid Bimgilot Midbar Yehudah', in *Iyunim Bimgilot Midbar Yehudah le-Zekher A. Sukenick* (Jerusalem, 1957), p. 70.
58. Schürer, *History* (revised), Vol. 2, p. 551.

SECTION B

From theory to practice: the struggle for supremacy

5

The first phase (c. 135 B.C.E. – c. 100 C.E.)

The destruction of the second Temple in 70 C.E. necessarily influences perceptions of the entire course of Jewish history during the period of late antiquity. At a stroke, that event deprived Israel of the most vivid expression of its sacred association with God and of the most compelling of its symbols of national distinctiveness. So great was the calamity of the Destruction that the date of its occurrence has traditionally been regarded as an authentic historical watershed. Its immediate impact was to stimulate anguished reflection on the specific and/or generic failings which were considered to have been its cause; more hesitantly, but more fundamentally, it also generated profound re-assessments of every aspect of Jewry's national thought and practice. Thus it was that with the fall of Jerusalem the Jewish people and its religious culture began to embark upon a course which was eventually to prove revolutionary. However irregular and hesitant the initial steps in that transition, their cumulative effect was decisive. Post-Destruction Judaism, largely under the impact of the Destruction itself, differed in almost all essentials from the civilisation by which it was preceded and out of which it grew.

It is tempting to apply the same gauge when measuring the domestic political effects of the Destruction. At that level, the events of 70 C.E. could arguably be portrayed as marking – in addition to all else – a constitutional turning-point. They crippled the authority of the priesthood as fatally as the precipitate death of Agrippa I in 43 or 44 C.E. had enfeebled the prestige of Jewry's native royalty. In thus creating a political hiatus, the Destruction also seems in retrospect to have immediately upset prior relationships between the three *ketarim*, depriving the *kehunah* and *malkhut* of functional expression and, thereby, leaving representatives of the *keter torah* in command of whatever autonomous power Jewry was still in a position to wield. Those new circumstances, it could be argued, enabled early rabbinic notions of power and its distribution to become normative principles of Jewish life. They also facilitated the process whereby early rabbinic proponents of that outlook legitimised their communal primacy, adding political supremacy to whatever spiritual authority their scholarship was deemed to impart.

Like most other schematic interpretations of historical developments, that presentation threatens to simplify what was an intrinsically complicated process. In so doing, it also distorts the data on which it relies. At both ends of the chronological spectrum, the struggle between the *ketarim* was far more protracted. The Destruction did not immediately result in the total elimination of the *kehunah* and the *malkhut* as forces in all subsequent Jewish politics, and hence did not – of itself – automatically ensure the communal hegemony of the *keter torah*. More to the point, spokesmen for the governmental primacy of the latter domain had in any case not awaited the Destruction before formulating their own programme of political supremacy and attempting its implementation. Some time before the final end of the second Jewish Commonwealth, they had aspired to dominate the internal life of the polity as a whole and, as organised within the framework of the Pharisaic party, had invoked the name of the *torah* when challenging the traditional government of kings and priests. Their rabbinic successors, however much they may have intensified that campaign, did not therefore initiate radically new departures. Instead, they in effect only refined and developed arguments which had already tended to dominate much of the very shape and texture of Jewish political behaviour.

The present chapter is designed to demonstrate that thesis. Concentrating on the constitutional implications of the positions respectively taken by the Pharisees and Sadducees prior to the Destruction, it will argue that those two parties projected (in addition to all else) contrasting political programmes. In so doing, they also acted as spokesmen for two distinct governmental domains. Whereas Sadducean doctrines tended to reflect the inherent prerogatives associated with the establishment of the existing *keter kehunah*, Pharisaic teachings asserted the claims to supremacy of the *keter torah* in its incipient and proto-rabbinic form.

Pharisees vs Sadducees: the confrontation defined

From a strictly constitutional perspective, conflicts between the Sadducees and the Pharisees during the later generations of the second Jewish Commonwealth appear to have been more concerned with means than with ends. At issue between the parties were not competing theories of sovereignty but conflicting perspectives on a tradition which both regarded as specifically Jewish and undeniably sacred. Significantly, their rival spokesmen did not put forward fundamentally divergent understandings of Judaism's covenantal heritage; neither did they propose diametrically opposite frameworks for the fulfilment of the obligations and duties which partnership in that holy commonwealth was believed to entail. Doctrinal dissent, although often fundamental, seems to have been expressed with remarkable discretion. Neither party can convincingly be shown to have adopted the tiresome expedient of pronouncing the other excommunicate. On the contrary, both appear to have acknowledged their joint birthright to complete membership in Israel's religious community and the enjoyment (at least in 'this world') of whatever privileges that status was deemed to bestow.[1]

When it came to specifics, too, far more united the two camps than divided them. Crucially, both regarded the Mosaic code as the basic constitutional referent of all Jewish behaviour, public as well as private. It would clearly be inappropriate therefore to attribute only to the Pharisees a belief in the Divine source of scripture's commandments and to describe their Sadducean opponents as either woefully ignorant of that legislative corpus or generally lax in its observance and transmission. Rabbinic sources of a later period, which thus tend to denigrate all Sadducees – including those who officiated as High Priests – have to be treated with considerable caution. At the very least, they need to be contrasted with other and older traditions (many themselves preserved in early rabbinic literature) which tender alternative characterisations. Studies of the relevant sources have suggested that no less than the Pharisees did the Sadducees take care to observe the strict requirements of the Mosaic rules governing ritual purity. Those who were priests were particularly rigorous in their insistence on the proper fulfilment of the well-preserved Temple rituals and learned in their elucidation of ancient Temple rites. If anything, Pharisees may have thought the (Sadducean) priesthood excessively punctillious in its attention to ritual purity and inordinately insistent on the retention of its exclusive mastery over some of the carefully-guarded technical skills appertaining to the Temple service.[2] Otherwise, however, charges of delinquency would be misplaced. By the last generations of the second Commonwealth, priests had developed their own framework of administrative councils and supervisory courts (perhaps generically referred to as the *beit din shel kohanim*);[3] their own – possibly independent – procedures for examining priestly genealogies (*Tosefta'*, *Sanhedrin* 7:1; cf. *Sifrei* Numb. 116 [p. 133]) and their own methods, some of which were summary and brutal, for dealing with infringements of their own ritual and cultic standards. As *Mishnah* (*Sanhedrin* 9:6) was later to record:

A priest who served while in a state of impurity is not brought before *beit din* by his fellow priests, but the young priests remove him from the Temple court and split his skull with logs.

Against that background, it seems somewhat anachronistic to suggest that the Pharisees were devotees of a 'religious' constitutional perspective, whilst the Sadducees advocated a 'statist' view of government. Once academically fashionable, that view seems to have been unduly affected by the modern European experience of conflict between Church and State.[4] Primary sources paint a more circumscribed picture. What they suggest is that disagreements between the parties concerned something far different: the constitutional status of the instruments and methodologies upon which they each relied in order to interpret the Mosaic code, and thereby define and specify its provisions. On this matter, the literary portrait provided by Josephus in AJ 13:297 – although tantalisingly succinct – is generally thought to be pivotal.

The Pharisees [he relates] had passed on to the people certain regulations handed down by former generations and not recorded in the Laws of Moses, for which reason they are rejected by the Sadducean group, who hold that only those ordinances should be considered valid which were written down [in Scripture], and that those which had been handed down by former generations [lit. 'by the fathers'; *paradosis ton pateron*] need not be observed. And concerning these matters the two parties came to have controversies and serious differences.

Much of the interest generated by that passage has centred on the evidence which it provides for the contrasting attitudes of the two sides towards the legitimacy of unwritten *halakhot*. Pharisees, it has been claimed – notwithstanding their insistence on the ultimate supremacy of the written *torah* – characteristically asserted the legitimacy of unwritten transmission (later known as 'the oral law') as a medium for legislative inference and pronouncement. Sadducees, on the other hand – whilst certainly not the unbending literalists of some subsequent caricature – insisted that ordinances derived from Biblical exegesis were only authoritative if formally inscribed and properly deposited in an official archive.[5] Be that as it may, the paradigm of the three *ketarim* indicates a supplementary nuance. Specifically, it suggests that conflicts between the two parties were concerned as much with the institutional focus of whatever oral teachings were at issue as with their precise form. At stake, in other words, was not only the authenticity and accuracy of variant traditions but also – perhaps even more so – the legitimacy of rival constitutional franchises and their respective authority to declare what was and what was not Divine law.[6]

Reconstructed along those lines, conflicts between the Pharisees and Sadducees exhibit undoubted traces of an incipient struggle between the two distinct mediating frameworks which were later to be termed the *keter kehunah* and the *keter torah*. Sadducean teachings, in this view, can be said to have been rooted in the assertion that the custody of the Holy Bible was part of the priests' own provenance. Their status as trustees of that manuscript's literary authenticity seems to have been reflected in the designation of its recognised prooftext as the *Sefer ha-'Azarah* (lit. 'Scroll of the [Temple] Court'; *Mishnah, Mo'ed Qaṭan* 3:4; *Kelim* 15:6). As far as *kohanim* were themselves concerned, it probably followed that their responsibility for its correct transmission was equally ordained. Hence, even where oral elucidation of the text was unavoidable, it had to be in accordance with the *kehunah*'s own doctrines and traditions.

Essential to the position adopted by the Pharisees, on the other hand, was a view which articulated the quite separate authority of the *keter torah*. Mindful of the need to establish an authorised version of the Biblical text,[7] Pharisees were certainly not prepared to grant priests a hereditary monopoly over its exegesis. Teaching and transmission had to be regarded as matters for 'experts in the law', men who were excellent and/or accurate in its interpretation[8] and who appreciated that the non-priestly oral heritage which they claimed to have received from Moses (the 'traditions' of which Josephus speaks, and which may also be referred to in Matthew 15:2 and Mark 7:3, 5) constituted the proper key to the understanding of Scripture's true meaning.

Josephus himself suggested that Pharisees and Sadducees appealed to different social strata (AJ 13:298). Pursuing that line of enquiry in greater detail, Finkelstein demonstrated that their legislative programmes did indeed often reflect the conflicting economic interests of their respective memberships. ('The interpretations of the Law given respectively by priests and scribes were necessarily colored by their diametrically opposed social connections. The priest in his decisions followed the patrician precedents and sympathies of the Temple, the scribe the inherited ideas of his plebian class.').[9] Nevertheless, closer examination has cautioned against a simplistic exercise in classification, whereby all priests would be dragooned into the ranks of aristocratic Sadducees and all Pharisees into a close-knit circle of like-minded plebeians. What has been noted, rather, are the ragged edges of both groupings and the extent to which their memberships in fact confounded conventional categorisations of caste, class, and residence. True, and as Le Moyne points out, 'there exists no source which refers to Sadducees [or the "Boethesians", their fellow-travellers] who were demonstrably not priests'. Nevertheless, the equation cannot be easily reduced to an axiom of analysis. As the case of Joshua ben Gamla' illustrates, not even all High Priests were necessarily Sadduceans.[10]

Similarly heterogeneous, it might be suggested, were the family affiliations of the lower classes of individuals who supported the rival claims of the two domains later to be designated the *keter kehunah* and the *keter torah*. Patronage of the former, as represented by the Sadducees, was not always dependent upon personal possession of priestly lineage; neither, conversely, was advocacy of the superiority of the *keter torah* necessarily a corollary of non-priestly status. In both cases, individual allegiances might have been far more dependent on philosophical and ideological affinity than on genetic circumstances. According to later talmudic accounts, early Pharisaic leaders deliberately discounted the relevance of pedigree as a yardstick of party affiliation when drumming up support for the *keter torah*, pointedly noting that 'pupils of Aaron' were superior to his sons (TB *Yoma'* 71b). To judge by the quantitative prominence of attested priests in scattered roll-calls of Pharisaic leadership, that message certainly struck a responsive cord.[11] But there is no reason to assume that all of the traffic moved in one direction. Awe of the majesty always inherent in the *keter kehunah*, combined perhaps with sympathy for the exegetical principles postulated by its current representatives, could – at the same time and perhaps in equal measure – have induced several non-priests to gravitate towards the Sadducean camp.

The focus of conflict

One inference of this depiction is that Sadducean representatives and supporters of the *keter kehunah* constituted virtual mirror-images of their Pharisee opponents. However much their theologies may have differed in several essentials (including, as Josephus was the first to point out, Divine retribution, free will, and resurrection; BJ 2:162–5; AJ 18:12–16), when presenting their rival cases the two camps employed recognisably parallel means. Both appealed to the identical scriptural basis of religious authority and both developed comparable – albeit incompatible – traditions of Biblical exegesis. Above all, both camps shared an overwhelming devotion to the maintenance of Israel's distinctive form of worship and – therefore – an abiding commitment to the rigid observance of the Temple service. In sum, not only did Pharisees and Sadducees share much common ground; even when differing they largely addressed the same concerns and had recourse to similar conventions.

Whether or not they were ever able to institutionalise that circumstance, and meet together in regular sessions of the same national tribunal sometimes referred to as the *sanhedrin* is (as we have seen) a much debated issue. If so, then (as Hoenig suggests) it might reasonably be supposed that their views were presented to that body in a consolidated form by the public personalities jointly referred to in Mishnaic sources as *zugot* ('pairs'). Individually entitled the *nasi'* ('president', or leader of the majority, which Hoenig hypothesis was a Sadducee post until the era of Simeon ben Sheṭaḥ) and *'av beit din* ('chairman of the court', leader of the minority party), the *zugot* thus acted as rival spokesmen for contesting exegetical outlooks and legislative programmes.[12] But even if a formal and quasi-parliamentary situation of that sort did not prevail, the two parties certainly seem to have understood each other well enough to co-operate informally. At moments of acute national crisis, Josephus reports, their mutual comprehension permitted some degree of pragmatic co-ordination.[13] Scattered references in tanna'itic texts (e.g. *Mishnah, Yadayim* 4:6–8 and *Tosefta', Yadayim* 2:20) suggest that their spokesmen were also able to conduct *ad hoc* dialogues, and to confront each other in direct debates on matters of common concern.

Even so, exchanges between Pharisees and Sadducees could never be entirely academic. Neither could they be conducted in the cordial atmosphere of congenial scholasticism. Even when limited to the purity regulations, their debates affected fundamental political concerns. The interpretation of the Divine command on such matters, it is worth repeating, was intimately bound up with authority. God's revealed word to His people could only be mediated by those who possessed a legitimate mandate to do so. What is more, that mandate conferred power as well as prestige. Ultimately at stake was not merely an understanding of Revelation, but control over the law which it prescribed. On that score, too, second Commonwealth representatives of the embryonic domains of the *kehunah* and the *torah* seem to have been of like minds. Speaking of the Sadducees, Bowker has posited that, when they

> denied the validity, both of the method of Hakamic [i.e. Pharisaic] exegesis, and of the support which they gave to traditional ways of doing things, and when they insisted on the application of the literal text of the Torah wherever possible, they were in fact creating another isolation – in addition to the geographical isolation of the Temple as an enclave of holiness, they were in fact isolating Torah from the lives of the people, since it was not in fact possible to apply the literal text of the Torah without interpretation.[14]

Mutatis mutandis, it is here suggested, Pharisees approached issues in precisely the same way. Like the Sadducees, they too attributed to their exegetical activity a dimension which was pragmatic rather than theoretical and political as well as intellectual.

Exactly when debates between the Pharisees and Sadducees assumed critical national importance is difficult to ascertain. Josephus, although remarking that the parties themselves date 'from the most ancient times' (AJ 18:11; a notoriously unhelpful phrase, the imprecision of which has provided scope for vastly differing conjectures),[15] does not dissect the divergencies in Pharisaic and Sadducean outlooks until his chronicle reaches the life and times of Jonathan the Maccabee (AJ 13:171–3). More to the point, he reserves his first mention of their **political** rivalry until he has worked his way down to the period of John Hyrcanus (AJ 13:288–98). Levine accounts for that arrangement by positing that not until the latter period did Hasmonean rulers begin to experience the domestic and diplomatic pressures which necessitated a choice between the two factions.[16] But even if that is the explanation, it does not necessarily obviate the argument that the intellectual forbears of both sides had previously been prone to resort to force in order to influence the course of Jewry's cultural destiny. On the contrary, it has been suggested that proto-Pharisees and proto-Sadducees had cultivated forceful versions of their religious-cum-political doctrines even prior to their joint participation in the grand Maccabean coalition against the Seleucids and the latter's Jewish supporters. Indeed, not the least of their joint contributions to that campaign stemmed from their shared status as heirs to traditions which regarded political militancy as an appropriate vehicle for the promotion of a specific religious programme.[17]

Victory in the Maccabean war, together with the renewed round of civil strife by which it was soon followed, merely permitted this strain to become even more pronounced. By 100 B.C.E. – at the very latest – Pharisaism had, in Bickerman's words, become 'a belligerent movement that knew how to hate'.[18] Its adherents certainly acted in that spirit shortly thereafter. Even if, like the Essenes, they were temporarily forced into political exile during the reign of John Hyrcanus, they did not permanently follow the sectarian path of withdrawal from the political fray. Instead (and as is recorded by the reports preserved in TJ *Berakhot* 7:2) they attempted to meet the challenge of political rivalry head-on, even to the extent of armed insurrection. In quick stages, they proceeded from the organisation of their ranks to open rebellion against the Sadducean policy, and person, of Alexander Yannai. According to such retrospective accounts as Leviticus *Rabbah* 35:10, it was during the reign of his widow and immediate successor, Queen Alexandra Salome (76–67 B.C.E.) that their efforts were crowned with significant – albeit temporary – success.

Arguably, the ferocious uncertainty attendant upon Herod's reign (37–4 B.C.E.) subsequently forced most Pharisees to adopt a far lower profile. As much is suggested by the intensely introspective character of the Mishnaic traditions said to have originated in that period, whose portrait is of a party undergoing a process of consolidation and internal development: refining its doctrines; fostering its own brand of exegesis; and closely scrutinising the consequent halakhic inferences. Neusner to the contrary, however, it nevertheless remains doubtful whether the dangerous ambience of the times dictated that, under Hillel's leadership, all Pharisees completely abandon their political ambitions for 'more irenic and quietist paths'.[19] Only a minority of their number – perhaps the *ḥaverim* of Mishnaic description – went to the extreme of virtually cutting themselves off from the rest of the nation (a category which includes, of course, most other Pharisees too) and grouping themselves into exclusive table-fellowships, distinguished by their special concern for the extended and scrupulous lay observance of purity laws. But the majority, although now subdued and fractured into various sub-divisions (as is recalled in ARN 'B', 37; [ed. Schechter, p. 109 and n. 4]), retained their older tradition of communal activism and thus remained a recognisably distinct party.[20] They still believed it imperative that the entire nation be induced to acknowledge the intrinsic validity and sanctity of Pharisaic traditions and made to follow Pharisaic practice and rulings.

What can be said is that, despite the intensity and persistence of their preparations for power, first-century Pharisees had few grounds to expect that they might soon be able to translate their aspirations into reality. In starkly political terms, theirs was really something of a forlorn cause, allowing them to hope for little more than a spectatorial role on the fringes of power. That status hardly seems to merit the aura of burgeoning triumph conveyed by Josephus in his *Antiquities* and *Life*. At several points, it has been shown, those accounts of massive Pharisaic popularity and influence prior to 70 C.E. conflict with the more restrained sketch earlier outlined in *The Jewish War*. Equally serious is the dichotomy between their portrait of a party maturing in the final century before the Destruction towards the threshold of supreme authority and the grimmer reality of what amounted – almost until the very end – to a Sadducean domination of contemporary public affairs.[21] All other evidence indicates that, prior to the outbreak of the Great Revolt, the Pharisees' proximity to the centres of national power was at best occasional and never corporate. Were he an acknowledged legal expert, a Pharisaic *mufla'* ('assessor'; *Mishnah, Horayot* 1:4) might – in a personal capacity – occasionally have been admitted into the councils of a national '*beit din*'.[22] If endowed with outstanding academic status, 'a teacher of the Law' (the designation accorded to Rabban Gamli'el I in Acts 5:34) might similarly have participated in the day-to-day affairs of the '*sanhedrin*'. But even thus to enumerate possible moments of Pharisee influence on those bodies (if they ever in fact existed) is to demonstrate the extent to which they were fleeting and exceptional. As a rule, and as we have seen (above p. 100), not excepting the reign of Agrippa I, the Sadducees were the party which wielded whatever autonomous power and authority the Jews of Judea could in that period hope to command.

Most crucially was this so where the Temple was concerned. By any standards, that was the most vitally important of Israel's institutions. As the nexus of all sanctity, it also manifestly constituted the central focus for all national affections. Of all the many identified groupings in second Commonwealth Jewry, only the Essenes might possibly have posited a communal surrogate for the existing shrine. Every other, including the Pharisees, acknowledged that the present structure and its cultic rituals continued to possess an atoning power for which no substitute was possibly conceivable. Whoever would wish to control the polity had perforce first to control its Temple.

But it was precisely within those precints that the Pharisees were on their weakest ground. Like other circles of cognoscenti, they did stalk the Temple concourse and approaches, thereby hoping to publicise and popularise their teachings.[23] Nevertheless, they possessed no independent following of overriding numerical significance (a simple count of heads would probably indicate that Pharisee 'scribes' or 'sages' in Jerusalem were considerably outnumbered by such Temple auxiliaries as priests, levites, musicians, and guards). More to the point, within the Temple itself the Pharisees could claim no official *locus standi*. Accordingly, it was quite out of the question that they might effect an institutional displacement by arrogating to themselves the performance of those cultic rituals which were an exclusive priestly monopoly. Scripture had explicitly instructed priests – and only priests – to 'keep charge of the holy things and the charge of the altar' (Numb. 18:7). As tanna'itic literature was itself to acknowledge, that injunction could mean but one thing: 'All matters pertaining to the altar shall be performed only by you [Aaron] and your sons' (*Sifrei* Numb. 116 [p. 133]).

Ample scope did exist, however, for an alternative approach. The ambience which foreclosed a direct Pharisaic onslaught on both Temple servants and Temple service did not preclude a critique of the behaviour of the former and the performance of the latter. Even when priests were acknowledged to possess exclusive functional prerogatives in cultic matters, it was still possible to deny them a monopoly over the determination of what might be considered correct ritual practice. Admittedly, this was a somewhat oblique challenge and, particularly in relation to the Temple service, not altogether an original one.[24] But from the perspective of Pharisaic purposes, it must have possessed one distinct polemical advantage:

by emphasising the need for the detailed scrutiny of cultic rites, it altered the focus of debate with the Sadducees and shifted attention to precisely those areas in which the Pharisaic 'experts on the law' felt themselves to be most competent. By virtue of their scholarship, the latter could claim to be better informed than priests themselves as to the correct understanding of the relevant Scriptural purity laws, and hence better qualified to supervise the manner whereby they were being carried out. Priestly conduct within the Temple, accordingly, could be assessed – and found wanting – in the light of criteria established by the '*ḥakhamim*' themselves (*Mishnah, Pesaḥim* 5:8; *Tosefta', Pesaḥim* 3:12). By extension, all actions carried out under the aegis of the *keter kehunah* had to pass the test of independent – and extra-priestly – scrutiny by representatives of a newly assertive *keter torah*.

Arguably, *Megilat Ta'anit* exaggerates the extent to which both priests and Sadducees were prepared to succumb to Pharisaic wishes in such matters.[25] *Mishnah* and *Tosefta'* probably do so too. (Is it likely, one wonders, that all High Priests would have unhesitatingly subscribed to the Pharisees' understanding of the Temple service on the annual Day of Atonement – especially if required to do so in the dead of night by a collegium [the '*ziqnei beit din*', *Mishnah, Yoma'* 1:2] which possessed no standing whatsoever in the priesthood's own adjudicatory system? On the basis of one reported conversation [*Tosefta', Nidah* 5:3, repeated with some variations in TB *Nidah* 33b] is it possible to generalise about the regularity with which all Sadducean women might have consulted 'a sage' [*ḥakham*] on matters of menstrual impurity?) But even if allowances do need to be made for some literary licence, Pharisaic intentions remain as important as Pharisaic accomplishments. For all their biases, the sources do not necessarily distort the radical impulse which, certainly by the very last generations of the second Temple period,[26] had begun to characterise much of Pharisaic *halakhah*. Certain ritual functions, its sages now taught, could legitimately be carried out by most categories of laymen and – as if to emphasise even further the intended encroachment on the priestly preserve – in some cases performed outside Jerusalem too.[27] Even where that was not the case, actions undertaken by members of the *keter kehunah* were deemed to be subject to lay control.[28] Ultimately, law-making was the prerogative of the *keter torah*.

What is especially remarkable about that claim is the range and scope of severely practical topics to which (perhaps concurrently) it came to be applied. Even as rigorously collated by Rivkin,[29] the 'unambiguous' tanna'itic chronicles of clashes between Pharisees and Sadducees transcribe an extensive sample of disputes covering several specific aspects of correct behaviour in the private and public Jewish domains. Contention between the two sides, it transpires, was not limited to either the minutiae of ritual purity laws (*Mishnah, Yadayim* 3:5, 4:6, 7) nor to the details of the Temple ritual (*Mishnah, Parah* 3:7; *Tosefta', Ḥagigah* 3:35; *Yoma'* 1:8). Their respective spokesmen were also said to have crossed swords with respect to some of the nuances of female inheritance (*Tosefta', Yadayim* 2:20 and TB *Bava' Batra'* 115b–116a); bills of divorce [*Mishnah, Yadayim* 4:8]; the examination and punishment of witnesses (*Mishnah, Makot* 1:6; *Tosefta', Sanhedrin* 6:6); and the determination of the dates of festivals (*Mishnah, Menaḥot* 10:3, *Tosefta', R'osh ha-Shanah* 1:15).

To accept that the texts do not necessarily contain the *ipsissima verba* of the contestants is not to deny the authenticity of their thrust. Indeed, far from confusing the issues between the parties,[30] the available information – precisely because it contrasts so vividly with Josephus' emphasis on differences in the more abstract realm of doctrinal belief – seems only to clarify them. It demonstrates the extent to which, by the eve of the Destruction, the Pharisees had transposed a series of religious opinions into a corpus of constitutional statements affecting matters civil as well as sacerdotal. By the same token, and as Alon pointed out,[31] it also reflects the degree to which they considered their legislative agenda to constitute a programme of communal government as well as a prescription for personal salvation. In directly challenging Sadducean interpretations on so heterogeneous a spectrum of the Biblical code, Pharisaic sages were not therefore merely attempting to score random exegetical points at their opponents' expense. Confident that their legal expertise encompassed the totality of day-to-day Jewish life, they were projecting their own emergent version of the *keter torah* as an alternative framework of government to the *keter kehunah*, and thereby articulating their own right to proclaim law on every aspect of the polity's affairs.

The contribution of Rabban Yoḥanan ben Zak'ai

According to rabbinic traditions, undoubtedly the most forceful individual exponent of that programme was Rabban Yoḥanan ben Zak'ai. As reconstructed from those sources, his biography virtually constitutes a record of its successful implementation. *Nasi'* (if that) for barely a decade, his partisan legislation and polemics shaped Judaism's religious and political agenda for centuries. More than any other single individual, Yoḥanan is credited with both delivering a *coup de grâce* to the Sadducean hierocracy and ensuring the transition from antebellum Pharisaism to postbellum rabbinism. Indeed, and as is argued by Neusner, Yoḥanan himself very much personified the shift.[32]

While Yoḥanan is chiefly revered and remembered by the rabbinic sources for his contributions to Jewish life after the Destruction, his commitment to the Pharisaic cause is also said to have anticipated that tragedy. He had apparently emerged as one of the party's leaders some time before 70 C.E., by which date he had already served a lengthy apprenticeship – occasionally as Rabban Simeon ben Gaml'iel's right-hand man – in both Galilean and metropolitan affairs. Prominence of that order cannot be attributed to the distinction of Yoḥanan's background. Although very little is revealed about the private circumstances of this remarkably public personality, the very silence of the sources as to his socio-economic position (even his attested priestly lineage has been doubted)[33] makes it unlikely that his distinction owed very much to genetic criteria. Of far greater importance seem to have been three other qualifications. One was the enormous breadth of his intellectual interests, which encompassed matters esoteric as well as practical;[34] a second was his reputation as a prominent teacher. The third was the force and vitality with which he had shown himself prepared to lead other *ḥakhamim* in their attacks on the Sadducees and thus to champion the validity of an independent (i.e. non-priestly) interpretation of the Scriptural code.

The records of Yoḥanan's several disputes with Sadduceans and/or priests prior to 70 C.E. reinforce the thrust of emerging relationships between the rival domains. Specifically, those transcriptions accord with the pattern of encroachment already noted to have been characteristic of the *keter torah*'s strategy *vis-à-vis* the *keter kehunah*. As recalled in the rabbinic literature (his name occurs in neither Josephus nor the New Testament) Yoḥanan's confrontations with his opponents invariably concerned material contentions on a range of specific civil and cultic topics. Even if those disputes did tend to be concerned with the correct exegesis on matters of procedure rather than substance,[35] their import and impact was nevertheless considerable. More often than not, they were generated by issues which champions of the *keter kehunah* must conventionally have regarded to fall fair and square within their own domain's terms of reference. Yoḥanan, if the rabbinic accounts are to be believed, blatantly contested that interpretation. He challenged priestly and/or Sadducean traditions on the status of rulings handed down by the municipal courts in cases which concerned civil law and commercial transactions (*Mishnah, Ketubot* 13:1, 2); he opposed them on specific details relevant to the laws of uncleanliness (the *ṭevul yom*; *Tosefta', Parah* 3:8) and the precise dating of the Pentecost festival (TB *Menaḥot* 65a). He also questioned priestly rights to consume certain parts of the sacred offerings; passed judgement on the validity of certain women to be considered permitted marriage partners for priests (*Mishnah, 'Eduyot* 8:3) and insisted on the priestly obligation to pay the Temple dues prescribed in Exodus 30:13 (*Mishnah, Sheqalim* 1:4).

Quite as important as the formal substance of those debates is the acerbic tone in which the retrospective records remembered them to have been conducted. Altogether, Yoḥanan emerges from the relevant sources as a testy personality possessed of both a sharp tongue and an almost volcanic disposition. When defending his own brand of exegesis he seems to have liberally indulged both traits. As a disputant, Yoḥanan is said to have made his reputation with a series of seemingly effortless (and ironically sarcastic)[36] ripostes, of the sort which friends will always remember and enemies can never forget. Moreover, and in order to get his way, he was not above sharp practice and (on at least one occasion, *Tosefta', Parah* 3:8) physical molestation. Quite apart from greatly embittering relations between the Pharisees and Sadducees, behaviour of that sort (if it occurred) must also have sharpened even further the lines now separating the *keter torah* from the *keter kehunah*. At the very least, it served notice of the lengths to which the spokesmen for the former were now prepared to go in order to assert the dominance of their domain over the entire Jewish polity.

It is tempting to trace an exacerbation of that trend – to a degree which almost defies credulity – in Yoḥanan's activities on the very eve of the Destruction. Particularly is this so once attention is concentrated, as must inevitably be the case, on the cluster of rabbinic sources which purport to describe the course and content of his ventures into what would today be called personal diplomacy. Notwithstanding differences in several important details, all tell roughly the same tale: at some point during the last stages of the

Roman siege of Jerusalem, Yoḥanan managed to outwit the zealots then in control of the city, make his way to the enemy camp and obtain an audience with Vespasian. Subsequent to an even more explicitly miraculous interlude, the Roman commander (soon to be Emperor) benignly expressed his willingness to commence negotiations. Yoḥanan seized the opportunity to make several requests, principal among which, according to the earliest sources (ARN 'A' 4:22–4; 'B' 6:19; TB *Giṭin* 56a–b), was clemency for 'Yavneh and her sages' – a petition which is traditionally regarded to have been a landmark in the history of rabbinic Judaism and which, from the perspective of our own study, must be understood to have exerted a crucial influence on the immediate survival of the *keter torah* and its subsequent national status. However, unless we are to believe a later revision of the tale (Lamentations *Rabbah* 1:5 no. 31), he did not investigate the possibility that the Romans might altogether raise their siege; neither did he apparently make any plea for the retention of the Temple, its service or its priestly officers.[37]

To dwell on this point is not necessarily to accept the rabbinic sources at their dubious face value (in fact, as Saldarini has shown, the thick varnish of legend with which even the earliest accounts are coated altogether detracts from their historical utility, too).[38] Still less is it to suggest that the historical Yoḥanan might have exploited Jewry's greatest national tragedy in order to cripple the *keter kehunah*. The importance of the account lies elsewhere: in the fact that, in their earliest versions of the tale, early rabbinic sources were prepared to leave open the implication that Yoḥanan might – consciously or otherwise – have been thus capable of attempting to further the ends of his own party and ensuring, to the best of his considerable ability, the communal supremacy of the *keter torah* which it championed.

Yoḥanan's activities after 70 C.E. (the records of which are considered much more reliable) go far towards explaining why that portrait might have been considered viable. Then, too, what was most distinctive about his activities and legislation is the extent to which they proclaimed an extension of the arc of the *keter torah*'s influence and, *pari passu*, a reduction in that of the *keter kehunah*. Yoḥanan, thus portrayed, did not merely re-interpret and adapt older Pharisaic teachings in the light of drastically changed circumstances. His true contribution was to extend them. Prior to the Destruction, representatives of the *keter torah* had emphasised the extent to which the world of Israel (indeed, of all mankind) rested on a tripod consisting of the books of the *torah*, the Temple rites and acts of piety (*Mishnah, 'Avot* 1:2). After 70, and largely under Yoḥanan's influence, both the sequence and the content of that formula underwent substantive change. The sages of the new age taught that – notwithstanding the loss of the Temple – the nation would and could endure. Its foundations now consisted of *torah*-study, performing the commandments and, perhaps especially, undertaking acts of compassion. In the words of the tradition recorded in ARN 'A' 4 (ed. Schechter 12b):

Once as Rabban Yoḥanan ben Zak'ai was coming out of Jerusalem, Rabbi Joshua followed after him, and beheld the Temple in ruins. Woe unto us, Rabbi Joshua cited, that this place, the place where the iniquities of Israel were atoned for, is laid waste. 'My son', Rabban Yoḥanan said to him, 'be not grieved. We have another atonement as effective as this, and what is it? It is acts of loving kindness [*gemilut ḥasadim* cf. *'Avot* 1:1], as it is said: "For I desire mercy and not sacrifice."' [Hosea 6:6].

Given that outlook, it is hardly surprising to learn that Yoḥanan initiated several legislative steps designed to meet the requirements of his times. In the absence of a Temple, liturgical practice, especially, became the subject of an entire series of *ad hoc* decrees (*taqanot*), five of which are specified in *Mishnah*. It was Yoḥanan, we are there told, who decided that some of the rituals hitherto reserved exclusively for the shrine could now be practised elsewhere: the *shofar* could be blown even when the New Year occurred on the Sabbath (*R'osh ha-Shanah* 4:1); and 'in memory of the *miqdash*', the *lulav* could be taken throughout the festival of Tabernacles (idem. 4:3). According to the same source, he also determined (or publicised) when precisely new produce could be eaten now that the *'omer* was no longer brought to Jerusalem (idem. cf., however, R. Judah in *Menaḥot* 10:5), when testimony concerning the sighting of the new moon of *Tishrei* could be accepted and where it might be delivered (*R'osh ha-Shanah* 4:4).

The implications of the *taqanot* attributed to Yoḥanan far exceeded their ostensibly limited range. True, and as is often pointed out, they leave untouched the entire field of civil legislation and affect only a marginal portion of cultic law. (That remains true even when *Mishnah*'s list of *taqanot* is supplemented by the four added in TB *R'osh ha-Shanah* 31b; the latter concern the mode of priestly footwear when blessing the people; permission for new-moon witnesses to travel on the Sabbath; the offering now demanded of a proselyte; and the disposal of the fourth-year fruits). Even as they stand, however, Yoḥanan's decrees constituted substantive encroachments on the priestly domain – which is doubtless one reason why several were later remembered to have aroused priestly ire (TB *R'osh ha-Shanah* 29b). Opponents no less than his supporters must have appreciated their thrust. By assuming a prerogative to legislate for the continued performance of actions which had previously been dependent on the sacrificial cult and its timing. Yoḥanan was in effect heralding a seismic shift in the very axis of Jewish religious observance as well as the auspices under which its practice was to be determined.[39]

Tosefta', R'osh ha-Shanah 4:3 is emphatic that:

> These things Rabban Yoḥanan ben Zak'ai ordained when the Temple was destroyed, and when it will be rebuilt, these matters will return to their former condition.

It is therefore doubtless stretching the evidence too far to suggest that, after 70, Yoḥanan 'may have prepared to declare in abeyance all those parts of the law which depended on the Temple for their performance or importance'. More accurate is the contention that his innovations generally declared only temporary modifications in the form of public ritual.[40] They were not necessarily intended to herald the disappearance of the priesthood or to erase the Temple cult from the national consciousness. Nevertheless, their cumulative effect was undoubtedly substantial. In demonstrating that the *keter torah* now possessed the capacity to act as the arbiter (perhaps the sole arbiter) of the nation's ritual life, Yoḥanan had come perceptibly close to suggesting that nascent rabbinism had arrogated to itself most of the privileges of the *keter kehunah*. In effect, he was also proclaiming the right of the *keter torah* to legislate for the entire Jewish polity, and not simply for that section of the population which had already accepted the rigours of Pharisaic discipline.

That does not appear to have been a systematically orchestrated programme. Neither was it necessarily one with which all of Yoḥanan's Pharisaic colleagues (especially those who were themselves of priestly descent) readily concurred.[41] Several *ḥakhamim* of the age initially reacted to the shock of the Temple's destruction by emphasising an introspective strain within Pharisaism. Strengthening their view might have been the realisation that the *keter kehunah* was not the only casualty of the Great Rebellion. Its aftermath had also weakened the *keter torah*. Pharisees, too, must have been slaughtered in 70 C.E.; even those who survived were dispersed and their nominal leader, Rabban Gaml'iel, reportedly forced underground (TB *Ta'anit* 29b). Those conditions were hardly propitious for a new round of internecine conflict against the *keter kehunah*; they seemed rather, to necessitate a programme of almost sectarian retrenchment on the part of Pharisaic champions of the *keter torah*.

'Eli'ezer ben Hyrcanus in many ways typified the latter point of view. Admittedly, he is depicted as one of Yoḥanan's most faithful students in Jerusalem and – prior to his establishment of his own academy at Lydda – one of his teacher's closest colleagues at Yavneh. Nevertheless, the two men emerge from the rabbinic traditions as very much personalities apart. Later sources suggest that they were raised in different backgrounds and tended to hold contrasting political views; earlier attestations indicate that – very soon after 70 C.E. – they had reached variant conclusions regarding the future direction of the Pharisaic party. In matters of halakhic procedure, 'Eli'ezer advocated a methodology at variance with that now favoured by the majority of sages – an advocacy which was ultimately to result in his ostracisation. As far as communal policy was concerned, he also recommended a strategy whose inference was that the *keter torah* withdraw into itself.[42] He was, it is true, prepared to rationalise and in some cases even make more lenient certain details of Pharisaic activities (simplifying, for instance, the giving of the 'wave' offering, extending the provisions of a sabbath *'eruv*; relaxing the procedures for nullifying vows).[43] But his surviving halakhic heritage does not indicate that 'Eli'ezer subjected the entire Pharisaic experience to new scrutiny in the light of the tragedy which had recently taken place. On the contrary, it reflects a profound anticipation that such scrutiny would essentially have been out of place. In any case, he seems to have reasoned, Jews had to believe that a third Temple would soon be built. In all essentials, practice in the new shrine would largely conform to the pattern recollected from the days of the old. Until then, it was really just a matter of sitting things out whilst acting piously and in purity. Hence, in halakhic matters, 'Eli'ezer could be – and was – essentially conservative. From his point of view, there was no call to extend – still less to radicalise – previous exegetical practice in order to find Scriptural support for new *halakhot*. Neither was there any need to abandon the perspective (arguably Shamma'itic in its essentials; see TJ *Beṣah* 1:4) which had regarded the tradition and doctrines hitherto handed down as the foundation and essence of post-destruction *halakhah*.

Yoḥanan's was a completely different approach to the demands of his times. No less than 'Eli'ezer did he mourn the destruction of the Temple, seeing it as an immense personal tragedy.[44] Unlike the vast majority of his contemporaries, however, he left not a single recorded recollection of the Temple service as he must have seen it prior to 70 C.E. One possible interpretation of that fact is that where some of his colleagues were still looking back, Yoḥanan insisted on looking forward.[45] The real issue confronting his age, he seems to have appreciated, was whether the Pharisees were to continue to remain a sect – and thus to put into practice an exclusivist ethic – or whether they might seize the opportunity to head what Shaye Cohen has recently termed a 'grand coalition' of Jewry.[46] To judge by his legislative programme, Yoḥanan advocated the latter course, deliberately arrogating to the academy of Yavneh the right to exercise much of the judicial and legal authority said to have been formerly held by the *sanhedrin* in Jerusalem.[47] In thus projecting an image of nation-wide power, Yoḥanan accomplished far more than the transition from Pharisaism to the Judaism of the early rabbinic period. Because regulations which had previously been of immediate and practical relevance to a limited sect were now decreed applicable to the entire nation, he had also generated a momentous expansion in the potential power and authority of the *keter torah*. As the next chapter will show, it was with those advantages to hand that Yoḥanan's successors were able further to expand the influence of their domain, in the process subordinating that of both the *malkhut* and the *kehunah*.

NOTES

1. Compare the restrained interpretation of *Mishnah, Sanh*. 10:1–3 in E.P. Sanders, *Paul and Palestinian Judaism: A Comparison of Patterns of Religion* (Phila., 1977), pp. 147–52 with V. Eppstein, 'When and How the Sadducees were Excommunicated', *JBL*, 85 (1966), pp. 213–23. See, too, TB *Ḥulin* 5a recalling that Pharisees did not invalidate the sacrifices of 'sinners' unless they were idol-worshippers or violated the Sabbath in public.
2. In general, V. Tcherikover, *Hellenistic Civilisation and the Jews* (Phila., 1959), pp. 262–5 and B.Z. Luria, 'Be-Sodam Shel ha-Kohanim', *Bet Miqra'*, 70 (1977), pp. 284–6. The secret knowledge of priests included

both technical skills (*Mishnah*, *Yoma'* 3:11; *Tosefta'*, ibid. 2:5–8), and miscellaneous items of information crucial to the Temple service (e.g. the pronunciation of the name of God; TB *Qidushin* 71a; TJ *Yoma'* 3:7, 40d). On excessive priestly zeal in purity matters, *Tosefta'*, *Kipurim* 1:12 (Lieberman, TK, *Mo'ed* [N.Y., 1962], pp. 224–5).

3. D. Tropper, 'Bet Din Shel Kohanim', *JQR*, 63 (1972–3), p. 209:

   For the *Bet Din shel Kohanim*, rather than being this single individual body heretofore envisioned by scholars, seems to have been a bureaucratic complex of priestly offices, agencies, and courts, each performing its unique functions in its personal hall of session, functionally and geographically independent of its fellow agencies.

   Antagonism between the 'sages' and this body is recorded in *Mishnah*, *Ketubot* 1:5.

4. J. Wellhausen, *Die Pharisäer und die Sadducäer* (2nd edn; Hanover, 1924), pp. 17ff. Cf. Tcherikover, pp. 264–5; Schürer, *History* (revised), Vol. 2, pp. 394–414; Urbach, *Sages*, p. 580 and Alon's strictures on Dubnow in *Jews, Judaism and the Classical World*, p. 3.

5. Perhaps literally '*ketuvah u-munaḥat*', see S. Lieberman, *Hellenism in Jewish Palestine*, p. 86 and E.E. Urbach, *Ha-Halakhah*, pp. 76–7. The inference that the Sadducees did not therefore limit their own textual interests to the Pentateuch is examined in J.M. Baumgarten, 'The Unwritten Law in the pre-Rabbinic Period', *JSJ*, 3 (1972), pp. 26–7. Contrast: R. Leszynsky, *Die Sadduzäer* (Berlin, 1912), pp. 23ff and R. Travers Herford, *The Pharisees* (London 1924), pp. 36ff.

6. For a somewhat different formulation, see A.I. Baumgarten, 'The Pharisaic *Paradosis*', *HThR*, 50 (1987), p. 71:

   The terms paradosis of the elders and of the fathers were deliberate attempts by the Pharisees to give their tradition a pedigree it might have seemed to lack. As such they hoped to defend their tradition at a vulnerable point and raise it from merely that of a school to the patrimony of the nation.

7. *Sifrei* Deut. 356 (see also the sources cited in Finkelstein's notes, p. 423 and Lieberman's analysis in *Hellenism*, p. 22), speaks of an occasion when 'three books were found in the *'azarah* [...] the sages [*ḥakhamim*] discarded [the reading of] the one and accepted [the reading of] the [other] two'.

8. Whence Josephus' designation of the Pharisees as *akribeia*. See A.I. Baumgarten, 'The Name of the Pharisees', *JBL*, 102/3 (1983), pp. 411–28; who argues that the name *paroshim* (meaning 'those who specify') may have been one of the original party designations. Only in later rabbinic literature did the term '*perushi*' come to possess pejorative overtones, perhaps connoting extreme ascetics. Cf. below, n. 14.

9. L. Finkelstein, *The Pharisees: The Sociological Background of Their Faith* (3rd, edn., Phila., 1962), Vol. 1, p. 265 and Vol. 2, pp. 63ff. See also W.W. Buehler, *The Pre-Herodian Civil War and Social Debate: Jewish Society in the Period 76–40 B.C. and the Social*

Factors Contributing to the Rise of the Pharisees and the Sadducees (Basel, 1974).

10. J. Le Moyne, *Les Sadducéens* (Paris, 1972), pp. 177–218; 236–8, 249–94 and 334–48. Second Commonwealth priests, he also shows, were far from constituting a genetically self-contained and economically homogeneous caste: their national influence was extended by recourse to inter-tribal marriages, just as their unity was threatened by intra-priestly economic rivalries (some of which reached violent proportions).
11. For precise data: Trifon, pp. 20–21. Particularly noteworthy is the anachronistic attribution of the title *rabi* to [the High Priest] Ishmael b. P'ari in *Mishnah, Soṭah* 9:15.
12. Hoenig, *Sanhedrin*, pp. 44–52. On priestly traditions of exegesis as reflected in tanna'itic literature. J.N. Epstein, *Mevo'ot le-Sifrut ha-Tana'im* (Jerusalem, 1957), pp. 512–13.
13. E.g. his account of their joint consideration of the demands presented by Florus immediately prior to the Revolt (BJ 2:411) and of their joint membership of the first revolutionary government thereafter.

    On co-operation between Simeon b. Gamli'el and the High Priest Ḥanan b. Ḥanan, see: M. Stern, 'Ha-Manhigut Bikvuṣot Loḥamei ha-Ḥerut be-Sof Yemei Bayit Sheini', *Ha-Mered ha-Gadol* (ed. A. Kasher; Jerusalem, 1983), p. 300.
14. J. Bowker, *Jesus and the Pharisees* (Cambridge, 1973), p. 18. The same source (pp. 13–15) also notes the 'measure of association' between *Perushim* and *Ḥakhamim* '(at least by their opponents)', and suggests that the term may have referred to persons who adhered to a particular degree of holiness.
15. The spectrum ranges from as early as the reconstruction of the Temple (Tchernowitz) to as late as the Herodian period (Holscher). See the review of the literature in H. Mantel, 'The Pharisees and the Sadducees', *The World History of the Jewish People*, Series 1, Vol. 8 (ed. M. Avi-Yonah and Z. Baras; Jerusalem, 1977), pp. 100–4.
16. L. Levine, 'Ha-Ma'avak ha-Poliṭie Bein ha-Perushim la-Ṣedukim Bitqufah ha-Ḥashmona'it', *Peraqim be-Toledot Yerushalayim Bimei Bayit Sheini* (eds. U. Oppenheimer, et al; Jerusalem, 1981), pp. 74–6. Cf. J. Goldin, 'The First Pair', *AJS review*, 5 (1980), pp. 44–5: 'the formerly inchaote groups then became distinct parties, crystallised and organised, their main beliefs on certain issues standing out clearly as platforms, and in debate with each other'.
17. R.T. Beckwith, 'The Pre-History and Relationships of the Pharisees, Sadducees and Essenes: A Tentative Reconstruction', *Revue de Qûmran*, 41 (1982), pp. 3–46, and A. Rofé, 'R'eishit Ṣemiḥatan Shel ha-Kitot Bimei Bayit Sheini', *Kathedra*, 49 (1988), pp. 13–22.

18. E. Bickerman, *From Ezra to the Last of the Maccabees* (N.Y., 1962), p. 168.
19. J. Neusner, *From Politics to Piety*, pp. 91ff. For a summary of the scholarly consensus, which seems to reject Neusner's view, see E. P. Sanders, *Jesus and Judaism* (London, 1985), pp. 184–8 and 195–8. Contrast, however, E. Rivkin, *A Hidden Revolution: The Pharisees' Search for the Kingdom Within* (Nashville, 1978), p. 256 ('Following the death of Salome Alexandra, the Pharisees acknowledge [sic] autonomy of the secular state in return for autonomy in the religious sphere'), and the more restrained reconstruction in L. I. Levine, ''Al ha-Me'oravut ha-Poliṭit Shel ha-Perushim Bitqufat Hordus u-Vimei ha-Neṣivim', *Kathedra*, 8 (1978), pp. 12–28.
20. Note Josephus' references to the Pharisees as a *suntagma* in BJ 1:110. On the difference between a sect and a party, Sanders, *Paul and Palestinian Judaism*, p. 267 and n.
21. The subject has been most thoroughly examined in S. J. D. Cohen, *Josephus in Galilee and Rome: His Vita and Development as a Historian* (Leiden, 1979). 'Our analysis of the shifts in the motives of the works of Josephus has allowed us to trace the development of the historian from a Roman apologist to a religious nationalist' (p. 240).
22. E. E. Urbach, 'Class Status and Leadership in the World of the Palestinian Sages', *Proceedings of the Israel Academy of Sciences and Humanities*, Vol. 2 (1968), p. 41 and note 6.
23. Thus, in addition to the tradition that Rabban Yoḥanan ben Zak'ai taught in the shadow of the Temple [walls] (TB *Pesaḥim* 26a), one notes the presence in the same surroundings of the Essene master Judah (BJ 1:78), and of Jesus of Nazareth (John 8:12–20). The location, one suspects, was not chosen at random. The Temple steps were certainly the best place to attract an audience, particularly during the pilgrim seasons when many devotees might in any case have wished to combine their ritual obligations with their scholastic inclinations. S. Safrai, 'Relations between the Diaspora and the Land of Israel', *Compendia Rerum Iudaicarum ad Novum Testamentum*, Vol. 1(a) (eds. S. Safrai, M. Stern; Assen, 1974), p. 193.
24. As Morton Smith has pointed out, the Pharisees had no monopoly on the claim that laymen can be better informed than the priesthood about correct conduct in the Temple. It had been foreshadowed at the very beginning of the second Commonwealth, was to be expressed by some members of the Dea Sea sects and is made explicit in Mark 11:15ff. In each case 'a layman, relying on his own knowledge and interpretation of the sacred law, purifies the temple from the pollution for which the priests have been responsible'. M. Smith, 'The Dead Sea Sect in its Relation to Ancient Judaism', *New Testament Studies*, 7 (1961), p. 353.
25. Compare, however, the analysis of such Pharisaic victories as were

celebrated on 27th Marḥeshvan in H. D. Mantel, 'Megilat Ta'anit we-ha-Kitot', *'Anshei Keneset ha-Gedolah* (Tel Aviv, 1983), p. 221.

26. According to Büchler, a decisive turning-point was reached in 62/63 C.E., when the much-maligned Sadducean High Priest Ḥanan ben Ḥanan was deposed. Thereafter, Pharisaic pronouncements became particularly militant. *Ha-Kohanim we-'Avodatam be-Miqdash Yerushalayim ba-'Asor ha-Shanim ha-'Aḥaron she-Lifnei Ḥurban Bayit Sheini* (trans. N. Ginton; Jerusalem, 1966), pp. 14–15.
27. Particularly instructive is one recent analysis of ten of the tanna'itic texts commencing with the formula *ha-kol* (lit. 'Anybody [can do such-and-such]'. Apparently pre-dating the Destruction, all demonstrate the manner in which 'early' Pharisaic *halakhah* had begun to dilute the priestly prerogative, making the performance of certain rituals conditional upon knowledge (which an extension of literacy made more widely available) rather than on ancestry. M. Bar-Ilan, *Ha-Pulmus Bein ha-Ḥakhamim la-Kohanim be-Shelhei Yemei Bayit Sheini* (unpub. Ph.D. thesis, Bar-Ilan University, 1982). The subjects of his study, in their order of analysis, are: *Mishnah, Yoma'* 6:3 (the despatch of the sacrificial lamb on the Day of Atonement); *Tosefta', R'osh ha-Shanah* 2:5 (the blowing of the *shofar* on the New Year); *Tosefta' Megilah* 2:7 and *Mishnah Megilah* 2:4 (the reading of the Scroll of Esther); *Mishnah, Nega'im* 3:1 (the inspection of *nega'im*); *Mishnah Parah* 5:4 and 12:10 (rites connected with the ceremony of the red heifer); *Tosefta' Nega'im* 8:1 (the purification of lepers); *Mishnah Ḥulin* 1:1 (the slaughter of *ḥulin* sacrifices); and *Mishnah Giṭin* 2:5 (writing bills of divorce).
28. *Mishnah, Nega'im* 3:1; see the discussion in J. Neusner, *A History of the Mishnaic Law of Purities*, Vol. 8 (Leiden, 1975), pp. 2, 139–44.
29. Rivkin, *Hidden Revolution*, pp. 125–75; compare the less restrictive discussions in S. Lauterbach, *Rabbinical Essays* (Cincinnati, 1951), pp. 23–162 and S. N. Zeitlin, 'Ṣedukim we-Perushim', *Ḥorev*, 3 (1936) pp. 57–89. The sources in Josephus and the *Mishnah* which record confrontations between the two parties are conveniently reproduced in Schürer, *History* (revised), Vol. 2, pp. 382–7. More comprehensive are the translations of rabbinic and non-rabbinic texts in Bowker, *Jesus and the Pharisees*, pp. 77–179.
30. J. Lightstone, 'Sadducees *versus* Pharisees: The Tannaitic Sources', *Christianity, Judaism and Other Greco-Roman Cults* (ed. J. Neusner; Leiden, 1975), part III, pp. 206–17.
31. G. Alon, 'The Attitude of the Pharisees to Roman Rule and the House of Herod', *Jews, Judaism*, p. 21.

    The Halakhah of the Pharisees is directed to the welfare and improvement of society [...] and embraces [...] besides religious precepts, basic principles in the sphere of law – both civil and criminal – and even communal and state legislation, including ordinances affecting the monarchy.
32. Josephus lobbied for Roman recognition of Pharisaic hegemony. But it

was Yoḥanan, 'above any other in his generation', who 'was responsible for the ultimate prevalance of Pharisaic Judaism, which was made possible by Roman encouragement and, in unequal measure, by the Pharisaic policy and program'. J. Neusner, *A Life of Rabban Yohanan Ben Zakkai, ca. 1–80 C.E.* (Leiden, 1962), p. 127.

33. The sources which dispute the case (notably *Shabbat* 34a and *tosafot* on *Menaḥot* 21b), have most recently been summarised in Trifon, *Ha-Kohanim* [...] pp. 131–45 (who argues that he was a priest). Her case is supported by D. Schwartz, 'Ha-'Im Hayah Raban Yoḥanan ben Zak'ai Kohen?', *Sinai*, 88 (1981), pp. 37–9.
34. E. E. Urbach, 'Ha-Mesorot 'Al Torat ha-Sod Bitqufat ha-Tana'im', *Meḥqarim be-Qabalah u-ve-Toledot ha-Datot, Mugashim le-Gershom Scholem* (ed. Urbach et al.; Jerusalem, 1968), Hebrew section, pp. 1–28.
35. As is argued by Trifon, *Ha-Kohanim*, pp. 131–68. However, compare the analysis of Yoḥanan's decision to abrogate the rite of the *soṭah* (reported in *Mishnah, Soṭah* 9:9 and *Tosefta', Soṭah* 14:2) in S. Safrai, *'Ereṣ Yisra'el we-Ḥakhamehah Bitqufat ha-Mishnah we-ha-Talmud* (Jerusalem, 1983), pp. 190–1.
36. For his use of the *pluralis sociativus ironicus*, see D. Daube, 'Three Notes Having to Do with Johanan ben Zaccai', *JTS*, XI (1960), pp. 53–62.
37. S. J. D. Cohen, 'The Destruction: From Scripture to Midrash', *Prooftexts*, 2 (1982), pp. 18–39 and A. J. Saldarini, 'Varieties of Rabbinic Response to the Destruction of the Temple', *SBL Seminar Papers*, 21 (1982), p. 456.
38. A. J. Saldarini, 'Johanan Ben Zakkai's Escape from Jerusalem: Origins and Development of a Rabbinic Story', *JSJ*, 6 (1975), pp. 189–204.
39. D. Goodblatt, 'Yehudei 'Ereṣ-Yisra'el ba-Shanim 70–132', *Histoṛiah Shel 'Am Yisra'el*, Vol. 11, 'Yehudah we-Roma''; (ed. U. Rappaport; Jerusalem, 1983), pp. 168–71.
40. Compare Neusner's claims in *Development of a Legend. Studies in the Traditions Concerning Yohanan ben Zakkai* (Leiden, 1970), p. 7, with the more restrained version in his *Ben Zakkai*, p. 161.
41. Büchler noted that seven of those sages who were also priests were not affiliated with Yoḥanan's academy at Yavneh. Alon added another five. Trifon conjectures that the reasons are to be sought in their opposition to Yoḥanan's policies, not in his antipathy towards them (*Ha-Kohanim*, p. 157, n. 64).
42. Compare, B. Z. Bokser, *Pharisaic Judaism in Transition* (N.Y., 1935); Y. D. Gilat, *R. Eliezer ben Hyrcanus. A Scholar Outcast* (Ramat Gan, 1984), and J. Neusner, *Eliezer ben Hyrcanus: The Tradition and the Man* (2 vols; Leiden, 1973). The specifics of 'Eli'ezer's *nidui* are examined in comparative context in G. Leibson, ''Al Mah Menadin', *Shenaṭon ha-Mishpaṭ ha-'Ivri*, 2 (1976), pp. 313–14.
43. Gilat, pp. 459ff; Neusner, *Eliezer*, pp. 287–330; 387–97.

44. 'When Rabban Yoḥanan ben Zak'ai heard that Jerusalem was destroyed and the Temple up in flames, he tore his clothing and his disciples tore their clothing, and they wept, crying aloud and mourning.' ARN 'A', 4 (Schechter 12b).
45. Safrai, *'Ereṣ Yisra'el*, p. 189. As Neusner points out, it might also be indicative of Yoḥanan's status as the initiator of new departures that, while he himself is often cited by his pupils, he never quotes his own masters.
46. Rather than view the sages as a party triumphant which closes the ranks, defines orthodoxy, and expels the unwanted, I suggest that we look at Yavneh as a grand coalition of different groups and parties, held together by the belief that sectarian self-identification was a thing of the past [...]

    S. J. D. Cohen, 'Yavneh Revisited: Pharisees, Rabbis and the End of Jewish Sectarianism', *SBL Seminar Papers*, 21 (1982), pp. 45–61. Perhaps; nevertheless, the rabbis had no doubts about who the leaders of that 'coalition' had to be.
47. Alon, *Jews, Judaism* [...], pp. 269–313; on different legislative agenda, J. Neusner, 'The Formation of Rabbinic Judaism: Yavneh (Jamnia) from A.D. 70 to 100', *ANRW*, 19:2 (1979), pp. 3–42.

6

Rabbis and priests (c. 100 C.E. – c. 300 C.E.)

Between the beginning of the second century C.E. and the end of the fifth, the face of Jewish communal government changed quite as much as did the norms of Jewish religious thought and practice. In the process, the balance of forces between the three *ketarim* was fundamentally transformed. Notwithstanding the failure of Bar Kokhba's revolt against Roman rule in Judea between 132 and 135, other instruments of the *keter malkhut* did manage to recover some of that domain's ancient prestige and influence. Conversely – although by no means immediately – the domestic authority of the *keter kehunah* became severely curtailed. Most dramatic of all, however, was the alteration in the communal status of the *keter torah*. By the end of the period, in both *'Ereṣ Yisra'el* (Palestine) and *Bavel* (Babylonia), all facets of Jewish life had become affected by rabbinic patterns of thought and influenced by rabbinic institutions of scholarship and justice. Admittedly, in neither region did rabbis and their disciples necessarily constitute the majority of the local Jewish population. Nevertheless it remains (in Neusner's words) 'an extraordinary fact' that 'the handful of masters of ca. 140 A.D. had become by 640 A.D. so powerful a force as to affect all Babylonian Jewry and to dominate a substantial and important part of its everyday affairs'.[1] In large measure, the comment is equally true of the situation in *'Ereṣ Yisra'el*.

As the rabbinic sources themselves indicate, that transformation was not accomplished in steady sequential stages. Rather, the process was untidy, erratic and – other than by its most ardent advocates – entirely unpredicted. Nothing inherent in Jewry's post-Destruction situation automatically guaranteed the popular acceptance of the *keter torah*'s claims to hegemony over every aspect of national life. If anything, that domain laboured under the burden of several initial handicaps. Its primary instruments, the sages, possessed no easily recognisable power-base from which they might have launched a campaign of communal conquest. Not until comparatively late into the early rabbinic age did they possess the cohesion necessary for the formulation of a coherent programme designed to accomplish that end. Although historians know far less than they would like to about precise rabbinic standings in individual localities, one facet of their condition is clear. Whatever corporate authority the *keter torah* eventually managed to deploy in both *'Ereṣ Yisra'el* and *Bavel* was not easily obtained. In both regions, the struggle for prominence was very much uphill and its success largely dependent on the dogged tenacity of the comparatively few individuals by whom it was waged.

The *keter torah*: disadvantages and disarray

If the magnitude of the rabbis' ultimate achievement is to be assessed, appropriate note must first be taken of the distinctly unfavourable complex of circumstances in which it was nurtured. Rabbinic interpretations of normative Jewish religious behaviour carried little inherent authority immediately after the Destruction. Attached though most Jews may have been to the ancient rites of the Sabbath and circumcision, and steadfast though the majority were in the observance of the Biblical commandments affecting their diet and sexual relations, few were immediately predisposed to perform such practices in accordance with the rigid dictates of Pharisaic *halakhah*. Even before 70 C.E. Judaism – broadly defined – had encompassed a variety of sects; in response to the pressures of demographic dispersion, it had also tolerated several forms of ritual (in extreme cases, cultic) expression.[2] The destruction of the Temple intensified such tendencies. With its shrine in ruins, the nation was deprived of the most prominent of its centripetal nexi and the most tangible focus of its cohesive affections. Artistic motifs unearthed by archeological investigations of individual synagogues have been said to demonstrate the striking heterogeneity of post-bellum Jewish culture.[3] Written sources, although more guarded, also bear witness to a degree of religious liquefaction which necessarily impeded the efforts of the rabbis to assert the pre-eminence of their own practices and beliefs.

Disparity must have been further exacerbated by the incremental influence of contemporary political and economic developments over which rabbinic control was still more marginal. Even after the crushing disaster of 70 C.E., Jews hardly constituted perennially persecuted fugitives. Subsequent moments of intense anti-Jewish frenzy – however lethal when they did occur – were blessedly intermittent. In *'Ereṣ Yisra'el*, the draconian legislation of 135–8 associated in rabbinic memories with the name of Hadrian must be contrasted with the lengthier periods of toleration subsequently enjoyed under Septimus Severus (193–211) and Elagabalus (218–22); similarly irregular were the incidences of legislative restrictions on the pursuit of Jewish learning and the practice of Jewish rites in Mesopotamia. Although heavily taxed and politically segregated, Jewish communities in both regions were generally accorded a broad measure of internal autonomy. That condition certainly facilitated the participation of many Jews (and particularly urban Jews) in several of the economic developments which were gradually changing the social complexion of the entire Middle East.[4] It probably also goes far towards explaining the great flowering of Jewish culture to which the surviving artistic and literary evidence of the early rabbinic period bears eloquent witness. Of themselves, however, political stability and economic prosperity provided no guarantees that the people of Israel and its religion would necessarily continue to constitute a conglomerate unit of analysis. If anything, because those benefits were unevenly distributed and experienced, quite the contrary was the case. The material survival and development of atomistic Jewish communities – precisely because they were such – might also have entailed their separation into distinct entities each in possession of its own traditions and rituals.

Particularly jealous of their own distinctiveness were Jewry's oldest diasporas, located in the Mesopotamian regions generically designated *Bavel* (Babylonia).[5] Subject to gentile authorities (initially Arsacid and subsequently Sasanid) entirely distinct from Roman rule of Palestine, they forged a sense of regional identity which persisted long into the rabbinic period. Indeed, much of Jewry's inner constitutional history during the first five centuries of the Christian era consists of *Bavel*'s claim to a collective status equal to that of *'Ereṣ Yisra'el*, and hence commensurate with its increasing demographic preponderance and intellectual vitality.[6] As early as the middle of the third century, even so ardent a believer in *'Ereṣ Yisra'el*'s *genius loci* as R. Simeon ben Laqish (usually known by his *nom de guerre* as 'Reish Laqish') had to acknowledge *Bavel*'s enormous – and continued – contribution to the preservation of Jewish scholarship and hence to the survival of Jewish peoplehood.

When *torah* was forgotten in Israel [he recalled] Ezra came up from Babylon and established it; when [some of it] was again forgotten, Hillel the Babylonian came up and established it; when once again [some of it] was forgotten R. Ḥiyya' [*tana'*; end 2nd cent.] and his sons came up and established it. (TB *Sukah* 20a).

In part due to the problems affecting the Roman Empire as a whole, *Bavel*'s efforts to establish its independence ultimately succeeded. Nevertheless, priorities long remained confused and confusing. *'Ereṣ Yisra'el*, even when perforce relegated to a position of economic and administrative inferiority, could still draw upon the vast reservoir of ingrained affection and prestige exemplified in the saying that 'a small group of students within *'Ereṣ Yisra'el* is dearer to me [God] than a Great Sanhedrin outside' (TJ *Nedarim* 7:13). Its political and religious leaders were determined to exploit such sentiments, and their jurisdictional conflicts with the authorities of *Bavel* over such crucial issues as the determination of the calendar (TB *Berakhot* 63a–b and parallels) consequently continued to be an endemic irritant. Not until the enforced abolition of the Patriarchate of *'Ereṣ Yisra'el* in 429, just four years after the death of the *nasi'* Gamli'el VI, were such bones of contention laid to rest.

Three centuries earlier, however, no single governmental agency could reasonably have expected to assume unitary political control over the management of Jewish internal affairs. That the *keter torah*, as represented by the rabbis, might have done so was especially unlikely. Even when most numerous,[7] the *tana'im* – and even the *'amora'im* – of talmudic description possessed very few of the assets usually deemed necessary for the attainment of political power. Initially, the small groups of Palestinian scholars who fled to *Bavel* in the wake of the Bar Kokhba' debacle were penurious parvenus; not until some of their successors had themselves begun to amass fortunes in land and commerce did they begin to cut more prosperous figures and thus to share some of the standing enjoyed by the established magnate families of the region.[8] Even in *'Ereṣ Yisra'el*, where the earliest *tana'im* could presumably hope to capitalize on some of the prestige for piety formerly accumulated by their Pharisaic antecedents, their social status was similarly low. With the shift of the local Jewish demographic axis towards the Galilee after 135, sages were there too reduced to the status of penniless refugees. Ekeing out an existence as manual labourers or self-employed craftsmen, they possessed none of the economic status enjoyed by non-rabbinic farmers and tradesmen, to whom the local populace was understandably inclined to defer. Consequently, one study of Roman Galilee has recently argued, the civil authority of rabbis in that region was virtually negligible for the first two hundred years after the Destruction; their religious influence, too – despite 'a mild flourish' between revolts – 'died away after Bar Kokhba, and was only resuscitated at a much later date in the early third century [C.E.]'.[9]

Material disadvantages of that magnitude could not easily be repaired by appeals to other sources of authority. As a group, rabbis were unable to claim a historically sanctioned *locus standi* within any of the traditional frameworks of Jewish government. Most obviously, and much to the disdain of a culture often obsessed with pedigree,[10] they lacked the social distinction which prestigious lineage (*yiḥus*) traditionally conferred on both priests and Davidides. In neither *Bavel* nor *'Ereṣ Yisra'el*, moreover, were they particularly favoured by Jewry's gentile overlords and hence in a position to muster easily instrumentalised coercive or deterrent authority. Although some third-century scholars in *'Ereṣ Yisra'el* were appointed Roman officials (and one head of the Nehardean academy, R. Sheila', did once receive from his Babylonian overlord the right to administer capital punishment),[11] such cases were few and far-between. In the main, the influence of the rabbis, such as it was, depended entirely on their own teachings and personalities, and necessarily varied from case to case. Hence, it would be inaccurate to generalise from the reputations (quasi-totemistic in some accounts) which some individuals were granted as pietists and even magicians. Even amongst those Jews who were not pronounced *minim* (heretics), and hence outside the obvious orbit of rabbinic influence, the authority of the rabbis had to be asserted; it could not be automatically assumed. As the talmudic record frequently laments, non-rabbinic Jews had persistently to be wooed. The much maligned *'amei ha-'areṣ* of *'Ereṣ Yisra'el*, to take the most outstanding case, could not simply be brow-beaten; eventually, they had to be won over.[12] To disregard that situation is both to telescope the length of the rabbinic enterprise and to miss much of its essentially political thrust.

Prominent among the proposed antidotes to non-rabbinic indifference and anti-rabbinic opposition was a sense of corporate rabbinic unity, such as had been fostered by Pharisaic *ḥavurot* in second Commonwealth times. Building upon the precedents of that experience, *tana'im* and *'amora'im* did indeed emphasise the virtues of scholastic fraternity.

'Form groups [*kitot, kitot*] and occupy yourselves with the *torah*', runs one piece of advice incorporated into a lengthy panegyric on learning in TB *Berakhot* 63b, 'for the knowledge of the *torah* is acquired only in an association [*ḥavurah*].'

In order to instrumentalise such teachings, rabbis also established and maintained an extended system of social welfare, comprehensive enough to supplement the spiritual and material needs of their own kith, kin and kind from the cradle to the grave.[13] Nevertheless, and notwithstanding the prominence which such activities undoubtedly deserve, as determinants of rabbinic cohesion their effect was limited; by and large, the *keter torah* remained a distinctly heterogeneous domain. Though they might appear from afar and in retrospect as a single entity, some corrective is surely necessary to the impression – subsequently nurtured by generations of pious hagiography – that 'the sages' comprised a monolithic unit.[14] If anything, the inner life of Jewry's scholastic elite was (in talmudic times as much as in others) frequently characterised by bickering feuds, brittle alliances and fumbling attempts at co-ordination.

One initial reason for that state of affairs was the absence of a single administrative focus of *torah* allegiance immediately after the Destruction. Whatever the authority attained by the *beit din* which Rabban Yoḥanan ben Zak'ai established (or strengthened) at Yavneh, it was not the only institution of its kind. Even when Rabban Gamli'el II presided over that body (probably until 115 or 117 C.E.), several other *batei din* simultaneously dispensed parallel forms of rabbinic justice; similarly, many of the outstanding scholars of the time continued to hold individual court to their own disciples – as did rabbis Ṭarfon and 'Aqiva' at Lod and rabbis 'El'azar ben 'Azareyah and Yoḥanan ben Nuri at Sephoris. Altogether, one detailed study has recently demonstrated, rivalry between 'southern' (i.e. Judean) and 'northern' (Galilean) scholars persisted long into the talmudic period, affecting scholastic allegiances and even modes of exegesis.[15]

The existence of the two separate, often rival, centres of academic life of *Bavel* and *'Ereṣ Yisra'el* subsequently added a further layer of complexity. Certainly, by the third century scholars everywhere did share a common adherence to the *halakhah* as eventually codified (perhaps, originally, for didactic purposes) in the *Mishnah*. Nevertheless, local patriotism remained pronounced. Rabbis educated in one of the two great regions frequently complained of the moral shortcomings and ritual deficiencies which they claimed to have observed in the other and familiarity, fostered by the shared phenomenon of trans-migration, seems hardly to have bred respect. The masters of *'Ereṣ Yisra'el* long preserved their traditional reluctance 'to teach *'agadah* to either a Babylonian or a man of the south [*dromi*], since they are rude and possess little *torah*' (TJ *Pesaḥim* 5:3). The common populace was no more hospitable. Not surprisingly, therefore, Babylonians tended to keep themselves to themselves. Even those who came to *'Ereṣ Yisra'el* for extended periods of study preferred to congregate in their own synagogues and thus preserve the purity of their own customs. More heeded the advice of R. Judah bar Ezekiel (the fourth-century founder of the Pumbediṭa' academy) to postpone 'ascent' to *'Ereṣ Yisra'el* until the arrival of the Messiah (TB *Ketubot* 110b–11a; exegesis on Jer. 27:22).[16]

To these circumstances must be added, within both *Bavel* and *'Ereṣ Yisra'el*, antagonisms of a more specifically personal nature. The robust tone which often characterises the give and take of recorded talmudic discourse (itself termed, significantly, 'warfare' in TB *Sanhedrin* 111b) was not solely a reflection of incisive academic exchanges between brilliant minds at variance over points of law. It also bore witness to more mundane antagonisms. Some intra-rabbinic conflicts were generated by the development of alternative scholastic traditions (exegetical and mystical, as well as legal); others by jurisdictional affiliations.[17] In yet a third category, the conventional façade of mutual deference and regard was punctuated by the sort of tensions which seem to thrive in academic society everywhere. Members of rabbinical convocations acted with unrestrained viciousness towards defecting colleagues when aquiescing in Patriarchal bans of excommunication (*nidui*).[18] In extreme cases, vendettas were carried beyond the grave. Two sources report that:

After R. Mei'ir's death, R. Judah said to his disciples: 'Let not R. Mei'ir's disciples enter here, because they are disputatious and would not come to learn but to overwhelm me with *halakhot*.' (TB *Qidushin* 52b and *Nazir* 49b)

The formation of communal strategy

Throughout the period here reviewed, rabbis prided themselves on their status as an intellectual and religious elite. Very few, however, cultivated the sort of introspective ethos which might have cut them off from their co-religionists. On the contrary, because they considered the scholar and the sage to be the very paradigms of correct Jewish behaviour, they wished to transform all Jews into men like themselves. Hence, they did not congregate in cocooned and self-contained clusters, individually sequestered from the hurly-burly of the real world and collectively indifferent to the material concerns of all non-scholastic aspects of Jewish life. Instead, most rabbis in most periods (there were, of course, exceptions), deliberately fostered an outward-looking programme of involvement in the lives of communities which they attempted to lead. Furthermore, much of their work in the academies, the courthouses and the market-places was undertaken with the express purpose of moulding those communities in the image which the rabbis themselves had defined and designed. Cultivating the ethos of scholarship and piety which they sought to embody, *tana'im* and *'amora'im* embarked on a campaign of communal conquest. Although their aspirations undoubtedly owed far less to material ambition than to religious belief, they were hardly less blatant for being thus inspired.

It is in that broad sense that a significant proportion of the early rabbinic enterprise might be described as overtly political. Although not primarily politicians, several rabbis (albeit, again, some more than others) did unquestionably strive to attain communal power, regarding their own influence over the inner life of Jewry as a necessary prerequisite to their nation's salvation. That is not to suggest that all talmudic representatives of the *keter torah* in either *'Ereṣ Yisra'el* or *Bavel* might posthumously be dragooned into membership of a self-conscious political party, nor even an articulate faction. At several points in time they did, however, approximate to a political 'connection' – a group of like-minded men united by intimate personal association, an extended tradition of continuous scholarly exchange and a common core of assumptions about the way in which the Jewish world ought to be governed and its affairs run.[19] It was thus constituted that they asserted the superiority of the *keter torah*, which they claimed to represent, over the domains of the *kehunah* and the *malkhut*, from which they were generally excluded.

Precisely when that programme was inaugurated (if, indeed, it ever was formally inaugurated) must remain a matter of speculation. Perhaps, as Shaye Cohen has suggested, a conscious decision to forswear sectarianism in favour of communal conciliation was taken as early as the Yavnean period of post-Destruction history.[20] If so, it seems for long to have remained largely inconsequential. Although the *tana'im* did then certainly apply themselves with energy and enthusiasm to the task of teaching Israel *torah*, they were initially reluctant to take an active part in public administration at any level. Scholarship and its dissemination were their primary missions; other commitments – especially any as onerous as judicial arbitration – were denigrated as undesirable distractions. That attitude could only have hardened in the wake of the Bar Kokhba' uprising, when the cream of *'Ereṣ Yisra'el*'s scholarly class was slaughtered and when local Roman restrictions on *torah* study imperilled its very existence. Particularly sensitive to the danger, R. Simeon bar Yoḥ'ai was especially determined to avert its occurrence. Contemplating the academic desolation of his times, one of his very few consolations was the fact that 'I do not know how to judge' (TJ *Sanhedrin* 1:[18a]).

Although such sentiments died hard,[21] within just a few generations after Bar Kokhba's defeat their force was definitely on the wane. By the third century, in both *'Ereṣ Yisra'el* and *Bavel*, rabbinic instruments of the *keter torah* had begun to take an active part in virtually every facet of local Jewish affairs, in the process becoming almost as indispensable to the efficient administration of public life as they were to the provision of private counsel. Thus, in addition to now furnishing halakhic instruction and moral guidance to what the talmudic sources portray as ever-widening circles of devotees, they also functioned as wardens of local charity chests (*parnasim*), as market administrators, as tax-assessors on behalf of the Patriarch and Exilarch, and (not least) as holy men. By virtue of their almost occult intimacy with the Deity, they could defend cities, generate rainfall in times of drought and – at least so the injured parties complained – deprive local mafiosi of their livelihoods.[22]

Most intimately were rabbis involved in the life of the communities, however, when they acted as judicial bureaucrats and clerks of courts. Indeed, it was as *jurisprudentes* that their local influence was most pervasive. By virtue of their intimate acquaintance with the intricacies of national Jewish law (not just regional custom), they were considered ideally qualified to weigh the merits of a litigant's case, cite relevant precedents, apply halakhic principles and, ultimately, provide equitable judgement. Hence, although most rabbinic *batei din* functioned only in an arbitral capacity, their communal authority ultimately belied their unofficial status. So too did that of the scholars by whom they were staffed, either singly or in groups of three. Jews who submitted their spiritual and civil affairs to the judgement of rabbinic courts (even where others were often available) did so in the full knowledge that they were thereby empowering rabbis to define their personal status, dispose of their property and direct their commerce. In a sense, the rabbis had thus become the *intendants* of their time.[23]

Much of the impetus for that development was generated by the institutional and personal interests of figures beyond the arc of the *keter torah* itself. Indeed, active rabbinic involvement in communal affairs could never have occurred without the sustained encouragement provided by successive Patriarchs in *'Ereṣ Yisra'el* and Exilarchs in *Bavel*, who (as the next chapter will argue) now represented the *keter malkhut*. It was the latter who invited rabbinical scholars to staff their courts and bureaucracies – on their behalf and at their command – principally because there was no other group comparably qualified (and subordinate) available to do so. Nevertheless, what is significant in the present context is the alacrity with which, by the third century, rabbis in both regions had begun to respond to that invitation. Theirs was not an unwilling compliance with the Patriarchal or Exilarchic will. Rather, and in the most interesting of cases, their acceptance of public office articulated a wider purposes. To an extent, some now claimed, their sense of communal responsibility left them no choice. Israel, after all, could not remain 'as sheep that have no shepherd' (*Sifrei Zuṭa'* [p. 206], exegesis on I Kings 22:17). Responding to the declaration of a tanna'itic convocation in Lydda that *talmud* (study) takes precedence over *ma'aseh* (lit. 'performance'; possibly referring to involvement in communal affairs), later 'rabbis of Caesarea' are said to have attached one important reservation: they could agree to this only 'when others are available to serve the community. If no one else is available, public service takes precedence.'[24]

It would be ungenerous to attribute the shift thus enunciated entirely to individual avarice or ambition. Admittedly, public service on behalf of the current Patriarch or Exilarch did promise certain financial rewards which, however meagre, very few of the early rabbis could afford to disdain.[25] But in addition to that consideration, interests of a corporate nature also came into play.

Significantly, it has been noted, the rabbis' readiness to accept public office coincided with a perceptible softening in their attitude towards their social milieu. In *'Ereṣ Yisra'el*, especially, they became progressively tolerant of *'amei ha-'areṣ* (previously a target of regular, and blatantly reciprocated contempt);[26] in general, they also displayed an increasing flexibility and lack of formalism in their religious demands, most even supporting Patriarchal initiatives designed to relax some of the restrictions of the sabbatical year laws. It must remain an open question whether the sole purpose of such modifications was to win public acceptance, 'because the prosperous farmers of these Galilean villages were prepared to accept rabbinic and secular leadership only when such changes had come about'.[27] What they do indicate, however, is the extent to which, especially after the Bar Kokhba' war, rabbinic perspectives had shifted (in Neusner's words) from a 'cultic to a communal conception'.[28] Without abandoning Pharisaism's insistence on the scrupulous observance of the purity laws, late tanna'itic traditions no longer regard those as the pivotal focus of all halakhic attention.

Of all the various amora'ic proponents of early rabbinic communal involvement, undoubtedly the most prominent was R. Yoḥanan (b. Napaḥa') of Tiberias (c. 180–c. 279). Renowned for his scholarship in *Bavel* as well as his native land, Yoḥanan's name and fame bestride the Jerusalem Talmud upon whose ultimate format his personality and pronouncements left a permanent – although not exclusive – imprint. In the history of the *halakhah*, R. Yoḥanan's importance is judged to have lain in his status as a double buckle; his teachings forged a junction between the traditions of *'Ereṣ Yisra'el* and of *Bavel*; at the same time, and perhaps even more decisively, his legal analyses also ensured continuity from the *mishnah* of the *tana'im* to the *talmudim* of the *'amora'im*.[29] Equally important, certainly in his own age, was his contribution to the formulation of the *keter torah*'s communal strategy. More than any other teacher of his age, R. Yoḥanan was determined to ensure that his numerous students and disciples did not quarantine themselves into academic ivory towers. *Talmidei ḥakhamim*, he argued, had to regard themselves as 'builders of the world'; those who refused to interrupt their studies when approached by widows and orphans would be regarded by Scripture as agents of its destruction.[30]

One essential prerequisite to the successful implementation of that programme was the insistence on an appropriately dignified rabbinic comportment, a subject upon which Yoḥanan's counterparts in *Bavel* had already expressed strong views.[31] Another was the maintenance of close relations with the Patriarch, without whose co-operation and assent no rabbi in *'Ereş Yisra'el* could ever aspire to gain and maintain public office (see below, chapter 7). Above all, however, it required a willingness on the part of the rabbis themselves to fulfil public functions beyond those of teachers and scholars. Yoḥanan himself set an outstanding example: he regularly presided over the *beit din* of Tiberias (then the most important in the land) and issued authoritative, sometimes liberal, pronouncements on matters of public concern and current interest.[32] Largely, it must be assumed, under the influence of their master, Yoḥanan's pupils adopted the parallel course of direct entry into the lower echelons of public service. Despite some residual reluctance, several assumed a variety of judicial and administrative public responsibilities in localities throughout the Galilee, and occasionally beyond; others instituted a system of qualifying examinations for such posts. At least two, rabbis 'Ami and 'Assi, explicitly became known as 'judges of [*dayanei*] *'Ereş Yisra'el*'. As Kimelman points out, one consequence was a shift in certain rabbinic priorities: public service now attained the status of a virtue (halakhically equivalent in certain ritual matters, according to R. Jeremiah, even to *torah* study).[33] Equally substantial was the impact on the wider rabbinic image. The administrative and judicial prominence attained by Yoḥanan and his disciples helped to position the *keter torah* of *'Ereş Yisra'el* at the very nexus of local Jewish communal affairs. Thus placed, its corporate influence on Jewish autonomous government could parallel that which rabbinic representatives of the domain had simultaneously begun to exercise in the communities of *Bavel*.

The resilience of the *keter kehunah*

The rabbis were not the only group in post-Destruction Jewry attempting to gain (or retain) communal influence. Primary amongst other contestants to whatever rulership was still available were genetic members of the *keter kehunah*. Priests certainly continued to constitute a communal force of some power and cohesion after 70 C.E. Admittedly, their corporate prestige must have suffered an immediate blow once the most tangible focus of their national standing had been razed to the ground. Nevertheless, even with the Temple destroyed, *kohanim* retained their distinctive identity. They did not all share the fate of the Sadducean party, which apparently withered away during the economic dislocations and social turbulence which punctuated the final years of rebellion and defeat.[34] Moreover, Trifon's re-appraisal of the available materials demonstrates that some corrective is necessary to the simplistic impression that, as soon as Jerusalem succumbed to the might of Rome, the priesthood was instantly stripped of all communal influence. Thus to anticipate the enfeeblement of the *keter kehunah* is, she argues, seriously to underestimate that domain's reservoirs of strength. More noteworthy is the speed and extent with which the post-Destruction priesthood recovered from its earlier setbacks.[35]

Most pronouncedly was this so in matters material. Indeed, comparatively soon after 70 C.E. priestly wealth had once again become proverbial. Admittedly, the absence of precise information renders all generalisations dangerous. Nevertheless, what is known of the situation in *'Ereṣ Yisra'el*, at least, certainly seems to substantiate the impression created by the majority of contemporary cliches. As the late Professor Lieberman pointed out, almost the only *tana'im* known to have been prosperous were of priestly descent (the exceptions invariably being members of the Patriarch's immediate entourage).[36] Non-rabbinic priests were equally prominent within their own societies; by the late second century, at the latest, they constituted what Kimelman has more recently termed a distinct 'oligarchy'. Especially was that so in some of the more important Galilean settlements, where post-Destruction priests had quickly carved out several well entrenched positions as, amongst other things, landlords, tax-farmers and elementary-level-teachers-cum-synagogue-administrators (*ḥazanim*).[37]

One indication of the privileged status which could still be enjoyed by the post-Destruction priesthood is provided by the history of tithes. Long after 70 C.E. even in *Bavel* pious Jews continued to set aside some of the traditional priestly levies (*matnot kehunah*). In *'Ereṣ Yisra'el*, such dues as *ḥalah, bikurim, terumot, ma'asarot* and *bekhorot* were likewise a regular item in household budgets.[38] Indeed, they were still being regularly paid, on a voluntary basis, at the very height of the third-century economic crisis. That phenomenon cannot be attributed solely to pious self-sacrifice, born out of a generous population's instinctive and wistful desire to keep alive the memory of Israel's former practices. Rather, it must be seen as a reflection of the degree to which *kohanim* continued to retain much of their ancient aura of sanctity. For as long as that situation lasted, it also ensured the retention and extension of corporate priestly authority.

At bottom, the status of the *keter kehunah* and its representatives in the Jewish world was rooted in theological conviction and sustained by intense reverence for Jewry's Divinely ordained form of cultic worship. Whether – and if so, for how long – some Jews continued to offer sacrifices on the Temple mount after 70 C.E. has long been debated. That many continued to observe the custom of three annual pilgrimages to the site seems beyond doubt.[39] Until such time as both practices were finally abandoned, *kohanim* must have retained their claims on national loyalties. If nothing else, they remained the living descendants of men who had traditionally instrumentalised the Temple ordinances and had thereby brought the community into close and regular contact with the Divine.

As far as can be judged, that was certainly the self-image cultivated by the priests themselves. Jews of attested priestly descent – a category which long included a high proportion of rabbis in both *'Ereṣ Yisra'el* and *Bavel* – continued to cherish the attestation of their distinctive ancestry (*yiḥus*). In regions as far-flung as the Yemen, they also preserved residual traces of their pre-Destruction division into *mishmarot* and *ma'amadot*.[40] The more immediate insistence with which priests also proudly flaunted their ritual cleanliness after the Destruction (notwithstanding the absence of a red heifer; TB *Bekhorot* 30b) similarly suggests that, in their own minds, they remained a distinctive element within the nation as a whole. Anecdotal materials further indicate the extent to which they might also have insisted on the retention of their former status. When, shortly after the Destruction, Rabban Gamli'el demanded that R. Ṭarfon (himself a *kohen*) explain his late arrival at a session of the academy, the following dialogue is reported to have ensued:

Rabbi Ṭarfon answered: 'I was engaged in service [*'oved*; from the noun *'avodah*, a term invariably applied in the Bible and tanna'itic literature to the conduct of the Temple ministrations].'

Rabban Gamli'el said to him: 'You speak in riddles. Is there such a thing nowadays as the *'avodah*?'

He answered: 'Scripture says: "I give you the priesthood as a service of gift" [Numb. 18:7]. The intent of this verse is to make the eating of hallowed foods outside the Sanctuary equal to conducting the Temple rites inside the Sanctuary.' (*Sifrei* Numb. 116 [p. 133]).

There was more to such incidents than the ingrained snobbery of a small and politically insignificant caste of diehards, wistfully recalling better days. What the sources also suggest is that, notwithstanding the Destruction, priests continued to regard themselves as integral – even essential – components of the Jewish polity. Accordingly, they would have posited, no Jewish political organisation would be complete unless it allowed for their representation in as complete a manner as current circumstances would allow. By and large, of course, their options were restricted to their immediate and local vicinities. But, as Goodblatt has suggested, with the outbreak of Bar Kokhba's revolt against Rome in 132 C.E. they conceivably set their sights considerably higher. Priests, he argues, did not necessarily initiate that adventure. But the priesthood – as an estate – does seem to have constituted the most prominent (and unified) source of corporate support for a rebellion which proclaimed the recapture of Jerusalem and the reconstruction of the Temple to be its primary strategic aims.[41]

One can only guess how, had Bar Kokhba's gamble succeeded, the priests of his day might have accommodated themselves to his highly charismatic style of leadership. However, if we are to judge by what transpired during the insurrection itself, some tough bargaining might have been expected to ensue. With the outbreak of revolt, priests seem to have extracted from Bar Kokhba' a fairly stiff price for their support: the prevention of the disturbances which had so shaken society between 66 and 70; an intensification of Jewish anti-Christian polemic; and – perhaps above all – the recognition of a priestly figure as co-ruler in whatever regime was eventually to be established. Numismatic discoveries have shed particularly interesting light on the latter issue. Some of the Bar Kokhba' coins carry the name of a personage, identified only as '*'El'azar ha-kohen*', alongside that of the *nasi' yisra'el* himself.[42]

Whereas the priests thus seem to have granted Bar Kokhba' support and legitimacy, the attitude of the rabbinic leadership of the age was far more circumspect. With the outstanding – but singular – exception of R. 'Aqiva', no contemporary representative of the *keter torah* is recorded to have shown enthusiasm for Bar Kokhba's venture. Some were rudely sceptical; most chose to wait on the sidelines, refusing to commit themselves one way or the other.[43] In part, their hesitations might be attributed to theological uncertainties: was Bar Kokhba' indeed the sort of personality envisaged by their messianic expectations? could any justification at all be found for rebellion against a power evidently chosen by Providence to punish Israel for its sins? At the same time, however, considerations of a less speculative nature might also have played a role. One was the difficulty of gauging the realistic chances of Bar Kokhba's success against the fabled – albeit temporarily enfeebled – might of Rome. Another was tanna'itic reticence to encourage an enterprise which (quite apart from its other risks) also threatened to place the *keter torah* in political isolation. The *tana'im* of 132–5 might have feared precisely the same unitary combination of *kehunah* and *malkhut* which their Pharisaic forebears had found so troublesome during the Hasmonean age. That was not necessarily a reason for them to oppose the revolt or collaborate with the Romans. It might, however, have helped to generate an ambivalence which, in practical terms, was almost as debilitating.

For there can be no doubt that the attitude of the early rabbinic *keter torah* towards the contemporary *keter kehunah* was indeed ambivalent. Much though they contested many of the communal prerogatives claimed by priests, the sages and their disciples never considered the Temple beyond recovery. Nor, therefore, was the priesthood in any way superfluous. For them, too, the Destruction was in every way a calamity – personally, nationally and universally.[44] Even in its present state of ruin, the shrine commanded an awe as eternal as the honour due to the Sabbath (TB *Yevamot* 6a–b, commentary on Leviticus 19:30); since the Almighty Himself thrice nightly expressed His remorse at the conflagration of His own house and the dispersion of His people, its reconstruction was necessarily an essential pre-requisite to Israel's Redemption.[45] Hence, there could be no question of abandoning the frameworks of reference which the Temple and its ritual had for almost a millennium inculcated into Jewish thought and practice. On the contrary, *Mishnah-Tosefta'*, especially, are framed in a distinctively 'priestly' form. Cultic perspectives permeate even the very structure of that corpus and its division into its six separate orders; similarly, cultic matters dominate all early rabbinic lists of *gufei torah* ('the essence of the *torah*'). Nowhere do the rabbis deny that true Jewish religious expression would ultimately depend on the re-instatement of the sacrificial system. If anything, Sanders has suggested, their general tendency was to amplify the role which the Pentateuch attaches to the cult.[46]

By the same token, no rabbi of our period could ever completely disregard the inherent respect corporately owed to the priesthood.

True, its past contributions to Jewish welfare could easily be denigrated (according to one frequently cited *beraitah*, the misdemeanours of second-Temple priests were widely believed to have caused the Sanctuary itself to cry out in despair; e.g. TB *Pesaḥim* 57a). Nevertheless, that caste remained in possession of its inherited sanctity. Consequently, whatever the extent of the fears possibly aroused in rabbinic circles by the constellation of forces which supported Bar Kokhba' between 132 and 135 – whatever, for that matter, the strength with which those same fears might have resurfaced over two centuries later, when, in 363, the Emperor Julian mooted a reconstruction of the Jerusalem Temple[47] – traditional constitutional parameters had to be preserved. Priestly rights to distinctive priorities were, as the school of R. Yishma'el was reported to have taught (TB *Giṭin* 59b), irrevocably rooted in the injunctions laid down in Leviticus 21:8 . Indeed, those privileges were now embellished by the generic designation of priests as the Almighty's personal agents.[48] Even after 70 C.E., their blood still entitled *kohanim* to play the predestined intercessionary roles considered ultimately indispensable to Israel's well-being.

At a very basic level, rabbinic adherence to such principles could be translated into a determination to ensure that some members of the priestly caste were always at hand in order to fulfil their original sacerdotal functions when time should be ripe. (A circumstance which has been said to account for occasional rabbinic attempts to discourage their emigration from *'Ereṣ Yisra'el*, even after the failure of Bar Kokhba's revolt.)[49] What it also involved was the appropriate representation of priests in the actual exercise of whatever power and authority Jews themselves could still command. Early rabbinic political theory, admittedly, intimated that priestly participation in the *sanhedrin* was nothing more than desirable (*Sifrei* Deut. 153 [p. 206], cf. *Mishnah, Sanhedrin* 4:2). But early practice – certainly in *'Ereṣ Yisra'el* – seems to have been very different. One indication is provided by the records of the principal appointments to the senior ranks of rabbinical councils in the same region. A reconstruction of the relevant lists indicates that, until as late as the second century, the position of *'av beit din* (or its equivalent), was reserved for scholars who were also priests. Only the patriarch Rabban Simeon be Gamli'el was able to break that tradition when apportioning the position to R. Natan, the son of the Babylonian Exilarch.[50]

The rite of scholarship and the sanctity of the scholar

Priestly influence of such scope could hardly be revoked by the simple expedient of rabbinic fiat. Even had post-bellum representatives of the *keter torah* in any way wished to abrogate the *kehunah* or its benefits – and, it must be repeated, they most certainly did not – the rabbis were quite simply in no position to issue independent directives on such matters and expect them to command immediate and practical effect. Instead, they adopted an entirely different tactic, one which was no less subtle for being radical. Rather than suggesting that priestly dues be altogether annulled, they intimated that the most prestigious be transferred to their own domain. By virtue of their devotion to the study of the *torah*, they taught, sages and their students were in effect performing a ritual function which could be described as quasi-priestly in form. Consequently, scholars were entitled to the respect once bestowed upon *kohanim* and worthy of the same communal consideration.

Claims such as those did not indicate that the early rabbinic *keter torah* was demanding exclusive liturgical or sacerdotal privileges. At no point in the entire talmudic period did the rabbis claim a monopoly on the performance of Jewish cultic practice. Instead, they throughout rested their case for communal authority on the entirely different base of their proven scholastic prowess. It was because they were Masters of the Law that the *ḥakhamim* considered themselves eminently qualified for public office. Indeed, their shared commitment to academic excellence in the *halakhah* constituted their own most fundamental claim to also be holy men. All sages shared the belief that the true path to a proper understanding of God's expectations (governmental as well as ritual) lay through constant analysis of His sacred texts. Even homiletical teachings, they maintained, had to be based upon precise – sometimes minute – scriptural references. Legal decisions were certainly expected to accord with the rigorous criteria mandated by established hermeneutical principles. Only if thus substantiated might the resultant admonitions and deductions be categorised as *miṣwot*, precepts which carried the full weight and support of God's own command.

Study of the *torah*, the rabbis insisted, was itself one such *miṣwah*. Sages as early as Hillel and Shamm'ai (*'Avot* 1:13, 16), had enjoined Jews to set aside fixed periods for that purpose and warned that whoever did not 'is deserving of death'. By the time of the redaction of the *Mishnah* (at the latest), that position had considerably hardened. *Talmud torah*, it was then declared, possessed no fixed measure; its pre-eminent status amongst the precepts was indicated by its equality with all the other activities 'the fruits of which a man enjoys in this world while the capital remains for him in the world to come' (*Mishnah, Pe'ah* 1:1 and TB *Shabbat* 127a). Admittedly, there did long remain a measure of tension between 'learning' (*talmud*) and 'practice' (*ma'aseh*) which gave rise to intense scrutiny. But not even the reported tanna'itic consensus that scholarship was most purposeful when it led to correct performance[51] required all study to be entirely instrumental. Pharisaic masters had long since bequeathed to rabbinic halakhic methodology a tradition which had often emphasised the theoretical, rather than the entirely pragmatic and practical;[52] and its effect was to be felt well into the tanna'itic age. Sayings attributed to R. Simeon bar Yoḥ'ai, in particular, suggest that during the second century study could still be regarded as almost an end in itself. If nothing else, he was adamant in his insistence that learning takes precedence over all other actions; as a *miṣwah* it simply has no equal.[53]

Marmorstein has suggested that the accentuation of the scholarly ethos in early rabbinic society can be directly attributed to the 'Hadrianic' persecutions of 137–8 C.E. With the academic community in *'Ereṣ Yisra'el* then virtually decimated, and with the personal privations of prospective students so marked, the sages (he argues) were compelled to promulgate a doctrine of academic single-mindedness far in excess of any that more benevolent circumstances might have required.[54] Certainly, the subsequent rabbinic devotion to study articulated something far more compelling than a quest for intellectual satisfaction. Rav (the third-century founder of the great Babylonian academy at Sura') was to stress the religious facet of his academic calling when categorising the 'love' of *torah* as a superior form of worship.[55] But even his position was by no means unique. In *'Ereṣ Yisra'el* as well as in *Bavel*, study for its own sake (*lishmah*) in effect came to be regarded – at least in some circles – as a self-contained form of devotional expression. In third-century Tiberias, rabbis 'Ami and 'Assi reportedly refused to succumb to the ritual diversions supplied by any of the thirteen available local synagogues (TB *Berakhot* 8a); in fourth-century *Bavel*, Rav was to chastise his student, Rav Hamnuna', for interrupting his studies in order to say his prayers, brandishing him for all time as one of the miscreants who 'forsake eternal life and occupy themselves with temporal needs' (TB *Shabbat* 10a, see also TB *R'osh ha-Shanah* 35b).

Significant though the sharpening in emphasis undoubtedly was, the perspective itself cannot be described as altogether innovative. Tanna'itic statements on the value of *torah* study – especially as reflected in *'Avot* – had also been distinguished by their emphasis on its inherent sanctity. As much is indicated by the numerous aphorisms attributed to the period of the early sages which speak of that activity as a ritual. By pondering the Law and exploring its limitless nuances, they had intimated, the student of *torah* stimulates and concretises an intimate relationship with his Maker. In effect, he thus achieves communion with his God. The *Shekhinah* (Divinity) is itself present whenever two persons discuss the *torah* (*'Avot* 3:2); every act of study re-enacts the theophany on Mount Sinai.[56] As a regulated – and even disciplined – experience, learning had thus been recognised to be far more than a skill whose purpose is the assembly and deployment of information. Essentially, it had already been transposed into a form of sacrament, one of the means whereby man attains piety and might thereby scale otherwise unobtainable heights of holiness. By the age of the third-century *'amora'* 'Ula' (whose frequent travels between *'Ereṣ Yisra'el* and *Bavel* enabled him to transmit the teachings of both regions) it had apparently become common knowledge that: 'now that the Temple was destroyed, God Himself has nothing in this world but the four cubits of *halakhah* alone' (TB *Berakhot* 8a).

With those postulates to hand, study of the *torah* could be invested with a degree of sanctity which previous generations had reserved for the shrine and cultic worship. In a general sense, all *torah* was thus designated *'avodah* (e.g. the exegesis on Deut. 11:13 in *Sifrei*, Deut. 41 [pp. 87–8]). Still more specifically, *torah* scholarship could also be described as a surrogate for the cultic ritual – and a superior one at that. A source as early as *'Avot de Rabi Natan* (4:18) speaks of 'the study of *torah*' being:

> More beloved of God than burnt offerings. For if a man studies *torah* he comes to know the will of God [Proverbs 2:5] [...] Hence when a sage sits and expounds to the congregation, Scripture accords it to him as though he had offered up fat and blood on the altar.

The amora'ic contribution was to accentuate the shift in focus from the activity to the actor.[57] Moreover, the movement seems to have been deliberate. For if the scholarly examination of the *torah* constituted Judaism's most sublime avocation, the scholar had necessarily to be regarded as the embodiment of Jewry's highest aspirations. By virtue of his academic proficiency and attainments, the *ḥakham* in fact personified the very essence of the *torah*'s own sanctity and incorporated the holiness of the texts to which he was entirely devoted. Babylonian academicians apparently found it debatable whether or not the talmudic texts were themselves to be classified as *torah*, whose study necessitated the recital of a prior blessing (TB *Berakhot* 11b). What none questioned, however, was the proposition that the students of the law were best fitted to act as Israel's administrative and moral prefects. Mastery of the sacred canon deserved to be transmuted into mastery within and over the community; the greater the scholarship of the sage, the more pronounced his communal authority had to be. Unless and until they could also prove their academic excellence before the bar of rabbinic learning, other claimants to power – no matter how distinguished their pedigree – were necessarily inferior.

Judged by those standards, priests cut particularly poor figures. At least, such was the impression deliberately cultivated by the authors of the *talmudim*. Although meticulous in their acknowledgement of the dignity owing to the priesthood as an institution, the rabbis made no bones about their disapproval of priests as individuals. On the contrary, the denigration of *kohanim* became something of a favoured motif in early rabbinic literature, leaving an imprint on virtually every one of its various strata. In conformity with the conventions of talmudic style, several of the barbs were decked out in the guise of seemingly innocuous history or exegesis. But even when thus made to look more like retrospective criticisms than contemporary attacks, their meaning is not difficult to penetrate. Low brows as well as high in a typical rabbinic audience would have appreciated the nuanced relevance of those *obiter dicta* which stress the misbehaviour of pre-Destruction priests and emphasise their disproportionate share in the blame for Israel's most crushing disaster.[58] Only the most illiterate, one suspects, might have been insensitive to the innuendoes behind rabbinic reconstructions of Biblical stories, several of which suggest that moral failings are in some way a congenital fault of the priestly breed.[59] For those who may still have been ignorant of the message being conveyed, there was the resort of more explicit language. Random talmudic passages indicate that priestly deportment was altogether to be considered a byword for arrogance, a posture made particularly objectionable by the alleged fact that several priests were neglectful of some *miṣwot* and downright ignorant of others.[60]

Even as early a *tana'* as Rabban Yoḥanan ben Zak'ai, it will be recalled, had shown how such charges could be exploited for all their political worth. Prior to the Destruction, he had argued that the superior halakhic wisdom of the sages entitled them to supervise priestly conduct of certain cultic functions. After 70 C.E. several of his teachings had further suggested that scholastic prowess altogether superseded priestly blood as a prerequisite for the performance of ritual activity. Building on those premises, Yoḥanan's successors were still more explicit. Specifically positing the superiority of *torah* scholarship to any other qualification for public service, they ultimately came to regard scholars as inherently superior to priests in every way. Indeed, priests were barely entitled to be considered as such unless they were also *talmidei ḥakamim*;[61] conversely, sages – by virtue of their academic status – deserved to be accorded the honours and rights previously bestowed upon priests. R. 'Eli'ezer ben Jacob (a second-century *tana'* in *'Ereṣ Yisra'el*) was reported to have proclaimed that:

> Whoever provides hospitality to a *talmid ḥakham* and shares with him his wealth is considered as though he had offered up the daily offering. (TB *Berakhot* 10b, exegesis on II Kings 4:9).

In fourth-century *Bavel*, it was apparently axiomatic that: 'Just as a priest takes first, so a sage takes first' (TB *Nedarim* 62a).

Undoubtedly, the evolution of those positions too was a prolonged process. Some of the first steps seem to have been only tentative. In their earliest form, and particularly in *'Ereṣ Yisra'el*, they might have amounted to little more than attempts to restrict the award of *terumot* to those priests whose status as *ḥaverim* had already been ascertained or, in the third century, of *ma'asarot* to persons who were undeniably scholars.[62] Somewhat more advanced was the Babylonian discovery of a precedent in second-Temple times for the direct transfer of such priestly gifts to the non-priestly masters who had then taught *kohanim* some of the niceties of their own cultic trade (TB *Ketubot* 106a, citing traditions in the names of both Rav and Samuel). Ultimately, however, even the pretence of such finer distinctions seems to have been disregarded. *Talmidei ḥakhamim*, solely because they were such, eventually posed as rightful recipients of priestly benefits – regardless of their precise genealogies and areas of academic specialisation. In *Bavel*, especially, members of the *keter torah* put forward the proposition that, where material benefits were concerned, they and their colleagues had to all intents and purposes succeeded to the prerogatives once thought exclusive to the *keter kehunah*.[63]

Particularly forthright was the consequent rabbinical claim rightfully to enjoy whatever financial concessions local gentile authorities were prepared to make to 'priests of a recognised religion' (or, in *Bavel*, 'servants of the fire'; see TB *Nedarim* 62b). Enlisting the full scope of their exegetical skills, rabbis and their disciples regularly claimed exemption from several of the taxes imposed upon those of their brethren who were not members of their own scholarly estate.[64] Popular opposition to such concessions, it must be admitted, was often strong. But it would be ineffective for as long as rabbis could convince Patriarchs and Exilarchs of the justice of their case (alternatively, provided Patriarchs and Exilarchs considered it in their own political interests to support the rabbis). One paradigmatic case, according to TB *Bava' Batra'* 8a, occurred in third-century *'Ereṣ Yisra'el*:

It once happened that a poll tax [*kelila* = *aurum coronarium*] was imposed on Tiberias. They [the local populace] came before *Rabi* [Judah II] and said: 'The *ḥakhamim* should also contribute.' He said to them: 'No.' They said to him: '[In that case] we shall flee.' He replied: 'Flee.' Half fled and the authorities reduced the tax by half.

The [remaining] half came before *Rabi* and said: 'The *ḥakhamim* should share in paying.' He said, 'No.' [They said], '[In that case] we shall flee.' [He said:] 'Flee.' They all fled, and only one fuller remained. The authorities imposed [the entire tax] on the fuller. He too fled, and the tax was cancelled.[65]

As the discussion which introduces the above account makes explicit, the rabbinic demand for tax exemptions was never intended to articulate only the narrow interests of Israel's scholastic elite. Rather, it was projected as a touchstone of national confidence in the overall protective qualities of the *torah* and its ability to provide security for the nation as a whole. Therein lay the true import of the statement that: 'rabbis do not require protection' (and therefore need not contribute, in this particular instance, to the upkeep of the city walls). Study of the *torah*, was the implication, guarantees much more than spiritual and material rewards for the scholar himself; it also promises Divine salvation to every other segment of the nation which supports students and is otherwise associated with them. The pursuit of scholarship, in fact, possesses the power to induce supernatural redemption – particularly when allied with other forms of communal service. Hence: 'If a man occupies himself with the study of the *torah*, works of charity, and prays with the community', says God, 'I account it to him as if he had redeemed Me and My children from among the nations of the world' (TB *Berakhot* 8a). In an extended sense, popular study could even be described as a form of atonement. Hence:

Whoever occupies himself with the study of the *torah* needs no burnt offering nor sin-offering, no meal offering nor guilt offering. (Rava' cited in TB *Menaḥot* 110a)[66]

As Neusner has pointed out, the programmatic corollary of all such teachings was that the *keter torah* of the sages had replaced the *keter kehunah* of the priests as the principal arbiter of Israel's collective destiny. From being an act of personal piety, scholarship had been transformed into a determinate of national fortune, one which replicated the influence of the cultic ritual.

The study of the Torah substitutes for the ancient cult and does for Israel what sacrifice did then: reconcile Israel to its father in heaven, wipe away sin, secure atonement, so save Israel. These deeply mythic convictions gave concrete expression to the view that the Torah not only sanctifies, but saves.[67]

Therein lay the thrust of the anonymous homily preserved in *Tanḥuma'* (*'Aḥarei*, 10):

When the Temple is not in existence, how shall you find atonement? Occupy yourselves with the words of the *torah*, which are comparable to the sacrifices, and they shall make atonement for you [...]

One possible lesson to be learnt was retrospective: learning had always been more important than the cult (thus, acording to the 'additional opinion' appended to the long catalogue of second Commonwealth deficiencies attributed to Yoḥanan ben Zak'ai in *Mekhilta'* [*de-Ba-Ḥodesh*; ed. Lauterbach, II, pp. 194–5], the Temple had itself been destroyed because Israel had neglected *torah* study). Still more powerful, however, was the subsequent projection of those priorities into the future. Scholarly examination of the sacred texts could in effect now be predicated as a route to national regeneration. It was the hum of children's voices in the schoolhouse which ensured Israel's salvation.[68] What is more, through *torah* study the sage and his students took their place at the very forefront of the messianic process. In the words of one particularly resonant passage:

R. 'Alekhsandri said: 'He who studies the *torah* for its own sake makes peace in the Upper [Divine] family and the Lower [human] family [...]' [Is. 27:5]. Rav said: 'It is as though he built the heavenly and the earthly Temples [...]' [Is. 51:16]. R. Yoḥanan said: 'He also shields the whole world [...] and Levi said: 'He also hastens the Redemption, as it is written, ''and say unto Zion thou are my people''' [idem]. (TB *Sanhedrin* 99b)[69]

NOTES

1. J. Neusner, *A History of the Jews in Babylonia*, Vol. 5 (*Later Sasanian Times*; Leiden, 1970), p. 329.
2. M. Smith, 'Palestinian Judaism in the First Century', *Israel: Its Role in Civilization* (ed. M. Davis; N.Y., 1956), esp. pp. 79–80.
3. At the very least, the evidence indicates that Jewish residents in *'Ereṣ Yisra'el* as well as the diasporas were not all living in absolute conformity to rabbinic law. Some were engaged in religious and magical activities which the rabbis might at best have tolerated, but which they would never in the first place have initiated. M. Smith, 'Goodenough's Jewish Symbols in Retrospect', *JBL*, 86 (1967), pp. 53–68. Compare, however, the blanket condemnation, based on a study of the evidence of Beth She'arim, in E. E. Urbach, 'Hilkhot 'Avodah Zarah we-ha-Meṣi'ut ha-'Arkhiologit we-ha-Hisṭorit ba-Me'ah ha-Sheniyah u-va-Me'ah ha-Shelishit', *Eretz Israel*, 5 (1959), pp. 189–205.
4. On *'Ereṣ Yisra'el*: M. Avi-Yonah, *The Jews Under Roman and Byzantine Rule* (Jerusalem, 1984), esp. pp. 45–51; on Babylonia: G. Widengren, 'The Status of the Jews in the Sassanian Empire', *Iranica Antiqua*, 1 (1966), esp. pp. 124, 128–31.
5. On the geography of the territory, see the discussion recorded in TB *Qidushin* 71b–72a and A. Oppenheimer, *Babylonia Judaica in The Talmudic Period* (Wiesbaden, 1983), p. 256.
6. Several of the many rabbinic sources on this subject are collated in M. A. Tannenblatt, *Peraqim Ḥadashim le-Toledot 'Ereṣ Yisrael u-Bavel Bitqufat ha-Talmud* (Tel Aviv, 1966), pp. 13–22.
7. On the basis of the index appended to H. Albeck, *Mav'o la-Talmudim* (Tel-Aviv, 1969), pp. 669–81, it has been estimated that the **total** number of *'amora'im* in *'Ereṣ Yisra'el* between 225 and 375 C. E. was 367 (of whom 135 were active 280–310 C. E.); and in *Bavel* prior to *circa* 500 C. E. to have been just under 400 (of whom 98 are dated to the years 300–335 C. E.). Y. L. Levine, *Ma'amad ha-Ḥakhamim be-'Ereṣ Yisra'el Bitqufat ha-Talmud* (Jerusalem, 1986), pp. 40–3.

   In a spurt of filial devotion and fraternal harmony, my sons have laboriously computed the information contained in R. Halperin, *'Atlas 'Eiṣ-Ḥayim*, Vols. 3 & 4 (Jerusalem, 1980) and reached somewhat higher numbers: viz.:

Total **named** *tana'im* (circa 60 B.C.E.–225 C.E.): 223:
Total **named** *'amora'im* (circa 225–circa 500 C.E.): 1421.

The breakdown of the latter figure is as follows.

'Generation'	*'Ereṣ Yisra'el*		*Bavel*	
1st	(225–250 C.E.)	66	(until 250 C.E.)	30
2nd	(250–280)	115	(250–300)	139
3rd	(280–310)	183	(300–335)	182
4th	(310–340)	148	(335–370)	131
5th	(340–375)	148	(370–410)	113
6th	(375–405)	40	(410–450)	78
7th	—	—	(450–500)	48

8. L. Jacobs, 'The Economic Conditions of the Jews in Babylon in Talmudic Times Compared with Palestine', *Jewish Journal of Sociology*, 2 (1957), pp. 349–59. On the later wealth of Babylonian sages see M.Beer, *'Amor'ai Bavel* (Ramat Gan, 1982), pp. 258–71, and below, chap. 7.
9. M. Goodman, *State and Society in Roman Galilee, A.D. 132–212* (Totowa, N.J., 1983), pp. 101–4, 110–11, 126, 160. Not until the late third century, he argues, do rabbis seem to have been empowered to reprimand negligent local community leaders and to concern themselves with 'all the needs' of the villages within their individual bailiwicks. Thereto, 'neither civil nor criminal cases [...] were decided by rabbis [...] There *were* Jewish courts in the villages and such cases *did* come before them, but their judges were not rabbis [...] The latter acted as *iurisprudentes* rather than as an alternative legal system.' Compare, however, G. Alon, *The Jews in Their Land in the Talmudic Age*, Vol. 1 (Jerusalem, 1980), pp. 181–4 and idem., 'Ga'on, Ge'im: (On the Social History of Eretz-Israel in the Period of the Tanna'im)', *Jews, Judaism*, pp. 344–53.
10. On the extent to which that was so in *'Ereṣ Yisra'el*: R. Yankelevitch, 'Mishqalo Shel ha-Yiḥus ha-Mishpaḥti ba-Ḥevrah ha-Yehudit be-'Ereṣ Yisra'el', *'Umah we-Toldotehah*, Vol. 1 (ed. M. Stern; Jerusalem, 1983), pp. 151–2; and below, chap. 9.
11. TB *Berakhot* 58a; instances of rabbis as Roman appointees in third-century *'Ereṣ Yisra'el* are discussed in S. Lieberman, 'Palestine in the Third and Fourth Centuries', *JQR*, 36 (1940), pp. 360–4 and Y. L. Levine, 'Tequfato Shel R. Yehudah ha-Nasi', *Ereṣ-Yisra'el mi-Ḥurban Bayit Sheini we-'Ad ha-Kibush ha-Muslemi*, Vol. 1 (ed. Z. Baras, et al.; Jerusalem, 1982), p. 96.
12. On the varieties of meaning attached to the term *'am ha'areṣ* and the extent of the phenomena it describes: A. Oppenheimer, *The 'Am Ha-Aretz: A Study in the Social History of the Jewish People in the Hellenistic Period* (Leiden, 1977), pp. 67–117.
13. The range of services which sages provided to each other in *'Ereṣ Yisra'el*

is outlined in Levine. *Ma'amad ha-Ḥakhamim*, pp. 32–40; for a reconstruction of the earlier Pharisaic cells, based on such early rabbinic recollections as are provided in *Tosefta', Bava' Batra'* 6:13 and *Semaḥot* 12:5, see A. Oppenheimer, 'Ḥavurot Shehayu Birushalayim', *Yerushalayim (Mivḥar Ma'amarim mi-Sifrei Yad Yiṣḥaq Ben-Ṣevi)* (Jerusalem, 1987), pp. 35–47.

14. J. Neusner, 'The Formation of Rabbinic Judaism', *ANRW*, 19:2 (1979), pp. 3–42.
15. J. Schwartz, *Ha-Yishuv ha-Yehudi bi-Yehudah mi-La'Aḥar Milkhemet Bar Kokhba' we-'Ad la-Kibush ha-'Aravi* (Jerusalem, 1986), pp. 216–26.
16. Idem., 'Tensions between Palestinian Scholars and Babylonian Amoraim in Amoraic Palestine', *JSJ*, 11 (1980), pp. 78–94.
17. Notably the tensions between those rabbis – *dayanim* (judges) who were attached to the Exilarch's court ('*debei reish galuta*'') and those who were not; M. Beer, *R'eshut ha-Golah be-Bavel Bimei ha-Mishnah we-ha-Talmud* (Tel Aviv, 1976), pp. 85–7.
18. Specific instances are examined in G. Leibson, ''Al Mah Menadin'', *Shenaṭon ha-Mishpaṭ ha-'Ivri*, 2 (1975–6), pp. 292–342. See also below, pp. 228–9.
19. Compare Neusner's suggestion (*Babylonian Jewry*, Vol. 3 [Leiden, 1968], pp. 102ff) that the rabbinate of *Bavel* might be defined as 'an estate, or a recognised group within Jewish society', and Beer, *'Amor'ai Bavel*, pp. 256–7.
20. S.J.D. Cohen, 'Yavneh Revisited: Pharisees, Rabbis and the End of Jewish Sectarianism', *SBL Seminar Papers*, 21 (1982), pp. 45–61.
21. And an aversion to using the *torah* 'as a spade to dig with' remained characteristic: M. Beer, 'Talmud Torah we-Derekh 'Ereṣ', *Bar-Ilan Annual*, 2 (1964), pp. 134–62; and (during the amora'ic period) Neusner, *Babylonian Jewry*, Vol. 3, pp. 126–30.
22. For one amusing instance see TB *'Avodah Zarah* 26a and S. Lieberman, 'Jewish Life in *Eretz Yisrael* as Reflected in the Palestinian Talmud', *Israel: Its Role in Civilization*, p. 89.
23. Levine, *Ma'amad*, pp. 66–70; J. Neusner, *Judaism in Society: The Evidence of the Yerushalmi* (Chicago, 1983), esp. pp. 120–69 and Neusner, *Babylonian Jewry*, Vol. 5, pp. 326–9. On the composition of the courts, S. Albeck, *Batei ha-Din Bimei ha-Talmud* (Ramat Gan, 1981), pp. 70–5.
24. TJ *Pesaḥim* 3:7 as interpreted in L. I. Levine, *Caesarea Under Roman Rule* (Leiden, 1975), pp. 95–6 (on the tanna'itic discussion itself, below n. 51). For references to the local communal activities of rabbis Hoshaiyah (second-century, who numbered Yoḥanan amongst his pupils) and 'Abbahu (third-century), see Levine, idem., pp. 88, 102–3 and the same author's 'R. Abbahu of Caesarea', *Christianity, Judaism and other*

Greco-Roman Cults: Studies for Morton Smith at Sixty, Vol. 4 (ed. J. Neusner; Leiden, 1975), pp. 67–76.

25. Thus, in third- and fourth-century Palestine, for instance, intra-rabbinic competition for administrative positions could become so intense that the Patriarch was forced to limit the number of appointments. Lieberman, 'Palestine', pp. 360–4.
26. Oppenheimer, *The 'Am Ha-Aretz*, pp. 188–95, noting changes in the attitude of the sages to members of that class 'even to the extent of vindicating them'. On previous 'manifestations of hatred', idem., pp. 172–88.
27. Goodman, *State and Society*, p. 180. Cf. Levine, *Ma'amad*, pp. 73–9. In *Bavel*, at least some rabbis fully appreciated the potential political consequences of their actions. As 'Abbayei (the principal of the Pumbeṭida' academy during the early part of the fourth century) is reported to have once remarked: 'The reason that the local inhabitants love the *talmid ḥakham* is not because he is superior but because he refrains from rebuking them in heavenly matters' (TB *Ketubot* 105b).
28. J. Neusner, *Judaism: The Evidence of the Mishnah* (Chicago, 1982), p. 112.
29. E. E. Urbach, *Ha-Halakhah: Meqorotehah we-Hitpatḥutah* (Jerusalem, 1984), pp. 197–205.
30. TB *Shabbat* 114a and Exodus *Rabbah* 30:13; R. Kimelman, 'R. Yoḥanan u-Ma'amad ha-Rabanut', *Shenaṭon ha-Mishpaṭ ha-'Ivri*, 9–10 (1983), pp. 331–2.
31. On R. Yoḥanan's insistence that scholars and their students maintain proper standards of dress and behaviour, Urbach, *Sages*, p. 606 and the sources cited in Levine, *Ma'amad* p. 30 fn. 45, 47. In *Bavel*, Samuel had already decreed that 'once a man is appointed to public office he is forbidden to perform [manual] labour' (TB *Qidushin* 70a; Kimelman, op. cit., p. 335 fn. 25).
32. Amongst the most famous, and contentious, of R. Yoḥanan's rulings were his grant of permission for women to study Greek (TJ *Pe'ah* 1:1); and his refusal to object to the practice of painting decorative murals (TJ *'Avodah Zarah* 3:3). See also the reasons which he reportedly gave for upholding Judah *ha-nasi*'s authority to repeal the prohibition against using gentile oil (TB *'Avodah Zarah* 36a and *tosafot* s.v. *'we-ha-tenan'*).
33. Kimelman, 'R. Yoḥanan', p. 335, fn. 42 and pp. 343–4.
34. For one analysis of these phenomena immediately prior to 70 see: M. Goodman, 'The First Jewish Revolt: Social Conflict and the Problem of Debt', *JJS*, 33 (1982), pp. 417–27.
35. D. Ben-Ḥayyim Trifon, *Ha-Kohanim mi-Ḥurban Bayit Sheini we-'Ad 'Aliyat ha-Naṣut* (unpub. Ph.D.; Tel-Aviv, 1985), pp. 75–82, 91–110, and 361–79.
36. Lieberman, TK, Vol. 8 (*Nashim*, N.Y., 1973), p. 762.

37. R. Kimelman, 'Ha-Oligarkhiah ha-Kohanit we-Talmidei Ḥakhamim Bitqufat ha-Talmud', *Zion*, 48 (1983), pp. 136–47 and the sources cited in Levin, *Ma'amad* p. 115 fn. 28. Compare, however, the reservations in Trifon, *Ha-Kohanim*, pp. 219–22.
On the *ḥazan* (as in *Mishnah, Shabbat* 1:3), E. Eber, *Elementary Education in Ancient Israel during the Tannaitic Period* (New York, 1956), pp. 53–4 and Goodman, *State and Society*, pp. 123–4.
38. Neusner, *Babylonian Jewry*, Vol. 2, chap. 2. See also A. Oppenheimer, 'Hafrashat Ma'aser Ri'shon ba-Meṣi'ut she-le-'Aḥar Ḥurban ha-Bayit ha-Sheini', *Sinai*, 83 (1978), pp. 267–87.
39. S. Safrai, 'Ha-'Aliyah la-Regel Lirushalayim la-'Aḥar Ḥurban Bayit Sheini', *Peraqim be-Toledot Yerushalayim Bimei Bayit Sheini* (eds. A. Oppenheimer, et al.; Jerusalem, 1981), pp. 376–93. Compare K. W. Clark, 'Worship in the Jerusalem Temple after A.D. 70', *New Testament Studies*, 6 (1960), pp. 269–80.
40. E. E. Urbach, 'Mishmarot u-Ma'amadot', *Tarbitz*, 42 (1973), pp. 304–27. Trifon (*Ha-Kohanim*, pp. 175, 188–9) calculates that no less than 40 per cent of the sages of *'Ereṣ Yisra'el* during the Yavnean period were of attested priestly descent, a proportion probably some ten times larger than their overall demographic weight. It remains to be proved whether this figure accounts for the priestly 'bias' of their attitudes (as she suggests it does). As will be argued below, *tana'im* did not have to be priests in order to respect the *kehunah* – although it certainly did no harm if they were so. I. Sonne has argued that in *Bavel* too, throughout the Talmudic period, 'priests [...] seem to have formed the majority of the learned nobility'. 'The Paintings of the Dura Synagogue', *HUCA*, 20 (1947), p. 272 fn. 22. See also L. I. Levine, 'R. Simeon b. Yoḥai and the Purification of Tiberias: History and Tradition', *HUCA*, 49 (1978), p. 173: 'For some three generations, from the mid-third to the early fourth century, the major figures of the Tiberian academy [then the most important in the land] were Babylonian rabbis who were also priests.'
41. D. Goodblatt, 'Ha-To'ar "Nasi" we-ha-Reka' ha-Dati-'Idei'ologi Shel ha-Mered ha-Sheini', *Mered Bar-Kokhba': Meḥqarim Ḥadashim* (eds., A. Oppenheimer, U. Rappaport; Jerusalem, 1984), pp. 113–32 and idem., 'Temikhat ha-Tana'im 'O Hashpa'at ha-Kohanim', *Kathedra*, 29 (1983), pp. 6–12.
L. Mildenberg argues that Bar Kokhba' failed to take Jerusalem: 'The Bar-Kokhba War in the Light of the Coins and Document Finds, 1947–1982', *Israel Numismatic Journal*, 8 (1985), pp. 27–33. See also M. Beer, ' 'Edut 'Aḥat li-She'eilat 'i-Ḥidush 'Avodat ha-Qorbanot be-Yamav Shel Bar-Kokhba', *Nezir 'Eḥav: Sefer Zikaron le-R. David Kohen, ha-Nazir* (Jerusalem, 1978), pp. 196–206.
42. The 'Elazar' of the coins is widely identified with the *tana'* 'El'azar ha-Moda'i; see the summary of the literature in Oppenheimer, 'Meshiḥiyuto

Shel Bar Kokhba', p. 158. Compare, however, Mildenberg, op. cit., p. 27: 'The document finds have not told us who the Elazar appearing on the silver and bronze coins was. However, they contain a clear warning that one should not rely on any of the traditional candidates.'

43. There are numerous indications that the majority of the *Tannas* contemporary to the Bar-Kokhba rebellion looked upon the power of Rome as a fated phenomenon against which it was impossible to rise, continuing the line of pro-Roman orientation inherited from Yohanan ben Zakkai.

G. S. Aleksandrov, 'The Role of 'Aqiba in the Bar Kokhba Rebellion', in J. Neusner, *Eliezer ben Hyrcanus: The Tradition and the Man*, vol. 2 (Leiden, 1973), p. 435. See also P. Schaefer, 'Rabbi Akiva and Bar Kokhba', *Approaches to Ancient Judaism*, Vol. 2 (ed. W. S. Green; Missoula, Michigan, 1980), pp. 117–19. But compare Y. Ben-Shalom's response to Goodblatt in *Kathedra*, ibid., pp. 13–28.

44. Such texts as *Mishnah, Soṭah* 9:12 and ARN 'A', chap. 4 and 'B' chap. 5 (ed. Schechter, pp. 18–19) all contradict R. Patai's 'Postscript' to the 1967 reprint of *Man and Temple* (N.Y. 1947), p. 224. Far more reasonable appear to be the arguments in R. Goldenberg, 'Early Rabbinic Explanations of the Destruction of Jerusalem', *JJS*, 33 (1982), pp. 518–25.

45. TB *Berakhot* 3a (but cf. *Diqduqei Soferim*, ad. loc., pp. 4–5, n. 5).

46. Compare the discussion in E. P. Sanders, *Paul and Palestinian Judaism: A Comparison of Patterns of Religion* (Phila., 1977), pp. 162–4 with M. Kadushin, *The Rabbinic Mind* (N.Y., 1972), pp. 343ff. On the structure of *Mishnah*: J. Neusner, *The Evidence of the Mishnah*, pp. 148ff.

47. For an account of this episode, about which contemporary Jewish sources remain discreetly silent, see Avi-Yonah, *Jews Under Roman and Byzantine Rule*, pp. 193–204.

The patriarch and the Sanhedrin must have regarded the imperial letters and proclamations as the harbingers of an impending revolution. The restoration of Jerusalem and its territory to Jewish rule, together with the re-erection of the Temple, would radically change the whole structure of Jewish public life. It would most likely bring about a restoration of the ancient form of government, headed by a high priest. (p. 196).

Early Christian explanations for the failure of the project are examined in C. Robert Phillips, 'Julian's Rebuilding of the Temple: A Sociological Study of Religious Competition', *Society of Biblical Literature: Seminar Papers*, 2 (1979), pp. 167–72.

48. *Sheluḥie de-raḥmanah*; see Ḥuna' (fourth-century Babylonian *'amora'*) in TB *Yoma'* 19a; *Qidushin* 23b and *Nedarim* 35b.

49. Avi-Yonah, *Jews Under Roman and Byzantine Rule*, p. 26.

50. S. Safrai, *'Ereṣ Yisra'el we-Ḥakhamehah Bitqufat ha-Mishnah we-ha-Talmud* (Jerusalem, 1983), p. 189 citing TB *Horayot* 13b–14a and TJ *Bikurim* 3.

51. According to *Sifrei* Deut. 41 (p. 85; see also TB *Qidushin* 40b), the issue was thrashed out by several *tana'im* in Lydda, where rival positions were

put forward by rabbis Ṭarfon, 'Aqiva' and Yosie ha-Galili. The ultimate consensus was that study (*talmud*) takes precedence over action (*ma'aseh*), since the former leads to the latter. Compare, however, Rav Papa' in TB *Yevamot* 109b and above n. 24.

52. L. Ginzberg, 'The Significance of the Halakhah', *On Jewish Law and Lore* (Phila., 1955), pp. 94–5, dates the genesis of this development to the disputes between the disciples of Hillel and Shamm'ai. See, particularly, his reading and explanation of *Tosefta', Ḥagigah* 2:9:

    This is what is meant by the declaration that, when there was an increase in the disciples of Hillel and Shammai, who had not sufficiently waited on their masters, disagreements multiplied. The disciples of earlier generations were primarily interested in practical and pragmatic studies and there were therefore few disagreements among them; but the disciples of Shammai and Hillel emphasized theoretical investigation, and this caused greater disagreement.

53. A. J. Heschel, *Torah Min Ha-Shamayim be-'Aspaklariah Shel ha-Dorot*, Vol. 1 (Jerusalem, 1962), pp. 123–6. More discursive is G. F. Moore, *Judaism in the First Centuries of the Christian Era: the Age of the Tannaim*, Vol. 2 (Oxford, 1927), pp. 239–47.
54. A. Marmorstein, 'Ma'alat Talmud Torah (be-Ma'amarei Rabi Shim'on bar Yoḥ'ai)', *Sefer ha-Yovel* [...] *B. M. Levin* (Jerusalem, 1939), esp. pp. 140–1.
55. M. Beer, 'Ha-Reqa' ha-Medini u-Fe'iluto Shel Rav be-Bavel', *Zion*, 50 (1985), pp. 166–7. In TB *Sanhedrin* 44b, Rav is said to have declared that 'the study of the *torah* is' – quite simply – 'more important than the *tamid* [daily whole offering]'.
56. E.E. Urbach, 'Ha-Mesorot 'Al Torat ha-Sod Bitqufat ha-Tana'im', *Meḥqarim be-Qabalah u-ve-Toledot ha-Datot, Mugashim le-Gershom Scholem* (ed. Urbach; Jerusalem, 1968), Hebrew section, pp. 1–28, has demonstrated how even the tanna'itic terminology employed to describe study was derived from Exodus 19:18. On the perspectives of tractate *'Avot*, see P.T. Viviano, *Study as Worship: Aboth and the New Testament* (Leiden, 1978).
57. See, e.g., the exegesis on I Sam. 3:14 debated by Rabah (bar Naḥmani?) and 'Abbayei in TB *R'osh ha-Shanah* 18a. Even more explicit, with reference to the textual materials to hand, is Lev. *Rabbah* 7:3: 'The Holy One blessed be He said: "Seeing that you are engaged in the study of the *Mishnah*, it is as if you were offering up sacrifices."'
58. E.g. *Tosefta', Menaḥot* 13:21; TJ *Yoma'* 1:1; TB *Pesaḥim* 57a and *Yoma'* 9a.
59. For examples (notably, the supposed fates of the Biblical Phineas and of the two sons of Eli, the Shilonite High Priest), see the extended analyses in M. Beer, ''Al Manhigim Shel Yehudei Ṣipori ba-Me'ah ha-Shelishit', *Sinai*, 74 (1974), pp. 133–8, and idem, 'Banav Shel 'Eli be-'Agadot Ḥazal', *Bar-Ilan Annual*, 14 (Ramat Gan, 1977), pp. 79–93. See also below, chap. 9, p. 243.

60. E.g. TJ *Sheqalim* 4:3 on their swank; TB *Bava' Batra'* 160b on their choleric nature; and TB *Sanhedrin* 90b on priests as *'amei ha-'areṣ*.
61. Trifon, *Ha-Kohanim*, pp. 47–8.
62. Alon, *Jews in Their Land*, I, p. 257 and A. Oppenheimer, 'Hafrashat Ma'aser R'ishon ba-Meṣi 'ut she-le-'Aḥar Ḥurban ha-Bayit ha-Sheini', *Sinai*, 83 (1978), esp. pp. 284–5.
63. See Appendix 1 in Beer's *'Amor'ai Bavel*, pp. 350–61 and his comparisons with the situation in *'Ereṣ Yisra'el*, fn. 38.
64. On the right of sages to claim the same exemptions from *liturgia* as had supposedly been enjoyed by the Levites in Pharaoh's Egypt, see: *Tanḥuma'*, Exodus, *Wayeira'*, 4.
In general (for *'Ereṣ Yisra'el*): Avi Yonah, *Jews Under Roman & Byzantine Rule*, pp. 117–19 and R. Kimelman, 'The Conflict between R. Yoḥanan and Resh Laqish on the Supremacy of the Patriarchate', *WCJS*, 7(3), 1981, pp. 7–18. On the situation in *Bavel* during the age of Shapur II: Neusner, *Babylonian Jewry*, Vol. 4 (Leiden, 1969), pp. 85–91 and Beer, *'Amor'ai Bavel*, pp. 222–57.
65. The technical difficulties raised by this account, as well as the justification for the attribution to Judah II rather than Judah I, are discussed at length in the footnotes to Kimelman, op. cit., pp. 8–10.
66. As Urbach remarks (*Sages*, p. 611), Rava's statement exceeds others cited in the same source. (i) It is not restricted to the study of *halakhot* on sacrifices; (ii) it omits the 'as if' clause usually present in such remarks.
67. J. Neusner, *Torah: From Scroll to Symbol in Formative Judaism* (Phila., 1985), p. 148.
68. See, e.g., the translation from Lamentations *Rabbah*, proem 2, and commentary, in idem., pp. 120–2.
69. Cited idem., p. 148.

7

Rabbis and appointed rulers (c. 100 C.E. – c. 400 C.E.)

An aura of superfluity pervades rabbinic polemic against the priesthood after the middle of the third century. Subsequent talmudic sources, whilst still insisting on the incorporation of the *keter kehunah* within a vastly superior *keter torah*, state their case almost nonchanantly, and without anything like the urgency or bitterness of earlier times. In retrospect, the modulation of invective is easily understood. As Trifon illustrates,[1] even though priests were never to be entirely disregarded as symbols of national concern, their bid for communal re-instatement was lost. Reduced to hovering on the margins of even ritual Jewish life, the *keter kehunah* was thus a party on the run. It possessed no viable defences against the aggressive ethos of scholastic piety now being promulgated inside and outside the academies in the name of the *keter torah*.

Entirely different were rabbinic relations with contemporary agencies of the *keter malkhut*, now jointly represented by successive *nesi'im* (Patriarchs) in *'Ereṣ Yisra'el* and *rashei galuta'* (Exilarchs) in *Bavel*. Together, holders of both positions – and it is significant that they occasionally shared the same title[2] – self-consciously represented a franchise of government distinct from the *torah* as well as the *kehunah*. Ultimately, they considered themselves independent of both. Their occasional need to co-operate with the sister domains did not generate a sense of inferiority. On the contrary, Patriarchs and Exilarchs boasted pedigrees as distinguished as those of the priests and redemptive capacities as stirring as those claimed by the rabbis. They could also parade the invaluable – and unique – advantage of official authorisation by the gentile suzerains upon whose favour Jewish lives and property were (under God) universally recognised to be entirely dependent. Even separately, those assets constituted potential obstacles to the progress of the rabbinic programme of communal conquest. Combined, they transformed the *keter malkhut* into a brake on its ultimate fulfilment.

Origins and development of the re-constituted *keter malkhut*

As a corporate entity, the *keter malkhut* represented by the Exilarchs and Patriarchs of the early rabbinic era has to be severely differentiated from the franchise of the same name which had existed at earlier periods of Jewish history. True, incumbents of both offices did sometimes attempt to mask the discontinuities in their institutional pedigree, principally by promoting the atavistic revival of Israel's ancient monarchical slogans. Most famously, they adopted the convention of belatedly tracing parallel, and probably spurious, descents from the royal Davidic line.[3] Where acknowledged, that *cachet* may indeed have been sufficiently evocative to bestow upon its owners the kind of respect which contemporary culture was wont to invest in proprietary dynasticism. But, even so, it could not entirely mask the novelty and limitations of their offices. Significantly, and like Bar-Kokhba', *nesi'im* and *rashei galuta'* did not adopt the Biblical title of *melekh*; nor, in any but the most guarded of terms, does rabbinic literature designate them the Davidic monarchy's exact constitutional equivalents.[4] For all the antiquity of their titles and assumed patrimony, neither Patriarchs nor Exilarchs constituted true institutional reincarnations of Israel's ancient monarchy. Rather, they represented functional extensions of Jewry's gentile overlords.

Because both the Patriarchate and the Exilarchate were the product of contemporary circumstances, they deserve to be treated in tandem. In origin, the two positions came into being for separate reasons and at different times. By the second century C.E. onwards, however (if not earlier), their incumbents were individually serving the remarkably similar – albeit antagonistic – interests of their respective Roman and Persian masters. In the bi-polar circumstances then prevailing in the Middle Eastern world, the rulers of both powers regarded their Jewish subjects with some ambivalence, a useful asset if handled correctly but a dangerous liability if not. That substantial Jewish communities straddled both sides of the political boundaries disputed by the two embattled empires was undoubtedly one inducement to keeping a careful watch on the affairs of this distinctive ethnic group. Neglect to do so invited the sort of embarrassment caused to Trajan by the Jews of Nisibis during his attempted invasion of Mesopotamia in c. 115–17. There was also the danger that Jews might be tempted to exploit great-power rivalry for the attainment of their own national aims (which was probably precisely the opportunity envisioned by the saying attributed to R. Simeon bar Yoḥ'ai: 'If you see a Persian horse tied to the gravestones in *'Ereṣ Yisra'el* await the coming of the Messiah.' Canticles *Rabbah* 8:10). On the other hand, Jewry's international connections could also be exploited for the benefit of Roman and Persian policies and economies. The latter consideration perhaps explains why neither power was averse to permitting its vassal princes – for that is in effect what both Patriarchs and Exilarchs were – from developing and maintaining a communications network which extended deep into each other's sphere of geographical influence.[5]

Within each region, Imperial interests of a more local focus also came into play. Recent scholarship is tending to substantiate the thesis (originally submitted by Derenbourg over a century ago) that the emergence of the *nesi'ut* as an arm of government in *'Ereṣ Yisra'el* owed little to native Jewish initiative and still less to ancient Jewish traditions.[6] Although the title *nasi'* did resonate with rich historical associations dating from both the first and second Commonwealths,[7] the office whose powers are described in third- and fourth-century sources – gentile as well as Jewish – seems to have been entirely the product of post-Destruction circumstances. What is more, it owed its foundation in that period to the interests of Roman authorities whose overriding concern was to prevent a repetition of the uncomfortable jolts administered to Imperial arms and prestige by successive waves of Jewish rebellion. One possible deterrent was to impose direct Roman rule over the unruly province: to appoint a Legate; to confiscate property; and to overawe potential troublemakers by permanently stationing in their land such hardened veterans as the troopers of the Tenth Legion ('Frentensis') and – even before the Bar Kokhba' war – the 'Ironsides' ('Ferrata') of the Sixth Legion. But those measures created too many administrative and strategic complications to be entirely satisfactory. Far cheaper (and, to judge by Imperial experience in other contexts, far more effective too) was the establishment of what amounted to a local *Judenrat*, a client regime composed of Jews who – although acceptable to Jewish sentiment – would be entirely responsible to Roman wishes.

Doubtless the selection of suitable candidates for that stewardship was tricky. In Imperial eyes, both priests and *ḥakhamim* were likely to be disqualified; the former because they were too intimately associated with the insurrections of both 66–70 and 132–5; the latter because they did not (yet) command the necessary corporate status and communal standing. More preferable would be members of Jewry's scholarly elite and non-priestly gentry, persons who possessed some influence amongst their compatriots but who had signalled their political value by carefully distancing themselves from the extreme nationalists during the revolts. Soon after the Great Rebellion of 66–70, Gamli'el II seems to have demonstrated precisely those qualifications; so too, immediately following 135, did his son Simeon II. Although the family did come from distinguished stock,[8] it is doubtful whether the pedigree of its members exerted more than a marginal influence on their elevation. Post-bellum Judea's first two Patriarchs seem to have been appointed *ad hominem* and in no way to have 'inherited' their office. Gamli'el II's immediate predecessor as President of the court at Yavneh (a position which he probably held from early in the 80s until *circa* 115) was not his father, Simeon I, but Rabban Yoḥanan ben Zak'ai. Simeon II's succession was interrupted – perhaps even delayed – by Bar Kokhba's assumption of the rank of *nasi'*. To interpret such 'interregnums' as signs that Simeon I and Simeon II were forced 'underground' during the two great revolts is, it seems, to force the evidence. More reasonable is the suggestion that the patriarchal office had not yet become an established feature of Jewish political life in *'Ereṣ Yisra'el*. Only once the family had proved its worth in Roman eyes was the Imperial administration prepared to foster the permanence of the position of *nasi'* and to transform it into a dynastic preserve.[9]

The origins and development of the office of the *r'eshut ha-golah* in *Bavel* have been traced to similar considerations. Other than as a curiosity, little value is now attached to the medieval tradition which dates the genesis of the position to the last years of the exile of Jehoiachin (II Kings 25:27).[10] No such institution can be proven to have existed before the latter third of the first century; in all probability it was then established by Vologases I, primarily in order to provide the Parthian empire with a puppet agency which might control the turbulent Jewish populations in central and northern Babylonia and secure their support for his throne after a period of strife. Like the *nasi'* of *'Ereṣ Yisra'el*, the *reish galuta'* of

Bavel was created in order to keep the Jews in line and their payments to the Imperial treasury flowing. Only provided they fulfilled those functions were officers of that name granted the plenitude of powers which enabled them to represent their respective communities and exercise an influence over Jewry's internal affairs.[11] For long thereafter, that remained the basic fact of every Exilarch's life. Indeed, the extent to which each incumbent was ultimately nothing more than the servant of the Empire became starkly apparent with the advent to power of the Sasanians in 226. Owing nothing to the Jews, Ardashir (the first ruler of his dynasty) could make a renewal of the Exilarch's obeisance a condition of his reinstatement and a necessary prelude to the confirmation of his office as a hereditary benefice.

Exilarchs and Patriarchs, then, both lived inherently precarious lives. To their foreign suzerains, they were essentially administrative and financial agents; Jews, however, regarded *nesi'im* and *r'ashei golah* as their own national delegates and representatives. Whichever the case, their powers and privileges were contingent on the skill, tact and discretion with which they could walk the twin tightropes of authority within the Jewish community and subservience to their gentile overlords. If they meekly succumbed to the will of the latter they would forfeit the Jewish respect which they cherished and, for political as well as psychological reasons, obviously required; on the other hand, too forcefully to champion Jewish rights was to run the possibly fatal risk of Imperial displeasure and, in extreme cases, to provoke ruthless retribution.

As much was indicated, at the very end of our period, by the ill-starred rebellion associated in Jewish tradition with the Exilarchate of Mar Zuṭra' II (*fl.* 510–20), reputed to be the last surviving member of the royal Davidic line. If legend is to be believed, Mar Zuṭra' attempted to counter the anti-Jewish activities of the Mazdakites by exploiting the political chaos and economic depression affecting their Empire. In quick succession, he renounced his fealty to the throne of Kavadh, organised his own guard of 400 warriors and – encouraged by the ease with which he defeated a Persian force – declared himself ruler of an independent Jewish state in the region of Maḥoza'. Within seven years, however, his experiment had collapsed. Corruption undermined the strength of Mar Zuṭra's own troops, who were ultimately defeated on the field of battle. Together with his grandfather, the Exilarch himself was taken prisoner and beheaded. Thereafter, his body was suspended from a cross on the bridge at Maḥoza', a grisly reminder of the perils courted by any Exilarch foolish enough to overstep the bounds of propriety imposed by his station.[12]

Notwithstanding the uncertainties of their personal and professional lives, most Exilarchs and Patriarchs enjoyed comparative tranquillity and comfort. However fervently they may have prayed for an end to Israel's political subjugation, the vast majority certainly made a virtue out of present national necessity. Some are occasionally reported to have utilised their academic gifts in order to provide intellectual stimulation (and perhaps even spiritual counsel) to individual Roman and Persian dignitaries;[13] several also maintained opulent courts modelled on the lavish styles of the potentates with whom they mixed. Almost all managed to accumulate personal fortunes which, by contemporary Jewish standards, were of fabled proportions. Most conspicuously of all, Patriarchs and Exilarchs took pleasure in the external symbols of their uniquely privileged positions. In third century *'Ereṣ Yisra'el*, for instance, the *nasi'* enjoyed the so-called *praefectura honoraria*; hereditary possessors of the office were in official Imperial correspondence styled *viri clarissimi et illustres* and in some instances even supplied with the services of a personal squad of 'Gothic' guards.[14] In Babylonia, the *reish galuta'* was accorded the honours due to other semi-autonomous vassal princes by the strict etiquette of Iranian courtly life. His right to wear the *qamara'* (apparently an official sash of Iranian office) demonstrated the extent to which he was usually assured of unambiguous royal backing for the implementation of his various commands.[15]

Such external signs of privilege were inexorably transmuted into tangible power over the internal lives of the Jewish communities under Patriarchal and Exilarchic charge. Admittedly, and probably because of the novelty of their offices, the exact extent of domestic authority available to the instruments of the *keter malkhut* immediately after the Destruction seems for some time to have been a subject of considerable confusion (indeed, it still remains so in some historical analyses).[16] Possessed of a mandate which their Roman and Persian masters perhaps kept deliberately fluid and experimental, the earliest *nesi'im* and *rashei galuta'* were constrained to grow into their offices. They felt their way as much *vis à vis* the rabbis and each other as with respect to their respective gentile overlords. Several of the intra-communal tensions which (as will be seen) punctuated the *nesi'ut* of both Gamli'el II and Simeon II were surely affected by the fact that both men were operating under conditions of institutional imprecision as well as political uncertainty.

By the third century, however, when they had mastered the knack of skilful political manoeuvre and judicious dynastic marriages, matters seem to have settled into a fairly established pattern in both *Bavel* and *'Ereṣ Yisra'el*. Even after the advent of the Sasanids, *rashei galuta'* managed to assert their formal authority to ratify the appointment of judges; to imprison malefactors (including, where necessary, rabbis; see TB *Bava' Batra'* 59a–b); and to supervise the activities of tax-collectors, market officials and all the other instruments whom they charged with the maintenance of civil order in Jewish communities.[17] *Nesi'im*, by the same period, had accumulated even more extensive powers: in addition to exercising many of the administrative and supervisory rights enjoyed by their colleagues in *Bavel*, they also determined the Jewish calendar (a crucial privilege exercised as early as the period of Gamli'el II);[18] proclaimed, or annulled, fast-days; ordained rabbis; promulgated the religious amendments and decrees categorised as *taqanot* and *gezeirot*; imposed, or lifted, bans of 'excommunication'; levied taxes for their official treasuries; and despatched their own apostles to the Diaspora.

Keter malkhut and *keter torah*: parameters of relationships

By and large, Patriarchs and Exilarchs exercised the prerogatives thus available to the *keter malkhut* in ways which benefited rabbinic representatives of the *keter torah*. Sharing the religious outlook of the rabbis, *nesi'im* and *rashei galuta'* never encouraged anti-rabbinic or non-rabbinic sectarianism. On the contrary, they fully accepted the normative authority of the *halakhah* and, as is most forcefully demonstrated by Rabbi Judah *ha-nasi*'s *Mishnah* (below, pp. 196–7), played what was sometimes a crucial role in its codification and dissemination. They also provided instruments of the *keter torah* with other forms of material assistance. Exilarchs and Patriarchs furnished rabbis with the authorisation necessary to ensure their legal immunity from compensation for erroneous judicial decisions;[19] they distributed Jewry's financial obligations towards the Roman or Persian administrations in ways which satisfied rabbinic claims to municipal tax exemptions;[20] they also took a personal interest in the welfare of rabbinic students and (as had already been the case in second-century *'Ereş Yisra'el*) contributed towards their maintenance.[21]

Those actions did not signify an admission that the *keter malkhut* was in any sense inferior to the *keter torah*; still less did they indicate that its individual instruments were prepared to abdicate their institutional identities. On the contrary, the mandate which Patriarchs and Exilarchs had received to pick and choose between men enabled them to establish a corporate presence which was entirely the *keter malkhut*'s own. Even those *nesi'im* and *rashei galuta'* who adopted rabbinical titles (although sometimes, in the former case, *raban* rather than *rabi*)[22] did not subsume themselves within the rabbinical estate. As wealthy landowners and magnates, they deliberately cultivated their eminence at the economic pinnacle of Jewish society;[23] in political matters, they similarly operated from a constitutional power-base which they unreservedly regarded to be theirs alone. Hence, even when agreeing with rabbinic definitions of proper Jewish behaviour (as was invariably the case), *nesi'im* and *rashei galuta'* tended to do so from positions of executive independence. Consequently, to describe the *nasi'* (even the second-century *nasi'*) as 'no more than any important rabbi'[24] is to miss, it would seem, the political subtleties of the relationship between the parties. What set apart talmudic representatives of the *keter torah* and the *keter malkhut* was the fact that they represented different constitutional interests and therefore spoke with different constitutional voices. Much in the manner of partners in an untidy three-legged race, the parties – although generally headed in the same direction – were often out of step and tripping each other up.

Besides, when helping to promulgate the decrees of rabbinical Judaism, Patriarchs and Exilarchs were acting in what they understood to be their own best interests. The favours which they bestowed on the rabbis were expected to produce substantive administrative returns. They cast individual *ḥakhamim* in the role of their own agents, men whose widely-canvassed spiritual assets and cerebral calibre might compensate for the absence of any other instruments which could have sustained the *keter malkhut*'s authority. Lacking their own police force, salaried civil service, or even a judiciary independent of local magnates, *nesi'im* and *rashei galuta'* looked to rabbis to fit all those bills. Specifically, the latter were to staff Jewish courts, supervise the smooth running of other administrative services and in outstanding instances (as exemplified by R. Naḥman ben Jacob, the fourth-century Babylonian *'amora'* who married the Exilarch's daughter, Yalta') even to serve as their 'viziers'.[25] Necessarily, such offices were reserved for the Patriarch's and Exilarch's nominees. Their recipients were therefore expected to exercise whatever authority they held on their patrons' behalf – and sometimes even in their names.[26]

Only within those parameters is it possible to talk of the emergence of a 'dyarchy' in Jewish communal life comprising shared – but separate – rule between instruments of the *keter malkhut* and the *keter torah*.[27] The two branches did find it politic to co-operate, most obviously at various Galilean locations in *'Ereṣ Yisra'el*, where rabbis and Patriarchs regularly joined council for administrative and judicial purposes in the conclaves sometimes (perhaps erroneously) designated a '*sanhedrin*'. Nevertheless, as the records appertaining to those meetings themselves show, the relationship was often tense and occasionally stormy. Perceptions of mutual advantage did not generate harmony; in fact, in *Bavel* as well as in *'Ereṣ Yisra'el*, the domains of the *torah* and the *malkhut* tended to operate in what was no more than uneasy harness, with their association marked by dissent as well as co-operation. Each franchise appreciated that it needed the other in order to further its own theological and political ends, and that their collusion was essential for the survival of their people and the preservation of its faith. Yet, at the same time, each was also determined, wherever possible, to deny the other an overriding advantage. Thus it was that several of the recorded dialogues of the period came to be characterised by tension, with champions of the two sides defending with some intensity the interests of the estates which they claimed to represent.

Not all brushes between groups of rabbis and their respective Patriarchs or Exilarchs reflected constitutional conflict. As described in the talmudic literature, several seem to have been almost mundane, and of the sort only to be expected when men of fiercely independent minds find themselves working in stifling proximity. Others were generated by *amour propre*. Once again, a case in point is provided by an incident in the life of R. Naḥman ben Jacob, the Exilarch's major domo. TB *Qidushin* 70a–b recounts in some detail the tensions aroused when Naḥman summoned to his 'court' R. Judah, the founder of the academy of Pumbediṭa', and then insisted that he present formal greetings to Yalta' – who, quite apart from being Naḥman's own wife was also the Exilarch's daughter. Only the prudence of the lady concerned, we are informed, prevented what was already an unpleasant incident becoming an ugly one too.

On occasion, however, clashes of a more fundamental nature can also be discerned. As represented by the Exilarchate and Patriarchate on the one hand and the rabbis on the other, the *ketarim* of the *malkhut* and the *torah* in time came to posit what Neusner has referred to as two different 'political theories of authority and legitimacy'; by the third century (although probably not before), each had also begun to project a totally different version of Jewry's covenantal past and a very different conception of its messianic future. Ultimately at issue, Neusner suggests, was a consideration of the conditions necessary to effect Israel's destined redemption. Taking their cue from Biblical sources, agents and embodiments of the *keter malkhut* redivivus in both *'Ereṣ Yisra'el* and *Bavel* portrayed that eventuality in highly personal terms. Even if only implicitly, all would ultimately have posited the future advent of an individual Messiah, much of whose authority would rest upon the Davidic ancestry which they themselves somewhat dubiously claimed to share.[28]

Rabbinic spokesmen for the *keter torah*, by contrast, adopted a far more republican view of both the nature of Redemption and its prerequisites. True salvation, they argued, could not be reduced solely to the mundane notion of the restoration of a Biblical monarchy. To attain full meaning, the messianic era had to encompass the establishment of the kingdom of heaven rather than the mortal monarchy currently being resurrected by instruments of the *keter malkhut*. Israel had to undertake a legal reformation in accordance with the *torah* communicated and defined by the rabbis, not as identified by the nation's princes. Once their tongues had been lubricated by large doses of strong wine, R. Ḥiyya's sons were even prepared to say as much to Judah *ha-nasi*'s face. 'The Son of David', they are reported to have mumbled into their cups, 'cannot appear before the two ruling houses in Israel shall come to an end' and (lest there linger any doubt about the targets of the reference) 'that is the Exilarchate in *Bavel* and the Patriarchate in *'Ereṣ Yisra'el*' (TB *Sanhedrin* 38a; see also R. Ḥanina' bar Ḥama' in ibid. 98a).

Outbursts such as that were not the norm. For the most part, rabbinic criticism of the *keter malkhut* (and especially its Babylonian variant) was more oblique – and the evidence consequently more recalcitrant. Rabbis, after all, needed the employment which only Patriarchs and Exilarchs could provide; in addition, the ever-present threat of gentile intervention (or worse) in intra-Jewish affairs imposed its own rule of discretion. But much though those pragmatic considerations muffled the sounds of conflict, absolute silence proved impossible to maintain. An early echo of the tussle, it has been suggested, can be discerned in *Mishnah 'Avot*'s two records of the chain of (Pharisaic) scholastic transmission. Passages 1:12–2:4 trace a direct line from Hillel's teachings of those of Rabban Gamli'el [I] and thence to those of his genetic descendants who were *nesi'im*; 2:8–14, however, designates Rabban Yoḥanan ben Zak'ai as the first recipient of that *torah* and his disciples as its authentic guardians.[29]

Notwithstanding the different political climates of *'Ereṣ Yisra'el* and *Bavel*, subsequent intra-communal tension between the two domains was exclusive to neither.[30] In both centres, rabbis criticised the dynastic pretensions of Exilarchs and Patriarchs, often giving vent to their antagonism through the refracting lens of deceptively innocuous Biblical exegesis. Equally comparable is the corporate rabbinic advocacy, in both *'Ereṣ Yisra'el* and *Bavel*, of an alternative style of collegial leadership. The frequency of allusions to those themes attests to their polemic purpose. In the very long term, they were arguably designed to resolve the tension between the underlying impulses towards republicanism and autocracy which, in some views, had been articulated as early as the Moses–Joshua succession described in the book of Deuteronomy.[31] More immediately pressing, however, was the determination of current constitutional precedence between the *keter torah* and the *keter malkhut*. In the disarmingly straightforward terms employed in third-century Palestine during a debate on this very subject between two brothers-in-law, R. Yoḥanan and Reish Laqish, the question was quite simple: did the sages of the age stand in need of the *nasi*'s honour, or did he require theirs?[32]

Varieties of strategic choice: 'usurpation', 'collusion' and 'attrition'

During the course of the period here reviewed, rabbinic spokesmen for the *keter torah* advocated various responses to that enquiry. Undoubtedly the most aggressive – albeit also the most infrequent – might be designated 'usurpation'. Designed to revolutionise the constitutional framework of post-Destruction Israel, it posited the transfer to the *keter torah* of whatever powers and prerogatives had traditionally been vested in the *keter malkhut*. Thereby, the latter domain was to be neutralised as an effective locus of authority in Jewish political life. Several of the actions unilaterally taken immediately after 70 C.E. by Rabban Yoḥanan ben Zak'ai suggest that such might have been his own design. Even if, as now seems likely, Yoḥanan did not himself then assume the title of *nasi'* (indeed, if we are to follow Goodblatt, could not possibly have done so since no position of that name yet existed), he certainly acted as one, arrogating to his seat at Yavneh the centripetal powers previously vested in Jerusalem's organs of sacerdotal and administrative government.[33] In so doing, he can be understood to have intimated that, due to the circumstances created by the Destruction, the *keter malkhut* should be regarded as constitutionally defunct as was the *keter kehunah*. The authority of both domains could now be incorporated within what he projected as the expanding sphere of the *keter torah*.

The strategy of usurpation thus adumbrated did not necessarily die a sudden death with Yoḥanan's own (possibly enforced) retirement to Beror Ḥayyil. It may subsequently have been revived by the small band of scholars who met in secret conclave in the Rimmon Valley (TJ *Ḥagigah* 3:1), during the nightmarish aftermath of the Bar Kokhba' revolt. In deciding, amongst other things, to intercalate the calendar – without the prior permission of Simeon II, or even his presence – members of the assembled group were expressly declaring their own institutional and political preferences. They were in effect pronouncing the office of the *nasi'* to be – not simply in temporary abeyance – but defunct.[34] Had the Roman authorities not wished matters otherwise, it might indeed have become so.

At the other end of the spectrum, can be discerned an inclination to pursue what is here termed a policy of 'collusion'. Broadly outlined, it required rabbis to bow to the obvious political strengths of the *keter malkhut* and to acknowledge that its instruments could not be dislodged as long as they continued to enjoy the backing of Jewry's gentile suzerains. Aware that intra-communal dissension might prove fatal to themselves as well as their domestic opponents, rabbis were to make a virtue out of necessity, principally by according the *nesi'ut* and *r'eshut ha-golah* visible marks of *keter torah* approval. At the very least, incumbents of those offices had to be granted the privilege of ceremonial precedence whenever they appeared in public; their offspring had also be honoured by consideration as eminently suitable marriage partners for the immediate members of the sages' own families.[35] It followed that deference to the *keter malkhut* ought further to be extended in other directions. Specifically, all rabbis had unhesitatingly to respect the Patriarch's unique right to determine the Jewish calendar (*Mishnah, R'osh ha-Shanah* 2:8–9); for that matter, they had to accept the binding force of whatever judicial actions may have been taken in his (or, where relevant, the Exilarch's) name. Position, rather than pedigree and even scholarship, was thus the true determinate of authority. At bottom, the power of the *keter malkhut* was sustained by the mere fact of its existence:

Whoever is appointed administrator of a community, even though he be the most worthless of persons, has the same status as the noblest. (*Tosefta', R'osh ha-Shanah* 2:3; TJ ibid., 2:9).

While instances of rabbinic collusion with the *keter malkhut* can be discerned in *'Ereṣ Yisra'el* as early as mid-tanna'itic times,[36] they become especially prevalent during the transition to the amora'ic period. Early during the third century C.E., one inducement may have been provided by the policies and personalities of such an outstanding *nasi'* as Judah I and *reish galuta'* as Mar 'Ukba'. Quite apart from themselves being scholars of considerable distinction (on Judah see below), both managed further to dilute much rabbinic suspicion and reserve when deliberately sustaining and supporting several of the interests and enterprises which the rabbis held most dear. But the influence of that circumstance was undoubtedly compounded by the more comprehensive fact that third-century Patriarchs and Exilarchs in general possessed a range of deterrent and compellant powers far in excess of those previously available to their predecessors. For that reason, too, they were likely to have enjoyed increasing deference. Especially was this so in *'Ereṣ Yisra'el*, where relations between the sages and their *nesi'im* were further affected by the depredations resulting from local economic exigences, themselves partly the consequence of political crises in Rome. At a time when the burden of Imperial financial impositions on the local Jewish population was widely acknowledged to be virtually intolerable – so much so that emigration was rife and public funding for scholars and students almost impossible to obtain – the conjunction of rabbis and *nesi'im* was considered to be as beneficial to Israel as the exploits of the Maccabeans in days of yore (TB *Megilah* 11a).

Under those circumstances, collusion between the *keter torah* and the *keter malkhut* for a time became a pronounced tone of much rabbinic life. In *Bavel*, the trend – although perhaps exemplified by R. Naḥman ben Jacob – had somewhat earlier been set by Samuel (died 254), who may possibly have been his teacher. One of the most distinguished and influential sages of the entire age, Samuel is reported to have been particularly assiduous in his cultivation of close relations with the Exilarch and his officials (TJ *Ta'anit* 4:2 and TB *Mo'ed Qaṭan* 16b); his famous declaration that 'the law of the land is law' certainly served (amongst other things) Exilarchic interests.[37] In *'Ereṣ Yisra'el* precisely the same mood was almost simultaneously adumbrated by R. Yoḥanan, whose emphasis on the monarchical *dignitas* expected of a *nasi'* became something of a fetish (e.g. his elucidation of Isaiah 33:17 in TJ *Sanhedrin* 2:6). Indeed, Yoḥanan seems to have regarded collusion to be a strategic rule of thumb. Not even his opposition to the taxes imposed on scholars by the *nasi'* Judah II could induce Yoḥanan to countenance the sort of public hue and cry raised by Reish Laqish; neither did he concur with the latter's suggestion that the rabbis disregard a Patriarchal proclamation of a fast day on the grounds that they had only belatedly been informed of the decision.[38] Adamant that 'we must follow [the *nasi*'s] lead' (TB *Ta'anit* 24a), Yoḥanan expressed the sentiments of an entire school of rabbinic thought which considered the maintenance of a concordat with the *nesi'ut* essential to the best interests of the *keter torah* too.

A third option was to adopt a stance here designated 'attrition'. Although less obviously audacious than attempted usurpation, it was also less forthcoming than collusion. As pursued by representatives of the *keter torah*, attrition in effect constituted a pragmatic course, designed less to establish a long-term pattern of relationships with the *keter malkhut* than to secure piecemeal concessions from its principal instruments. What its implementation required, accordingly, was not comprehensive assaults on the existence of the Patriarchate or Exilarchate, but probing – and often carefully selected – challenges to the manner in which individual *nesi'im* and *rashei galuta'* were allegedly exceeding the constitutional boundaries of their institutional privileges or exploiting them for their own personal advantage. Its ultimate purpose, then, was (in the words attributed to the third-century *'amora'*, R. 'Abbahu of Caesarea), to 'fence in' the officers of the *keter malkhut* and by thus clipping their wings to allow the *keter torah* gradually to encroach upon their various preserves (TJ *'Avodah Zarah* 1:1).

When practised, the policy of attrition was most obviously expressed through the medium of rabbinic confrontations with *nesi'im* or *rashei galuta'* over tangible specifics. In their bluntest form, they involved disputes over either the halakhic legality of certain Patriarchal/Exilarchic decisions and pronouncements or the suitability of some of their appointees to particular judicial and academic offices. In what seem to have been extreme cases, such tactics could be accompanied by the articulation of outspoken rabbinic insults concerning both the personal deportment of individual Patriarchs or Exilarchs and their ignorance.[39] Several of the exchanges, however, were couched in the more opaque language of Biblical exegesis. Exploiting their audiences' familiarity with the books of the Old Testament, rabbis employed those texts as a polemical quarry, reconstructing – and sometimes completely re-writing – Israel's ancient history in ways which implicitly vilified the contemporary equivalents of the nation's monarchical ghouls.[40] Equally to the point was the transformation into political slogans of judiciously selected Biblical verses (especially, towards the end of the third century, of Proverbs 8:15–16).[41]

From an institutional perspective, attrition certainly presented less of a radical threat to the *keter malkhut* than did attempts at outright usurpation. Because practised with alarming frequency, however, that policy in effect constituted an even more recurrent and insidious danger to the personal authority of individual Patriarchs and Exilarchs. One extreme example of the extent to which this was so is provided by the run of constitutional crises which plagued the *nesi'ut* in *'Ereṣ Yisra'el* during the second century. In what must have smacked suspiciously of a planned campaign of provocation, several rabbis – many of whom have been identified as close associates of R. 'Aqiva' – challenged Gamli'el II's authority to make independent decisions on a battery of crucial issues (the determination of the calendar; the delegation of authority to allocate firstlings; the liturgy). Having thus pushed their *nasi*'s patience beyond all reasonable limits, they then deposed him from office, only sanctioning his re-instatement on condition that he agreed to the appointment of two of their own number as constitutional watchdogs entitled the '*'av beit din*' and the '*ḥakham*'.[42]

As is so often the case with finely-balanced political arrangements of that sort, it very nearly came apart at its first testing. A new rabbinic conspiracy (led, significantly, by R. Natan and R. Mei'ir – themselves, *'av beit din* and *ḥakham*) almost brought about the deposition of Gamli'el's son and successor, Simeon II.[43] Exilarchs could be confronted with similar challenges, as was indicated by the curious third-century episode associated with the somewhat cantankerous personality of Geniva'. Himself apparently a member of a rabbinic seminary, Geniva' altogether thought it high time to put a stop to the practice whereby the *reish galuta'* appointed the principals of such institutions. The issue came to the boil when Mar 'Ukba' II designated one of his henchmen (Rav Ḥuna') as successor to Rav at the prestigious academy of Sura'. As protestations to rabbinical colleagues in *'Ereṣ Yisra'el* showed, Geniva' regarded the appointment as an improper encroachment on what was rightly the *keter torah*'s own preserve. Matters had to be rectified – if necessary, by a direct challenge to the Exilarch's authority.[44]

Rabbi Judah *ha-nasi'*

The three approaches here outlined were not pursued in strict sequence; neither did the sages of a particular generation unanimously select any particular course as part of their combined communal strategy. If anything, most rabbis at most periods seem to have been divided over the tactics to be adopted towards their local representatives of the *keter malkhut*; and in both *Bavel* and *'Ereṣ Yisra'el* sometimes to have coalesced into rival camps on the issue. Some configurations might have conformed to personal and administrative affiliations. Rabbis linked by marriage to the families of the *nasi'* or *reish galuta'*, it has been suggested, were more likely to advocate a policy of co-operation with their respective regimes. Conversely, those without judicial office claimed to be more free to express whatever feelings their consciences may have dictated than were those of their colleagues who, because they had stooped to accept such benefices, were professionally tied to the Patriarch's or Exilarch's own *camarilla*.[45] Nevertheless, those do not appear to have been the only determinants of rabbinic attitudes towards the *keter malkhut* in every case. As the contrast between R. Yoḥanan and Reish Laqish showed, much depended upon contrasting personal dispositions towards authority in any form; presumably, too, much also depended on individual readings of Israel's past. Not all of the biases apparent in contemporary Biblical exegesis need necessarily have been determined by current attitudes towards contemporary incumbents of the *keter malkhut*. On the contrary, in some cases, Biblical exegesis might have inspired those attitudes and generated their articulation.[46]

More amenable to synoptic analysis are the possible circumstances affecting the dominance of any particular rabbinic strategy at a specific juncture in time. At this level of enquiry, two considerations seem to have been especially influential: one external to the framework of the three *ketarim*, the other a consequence of its own internal dynamics. The first reflected Israel's situation of political subjugation; when gauging the extent to which they might assert their corporate will on Patriarchs and Exilarchs, rabbis in *'Ereṣ Yisra'el* and *Bavel* had carefully to assess the possible reactions of their respective gentile suzerains, and the degree to which the latter might – or might not – be willing to sanction a realignment in Jewish internal affairs. Blatant 'usurpation' was thus only a viable option for the rabbis during the very earliest stages of the *nesi'ut* and *r'eshut ha-golah*, when the form of Jewry's internal government was still sufficiently experimental to encourage the hope that the Roman and Persian authorities might permit an alternative. Even then, its risks probably outweighed its value. In Alon's reading, it was after assessing this consideration that Gamli'el II's rabbinic opponents concluded that discretion was the better part of valour, and therefore agreed to his re-instatement as *nasi'*. On the other hand, when embarking on his plan of campaign against Mar 'Ukba', Geniva' seems entirely to have misjudged the discretionary powers which the Sasanian government was prepared to grant to *rashei galuta'* – and to have paid for his error of judgement with his life.[47]

Rabbinic sources are far more explicit in their discussions of the intra-Jewish considerations which influenced rabbinic policy towards Patriarchal and Exilarchic representatives of the *keter malkhut*. Indeed, they often give the impression that the relationship was almost entirely determined by the sheer force of the relevant *dramatis personae*. As much is most pointedly illustrated by the manner in which they portray the life and times of the *nasi'* Rabbi Judah [Yehudah] I (late second and early third centuries C.E.). Undoubtedly the single most important personality in the entire talmudic corpus, Judah is in rabbinic literature often referred to simply as '*Rabi*' (alternatively, '*rabenu ha-qadosh*': 'our holy teacher'), an appellation which clearly acknowledges that he stands in a class quite different from either his predecessors or descendants in the post-Destruction *nesi'ut*. Retrospectively, he was to be placed on a par with some of the greatest men of Jewish history (TB *Megilah* 11a); in his own lifetime he is reported to have been associated with the fulfilment of Israel's messianic hopes (TJ *Shabbat* 16:1 and TB *R'osh ha-Shanah* 25a). Judah himself seems to have encouraged at least some of those sentiments, not least when reportedly advocating the abrogation of one day of national mourning (the fast of the ninth of Av; TJ *Megilah* 1:6; *Ta'anit* 4:9) and bathing on another (the 17th of Tammuz; TB *Megilah* 5b).

In the annals of rabbinic Judaism, Judah's claim to immortality most obviously rests on the enormity of his personal contribution to the final redaction of the *Mishnah* and its presentation as an authoritative basis of all subsequent halakhic rulings. But those achievements must surely be considered as much the consequence of his extraordinary stature as their cause. Judah I, we know, was not the only *tana'* of his age to recognise the need for a systematic classification of rabbinic traditions; neither was he the first of that circle to attempt their codification.[48] His uniqueness lay elsewhere: in the confidence with which he mastered, marshalled and deployed the available sources; and in the authority with which he determined to exercise his own critical judgement in their selection, emendation and presentation within the framework of an anthology which (it has been argued) was originally designed to serve pedagogic purposes. Those were the qualities which ultimately ensured that his codex would become far more than a mere summary of previously scattered rulings. As early as the sixth century it was apparent that Judah had in fact purposefully set out to adjudicate the Oral Law, and thereby determine the *halakhah*'s future development.[49]

In accounting for the benchmark status of R. Judah's *Mishnah*, talmudic traditions tend to emphasise the quality of the intellectual criteria which he brought to that undertaking. Particularly stressed are the excellence and number of his teachers; his own mastery of the *halakhah*; and his immense application to his studies (e.g. TB *Ketubot* 104a). Necessary though these attributes undoubtedly must have been as prerequisites to embarking upon the enterprise, it is clear that of themselves they did not guarantee its success. For R. Judah's anthology to win acceptance, the standard of its scholarship had to be buttressed by the author's administrative skill and political clout. As it was, some of Judah's younger colleagues in *'Ereṣ Yisra'el* were apparently so dissatisfied with his compilation that they thought it necessary to compile and/or preserve a more comprehensive *Tosefta'* (lit. 'supplement').[50] Their criticisms would undoubtedly have been more severe – and more widely-shared – had R. Judah not managed to convince his audiences, and particularly the Akiban segments of those audiences, that his substantial political credentials outweighed his marginal scholastic shortcomings. Whatever *Mishnah*'s alleged faults, it possessed the supreme advantage of bearing the imprint of a figure whose ability to enforce its dictates was far greater than any which his contemporaries could possibly have mustered.

Third- and fourth-century amora'ic traditions put their finger on this point when comparing Judah *ha-nasi* to Moses, arguing that the singularity of both men lay in their rare possession of both '[*torah*] wisdom and greatness' (*ḥokhmah u-gedulah*).[51] Translated into the terms suggested by the paradigm of the three *ketarim*, such sayings could be taken to mean that Judah in effect combined the virtues intrinsic to high office in the domains of both the *torah* and the *malkhut*. It was that assimilation of two symbolic systems, creating what was virtually a hybrid Caesaropapism, which explains the quite extraordinary range of his powers and prerogatives. The distinction of Judah's *nesi'ut* did not reside solely in the warmth of his relationships with the great and near-great of Roman high society, nor only in the intensity of his personal insistence on the maintenance of an unabashedly regal appearance and life-style.[52] What also set him apart from his predecessors and successors in the Patriarchate was his consummate skill in manipulating relationships with the rabbis of his times. It was thus that he attained and retained a mastery from which the supremacy of his office, and the acceptance of his *Mishnah*, seemed naturally to flow.

Arguably, Judah I was not solely responsible for that shift in the balance between the *ketarim* of the *torah* and the *malkhut*. In all probability, it was also encouraged by his Roman overlords. Fortuitously, Judah's accession to office coincided with the run of Imperial enactments which announced the Severans' decision to pursue an active policy of Roman-Jewish rapprochement.[53] From the *nesi'ut*'s point of view, far more important than the revocation of previously issued punishments were the decisions to provide Jewish courts with Imperial backing and to allow them to adjudicate cases involving capital punishment. As the principal of such courts, the *nasi'* was bound to benefit from the new status. Therein lay the silver lining in the clouds of crisis which increasingly affected the Empire as the third century progressed. 'With the attention of the Roman administration directed elsewhere', the Patriarch was left free to extend his control over many of the Jews in the Galilee 'in much the same way and for the same local cultural reasons as other leaders of eastern states at the same time'.[54]

Even more of the credit for Judah's success must be attributed to his father, Simeon II, from whom he inherited his office and much of his wealth. In the difficult aftermath of the Bar Kokhba' revolt, Simeon had managed both to mend relations with the Roman authorities and to augment the family fortunes, thereby consolidating the twin pillars of material power which Judah himself was to exploit to such good purpose. Moreover, he had deliberately embarked upon a policy of conciliation *vis-à-vis* his rabbis: appointing R. Mei'ir as *ḥakham* (TB *Horayot* 14a; TJ *Bikurim* 3:3); agreeing not to punish elders with the ban (*nidui*; TJ *Mo'ed Qaṭan* 3:1); and – perhaps most perspicaciously of all – despatching Judah himself to the 'Akiban' schools headed by rabbis 'El'azar b. Shamua', Simeon bar Yoh'ai and Judah b. 'Il'ai.[55] In sum, Simeon had not only managed to neutralise much of what Baumgarten has called the 'Akiban Opposition' to the *nesi'ut*, he had also re-constituted the office as the focus of all indigenous authority in both Roman and Jewish eyes.

Judah I's distinction lay in the energy and decisiveness with which he built upon these foundations. Driven by the twin furies of supreme self-confidence and urgent national necessity, he pressed home his advantages in a style which became unabashedly assertive. Much though he respected and honoured the rabbis and their scholarship, he was determined to ensure his own independence of their favour. One method of attaining that goal was to cultivate other loyalties and allegiances; non-rabbinical local magnates are reported to have been particularly impressed by his Roman contacts and, consequently, to have been the more easily enticed into the *nasi*'s court with the promise of honours, appointments and dynastic alliances.[56]

An alternative policy was to stretch his inherited Patriarchal prerogatives to their limits (and often beyond), thereby redefining the conventions of both permissible executive action and valid legislative discretion. In that, too, Judah I went further than any of his predecessors. Pleading impending economic calamity, he exempted several towns from tithes by excluding them from the boundaries of purity ascribed to *'Ereṣ Yisra'el*; arguing the existence of new political circumstances, he also reformed procedures regulating the announcement and proclamation of the new moon; stressing the need for bureaucratic rationalisation, he insisted that the *sanhedrin* accommodate the location of its sessions to changes in the residence of the *nasi'* and that the *beit din* acknowledge the Patriarchal right of supervision over the various communities of *'Ereṣ Yisra'el* and their religious and judicial institutions.[57] Possibly on the same administrative grounds, he may even have challenged the sacrosanct right of freedom of instruction, decreeing that: 'Pupils are not to be taught in the market place' (TB *Mo'ed Qaṭan* 16a–b).

It is hardly surprising to learn that several of these measures aroused severe opposition, in the face of which Judah occasionally thought it prudent to retract. Especially vociferous was rabbinic criticism of the unilateral manner whereby the Patriarch's decrees had been enacted. Some of the *nasi*'s opponents hinted at the charge that his courts were rigged (R. Simeon b. 'El'azar quoted in *Midrash Tana'im*, on Deut. 1:8); others that he 'honoured the rich' (TB *'Eruvin* 86a). That such comments managed to survive the censorship of the *nasi*'s own inner circle of supporters certainly attests to the depths of feelings which Judah's actions aroused during his lifetime, and continued to generate long after his death.[58] It does not, however, in any way diminish the extent of his success in pushing through his programme and thereby spreading the net of his authority throughout *'Ereṣ Yisra'el* – and even to *Bavel*. Ultimately, indeed, Judah managed to win the support of the vast majority of his rabbinical colleagues in both localities and, by stages to have conciliated all but a minority of his opponents. Perhaps the only person permanently to resist his will was the widow of one of his long-standing antagonists, 'El'azar b. R. Simeon bar Yoḥ'ai, who spurned his offer of marriage by caustically enquiring whether: 'a vessel which has been used for a sacred purpose might be used for a profane one?' (TJ *Shabbat* 10:5). Otherwise, however, Judah's success seems to have been complete.

Particularly was this so in his insistence that rabbinical appointments were to be considered an exclusively Patriarchal prerogative (TB *Sanhedrin* 13b). With that rule firmly in place, he set about displaying a judicious blend of the carrot of his munificence and the stick of his displeasure. Sages who were prepared to accept his authority served in renumerative offices and enjoyed the *nasi*'s own bounty. (TB *'Eruvin* 73a; *Beṣah* 28a). Those who opposed his will were made to realise that their chances of advancement, and hence of economic security, were minimal (TJ *Mo'ed Qaṭan* 3:1 and *Ta'anit* 4:2). One indication of the success of those tactics is to be found in the fact that Judah I never had to face the sort of rabbinic conspiracy which had disconcerted his father and grandfather. He even managed to ignore the earlier Patriarchal agreement to appoint a *ḥakham* and *'av beit din*, neither of which offices were filled in his own lifetime. Nothing could better illustrate the fact that, by appearing to ingratiate himself into the *keter torah*, the *nasi'* had in fact divided that estate, and in so doing established the supremacy – at least in his own day – of the *keter malkhut*.

The change in tone: operation and ordination

In a way, Judah I seems to have succeeded too much. The system of centralised rule which he created under the aegis of the *keter malkhut* was too dependent upon the force of his own personality to last. Indeed, if we are to accept the authenticity of his political will, Judah himself seems to have realised as much. According to that document, Judah did not advocate that the plenitude of his powers be automatically passed on to his own sons, either individually or in concert. Instead, 'Simeon, my [second] son', he is reported to have decreed, 'shall be *ḥakham*; Gamli'el my [eldest] son shall be *nasi'*; Ḥanina' ben Ḥama, shall preside [*yeishev ba-r'osh*]'.[59]

Notwithstanding this proposed division of powers, the nominal prestige of the *nesi'ut* was not immediately impaired. Measured by the yardstick of recognition by gentile suzerains, Judah's authority may even have been surpassed by that of his grandson (Judah II '*Yehudah nesi'ah*' fl. 230–70). Particular significance has in this regard been attached to the series of Imperial proclamations (and especially those issued by Constantine in 330, by Julian III in 363 and by Flavius Arcadius, the first 'eastern' Emperor, in 397) which specify the supremacy of the *nasi*'s political station. Even when tempered by Church criticism, all confirm that incumbents of the Patriarchal office were to be regarded as the principal representatives of Jewish interests throughout the Empire *vis-à-vis* the Roman and Byzantine authorities. In deference to their rank, they could despatch *apostoloi* abroad, enjoy tax concessions and deploy their own *gendarmerie*.[60] Thus defined, the status and powers of the *nesi'im* in *'Ereṣ Yisra'el* remained equivalent to those of their *keter malkhut* counterparts who occupied the Exilarchate in *Bavel*.

In several important respects, however, the appearance of institutional continuity was deceptive. Under Judah's successors, the effective **internal** power of the office began to decline. The predominant picture to emerge from recent studies of their franchise is one of continuing social prestige and economic strength, but of steadily contracting halakhic veneration. As early as the beginning of the fourth century, the *keter malkhut* could no longer claim a right to exclude representatives of the *keter torah* from several of the spheres of Jewish life which it had once considered its own exclusive preserves. In his own day, Judah I had managed to bestride both domains and thus – even when furthering the sectional interests of rabbis and promoting them to positions of local influence – to ensure that they were always subordinate to his will. But the communal consequences were reaped by his successor *nesi'im*, the majority of whom in any case seem to have lacked the scholastic attainments required in order to pronounce and enact their own *taqanot*.[61] Confronted with a rabbinate which – quite apart from its legal expertise – had by now come to enjoy administrative experience, later *nesi'im* possessed only the outer shells and forms of their domain's governmental authority. As far as the inner life of Jewry was concerned, the hegemony of the *keter malkhut* was suffering steady erosion and increasingly vociferous review. Although rabbis did still recognise the nominal rights of their *nasi'* (and, together with other prominent families, continued to vie for his attention and favour), they were no longer prepared to sanction exclusive Patriarchal control over the complete gamut of social and administrative affairs. To quote Levine:

> The Nasi was now challenged on issues directly affecting Jewish communal life. Social and economic policy, and not just strictly religious issues, were subject to scrutiny. This is a far cry from the Patriarchal–rabbinic disputes of earlier generations which, in the main, revolved around internal issues of the academy.[62]

Reports in talmudic literature testify to confrontations between rabbis and later *nesi'im* on a number of issues, prominent among which were: the promulgation of fast days in times of drought, calendarisation and the creeping 'Hellenisation' said to have become characteristic of the office. Ultimately, however, the litmus test of relations between the *keter torah* and the *keter malkhut* in *'Ereṣ Yisra'el* became the criteria and manner of Patriarchal appointments to judicial offices. No rabbi could ever hope to pose as a communal magistrate in the full sense of the term without verifiable proof of his authority to try cases involving the possible imposition of fines (TB *Sanhedrin* 13b); but the most desirable of judicial positions were precisely those hardest to come by. Pressures on the job-market first became evident at the turn of the third century when Judah I deliberately (and perhaps not altogether involuntarily) imposed a *numerus clausus* on the quantity of his judicial appointees; the shortage became acute when his successors, in an attempt to supplement their own shrinking revenues during a period of rampant inflation, began to sell such offices as were available to the highest bidders.[63] In both cases, rabbis found themselves being squeezed out of benefices which they had come to regard as properly their own. To add insult to injury, they were being supplanted by rivals who, their wealth apart, appeared to possess no obvious qualifications for their tasks. Indeed, according to the (admittedly tendentious) pen-portraits compiled by the rabbis themselves, the new appointees were an odious amalgam of place-seekers and hacks, altogether devoid of even the most rudimentary intellectual and moral attributes which Israel's judges were expected to possess.[64]

The rabbis' initial reaction, as expressed in reports of their opposition to Judah II between c. 230 and 270,[65] was to revert to the strategy previously designated 'attrition'. Reish Laqish, not unexpectedly, pitched himself with characteristic asperity into the very forefront of that particular campaign (TJ *Sanhedrin* 2:1); only marginally less insulting was the behaviour of Yossi of Beth Ma'on and of R. Yonah. During the course of a public sermon delivered in dangerous proximity to the current seat of the *nesi'ut* at Tiberias, the former is reported to have pointedly denigrated 'those of the house of the Patriarch who appropriate everything' (Genesis *Rabbah* 80:1). The latter apparently washed his hands of the same crowd when declining nomination to their ranks (TJ *Bikurim* 3:3). Towards the end of the third century, however, disdain was giving way to more forthright tendencies. Rabbis then advanced from occasional and peripheral comments on the personalities of Patriarchal appointees to concerted and direct attacks on the principle of the *nasi*'s unilateral voice in their selection. Claiming that scholars deserved at least an equal voice in ordination procedures, representatives of the *keter torah* thus replaced a strategy of 'attrition' with one of putative 'usurpation'.

One striking testimony to the manner in which this was so is preserved in a report found in TJ *Sanhedrin* 1:2, where R. Ba' ('Abba'; late third century) recollects three distinct stages in the local evolution of the process of appointment (*minui*):

Initially [a phrase which seems to refer to the period between c. 80 and c. 130 C. E.] each [of the sages] would appoint [*memaneh*] his own students. For example, Rabban Yoḥanan ben Zak'ai appointed R. Leizer ['Eli'ezer] and R. Joshua; and R. Joshua R. 'Aqiva'; and R. 'Aqiva' R. Mei'ir and R. Simeon [...] Subsequently [presumably mid-second century], they imparted honour to this [the *nasi*'s] house. They said: 'Any appointment issued by a *beit din* without the sanction of the *nasi'* is invalid [*'ein minuyo minui*]; but appointment by a *nasi'* without the sanction of a *beit din* is valid.' Subsequently [mid-third century?] they re-decreed [*ḥazru we-hitqinu*] that a *beit din* may appoint only with the sanction of the *nasi'*, and the *nasi'* may appoint only with the sanction of a *beit din*.

Garbled though this account might be in some details,[66] the importance of its general message remains unimpaired. As Waharftig has shown,[67] the recollection must be considered an authentic testimony to the development of a procedure which, because it affected so crucial a facet of communal life, had necessarily to reflect the relative standings of those by whom it was controlled. 'Decentralisation' (Waharftig's classification of R. 'Abba's first period), was a consequence of the institutional weakness which characterised the *nesi'ut* during the era of Yavneh. 'Centralisation', on the other hand, was subsequently facilitated by the growing strength of that office and constituted one of its expressions. As we might expect, Judah I had set the tone. It was he who selectively specified those of his prerogatives which he was prepared to impart to his chosen agents; and his *Mishnah* which contains no mention of the required presence of three persons who were themselves ordinands at the induction of a new appointee (which seems to have been prior convention).[68] To these items must be added other innovations which, although less explicitly attributed to Judah's own legislation, reveal unmistakable marks of his influence. In no source relating to events prior to his *nesi'ut* are any references made to a formal list of Patriarchal candidates for office (the *pitqah* in TJ *Bikurim* 3:3) or to different grades amongst potential and actual ordinands.[69]

The third stage delineated by R. 'Abba' departed from those guidelines in almost every important respect. Acting singly or as a collegium, rabbis refused to categorise judicial appointments as Patriarchal gifts; instead, they went far towards subsuming the entire process of *minui* within the framework of their own scholastic authority.[70] At the same time, they also began to intrude upon other sectors of the *nasi*'s former preserves. In quick succession, rabbis took upon themselves the authority to apppoint local *parnasim* and/or *archons* (significantly, sometimes with the admonition of Proverbs 8:15–16; see, e.g. the address reported to have been given by R. Ḥaggai of Tiberias [fl. 280–320] in TJ *Pe'ah* 8:7); to supervise the management of relations between *'Ereṣ Yisra'el* and Jewish communities in the Diaspora; and – not least significantly – even to conduct intercessionary *pourparlers* with resident Roman governors. One outstanding illustration is provided by the activities of R. 'Abbahu of Caesarea, altogether a highly politicised individual with cosmopolitan interests. But the instance was not unique. Consciously or otherwise, 'Abbahu's example was followed by rabbis Ḥanina' bar Ḥama' and Joshua b. Levi, who paid formal visits to the Roman pro-consul in Sephoris and by rabbis Jonah and Yossie, heads of the *beit wa'ad* in Tiberias, who (perhaps in 361) travelled to Antioch to meet with Ursicinus.[71]

The shift thus proclaimed in the balance of forces between the *keter torah* and the *keter malkhut* was neither temporary nor localised. Notwithstanding the revival of Patriarchal prominence immediately after the advent of Christian Rome, it persisted throughout the fourth century, thereby (according to some accounts) contributing to the publication of a fixed Jewish calendar and the redaction of the Jerusalem Talmud. Although the need to preserve a façade of unity did prevent a complete break between the parties, the Patriarchate was now decidedly the weaker. It was this enfeeblement, together with the general weakness of the Jewish community of *'Ereṣ Yisra'el* early in the fifth century, which contributed to the collapse of the Patriarchate under Imperial onslaught in 429.[72]

For all the differences between the two regions, there are indications that something like the same process was simultaneously under way in *Bavel*. Admittedly, and as Beer points out, the rabbinic criticisms of Exilarchs reported in the Talmud seem to have been guarded and reserved. Restricted almost entirely to private murmurings about the religious laxity, moral shortcomings and administrative cruelty of the *reish galuta*'s 'household', they stopped significantly short of the direct and public attacks on the *nasi*'s personal comportment so characteristic of their parallels in *'Ereṣ Yisra'el*.[73] Nevertheless, there too the change in relations between the two *ketarim* – although perhaps more subtle and less dramatic – is equally noticeable. As much is indicated by the state of affairs at the very end of the period covered by the Babylonian Talmud's chronicle. The academies, rather than the *reish galuta'*, were then issuing calendrial proclamations in accordance with regulations ordained in *'Ereṣ Yisra'el*, and the Exilarch Ḥuna' b. Nathan was invoking the authority of decisions reached by Rav 'Ashi, the long-time principal at Sura' (TB *Giṭin* 59a). Equally indicative of the new state of affairs is the fact that the latter assumed the title of *Rabana'* (perhaps thereto reserved for the Exilarch alone) and, together with two colleagues, constituted an official delegation 'at the gate of the King Yazdeger's court' (TB *Ketubot* 61a).

Talmudic sources, characteristically silent on events outside their own inner world, provide no reliable indication of the extent to which the timing and pace of that development might have been affected by simultaneous changes in the wider fabric of the Sasanian Empire.[74] Perhaps there was no cause for them to look that far afield. Internal developments within Babylonian Jewry, particularly as they affected relations between rival representatives of the *keter malkhut* and the *keter torah*, had been sufficiently dramatic to provide their own impetus to substantial change. Indeed, they had on occasions approached the stage of open corporate warfare. It is difficult to believe that those 'servants' of the Exilarchs who disgraced and injured rabbis (and, apparently, were responsible for the deaths of two principals of Pumbedita's academy, Rabah bar Naḥmani in 330 and R. Zevid in 385)[75] were acting either unilaterally or against the express wishes of their political masters. Similarly, the impression conveyed by some of the rabbis' own responses (e.g. that of Rav Sheshet in TB *Giṭin* 67b) is that their insults were intended to strike at personages far more exalted than the *bei reish galuta'*, who were their formal targets.

In both franchises, it seems, positions had some time earlier begun to congeal. Ever conscious of their stirring pedigree and innate powers, *rashei galuta'* probably resented the manner in which rabbis – notwithstanding the 'conciliatory' policies pursued by Rav and Samuel and, thereafter, Rava' – had perceptibly tended to encroach upon a range of social and administrative issues which had conventionally been considered exclusive Exilarchic preserves. Conversely, and as in *'Ereṣ Yisra'el*, rabbinic representatives of the *keter torah* had become increasingly vociferous in the articulation of communal postulates which, they held, merely reflected the station in Jewish national life which their piety and learning had made their due. Both cases, moreover, were worked out against the backcloth of an even more striking development. By the latter half of the third century, in neither *Bavel* nor *'Ereṣ Yisra'el* did representatives of the *keter malkhut* possess the advantage of exclusive bureaucratic articulation; the institutional frameworks controlled by *nesi'im* and *rashei galuta* were no longer the only ones existing in the Jewish world. On the contrary, they had been supplemented – and in many vital respects superseded – by the academies of learning, which were far more decidedly under rabbinic sway. As the next chapter will demonstrate, the significance of that development can hardly be exaggerated. At the very least, it enabled representatives of the *keter torah* to cultivate their own sense of corporate identity. More extensively, it also furnished rabbis with the power-bases necessary for the implementation of their strategy of communal control.

NOTES

1. *Ha-Kohanim*, pp. 231–43.
2. Of *nasi'*; Beer, *R'eshut ha-Golah*, pp. 6–9.
3. Ultimately, *nesi'im* claimed descent from the distaff line of David and *r'ashei ha-golah* from the male branch. The relevant sources are dated and their authenticity discussed in Liver, *Toledot Beit David*, pp. 37–41. Possible motives for the different patrimonies are analysed in A.I. Baumgarten, 'Rabbi Judah I and his Opponents', *JSJ*, 12 (1982), pp. 145–9.
4. At most, rabbinic literature could apply to the *nasi'* some of Scripture's ordinances with respect to kings; e.g. (in midrashic context) Genesis *Rabbah* 80:1 and (with reference to the guilt offering required by Lev. 4:22) *Mishnah, Horayot* 3:3 and the similar text in *Tosefta'* idem 2:2. Significantly, however, none of the available references to the *nasi'* in the book of Ezekiel is put to any polemic use. See: D. Goodblatt, 'Ha-To'ar "Nasi'" we-ha-Reka' ha-Dati-'Idei'ologie Shel ha-Mered ha-Sheini', *Mered Bar-Kokhba': Meḥqarim Ḥadashim* (eds. A. Oppenheimer, U. Rappaport; Jerusalem, 1984), pp. 115–16 and notes 10–12. On the possible reasons for Bar Kokhba's adoption of the title *nasi'*, rather than *melekh*, see: D. Flusser, 'Two Notes on the Midrash on 2 Sam. vii', *IEJ*, 9 (1959), p. 107.
5. Beer, *R'eshut ha-Golah*, pp. 11–32. See also Neusner's conjecture that the Exilarchate was created by the Arsacid authorities some time after 70 C.E., mainly in order to counteract the influence of the Roman-dominated Patriarchate established in *'Ereṣ Yisra'el. Babylonian Jewry*, Vol. 1 (Leiden, 1965), pp. 67–70, 74–6.
6. D. Goodblatt, 'R'eishitah Shel ha-Nesi'ut ha-'Arṣi-Yisra'elit ha-Mukeret', *Meḥqarim be-Toledot 'Am Yisra'el we-'Ereṣ Yisra'el*, 4 (1978), pp. 89–102 and idem., 'Yehudei 'Ereṣ Yisra'el ba-Shanim 70–132', *Hisṭoriyah Shel 'Am Yisra'el*, Vol. 11 ('Yehudah we-Roma''; ed. U. Rappaport; Jerusalem, 1983), pp. 155–84. Goodblatt analyses – and rejects – all other conjectures submitted since Derenbourg's work first appeared, as well as the authenticity of the chronology of the *nesi'ut* recorded in TB *Shabbat* 15a.
7. All of which are collated, and said to prove the antiquity of the

post-Destruction office, in H.D. Mantel, 'The Title *Nasi* in Jewish Tradition', *Studies in the History of the Sanhedrin* (Cambridge, Mass., 1965), pp. 1–53.

8. This is true even if we discount their supposed descent from Hillel (which is nowhere attested in the earliest sources). See the analysis of TJ *Ta'anit* 4:2 and Genesis *Rabbah* 98:13 in J. Liver, *Toledot Beit David*, pp. 28–32.
9. Compare Goodblatt (above n. 6) with Safrai, 'Ha-Khronologiah Shel ha-Nesi'im', *Ereṣ Yisra'el we-Ḥakhamehah*, pp. 119, 121, and (on the 'annulment' of the dynastic principle on the death of Gamli'el II), Urbach, *Sages*, p. 604.
10. Again, a striking exception is H. Mantel, ''Al R'eishitah Shel R'eshut ha-Golah', *'Anshei Keneset ha-Gedolah* (Tel Aviv, 1983), pp. 227–9.
11. G. Widengren, 'The Status of the Jews in the Sassanian Empire', *Iranica Antiqua*, 1 (1961), pp. 117–61.
12. The incident, reported in *Seder 'Olam Zuṭa'*, is reconstructed by Widengren, op. cit., p. 144, although he doubts the authenticity and precision of the tradition.
13. M.D. Herr, 'The Historical Significance of the Dialogues between Jewish Sages and Roman Dignitaries', *Scripta Hierosolymitana*, 22 (ed. J. Heinemann and D. Noy; Jerusalem, 1971), pp. 123–50, demonstrates the range of philosophical topics covered in these exchanges, which were not limited (either before or after 135 C.E.) to the *nesi'im*. On contacts between *rashei galuta'* and local Babylonian authorities (which are less well documented), Beer, *R'eshut ha-Golah*, pp. 54–6.
14. Mantel, op. cit., pp. 175–253 and L.I. Levine, 'The Jewish Patriarch (Nasi) in Third Century Palestine', *ANRW* 19:2 (1979), pp. 649–88. Virtually mandatory in all reconstructions is Origen's famous description of the powers of the *nasi*': 'How great is the power wielded by the ethnarch, granted by Caesar. We who have experienced it know that he differs in no way from a king of a nation', Letter to Africanus (XIV).
15. Widengren, op. cit., pp. 140–1 and (on the *qamara'* as an artefact of office) D. Goodblatt, ''Al Sipur ha-"Qesher" Neged Raban Shim'on ben Gamli'el ha-Sheini', *Ẓion*, 49 (1984), pp. 353–4.
16. The debate is surveyed in Goodman, *State and Society*, pp. 113ff.
17. The Exilarchs' powers are best delineated in Beer, *R'eshut ha-Golah*, pp. 29ff; for the demarcations of the spheres of Jewish life in which they were most likely to intervene, see: J. Neusner, 'The Rabbi and the Jewish Community', *Talmudic Judaism in Sasanian Babylonia* (Leiden, 1966), pp. 104–5.
18. Mantel, *Sanhedrin*, pp. 179–84.
19. According to Levine, *Ma'amad ha-Ḥakhamim*, p. 89, the dictum attributed to Rav and Shemu'el in TB *Sanhedrin* 5a ('If a man wishes to be free of liability for judicial error, he should acquire permission from

the Exilarch') also applied, *mutatis mutandis*, in *'Ereṣ Yisra'el*. Compare, however, Neusner, *Talmudic Judaism in Sasasian Babylonia*, p. 103 fn. 35.

20. In addition to the example from *'Ereṣ Yisra'el* cited above, p. 169, see also (regarding *Bavel*), Neusner, op. cit., p. 130.
21. Specific instances are documented in M. Beer, 'Talmud Torah we-Derekh 'Ereṣ', *Bar-Ilan Annual*, 2 (1964), pp. 152–3.
22. Compare Alon, *Jews, Judaism* (Jerusalem, 1977), p. 315 fn. 4 and G. F. Moore, *Judaism in the First Centuries of the Christian Era: The Age of the Tannaim*, Vol. 3 (Oxford, 1927), pp. 15–17.
23. In death, as well as life. See, e.g., the analysis of the evidence provided by the Beth She'arim catacombs in Levine, *Ma'amad*, p. 120 and of the *halakhot* permitting *nesi'im* to be accorded 'royal' burials in Mantel, *Sanhedrin*, p. 243.
24. Goodman, *State and Society*, p. 113.
25. Neusner, *Babylonian Jewry*, Vol. 3, p. 61; for a more detailed review of R. Naḥman's prominence, based on a review of judicial proceedings recorded in the three TB *Bava'* tractates, see Y. Gafni, 'Ma'asei Beit Din be-Talmud Bavli – Ṣurot Sifrutiyot we-Hashlakhot Hisṭoriot', *PAAJR*, 49 (1982), pp. 31–6.
26. J. Neusner, *Judaism in Society: The Evidence of the Yerushalmi* (Chicago, 1983), pp. 177–97 emphasises and illustrates the extent to which that was so in *'Ereṣ Yisra'el* as well as *Bavel*. In a more rigorous analysis of the terms *paqad* and *hinhig* in the TJ, Y. Levine has shown that even during the third century, a period of particularly intensive rabbinic involvement in local affairs in *'Ereṣ Yisra'el*, rabbis exercised very few prerogatives independently of the *nasi'*. 'Ma'amad ha-Ḥahkhamim be-'Ereṣ-Yisra'el ba-Me'ah ha-Shelishit', *WCJS*, 8 (2), 1982, pp. 5–8.
27. Compare Alon's reference to 'a diumvirate, or perhaps even a triumvirate', *Jews in Their Land*, I, p. 321; and Levine's strictures in 'The Jewish Patriarch', p. 681.
28. Neusner, *Talmudic Judaism in Sasanian Babylonia*, pp. 115–18 and *Babylonian Jewry*, Vol. 3, pp. 93–4.
    For Judah *ha-nasi*'s messianic projections see below pp. 196–7. That the Exilarch's Davidic descent could also give rise to messianic expectations, at least amongst his own relatives, is indicated by R. Naḥman's statement in TB *Sanhedrin* 98b and the application to Mar 'Ukba' (3rd century) of Jer. 21:12 in TB *Shabbat* 55a.
29. A. J. Saldarini, 'The End of the Rabbinic Chain of Tradition', *JBL*, 93 (1974), pp. 97–106, also comparing *'Avot* with the two versions in ARN. Cf. L. Finkelstein's earlier analysis in 'Introductory Study to Pirke Avot', *JBL*, 57 (1938), p. 27.
30. M. Beer 'Kavod u-Biqoret', *PAAJR*, 38–9 (1972), pp. 50, 56–7, points

out that the Patriarch was generally far more closely associated with the interests and modes of the *keter torah* than was the Exilarch. Nevertheless, local criticism of the former was usually far more direct than were the oblique attacks on the *bei reish galuta'*, (Exilarch's court) in *Bavel*.

31. Especially Deut. 31:7 and 31:23 (see TB *Sanhedrin* 8a). Analysis of this and other texts in M. Aberbach & L. Smolar, 'Jeroboam and Solomon: Rabbinic Interpretations', *JQR*, 59 (1969), pp. 118–32.
32. Genesis *Rabbah* 97:2; cited in R. Kimelman, 'The Conflict between R. Yoḥanan and Resh Laqish on the Supremacy of the Patriarchate', *WCJS*, 7 (3), 1981, p. 3.
33. Alon, *Jews in Their Land*, Vol. 1, pp. 107–18.
34. A.I. Baumgarten, 'The Akiban Opposition', *HUCA*, 50 (1979), pp. 179–97, suggesting that similar motives might have lain behind subsequent meetings (also attended by persons identifiable as 'Akibans') at Yavneh or 'Usha'.
35. On dynastic marriages in *'Ereṣ Yisra'el*, Levine, *Ma'amad*, p. 129. On the attribution to the *r'osh ha-golah* of the precedence over a high priest traditionally reserved for a king; Beer, *R'eshut ha-Golah*, p. 171.
36. Notably on the part of R. Judah bar 'Il'ai, whose relations with Simeon II were particularly close; Levine, *Ma'amad*, p. 105.
37. Neusner, *Babylonian Jewry*, Vol. 2, pp. 92–125. Moreover, Samuel's example was emulated by Rava', whose administrative contacts with the Exilarch during his headship of the Maḥoza' academy are frequently alluded to (see the sources cited in Beer, *R'eshut ha-Golah*, p. 105 n. 44).
38. R. Kimelman, 'R. Yoḥanan u-Ma'amad ha-Rabanut Bitqufat ha-Talmud', *Shenaṭon ha-Mishpaṭ ha-'Ivri*, 9 (1983), pp. 354–8.
39. For *Bavel*: Beer, 'Kavod u-Biqoret', pp. 50–8; for examples in *'Ereṣ Yisra'el*: Aberbach & Smolar, op. cit., p. 125.
40. E.E. Urbach, 'Ha-Melukhah ha-Miqra'it be-'Einei Ḥazal', *Sefer Seligman*, Vol. 1 (ed. J. Zakovitz, et al.; Jerusalem, 1983), pp. 439–51.
41. 'By me [i.e. the *torah*] kings reign and princes decree what is just.' Sensitive to the need for a suitable Biblical retort, Exilarchs cited Jeremiah 30:21: 'And their nobles shall be of themselves and their governor shall proceed from the midst of them.' See, e.g., R. Naḥman b. Jacob in TB *Sanhedrin* 98b.
42. Relevant texts are analysed in Alon, *Jews in Their Land*, Vol. I, pp. 317–21 and R. Goldenberg, 'The Deposition of Rabban Gamaliel II: An Examination of the Sources', *JJS*, 23 (1972), pp. 167–90.
43. That, at least, is the impression given by TB *Horayot* 13b–14a. Note, however, the critical comments in D. Goodblatt, ''Al Sipur ha-''Qesher'' Neged Raban Shim'on ben Gamli'el ha-Sheini', *Zion*, 49 (1984), pp. 349–74.
44. TB *Giṭin* 31b and 62a; compare the reconstructions in M. Beer, 'Rivo

Shel Geniva' be-Mar 'Uqba', *Tarbitz*, 31 (1962), pp. 281–6, and Neusner, *Babylonian Jewry*, Vol. 3, pp. 75–81.

45. On rabbis who (like R. Yoḥanan) were considered *debei nesi'ah*; see Levine, *Ma'amad*, pp. 104–5 and, for other patterns of alignment, his 'The Jewish Patriarch', p. 608.
46. A point made to me by Professor I. Twersky; see also A. Büchler, 'The Conspiracy of R. Nathan and R. Meir against the Patriarch Simon ben Gamaliel', *Studies in Jewish History* (eds. I. Brodie and J. Rabbinowitz; Oxford, 1956), pp. 160–78.
47. On the 'public interest' which induced a compromise with Gamli'el: Alon, *Jews in Their Land*, Vol. I, p. 320; on Iranian support for Geniva's execution (TB *Giṭin* 7a), Neusner, op. cit., p. 81.
48. Note, particularly, the (perhaps conciliatory) credit which Judah himself reportedly gave R. 'Aqiva': ARN 'A' 18 (ed. Schechter, p. 67). In general, Urbach, *Ha-Halakhah*, pp. 184–91.
49. A. Goldberg, 'Darko Shel R. Yehudah ha-Nasi', be-Sidur ha-Mishnah', *Tarbitz*, 28 (1959), pp. 260–70.
50. On the role of rabbis Ḥiyya' and Hoshaiyah in the latter compilation: D. Weiss Halivni, 'The Reception Accorded to Rabbi Judah's Mishnah', *Jewish and Christian Self-Definition*, Vol. 2 (ed. E. P. Sanders, et al., Phila. 1981), pp. 206ff. Also noted is the fact that the spread of R. Judah's *Mishnah* was slower in *'Ereṣ Yisra'el* than in *Bavel* and the extent to which some of its decisions were neatly side-stepped by later *'amora'im*.
51. TB *Giṭin* 59a. In his remarks on the parallel in TB *Sanhedrin* 36a, R. Solomon b. Isaac (*Rashi*, 1040–1105; the greatest of all medieval commentators on the Talmud) adds: 'Moses was superior to all Israel in *malkhut* and *torah*, so was *Rabi* [Judah I] in the *nesi'ut* and *torah*.'
52. Avi-Yonah, *Jews Under Roman and Byzantine Rule*, pp. 57–60.
53. For the chronology: Levine, 'The Jewish Patriarch', pp. 655–6 and 685–6.
54. Goodman, *State and Society*, p. 116.
55. All identified as 'Akibans'. On education as 'the functional equivalent of a dynastic marriage': A. I. Baumgarten, 'The Politics of Reconciliation: The Education of R. Judah the Prince', *Jewish and Christian Self-Definition*, pp. 213–25. On Simeon's success compare Avi-Yonah, op. cit., p. 57 and Y. L. Levine, 'Tequfato Shel Rabi Yehudah ha-Nasi'', *Ereṣ Yisra'el, mei-Ḥurban Bayit Sheini we-'Ad ha-Kibush ha-Muslemi*, Vol. 1 (eds. Z. Baras, et al; Jerusalem, 1982), pp. 102–3.
56. E. E. Urbach, 'Class Status and Leadership in the World of the Palestinian Sages', *Proceedings of the Israel Academy of Sciences and Humanities*, Vol. 2 (Jerusalem, 1968), pp. 70–4.
57. Respectively: TJ *Demai* 2:1 (and Avi-Yonah, *Jews Under Roman and Byzantine Rule*, pp. 104–5); TJ *R'osh ha-Shanah* 2:1; and Urbach, 'Class Status', p. 70.

58. A.I. Baumgarten, 'Rabbi Judah I and his Opponents', *JSJ*, 12 (1982), pp. 135–72 shows that some anti-Patriarchal sentiments, based on criticism of Judah's actions, can occasionally be seen to have persisted for two generations. Some of the opposition literature might also have been more systematically preserved. Baumgarten, 'The Akiban Opposition', *HUCA*, 50 (1974), p. 192, also cites Lieberman's comment that *Sifrei Zuṭa'* was 'definitely edited by a *tanna* who objected to the school of R. Judah'.
59. TB *Ketubot* 103b; cf. the version in TJ *Ta'anit* 4:2. For interpretations of these passages, and especially of the titles referred to, see Mantel, *Sanhedrin*, pp. 133–4, 206–12 and Levine, *Ma'amad*, pp. 45–6. Ḥanina' b. Ḥama's position is particularly curious; it is not clear whether the reference was to the presidency of the academy of the *sanhedrin*, or simply reflected his primacy amongst potential ordinands (a primacy which Ḥanina' himself denied; he deferred to his older colleague, R. 'Afes). Whichever the case, it is noteworthy that Ḥanina' was not related to the *nasi'*, and had not been ordained during Judah's life-time.
60. For analysis of the relevant records preserved in the 'Codex Theodosianus', see A. Linder, *The Jews in Roman Imperial Legislation* (Jerusalem, 1988), pp. 96–100 and 129–63.
61. One indicator has been discerned in the decreasing number of *halakhot* which the TB and TJ cite in the names of individual *nesi'im*. The decline begins in the era of Judah II but gains momentum with Judah III (Judah *nesi'ah ha-sheini*; fl. 270–310) and Judah IV (*nesi'ah ha-shelishi*; fl. 320–40), the last Patriarch whom talmudic literature cites by name. For precise counts see: B. Rosenfeld, 'Mashber ha-Nesi'ut be-'Ereṣ Yisra'el ba-Me'ah ha-4 la-Sefirah', *Zion*, 53 (1988), pp. 240–2.
62. Levine, 'The Jewish Patriarch', pp. 684–5.
63. S. Lieberman, 'Palestine in the Third and Fourth Centuries', *JQR*, 36 (1946), pp. 361–2; compare the rationale behind Judah's belated advice to his son to appoint a large number of communal functionaries simultaneously. TJ *Ta'anit* 4:2.
64. Avi-Yonah, *Jews Under Roman and Byzantine Rule*, p. 119 shows how rabbis often adduced Biblical verses (Exodus 20:23; Isaiah 1:15; Habbakuk 2:19) to illustrate the failings of the new appointees. Further details in Alon, 'Those Appointed for Money', *Jews, Judaism*, pp. 374–434.
65. Catalogued in A. Marmorstein, 'L'Opposition contre le Patriarche Juda II', *REJ*, 64 (1912), pp. 59–66.
66. Particularly regarding the first stage; see, e.g., Levine, 'The Patriarch', pp. 666–8.
67. S. Waharftig, 'Ha-Semikhah Bizman ha-Talmud', *Sinai*, 45 (1959), pp. 140–76; superseding A. Burnstein, 'Mishpaṭ ha-Semikhah ve-Qoroteihah', *Ha-Tequfah*, 4 (1919), pp. 394–426 and H. Albeck,

'Semikhah u-Minui u-Veit Din', *Zion*, 8 (1943), pp. 85–93 (both of which he cites) and J. Newman, *Semikhah (Ordination): A Study of its Origin, History and Function in Rabbinic Literature* (Manchester, 1950), which he ignores.

68. On the first see Waharftig, pp. 154–5, who notes the exclusion from Rav's powers an authorisation to permit firstlings (see also the reference to this as a Patriarchal prerogative in TB *Yoma'* 78a); on the second, Newman, pp. 4–5; comparing *Mishnah, Sanhedrin* 1:3 with the *beraitah* quoted in both TJ and TB.
69. Signified by the different titles of *rabi; mumḥe le-rabim; mumḥe mipi beit din;* and *zaqen*. Waharftig, pp. 150–2. Cf., Newman, pp. 51–7, Albeck, p. 87 and Mantel, *Sanhedrin*, p. 215.
70. Waharftig, p. 168.
71. TJ *Berakhot* 5:1 (But cf. Lieberman, op. cit., p. 341 n. 89), and – on 'Abbahu – Levine, 'R. Abbahu of Caesarea', pp. 67–76.
72. Rosenfeld, 'Ha-Mashber', pp. 254–5; see also Avi-Yonah, *Jews Under Roman & Byzantine Rule*, pp. 225–9.
73. Beer, *R'eshut ha-Golah*, pp. 179–84, suggests that the reasons for the differences lie in the fact that, unlike the *reish galuta'*, the *nasi'* was in any case regarded as a member of the rabbis' own fraternity. Consequently, they probably expected from him a higher degree of conformity.
74. Neusner, *Babylonian Jewry*, Vol. 4, pp. 76–7 suggests that:

    > From Shapur I's death, in 273, to the end of the minority of Shapur II, in about 325, the central government was distracted by, amongst other things, disastrous foreign wars, the suppression of the Manichaeans, dynastic struggles every few years, and finally the centrifugal effects of the weak regency.

75. The incidents are alluded to, respectively, in TB *'Avodah Zarah* 38b and *Bava' Meṣi'a* 86a (even though the latter source does not explicitly identify the informer as an agent of the Exilarch, Beer, [*R'eshut ha-Golah*, pp. 223–4] skilfully applies the principle of *cui bono* to indicate the latter's responsibility). Only marginally less shocking is the bodily harm inflicted on R. 'Amram (TB *Giṭin* 67b).

SECTION C

Ensuring hegemony

8

The institutionalisation of rabbinic authority

As portrayed in the talmudic account, the history of the early rabbinic *keter torah* is largely a record of the scholastic achievements and communal activities of individual sages. The prominence of their domain was not, however, entirely contingent upon the separate initiatives of egocentric personalities. What transformed a miscellaneous enterprise into a corporate achievement was the emergence of a permanent rabbinic administration and the establishment of educational frameworks whose influence transcended that of any single sage. From the organisational perspective, both were considerable advances. They equipped the rabbis with agencies for the co-ordination of their teachings and the synchronisation of their ideals. More to the point, they also provided the *keter torah*, in its entirety, with an institutional identity which was specifically its own. Rabbis thus became components of a bureaucratic framework organically distinct from its parallels in both the *malkhut* and the *kehunah*.

The academies of learning

Predominant among the organisational vehicles which promulgated the ideals and purposes of the *keter torah* during the early rabbinic period were the academies of learning. Interchangeably referred to in the literature of the times as *batei wa'ad* (houses of assembly), *batei midrash* (houses of learning), *yeshivot* (seats [of learning]; in Aramaic *metivta'ot*),[1] those institutions were characterised by the opportunities which they provided for the dedicated pursuit of the rabbinic mode of exegesis and analysis. They thus came to constitute the frameworks within which the Law – in all its nuances – might best be explored and mediated, and thereby created as well as transmitted. Even *Mishnah*, notwithstanding its codificatory style, occasionally evokes the incisive flavour of debates in the tanna'itic schools (e.g. *Pesaḥim* 6:5 and *Makhshirin* 6:8); to judge by the reports which fill the pages of the Jerusalem and Babylonian Talmuds, no less stimulating was the academic atmosphere which pervaded their amora'ic successors. In both periods, scholars and their students sought to perfect their understanding of the *torah* – primarily for its own sake. Unlike their equivalents amongst Greek sophists, they did not concentrate on the improvement of rhetorical style; neither did they study the *halakhah* solely for practical purposes. Although, as will be seen, senior members of rabbinic academies did often convene as courts of law, adjudication was not their primary function. In both *'Ereṣ Yisra'el* and *Bavel*, academies were set apart from all other institutions in contemporary Jewry by the fact that they furnished an environment singularly conducive to the speculative and hence uncluttered study of the *torah* in its purest form. Ultimately, they were seen effectively to articulate the independent focus of the *keter torah*, functioning as power-houses for the development of its ethos and as recruitment centres for the enlargement of its ranks.

As was the case with many other aspects of their enterprise, the sages of the talmudic period sometimes sought to claim for their scholastic institutions a pedigree even more distinguished than they in fact possessed. Most extravagantly, occasional aggadic embellishments on the Biblical text suggest that academies of some sort had functioned during the very earliest periods of the Israelite chronology.[2] With what appears to be a more refined historical sense, halakhic materials frequently assert the existence of *batei midrash* in second Commonwealth times. Particularly specific are the citations of such institutions as the loci for some of the crucial halakhic discussions in the period of Pharisaic legislation dominated by the names of Hillel, Shamm'ai and their pupils. (TB *Shabbat* 17a, see also *Yoma'* 35b). No less pertinent are *Tosefta*'s references to convocations of similar legislatures-cum-schools in the precints of the Temple immediately prior to its destruction (*Ḥagigah* 2:9; also *Sukah* 2:10 and 4:5).

In view of the high premium which all shades of second-Commonwealth Judaism are known to have placed on schooling, it would be rash to dismiss such attestations as retrospective fabrications. Although undoubtedly riddled with anachronisms and exaggerations,[3] they do serve as acknowledgements – and reminders – of the degree to which the earliest rabbinical academies were able to draw upon a tradition which had long recognised the need for an established system of public education, both primary and secondary. Certainly, rabbinic terminology was not altogether new. As early a source as Ecclesiasticus 51:23 (ed. Segal, p. 358) makes one mention of a *beit midrash* which (alongside, perhaps, the *yeshivah* referred to in verse 29 of the same chapter), possibly constituted a seminary in wisdom literature, catering to the sprigs of second-Commonwealth Jerusalem's native aristocracy.[4] During and immediately after the Hasmonean age, according to reports preserved in the talmudic literature, individual Pharisaic leaders had made careful provisions for a more extensive system of district elementary schools (also identified as *batei midrash*).[5] With the transition to rabbinic Judaism, it is also possible to verify the existence of what seems to have been a type of more advanced colloquia (as in the *beit wa'ad la-ḥakhamim* cited in *'Avot* 1:4) conducted in the privacy of individual homes.

Notwithstanding this range of facilities, until the second or third generation after the Destruction, *torah* scholarship seems largely to have been an unstructured affair. Indeed, the very multiplicity of titles employed to describe the component units of *torah* instruction during much of the tanna'itic epoch indicates the extent to which the framework then in existence was neither uniform nor systematised throughout the contemporary Jewish world. Rabbinic scholarship did certainly make great strides during that period, when academic convocations of rare congeniality and outstanding intellectual enterprise undoubtedly took place. But, with the possible exception of the Patriarch's own school,[6] most were provisional bodies. Little more than ad hoc convocations of virtuosi, they typically provided only occasional tutorials for whichever students were sufficiently conscientious (and adventurous) to gravitate towards a particular 'master' and his study sessions.[7] Mobility thus became a norm. According to *'Avot*, each student was prompted by Rabban Gamli'el to 'provide yourself a teacher' (1:16) and enjoined by R. Nehor'ai to 'wander to a place of *torah*' (4:14).

As numerous tales of the *tana'im* attest, this situation did possess one intrinsic merit: it permitted and fostered a quite remarkable degree of intimacy in several teacher–pupil relationships. But that gain was probably offset by equally obvious institutional drawbacks. Precisely because they were so intensely personal, most early academies (certainly in *'Ereṣ Yisra'el*, information about *Bavel* at this stage is too sparse to permit definitive judgement) operated erratically and spasmodically. Their existence, quite as much as their location and their scholastic programme, in effect depended on the presence, the inspiration and the inclinations of the 'master' with whose name they were associated and whose 'disciples' the students became. There was always the likelihood that with the principal's removal – because of death, voluntary migration or persecution – the entire academy would simply disband and the students be forced to apply to analogous bodies elsewhere. That indeed is precisely what seems to have occurred. Commenting on the Biblical commandment to pursue justice (Deut. 16:20), the *beraitah* cited in TB *Sanhedrin* 32b provides a lengthy – although not necessarily comprehensive – retrospective inventory of the opportunities which had been available to rabbinic students during the first and second centuries. Roughly arranged in chronological sequence, the passage is conventionally considered noteworthy because of its coverage of several geographical locations. Equally remarkable, however, is the spirit of individual initiative and peripatetic enterprise which it evokes and demands. Throughout, it admonishes students to follow each of the *ḥakhamim* to his own 'seat' (*yeshivah*):

> [...] to R. 'Eli'ezer at Lydda; to Rabban Yoḥanan ben Zak'ai at Beror Ḥayyil; to R. Joshua at Peki'in; to Rabban Gamli'el at Yavneh; to R. 'Aqiva' at Benei Beraq; to R. Mattia' [b. Ḥeresh] at Rome; to R. Ḥanania' ben Teradyon at Siknin; to R. Yossie at Sephoris; to R. Judah ben Beteirah at Nisibis [in northern Mesopotamia]; to R. [Ḥanania' the nephew of R. Joshuah ben Ḥanania'] in *Bavel*; to *Rabi* [Judah *ha-nasi*] at Beit-She'arim [...]

Not the least of the achievements of the first generations of *'amora'im* was to change that situation, principally by establishing the schools as durable sinews of Jewish public life. One step in that direction was taken when academies were sited in prominent urban centres – and often in specific buildings; another occurred when they were also endowed with the character of permanent agencies, in possession of their own, often regional, identities.[8] Goodblatt has recently warned that the pace of those developments has been drastically telescoped by subsequent historiography, medieval as well as modern. He notes, for instance, that even in late amora'ic times the term *yeshivah* continued to be applied to private study sessions. He also illustrates the extent to which the newer academies, very much like their predecessors, functioned as bureaux of public information and – more frequently – as courts of law.[9] Above all, he catalogues numerous references in the Talmuds to several *'bei rav'*, all of which attest to the continued proliferation of what he terms 'disciple circles'.

Nevertheless, it remains doubtful whether that is all that the Babylonian schools of the Sasanian age were. Gafni's terminological analyses of the talmudic occurrences of *yeshivah* and *metivta'* suggest that something far more drastic was occurring.[10] Increasingly, what came to distinguish the newer forums from their predecessors was the gradual institutionalisation of the scholastic aspect of their activities. Admittedly, itinerant students remained a common feature of Jewry's academic scene (see, e.g., Rav Yosef's report of the situation in fourth-century *Bavel*, TB *Bava' Batra'* 8a). Moreover, schools were still dependent for their foundation on the personal initiatives of their principals, whose individual inclinations affected their separate characters and (in some cases) their specific curricula too.[11] In those respects, little had changed. What had altered, however, was the degree to which the academies had acquired institutional resilience. Regarded as permanent establishments, they gradually came to possess identities which could (and did) transcend those of any particular sage.

In their institutional form, it has been argued, academies of this newer mould first emerged in *'Ereṣ Yisra'el* during the early part of the third century. In short sequence, independent *yeshivot* were then founded in Tiberias, Sephoris, Caesarea and Lydda.[12] Possibly, one impetus to that development was provided by the particularly unfavourable economic circumstances in which the students and scholars of the region then found themselves. At least some of them might have sought in the establishment of more durable frameworks their only release from their increasing dependence on the haphazard chance of occasional donations.[13] Equally significant, however, might have been the supplementary influences exerted by the life – and death – of R. Judah *ha-nasi'*. In anthologising the *Mishnah*, Judah had bequeathed to the world of Jewish scholarship a didactic tool which, in *Bavel* as well as in *'Ereṣ Yisra'el*, was generally recognised to be an indispensable (albeit still oral) pool of halakhic analysis and investigation.[14] On the other hand, it could be argued, Judah's death in 217 had released his students and colleagues from the intense centralisation which (as his exchange with R. Ḥiyya' reported in TB *Sanhedrin* 5a seems to show) his own multi-faceted authority had tended to impose. Supplied with his didactic framework, but released from his institutional straitjacket, members of the *keter torah* might thus have felt at liberty to establish and propogate their own corporate identity.

The Babylonian model

Whether or not the same conglomeration of causes can be said to have generated a parallel process in *Bavel* is difficult to ascertain. Significantly, however, the emergence of the great Babylonian *yeshivot* in their most articulated form is traditionally dated to precisely the same period. Geonic chronicles, for instance, retrospectively considered the death of Judah I to have been a turning-point in the rise to prominence of the great *r'ashei metivta'ot*;[15] more specifically, the Babylonian Talmud assigns to Rav (sometimes, because of his height, known by the sobriquet of ''Abba 'Arikha'') pride of place amongst the pioneers of academic institutionalisation in its own part of the Jewish world. According to that source, Rav – although of Babylonian birth – possessed considerable first-hand experience of emergent scholastic patterns in *'Ereṣ Yisra'el*. Moreover, he had been on particularly intimate terms with Judah I (TB *Ḥulin* 137b, *Giṭin* 59a), by whom he was authorised to hand down decisions in both ritual law and civil cases (TB *Sanhedrin* 5a–b; TJ *Ḥagigah* 1:8). Significantly, not until close to Judah's death does Rav seem finally to have made up his mind to leave his adopted home and return to his country of origin.

Rav's arrival in *Bavel* in 219 could hardly have been more timely. The accession to power of Ardashir I some six years later unleashed throughout the Persian Empire a wave of fanatical and missionary Mazdi zeal which threatened to engulf several Jewish communities; those of Elam, Media and Messene are said to have apostatised virtually *en masse*. Infused with a deep love of the *torah*, Rav seems soon to have appreciated that its intensive and organised study constituted Judaism's last line of defence.[16] Some purpose could be served by strengthening existing academies, a few of which, as at Nisbis and Ḥuzal, had been established by previous generations of Palestinian émigrés (indeed, Rav's first teaching appointment was as *'amora'* [assistant] to Rav Sheila' at Nehardea', an administrative and judicial centre in central Mesopotamia already favoured by several sages). Much more could be accomplished, however, by setting up new centres of learning in what had hitherto been academic wastelands. Thus it was that, after declining to succeed Rav Sheila' in Nehardea', Rav turned his attentions to the south Mesopotamian town of Sura', a locality not previously distinguished for either its scholars or its scholarship (TB *Ḥulin* 110a). There he established a school which became a model of its kind. Indeed the academy of Sura' was to flourish as 'a little sanctuary' (TB *Megilah* 29a), virtually without interruption, for almost 800 years.

Although outstanding, Rav's achievement was not the only one of its kind. Sura's fame and reputation – and even its principal's method of scriptural exegesis and legal analysis – were challenged by a range of parallel institutions situated elsewhere in central Mesopotamia and even in northern *Bavel* (Nisbis). Nehardea' remained particularly influential, not least perhaps because its scholars deliberately preserved specifically 'Babylonian' traditions of scholarship, and even of *halakhah*, in several respects distinct from those which Rav had imported from *'Ereṣ Yisra'el* and was disseminating to large audiences in Sura'. Indeed, far from being outshone, Nehardea' increased in fame and popularity during the first half of the third century, when Samuel – Rav's one-time colleague and frequent disputant in matters of talmudic law – became the principal of its academy. Thus called upon to exhibit administrative skills to match his scholarly attainments, Samuel proved more than equal to the task. Under his direction (he died in 254, seven years after Rav) Nehardea' attained an academic distinction which further augmented *Bavel*'s claims to be the true home of contemporary *torah* scholarship.[17] That tradition was further enhanced by the academic renown subsequently attained by the *metivta'ot* of Pumbediṭa' (founded by Judah bar Ezekiel c. 260 after the Palmyrenes had ravaged Nehardea'), of Maḥoza' (a southern suburb of the Imperial capital of Ctesiphon and seat of the Exilarch, where the academy was considerably expanded by Rava' after c. 325) and of Naresh (founded by the latter's pupil, R. Papa', after Rava's death in c. 352).

No single circumstance can account for the remarkable strength and resilience for which the great academies of the talmudic age were to become famous. Doubtless one contributory cause, even in *Bavel*, was the predominant tolerance of the gentile environment which, after an admittedly ambivalent start, allowed them to flourish.[18] Another, of equal relevance to *'Ereṣ Yisra'el*, was the financial support and moral encouragement which scholars and their students generally received from Patriarchs and Exilarchs, several of whom had their own pretensions to halakhic proficiency and all of whom (as has been seen) had an administrative interest in the health of institutions which furnished judicial cadres for their communal bureaucracies. But the benefits which accrued from those circumstances were undoubtedly augmented by the executive steps which the academies themselves took in order to maintain their own survival. Indeed, in immediate terms, it was the latter which ensured that the schools of *torah* scholarship (like many of the other great institutions of learning known to history) would become virtually autonomous bodies, governing their own affairs and regulating their own procedures.

Pedagogic forms and forums

Whilst it is impossible to be precise about either the timing or the pace of educational initiatives in the rabbinic academies of the talmudic age, their general thrust and direction can be outlined with some confidence. In what has the appearance of a deliberate drive towards rationalisation, most of the academies made conscious efforts to develop the sort of forms and procedures which are conventionally regarded as indispensable artefacts of all articulated scholarly bodies. Indeed, the largest of them may have felt compelled to do so. If nothing else, their sheer growth in size between the third and fifth centuries probably mandated at least some curbs on the extempore tendencies which (again, with the possible exception of the Patriarch's own schools) seem to have proliferated during the tanna'itic age of scholastic endeavour.[19] Admittedly, didactic theory, buttressed by the force of religious injunction, continued to insist on active student participation in classes: provided it was not considered overtly impertinent, intellectual enquiry was encouraged; so too was the employment of what in another context would have been termed the Socratic method.[20] But within those limits the general atmosphere of the schools seems to have become very much more rigorous.

Some indications of that process might possibly be discerned in those passages of talmudic literature which reflect the increasing intrusion into the academies of standardised conventions for the resolution of scholastic debates as well as judicial differences.[21] Equally prominent were a series of administrative developments affecting both the physical structure of classrooms and the allocation within them of human resources. In *'Ereṣ Yisra'el*, especially, the first generations of *'amora'im* exhibited a hightened awareness of the need for stratified seating arrangements in the lecture halls, primarily in order to facilitate the identification of student rank.[22] Elsewhere, they showed a detailed interest in the exact provisions of the timetable, thus allowing for the adequate preparation of classes and their review.[23] Altogether – and perhaps above all – they set about developing a strict hierarchy of staffing structures. Although the new academies still expected their principals to deliver a daily lesson (or lessons), their other duties were considerably eased. Occasional lapses of memory by senior lecturers could be repaired by recourse to a *tana'*; difficulties of comprehension on the part of students were overcome with the help of a bevy of *'amora'im*.[24]

Within the present context, more relevant than the exact origins of each of these initiatives (if initiatives they all were) is their cumulative contribution to the formulation of the corporate identity of the *keter torah*. By providing frameworks within which associates of that domain might develop and articulate forms and procedures which were specifically their own, the academies served instrumental needs which were altogether supplementary to their avowed scholarly purpose. Through the academies, sages and their students were able to add an institutional dimension to the self-awareness already evoked by their pietistic pursuit of textual analysis. Their status was reinforced by the application of procedural mechanisms (especially where they related to the ordination of scholars – see below, chap. 9) which the *keter torah* made exclusively its own. It was also articulated by the development of a singular titular code. Admittedly, very few of the academic titles – junior and senior – grafted on to the rabbinic lexicon after the third century seem to have been employed consistently or rigorously. (It has been aptly pointed out, for instance, that – as was often the case in subsequent periods of Jewish history – 'even in antiquity not all rabbis were Rabbis'.)[25] Nevertheless, what remains significant is the degree to which recourse was had to such terms as a mark of distinction. Referring to an earlier age, *Tosefta' 'Eduyot* 3:4 (in one variant) records that:

> He who has pupils, and whose pupils have pupils, is called 'Rabbi'. If his pupils excel [*nishtabeḥu*], he is called 'Rabban'. If these and these [pupils and the pupils of his pupils] excel, he is simply called by his name.[26]

Amora'ic practice, however, followed a reverse order. Generic designations of rank (in *Bavel*, generally, 'Rav'), then came into vogue as insignia of those members of the community who were devoting their time and energies to academic pursuits; they were even bestowed on student-companions who were not officially ordained Masters of the Law.[27] Quite apart from being the embodiments of Israel's supreme ideals of sacred scholarship, all were thus recognised to be members of a corporation, a structure different in form and kind from those possessed by the other ordained franchises of organised Jewish life.

For all that, rabbis of the amora'ic age did not constitute a sectarian coterie. Notwithstanding their occasional disdain for the mores and pursuits of their non-scholarly co-religionists, they did not seek to isolate themselves from the masses who did not (or could not) devote their lives to academic pursuits. Neither did they limit their contacts with ordinary men and women to the exhibition of their own miraculous skills or to the publication of *ex cathedra* rabbinic pronouncements on a range of topics whose span embraced both public deportment and the most intimate aspects of conjugal behaviour. Instead, the rabbis embarked upon a far more substantive programme of communal involvement, which – to a large extent – was deliberately designed to prevent their academies from becoming closed scholastic communities hermetically separated from the wider hinterland of contemporary Jewish life.[28]

It was as judges and as administrators that the rabbis most assiduously involved themselves in the public and private affairs of the community. As the abundance of talmudic case law indicates, in both *'Ereṣ Yisra'el* and *Bavel* the court and the market place were the spheres in which they attempted to make their influence most pronounced and persistent. Nevertheless, the evidence leaves no doubt that the rabbis themselves considered the legal and executive aspects of their communal activities to be ancillaries to their role as teachers. As they saw matters, whilst their primary personal obligation was to further their own understanding of the *torah*, their primary public duty was to transmit the fruits of their scholarship to their fellow-Jews. Only thus, in fact, could they prevent the *torah* from becoming an esoteric collection of arcane rulings, known only to the select and limited elite who were fortunate enough to be categorised as full-time cognoscenti.

Supplementary educational frameworks, specifically designed to cater to those segments of the community not formally enrolled in the regular academies, had long been prominent features of Jewish life. Public sermons (*derashot*) had been particularly frequent in tanna'itic synagogues, as were regular gatherings (usually on

Sabbaths) for the purposes of *torah* study and reading. They remained so into amora'ic times.[29] Concurrently with the development of specialised academies, however, such forums were considerably expanded and structured. Particularly was this so in *Bavel*, where the *kalah* was instituted as a fixed venue for popular study and the *pirqa'* developed into a stylised form of public lecture.[30] In addition to comprising major components of the academies' own agenda, both venues also became primary items in the communal diary. Absences from the *pirqa'* – even by ordained rabbis – could arouse considerable offence (TB *Berakhot* 28b and *Qidushin* 25a). Sessions of the *kalah*, when *metivta'ot* opened their doors to most of the general public throughout the months of *'Adar* and *'Elul*, are reported to have attracted vast numbers of students. (So much so, that the size of enrolment in fourth-century Pumbediṭa' gave rise to the charge that Rabah bar Naḥmani was deliberately abetting tax-evasions on a massive scale. TB *Bava' Meṣi'a* 86a, see also *Berakhot* 6a–b.)

In their fully developed form, the *kalah* and the *pirqa'* were deliberately intended to forge effective links between the academies and their teachers and the community at large. For that reason, neither medium was devoted solely to the occasional provision of devotional instruction designed (as it were) to recharge the spiritual batteries of those by whom they were attended. Although much of the *pirqa'* comprised parables and *'agadah*, those were not its only ingredients. Like the *kalah*, the public lecture was primarily designed to help laymen improve their exegetical skills and add to their understanding of accepted halakhic rulings. Conventionally, therefore, both gatherings were highly formal structures assuming (in Gafni's words) 'fixed patterns and contextual components'. So firmly did they become entrenched aspects of Babylonian life, that their forms and features lasted virtually without change until the very end of the Ge'onic period.[31]

Institutional autonomy

Individual associates of the academies undoubtedly derived some incidental economic benefits from the process of institutionalisation thus set in motion by rabbinic representatives of the *keter torah*. Scholars, as has already been noted, repeatedly insisted on a privileged right to exemptions from certain taxes; they also expected to receive some of the dues previously paid to priests. On the grounds that financial endeavours would consume time better devoted to scholarly pursuits, they further demanded – and were granted – mercantile preferences in the marketplace.[32] All such claims could doubtless have been presented in a more convincing manner once procedures had been developed for both the identification of beneficiaries and – where required – the verification of their credentials.[33] Nevertheless, the importance of the economic incentive in the development of a corporate rabbinic consciousness must not be exaggerated. The uncompromising Pharisaic tradition which denigrated the receipt of direct financial recompense for learning was never retracted; and no sage ever advocated a modification in the Mishnaic ordinance (*Bekhorot* 4:6) which prohibited the receipt of a salary in return for judicial service. Late into the amora'ic period, scholars still largely depended for their livelihoods on traditional resources, the most prominent of which were their own commercial acumen (which in many cases was considerable enough to arouse popular envy), donations from pious devotees and – perhaps the least speculative of all – the judicious selection of wealthy marriage-partners for themselves and their children.[34]

Whatever economic benefits as were to be gained from increasing bureaucratic articulation were more likely to have been institutional than individual. As Beer has shown, principals of the academies of *Bavel* – probably because they were regarded as chief executives of permanent foundations – began to solicit and collect endowments on behalf of their establishments. Drawing upon a reservoir of sympathy which seems to have been broad-based, they cultivated a variety of donors: nostalgic alumni, successful merchants and tradesmen and, perhaps the largest single category of all, rich and pious widows. What is significant about such benefactions is not only their frequency (itself a testimony to popular regard for scholarship) but also the institutional consequences which resulted from the manner of their collection. For one thing, by thus centralising fund-raising, principals of academies seem also to have made the entire process more efficient. Even when due note is taken of the improved economic climate, especially in *Bavel*, the sums now raised remain notably more substantial than those previously collected, either by individual *tana'im* who had solicited on their own behalves or by such intermittent expedients as the *magbit ḥakhamim* ('scholars' fund').[35] Secondly, and perhaps even more important, *r'ashei metivta'ot* seem to have been at pains to stress that they were acting quite independently of Exilarchic initiative or support. Some even established and thereafter maintained capital funds in order to make that point.[36] This was a step pregnant with corporate implications. Quite apart from pronouncing exclusive scholarly control over the distribution of the income thus gained, it also constituted a statement on the subject of scholarly security and autonomy. Now that academies were, at least to some extent, released from their previous degree of dependence on the whimsical largesse of individual Exilarchs and Patriarchs, their members were well placed to assert their institutional independence and to claim the liberties which they deemed that position to impart.

In part, that assertiveness found expression in a repetition of earlier demands that sages and their disciples be allowed to enjoy absolute academic freedom. As is indicated by the records of the famous incidents involving R. Joshua and R. 'Eli'ezer b. Hyrcanus (respectively, TB *Berakhot* 27b–28a and *Bava Meṣi'a* 59b), this issue was remembered to have been a cause of tension between Patriarchs and *ḥakhamim* in *'Ereṣ Yisra'el* as early as the incumbency of Rabban Gamli'el II. It became so once again during the period of Judah *ha-nasi*, whose imperious decree against what has been termed 'open-air' teaching was deliberately flouted by R. Ḥiyya'.[37] It was after Judah's death, however, that the issue was transposed into a trial of corporate strengths. Ever abrasive where the defence of rabbinical privileges was concerned, Reish Laqish seems to have been particularly keen to make that point. With what smacks suspiciously of malice aforethought, he chose to teach a law which stressed the Patriarch's subjection to even the most lowly of courts ('A *nasi'* who sins is administered lashes by a *beit din* of three [...]'); adding insult to injury, he then spurned the offer of reconciliation which Judah II, with the encouragement of R. Yoḥanan, decided to make.

'What do you think', Reish Laqish is said to have chided them 'that I would be afraid of you and therefore desist from the teachings of the Almighty?'[38]

Equally significant – and possibly even more portentious – was the rabbis' insistence on the academy's right to pick and choose its own governing body. While it is difficult to trace the steps whereby that claim was established in *'Ereṣ Yisra'el*, it is noteworthy that the Patriarchs who succeeded Judah I seem to have had no hand at all in the appointments to senior positions in the great academies established at various Galilean and coastal locations after *Rabi*'s death.[39] Precisely the same situation can be discerned, and documented in somewhat greater detail, in *Bavel*. There, according to Beer's interpretation of the incident involving Geniva' (above, chap. 7, pp. 194–5), the issue of academic autonomy had been raised as early as the second half of the third century, when 'Ukba', the *reish galuta'* of the time, appointed his kinsman R. Ḥuna' to be principal of the academy of Sura'. Thereafter, Exilarchic control over such offices were even more curtailed. Particularly was this so in Pumbediṭa'. Beer's detailed scrutiny of the sources relevant to successive successions to R. Judah b. Ezekiel (Pumbediṭa's founder and first principal) reveals that at no time between 297 and 352 is it possible to discern traces of the successful exercise of whatever influence *rashei galuta'* may have claimed in the matter. If anything, they seem to have been deliberately excluded from the consultations which preceded the appointments of both R. Ḥuna' b. Ḥiyya' and, later, 'Abbayei. In both instances, the ultimate selections (from a number of candidates) seem to have been made solely by a collegium of scholars who implicitly denied the Exilarch any constitutional *locus standi* in the process.[40] In thus behaving, members of the Pumbediṭa' academy were not merely expressing their regional pride. They were also shifting the boundaries of their own sphere of jurisdiction and redefining the entire balance of corporate relations between Babylonian representatives of the *ketarim* of the *torah* and the *malkhut*.

Authority, once thus claimed, was soon put to instrumental effect. Altogether, the amora'ic period witnessed the formulation of various executive and judicial stipulations, many of which further underscored the emerging cohesiveness of the rabbis and articulated their heightened sensitivity to their collective status. One outstanding example is provided by the revolution which occurred in the pronouncement and application of the mechanism of punitive isolation and contempt described as *nidui*. As Leibson has shown, prior to the third century that weapon had principally been employed in defence of the authority of the *keter malkhut*. Patriarchs, in particular, had found it to be a useful punishment which they had applied against *tana'im* who, in specific cases, had either rebelled against their regime or challenged their rulings.[41] That was no longer the case during the amora'ic period. Whereas Patriarchs (following the precedents established by Judah I) found it politic to have recourse to such milder instruments as the *nezifah* ('reprimand'), *nidui* itself came to constitute part of the rabbis' own armoury. What is more, only in part did they employ that weapon for what might be regarded as conventional disciplinary purposes, of the sort necessary for the preservation of internal unity (in order to enforce halakhic consensus within the rabbis' own ranks or to compel recourse to rabbinical courts and the acceptance of their decisions). More interesting are the instances in which they prescribed *nidui*, or the threat of *nidui*, in response to what were generically categorised (especially in Pumbediṭa')[42] as popular insults to the 'honour' due to *ḥakhamim*. By the end of the amora'ic period, Leibson reports, *nidui* had thus completely changed its character. No longer an administrative punishment of the last resort, it had become a loosely regulated response to real or imagined social misdemeanours.[43] Fashioned to serve the particularistic purposes of the very elite by whom it was administered, the sanctions it entailed were principally directed against the general public of the Jewish community. As such, *nidui* signified the extent to which the rabbis, as a group, considered themselves to be a distinct segment within that public and therefore collectively worthy of the dignities which the sanction of the *nidui* was expected to maintain.

The extent to which the Judaism of the talmudic rabbis had become 'normative' in both *'Ereṣ Yisra'el* and *Bavel* by the close of the talmudic age is still a subject of some debate.[44] Since the evidence presented here is based entirely on materials composed by the rabbis themselves, it cannot settle that issue. What those sources do mirror, however, is their authors' perceptions of their own communal environment. They show how deeply the proponents of rabbinic Judaism were imbued with a sense of the distinctiveness of their own mission in Jewish life, and how determined they were to embark upon a course which might translate their ideological convictions into the realities of power. Above all, they provide a chronicle of the steps which they took in order to articulate the *keter torah* and thus place it in a position from which it might challenge the supremacy traditionally attributed to the alternative domains of the *kehunah* and the *malkhut*. Those efforts, it has been seen, were not limited to occasional protests against Patriarchal and Exilarchic prerogatives, or even to more persistent encroachments on priestly privileges. Significant though the skirmishes which those issues engendered undoubtedly were, they effectively formed only a backcloth to the far more systematic development of a specifically rabbinic way of life. By cultivating their own ethos of scholarly application, the rabbis managed to invest the *keter torah* with a corporate personality. Moreover, by institutionalising their academies of learning they were able to supply that domain with the organised recruitment centres which ensured its resilience. It is to the halakhic mechanisms which they also employed in order to endow their own succession procedures with the sanctity and ceremony hitherto reserved to rival domains that attention must now be turned.

NOTES

1. On *beit ha-wa'ad* and *beit ha-midrash* as synonyms in *Mishnah* see J.N. Epstein, *Mavo' la-Nusaḥ ha-Mishnah*, Vol. 1 (2nd edn.; Tel Aviv, 1964), pp. 488–9.
2. E.g. TB *Yoma'* 28b; cf., however, the query at the end of Gen. *Rabbah* 63:6.
3. On the Hillel stories, S. Safrai, 'Tales of the Sages in the Palestinian Tradition and the Babylonian Talmud', *Scripta Hierosolymitana*, 22 (1971), pp. 220–1; on the *Tosefta'* passages, Levine, *Ma'amad ha-Ḥakhamim*, pp. 11–12.
4. Possibly corrupt, the text is also discussed in S. Mirsky, 'Le -R'eishit ha-Yeshivah u-Mahutah', *Ḥorev*, 5 (1939), p. 133 fn. 2.
5. See, e.g. the analysis of the talmudic sources which attribute particular prominence in this field to such Pharisaic personalities as Shim'on ben Sheṭaḥ and [the High Priest] Joshuah ben Gamla' in L. Greenwald, *Toledot ha-Kohanim ha-Gedolim* (New York, 1933), pp. 139–42 and S. Safrai, 'Ha-Ḥinuh ha-'Amami u-Mashma'uto ha-Datit we-ha-Ḥevratit Bitqufat ha-Talmud', *Ereṣ Yisra'el we-Ḥakhamehah Bitqufat ha-Mishnah we-ha-Talmud* (Jerusalem, 1983), p. 123.
6. S.J.D. Cohen, 'Patriarchs and Scholarchs', *PAAJR*, 48 (1981), p. 59 and n. 5.

   For a rejection of the view that Jesus ever established a school, or indeed fostered a teacher–pupil relationship with his followers on the rabbinic model, M. Hengel, *The Charismatic Leader and His Followers* (Edinburgh, 1981), pp. 51–6.
7. Whence the quantity of formulas that so-and-so 'went to learn [*halakh lilmod*] *torah* with so-and-so [often for twelve or thirteen years]'. See, the sources cited in Hengel, op. cit., p. 51 n. 50, and Levine, *Ma'amad*, p. 23 n. 4.
8. G. Hittenmeister, 'Beit ha-Keneset u-Veit ha-Midrash we-ha-Ziqah Beineihem', *Kathedra*, 18 (1981), pp. 37–44 and S. Safrai, 'Ha-Tafqidim ha-Qehilatiyim Shel Beit ha-Keneset be-'Ereṣ Yisra'el', *Beit ha-Keneset Bitqufat ha-Mishnah we-ha-Talmud* (Jerusalem, 1986), pp. 105–24.
9. 'In the Jewish communities of late antiquity what we would call academic and judicial functions were often combined in the same person or institution. Since the courts were administering what was believed to be divinely revealed law, legislation necessarily took the form of exegesis.'

D.M. Goodblatt, *Rabbinic Instruction in Sasanian Babylonia* (Leiden, 1975), p. 66. S. Albeck, *Batei ha-Din Bimei ha-Talmud* (Ramat Gan, 1980), pp. 117–22, also notes the extent to which academies were designated a *sanhedrin*, *beit din gadol* or, generically, as *batei din*.

10. Y. Gafni, '"Yeshivah" u-"Metivta"', *Zion*, 43 (1978), pp. 12–37 and his exchange with Goodblatt in idem., 46 (1981), pp. 52–6.
11. For instance, during the time of its first principal, R. Judah bar Ezekiel, the Pumbediṭa' academy was said to study only civil law (tractate *neziqin*). TB *Berakhot* 20a and parallels.
12. A. Oppenheimer, 'Batei Midrashot be-'Ereṣ Yisra'el be-R'eishit Tequfat ha-'Amora'im', *Kathedra*, 8 (1978), pp. 80–9.
13. M. Beer, 'Yissakhar u-Zevulun', *Bar-Ilan Annual*, 6 (1968), pp. 167–80.
14. S. Lieberman, *Hellenism in Jewish Palestine* (N.Y., 1950), pp. 83–99.
15. See, e.g., the citation from Sherira' Ga'on's *'Iggeret* (p. 74) in Y. Gafni, 'Sheveṭ u-Meḥoqeq: Manhigut Ḥadashah Bitqufat ha-Talmud be-'Ereṣ Yisra'el u-Bavel'. *Kehunah u-Malkhut: Yaḥasei Dat u-Medinah be-Yisra'el u-va-'Amim* (Jerusalem, 1987), p. 82. In general, M. Beer, 'Mi-Ba'ayot Hithawutah Shel ha-Metivta' be-Bavel', *WCJS*, 4 (1), 1967, pp. 99–101.
16. M. Beer, 'Ha-Reqa' ha-Medini u-Fe'iluto Shel Rav be-Bavel', *Zion*, 50 (1985), pp. 155–72. Whether Rav departed for *Bavel* in 189 or 219 has long been debated. Beer posits the latter date.
17. On the widespread influence of the academy of Nehardea' see TB *Ketubot* 54a; according to one account (*Mishnah, Yevamot* 16:7), R. 'Aqiva' had visited Nehardea' at the beginning of the second century C.E. and intercalated the year there.
18. A notorious exception, of course, is the destruction of the Nehardean academy by the Palmyrenes in 263. Even then, however, a replacement was soon found in the neighbouring town of Pumbediṭa'. Y. Fluersheim, 'Yesudon we-R'eishit Hitpathutan Shel Yeshivot Bavel Bimei ha-Mishnah we-ha-Talmud – Sura' u-Pumbediṭa'', *Zion*, 39 (1974), pp. 183–97. On the extent to which Babylonian *yeshivot* may have been influenced by local Christian institutions of learning see: Y. Gafni, 'Ḥiburim Nestorioniyim ke-Maqor le-Toledot Yeshivot Bavel', *Tarbitz*, 51 (1982), pp. 567–75.
19. Cohen, 'Patriarchs and Scholarchs', above n. 6. On numbers of students in *'Ereṣ Yisra'el* see e.g. TJ *Shabbat* 2:7; in *Bavel*, TB *Yevamot* 64b.
20. The religious duty of a student to participate in his master's lectures is stressed in TB *Sanhedrin* 7b. However, that there were limits is indicated by the report of the incident which brought about R. Jeremiah's temporary exclusion from the academy; TB *Bava' Batra'* 23b and *tosafot* s.v. *'we-'al da'*'. On the Socratic method, see TB *'Eruvin* 76a and *Ḥulin* 113a.
21. Particularly noteworthy are the insistence on a majority decision

(Z. A. Steinfeld, 'Le-Sugei ha-Rov be-Hora'ah', *Sidra*, 1 [1985], pp. 69–90) and on rabbinic compliance with academic decisions (G. Leibson, ''Al Mah Menadin', *Shenaṭon ha-Mishpaṭ ha-'Ivri*, 2 [1976], pp. 321–2). For illustrations drawn from the TJ; Neusner, *Judaism in Society: The Evidence of the Yerushalmi*, pp. 97–111.

22. See the references to seven 'rows' of pupils, graded in order of academic excellence, in TB *Bava' Qama'* 117a and to 24 rows in *Megilah* 28b. A similar arrangement (at least for the first seven pews) in Babylon in reported in TB *Berakhot* 57a. Earlier references to student 'benches' (as in TJ *Berakhot* 4:1 and TB *Berakhot* 27b–28a) do not specify any order of rank.
23. *Megilah* 28b; cf. *Horayot* 12a and the commentary ad. loc by Samuel Eliezer Edels (*Maharshaya'*; 1555–1631).
24. On the *tana'*, and the relatively low esteem in which his powers of deduction were held, *Megilah* idem; on the *'amora'* (sometimes termed *meturgeman*); TB *Berakhot* 27b; on daily lectures (morning and evening) TB *Shabbat* 136b. For all the wealth of material, a critical note is in order. Most of the sources are of Babylonian origin, and hence unreliable as accurate reflections of Palestinian practices. See Y. Gafni, 'Ha-Yeshivah ha-Bavlit le'Or Sugyat Bava' Qama' 117a', *Tarbitz*, 49 (1980), pp. 292–301.
25. S. J. D. Cohen, 'Epigraphical Rabbis', *JQR*, 2 (1981), pp. 1–17. Additional complications produced by the thick varnish of Geonic terminology (e.g. *reish sidra'*) are also noted in Goodblatt, *Rabbinic Instruction*, pp. 40–1 and 51–4, following Beer.
26. That, at least, is one version. An alternative, which inverts the sense of the passage, reads *nishtakheḥu* (forgotten) for *nishtabeḥu*. However, the latter reading seems to be substantiated by the citation from Sherira Gaon in Newman, *Semikhah*, pp. 10–11:

    In the earlier generation when they were very great [in knowledge] they were not in need of Rabbinical titles; not for the title of 'Rabban' nor 'Rabbi', nor 'Rab'; and this [the use of titles] has been spread from the students of Rabban Johanan ben Zakkai onward.
27. Thus, it has been shown that the term *ḥevraya'* came to denote groups of young scholars who served as student-companions to several of the sages of *'Ereṣ Yisra'el* between the early third and mid fourth centuries. Probably not ordained (a fact which accounts for their anonymity), they were renowned for their assiduous attention to their studies and their mastery of certain texts. In *Bavel*, the term was employed more loosely. M. Beer, ''Al Ha-Ḥevraya', *Bar-Ilan Annual*, 20–1 (1983), pp. 76–95.
28. On the differences, in this respect, between the academies of *Bavel* and the contemporary monasteries of Christian Iran, Neusner, *Babylonian Jewry*, Vol. 3, pp. 195–200. 'The academy did not retain its disciples, but always intended them to go back to the community, which it never supplanted in their lives.'

29. See, e.g. the sources collated in F. G. Hittenmeister, 'Beit ha-Keneset u-Veit ha-Midrash', pp. 37–44. For the amora'ic period see, e.g., TB *Giṭin* 38b.
30. S. K. Mirsky, 'Le-Sidrei ha-Yeshivot be-Bavel Bitqufat ha-'Amora'im', *Ḥorev*, 3 (1936), pp. 109–23 (emphasising study sessions on the Sabbath as the crux of the system); see also J. Z. Lauterbach, 'The Names of the Rabbinical Schools and Assemblies in Babylonia', *HUCA Jubilee Volume* (1926), pp. 211–22. Reviewing the sources, Goodblatt here too argues that the forum may have become institutionalised later than is often suggested; *Rabbinic Instruction*, pp. 155–70. On the *pirqa'*, see Goodblatt, op. cit., pp. 171–96, and compare I. Gafni, 'Public Sermons in Talmudic Babylonia: The Pirqa'', in *Yad la-Talmud: Selected Chapters* (ed. E. E. Urbach; n.d. [Jerusalem, 1984?]), pp. 39–42.
31. Idem., pp. 39–40. Hence, significantly, these institutions themselves generated an entire class of titles and ranks; *reish kalah*, etc.
32. The abundant material relating to *Bavel* is collated in Beer, *'Amor'ai Bavel*, pp. 222–57; for *'Ereṣ Yisra'el*, Levine, *Ma'amad ha-Ḥakhamim*, pp. 31–2.
33. As were (possibly) initiated by the Exilarch in order to determine whether R. Dimi was indeed a *ṣurba' de-rabanan*. TB *Bava' Batra'* 22a. Note also the insider/outsider dictum attributed to Rabah in TB *Yoma'* 72b (itself perhaps an echo of Rabban Gamli'el's ruling, reported in TB *Berakhot* 28a).
34. Neusner, *Babylonian Jewry*, Vol. 3, pp. 126–30 and Beer, op. cit., esp. pp. 258–71, who also notes that scholars were frequently named guardians of properties, whereby they gained access to liquid capital. For one example of the envy which rabbinic wealth might arouse, see TB *Bava' Meṣi'a* 73b.
35. M. Beer, 'Talmud Torah we-Derekh 'Ereṣ', *Bar-Ilan Annual*, 2 (1964), esp. pp. 148–9.
36. The most outstanding example appears to have been the fund (*shipura'*) apparently instituted at Pumbediṭa' by Rav Judah and subsequently maintained by Rabah, R. Joseph, 'Abayei and Rav (TB *Giṭin* 60b). Beer, *R'eshut ha-Golah*, p. 104 and n. 36.
37. S. Krauss, 'Outdoor Teaching in Talmudic Times', *JJS*, 1 (1949), pp. 82–4 and Alon, *Jews, Judaism* [...], p. 341 n. 84.
38. The incident is discussed in Levine, *Ma'amad ha-Ḥakhamim*, p. 127.
39. Thus, the report of the appointment of R. 'Abba' of Acco to the presidency of the Caesarean academy late in the third century (TB *Yoma'* 18a) stresses the role of R. 'Abbahu and his influence on the (unspecified) electoral body.
40. Beer, *R'eshut ha-Golah*, pp. 94–106, whose analysis of such sources as TB *Berakhot* 31a, 64a and *Horayot* 14a invalidates the contrary conclusions posited by Graetz.

41. Specific instances are analysed in G. Leibson, ''Al Mah Menadin', *Shenaṭon ha-Mishpaṭ ha-'Ivri*, pp. 298–314.
42. Whose scholars, in this instance too, see to have been particularly sensitive to their corporate status. See, e.g. the ruling attributed to Rav Joseph in TB *Mo'ed Qaṭan* 17a and Leibson, *op. cit.*, p. 341 n. 268.
43. Leibson's analysis (pp. 293–7) rejects the thesis (long a subject of halakhic contention) that the list of offences proscribed in TB *Berakhot* 19a was in any way comprehensive. Nevertheless, it is surely significant that the very first item there specified is '*'al kavod ha-rav*.'
44. Still valuable is the summary of the debate in M. Smith, 'Goodenough's Jewish Symbols in Retrospect', *JBL*, 86 (1967), pp. 53–68.

9

Patterns of succession and pageants of installation

Political theory conventionally distinguishes between three sequential steps in the process of public appointment. One is the identification of those members of the polity who possess prior rights to submit their candidacy for a particular position; a second is the determination of the mechanisms whereby individual credentials are verified and assessed; the third is the delineation of the procedures whereby designated incumbents are formally installed into office.[1]

Organised communities, whatever the nature of their regime, tend to make specific – often pedantic – provisions for rites of passage through all three stages. In part, the reasons are instrumental. Regularised patterns for the acquisition and transmission of authority constitute society's most convenient medium for the maintenance of political continuity and constitutional stability. Man's natural tendency towards competitiveness, runs the argument, is in the realm of public affairs best restrained by the knowledge that executive power, once conferred and confirmed in accordance with accepted conventions, cannot thereafter be lightly challenged. Fixed succession procedures thus function as constitutional safeguards; they reduce – even if they cannot entirely eliminate – the likelihood of unruly competition for place and position at the apex of government.

Equally important, although perhaps less immediately obtrusive, is a second facet of accession and succession procedures. Their existence and constant re-enactment help to perpetuate the institutional identities of the individual agencies to which they relate. They function, in this sense, as controlled reproductive mechanisms; they identify and specify the agencies of government to which society attaches importance and which it therefore wishes to preserve. In an ideological sense, they thus reflect political value concepts.

It was with the latter aspect of prescribed mechanisms for appointment and induction that early rabbinic authors were most deeply concerned. The succession and accession regulations which they laid down for each of the *ketarim* seem largely to have been framed with an eye to their possible effects on the status and standing of the *keter torah*. At each of the sequential stages of the appointment process, the perspective which informs the relevant analyses is thus essentially, although not entirely, insular. Often, rabbinic descriptions of accession procedures appear explicitly designed to constitutionalise the corporate independence of the rabbis' own franchise and to demonstrate its hegemony over both the *malkhut* and the *kehunah*.

Of the several obstacles which impeded the fulfilment of that aim, perhaps the most conspicuous stemmed from the institutional novelty of the *keter torah* in its early rabbinic guise. Notwithstanding the rabbis' claims to be the linear constitutional heirs of the Biblical prophets, the procedural lines of their descent remained uncomfortably haphazard and imprecise. Especially was this so when the mechanisms of rabbinic selection, appointment and induction were compared to verifiable parallels in the domains of the *malkhut* and the *kehunah*. Largely by virtue of their long chronology of institutional continuity, both the monarchy and the priesthood had been able to embellish and perpetuate an impressive range of such procedures within their own franchises. Moreover, the rituals whereby they were implemented had invested the relevant appointees with a nimbus of virtually autonomous sanctity. Priests and kings, as the Biblical texts would show, had assumed office at pageants originally mandated by God himself; indeed, it was precisely the rites of their induction which had conferred and confirmed the Divinely-inspired authority and independence of their positions in the higher reaches of Israel's traditional hierarchy of government. By contrast, the corporate ceremonial provisions available to rabbinic representatives of the *keter torah* seemed to be somewhat less resplendent. Even if rabbis could trace their own appointment rituals to Biblical precedents (which was doubtful) the lines of procedural continuity remained tenuous. Quite simply, the gaps in the institutional chronology of the *keter torah* were too glaring to be conveniently obscured and the changes in its personal composition too radical to be ignored.

Early rabbinic tradents were not content to solve that difficulty by the piecemeal invention of rites and formularies which the *keter torah* could call its own. Ever anxious to stress the antiquity of their own claims to supreme authority throughout Jewry, they characteristically preferred two other courses. One was to promote various theories of constitutional penetration. Traditional provisions concerning the selection of candidates for public office, and the verification of their credentials, were reinterpreted in ways which endowed representatives of the *keter torah* with a pre-eminent role in all such procedures. Even where appointments to the *keter malkhut* and the *keter kehunah* were concerned, rabbis and their constitutional equivalents were portrayed as participants (and, in some cases, as umpires) at every stage of the proceedings. A second method was to resort to a process of exegetical transfer. Biblical provisions for the appointment and induction of kings and priests were removed from their specific institutional contexts and applied to instruments of the *keter torah*. The symbolic grammar of royal and sacerdotal pageantry thus made available was deployed in rabbinic inductions and confirmations, and transposed into a vehicle for the proclamation that the *keter torah* too possessed a manifest identity which befitted its constitutional station.

The two techniques here outlined were not applied consistently or unanimously. As will be seen, preferences changed from region to region and were affected by shifting temporal circumstances. Nevertheless, they conform to a pattern which is particularly amenable to synoptic analysis. Even when concerned with issues of ostensibly historical and theoretical interest (in particular, the elevation of kings and high priests) early rabbinic writings on the appointment process remained commensurate with the notion that the *keter torah* was superior to both of the other domains. Indeed, that hierarchy was illustrated and emphasised at each successive stage of the process – candidacy, verification, and installation.

Criteria of succession

Although characteristically disjointed and scattered, early rabbinic references to the criteria required of candidates to senior public office are not entirely unsystematic. Woven into the wide range of halakhic and midrashic materials on the topic are several pronouncements which attempt to deduce coherent norms from a seemingly heterogeneous variety of attested succession rights and appointment procedures. Presented as self-contained statements of basic principles, they thus reflect the degree to which the framers of *halakhah* occasionally sought to attain (perhaps impose) uniformity on an area of Jewish life which the circumstances of national history might otherwise have rendered particularly haphazard.

Amongst the most apparent of such guidelines are those which proclaim an axiomatic preference for the principle of primogeniture. Various dicta explicitly derive criteria for succession to public office from *halakhot* which concern the hereditary transfer of private property. Scripture itself had expressly mandated the priority of firstborn sons when making provision for the distribution of family estates (Deut. 21:16–17). Senior positions of state, because they constitute public resources which are similarly scarce (indeed, even more so, since mono-regnalism obviously precludes their distribution among several heirs),[2] must also be allocated according to genetic priority. That was understood to be the reason why the Bible had specified that the high priesthood was to be delegated to the *kohen* 'greatest among his brethren' (*Sifra', 'Aḥarei Mot* 8 (5) on Leviticus 21:10); likewise, Jehoram had succeeded to the monarchy of his father Ahazziah 'because he was the firstborn' (TB *Keritut* 5b on II Chron. 21:3).

Not unexpectedly, such stipulations most commonly appear in rabbinic texts which comment upon criteria of candidacy to the very highest offices in the *kehunah* and the *malkhut*. Indeed, if we are to follow the rabbis' own reconstructions of Israel's constitutional history, it was to those cases that the principle of dynastic succession had most obviously to be applied. In its initial comment on R. Simeon's depiction of the three *ketarim*, *'Avot de Rabi Natan* ('B', chap. 48) had specified that both the priesthood and the kingship had at their very inception been delegated to the heads of two named families. All contemporary and subsequent rabbinic literature echoed that theme. Only the direct offspring of Aaron and David – provided they were male and their descent patrilineal – could inherit the highest offices which those two forefathers had originally possessed.[3] No non-Aaronide could possibly enter the *keter kehunah*; indeed, whatever their individual attainments and august station, all were designated by the Biblical sobriquet *zar* (Hillel, cited in TB *Shabbat* 31a, exegesis on Numbers 1:51). Admittedly, and as we have seen, matters were somewhat less rigorous with respect to the *keter malkhut*; in that case too, however, patrimony remained significant. Never accorded the messianic status attributed to the blood-line of David, 'a king of Israel' – notwithstanding the legitimacy of his rule – was also denied several of the ceremonial privileges allowed only to 'a king of Judah' (e.g. TB *Soṭah* 41b).

In theory, such criteria could not play a comparable role in the determination of candidacy to office in the *keter torah*. Unlike both the *kehunah* and the *malkhut*, the *torah* was not the private preserve of any particular caste; it had always been the common property of all Israel. As much was apparent from the terms of the original covenant (or covenants) whereby God had bestowed this, the most esteemed of all His gifts, on 'all of you [...] your captains of your tribes, your elders, and your officers [...] your children, your wives and your stranger that is in thy camp, from the hewer of thy wood to the drawer of thy water' (Deut. 29:9–10).[4] Even if it were true (as one minority rabbinic opinion contended, TB *Nedarim* 38a) that the *torah* had originally been granted only to Moses and his descendants, the convocation at Horeb had rendered all such claims to proprietary rights null and void. Deuteronomy 33:4 had explicitly depicted the *torah* as an 'inheritance' [*morashah*] of the entire congregation of Jacob; and in so doing had for evermore decreed that it was to be a domain open to the talented (*Sifrei* Deut. 48 [p. 112] and 345 [p. 402]). To deny any student the right to its teachings was to rob him of his birthright (TB *Sanhedrin* 91b); to regard it as a hereditary fiefdom was to emasculate its true character (TB *Nedarim* 81a). The *torah* was not the resource of an inbred brotherhood of cognoscenti, but a public well from which all who thirsted for its blessings could drink. Therein, as *'Avot de Rabi Natan* pointed out (loc. cit.), lay its most crucial singularity:

> The toil of the *torah*? Whoever wishes to assume it may do so, as it is said [Isaiah 55:1]: 'Ho, everyone that is thirsty, come for water.'[5]

All the relevant Biblical precedents seemed to confirm that message. With the possible – but problematic – exceptions of occasional scriptural references to the 'sons of prophets' (all in the books of Kings), there existed no Biblical supports for the supposition that the *keter torah*, as periodically instrumentalised, had ever become dynasticised.[6] On the contrary, every appointment in that domain to which the Bible attests had been made *ad hominem* and irrespective of hereditary considerations. Their sole determinant had been God's assessment of the individual candidate's personal qualifications. One outstanding example was provided by the fact that Moses 'our rabbi' had himself not been succeeded by his sons, but by Joshua. In the absence of explicit scriptural explanations for the choice, retrospective rabbinic *'agadah* took full advantage of the opportunity for homiletic amplification. Even those sources which do attribute to Moses the desire to see his titles and offices conferred on Gershom and Eliezer,[7] stress that the wish must have been considered entirely inappropriate. If nothing else, God is reported to have pointed out: 'Your sons sat idly by and did not concern themselves with *torah*' (Numbers *Rabbah* 21:14).

As far as tanna'itic tradents were concerned, the inference of all such examples had long been clear. The *torah* did not constitute a mystery whose secrets were accessible only to a genetic caste. On the contrary, the essential distinction of the entire domain known by that name lay in its refusal to attribute any normative value whatsoever to hereditary descent. The contrast with both the *malkhut* and the *kehunah* was pointed and apposite. In matters of *torah*, a commoner (*hedyoṭ*) had as much standing as a king (*Sifrei* Deut. 161 [p. 212]); and a *mamzer* (loosely translated as 'bastard') – provided he was a *talmid ḥakham* – took precedence over a high priest who was an *'am ha'areṣ* (in this sense: 'ignoramus'; *Mishnah, Horayot* 3:8 and parallels).

Appointments to public office had necessarily to be commensurate with such principles, especially when they concerned positions which the rabbinic *keter torah* regarded as its own particular preserve. Local magistrates and community wardens (*dayanim* and *parnasim*) provided obvious cases in point. Pure rabbinic theory certainly denied any suggestion that incumbency of either category of office could be dependent on genetic criteria. In practice, too, rabbis refused to give their blessings to Patriarchal nominees who, for all their upmarket origins, were alleged to be immoral or unlearned. As has been seen (above pp. 202–3), the issue became particularly contentious during the third and fourth centuries, when rabbis complained that Judah I's successors were altogether sacrificing considerations of equity and scholarship to those of wealth and pedigree.

Even if true, the accusation was in some respects misdirected. Some time before the third century, rabbinic practice had itself begun to diverge from rabbinic precept. Notwithstanding their continued fidelity to the concept of an academic society based upon equality of opportunity and promotion by merit, early rabbinic tradents had gradually come to propound notions of ancestral rights and privileges – even within the realm of the *keter torah*. Indeed, they had explicitly resorted to an appeal to genetic criteria in one of their earliest, and most blatant, attempts to expand their own influence at the expense of the Patriarchal *keter malkhut*. Therein, it might be suggested lies one of the waspish ironies in TJ's records of the attempted deposition of Rabban Gamli'el II, a man reported to have consistently harped on his own impeccable pedigree. In casting around for a possible nominee of their own, the cabal of rabbinic insurgents themselves felt it necessary to emphasise that academic ability had to be supplemented by the virtues of both wealth and *yiḥus* (genealogy). R. 'El'azar ben 'Azariah, we are informed, was chosen because he possessed the latter assets (being, besides all else, a tenth generation descendant of Ezra 'the priest'; see also TJ *Yevamot* 1:6). R. 'Aqiva', despite his scholarly attainments, did not; consequently – and much to his own regret – his potential candidacy never got off the ground.[8]

Arguably, the incident thus described was in every respect *sui generis*. Its geographical and institutional influence, certainly, seems to have been circumscribed. Throughout the period covered by the talmudic corpus, not one of the principals of the great *metivta'ot* of *Bavel* is known to have inherited his position from his father,[9] and even in *'Ereṣ Yisra'el* the phenomenon was – at that level – only occasional. Nevertheless, and as Alon demonstrated,[10] genetic criteria of succession do seem to have intruded into lower echelons of the *keter torah*. In *'Ereṣ Yisra'el* 'sons of sages' became a recognised category throughout the domain. Beneath their fathers, they were granted ceremonial precedence in various forums (*Tosefta'*, *Sanhedrin* 7:8–9) and generic priority over *r'ashei kenesiyot* as well as common folk (TB *Giṭin* 59b–60a). What is more, their candidacy for public office was also considered to be intrinsically preferential. In a remarkable example of exegetical transfer, *Sifrei* Deut. 162 (pp. 212–13), deliberately transmuted the rules of hereditary succession mandated for monarchs into a general principle, equally applicable at all levels of communal service:

> 'He and his sons' etc. [Deut. 17–20] – [teaches that] if he dies, his son takes his place. I possess [Scriptural support for the rule] only in this case [of a king]. Whence [do we know] that all of Israel's administrators [*parnasei yisra'el*] are succeeded by their sons? Scripture says: 'He and his sons in the midst of Israel.' Whoever [occupies a public post] in Israel is succeeded by his children.

In some respects, the process whereby hereditary succession thus began to become acceptable to at least some segments of the rabbinic *keter torah* might have been inevitable. As anlaysed by Weber, even societies which favour charismatic patterns of leadership often find it difficult to resist the encroachment of bureaucratisation and the tendencies towards dynasticism by which it generally seems to be accompanied. That apart, scholastic communities are notoriously prone to consider themselves especially conducive to the sort of hereditary reproduction facilitated by environmental circumstances. Children of great teachers, simply by virtue of their proximity to learned parents, often enjoy greater educational opportunities than other youngsters. (And various rabbinic traditions indicated that daughters could thereby benefit as well as sons.)[11] Some rabbis were apparently convinced that they ought to do so. In extreme cases, such as that provided by the wayward son of R. 'El'azar ben R. Simeon, this consideration – compounded as it seems to have been by a sense of residual collegiality – could override the obvious unsuitability of the prospective pupil, and even his unwillingness to attend the schools.[12] But even when all other things were equal, a tendency towards the establishment of a rabbinic caste, linked to its generational predecessors by hereditary considerations as much as any other, became a pronounced feature in some quarters of early rabbinic society. According to one source (ARN 'B', chap. 4 [ed. Goldin, p. 181]), the school of (*beit*) Shamm'ai had even advocated that *torah* education be restricted to those whose fathers – and grandfathers! – were themselves recognised scholars.

Rejecting the hypothesis that appointments to the second Commonwealth *sanhedrin* had also been hereditary, Alon dated the inception and apogee of that tendency in early rabbinic life to the period spanned by the second and fourth centuries C.E.[13] Moreover, he attributed its appearance to two complementary developments in the contemporary world of the sages in *'Ereṣ Yisra'el*. Teachers of *torah*, he suggested, then attained recognition as members of a distinct professional class (*'umanim*) rather than as devotees of a calling; at the same time, mastery of the Law was acknowledged to be a key qualification for entry to public service. Equally relevant, it might be suggested, was the simultaneous influence exerted on the process by the wider articulation and institutionalisation of the rabbinic *keter torah* to which reference has already been made in previous chapters. Those of the later *tana'im* and early *'amora'im* in *'Ereṣ Yisra'el* who fostered the intrusion of dynastic criteria into the rabbinic estate were imitating a phenomenon characteristic of other domains. Consciously or otherwise, 'sons of scholars' paralleled the 'sons of kings' mentioned in *Mishnah, Berakhot* 1:2 and *Shabbat* 6:9, as well as the 'sons of high priests' referred to (possibly as a generic for all priests) in *Mishnah, 'Ohalot* 17:5 and *Ketubot* 13:1–2. Genetic succession thus became a mark of corporate identity and a means of placing the *keter torah* on a par with its competitors for public esteem.

To the same end, and as was the characteristic rabbinic style in such matters, *'agadah* was also impressed into service and otherwise unexpected interpretations were put on certain Biblical episodes. Beer's analyses have shown that Hophni and Phineas (the sons of Eli); and Joel and Abiah (the sons of Samuel) provide two outstanding illustrations.[14] Both pairs were traditionally reputed to have been unworthy to succeed their fathers, and in early midrashic commentary (a category which includes the writings of Josephus and Pseudo-Philo) were in consequence roundly condemned as rogues. Indeed, not content with the somewhat summary allegations made in I Samuel 2:12 and 8:3, *tana'im* had tended to enumerate their shortcomings, often in scandalous detail. By the third century, however, the emphasis and tone of some of the comments had begun to change. True to their own past conventions, several sages did continue the earlier traditions of critical comment. But others, many of whom Beer identifies as part of the *nasi*'s immediate entourage (but not all; some were Babylonians) provided ingeniously different interpretation for the situations which the Bible describes. Refuting the allegations of knavery – and worse – which had previously been brought against the sons of Eli and Samuel, the sources now depicted their characters in more flattering colours.

Shifts of that magnitude cannot be attributed entirely to changing literary tastes. As Beer notes, it is difficult to avoid the conclusion that the texts which he cites reflect the eagerness of their rabbinic authors to justify and legitimise the growing prevalence of dynastic tendencies amongst their own circles. The very multiplicity of warnings about the dire consequences likely to ensue from a restriction of the *keter torah*'s ranks itself attests to the prevalence of a phenomenon which was eventually to become a prominent feature of almost all rabbinic life.[15]

Verification of candidacy

Although undoubtedly compatible with their communal objectives, the inclination of some rabbis thus to adopt genealogy as one of the criteria for the transmission of office in their own domain was not – in itself – entirely suited to their corporate purposes. Indeed, unless supplemented by other teachings, it could have been largely disfunctional. Even if universally adopted (and it is worth repeating that they were not), patterns of hereditary succession could only have transposed the *keter torah* into a pale imitation of the *keter kehunah* and the *keter malkhut*, endowed with one of their primary attributes but otherwise indistinct. Other means were required in order to ensure that the instruments of the *torah* were not equivalent in status to those of the monarchy and priesthood but essentially superior to them. Put another way , rabbis (and/or their functional predecessors) had to be shown to possess an inherent right to verify the credentials of candidates to office – as much in the *keter kehunah* and the *keter malkhut* as in the *keter torah* itself.

Of the several steps taken to legitimise that position, the first (logically if not always chronologically) was to posit a clear procedural hiatus between 'succession' (*yerushah*) and 'appointment' (*minui*). In the cases of the *keter kehunah* and the *keter malkhut*, the consequent distinction between necessary and sufficient categories of personal assets was made particularly explicit. Genetic succession, several texts pointed out, only conferred upon first-born sons a prior right to candidacy for the high priesthood or the kingship; primogeniture in no way guaranteed their ultimate possession of the offices. Transmission would not take place until their 'fitness' had also been ascertained. This was made explicit when a significant qualifying clause was added to the rule of thumb which – with specific reference to the highest appointments in the *keter kehunah* and the *keter malkhut* – equated the inheritance of public office and private property.

> 'He who has precedence in inheritance has precedence in rulership', the most explicit text now reads, '**provided** that he behaves in the manner of his fathers.'[16]

The caveat was not entirely a rabbinic invention. It could be substantiated – and was so in early rabbinic *'agadah* – by reference to Scriptural examples. After all, few of the successions to high office described in the Bible had been entirely automatic. Much though individual passages of the text had stressed the ritual primacy of first-born sons, several of its narrative portions had indicated alternative priorities. Arguably, it was possible to overlook the Genesis traditions which repeatedly depict instances of younger sons being preferred to older siblings (Isaac–Ishmael; Jacob–Esau; Joseph and his brothers; Ephraim and Menasseh). Ostensibly, those instances related to an embryonic period of Israel's constitutional history, prior to its governmental articulation. But later portions of the national chronicle were more difficult to sidestep. The book of Samuel, as we have already seen, was acknowledged to provide several adjacent lessons in the uncertainties of genetic succession, and the message conveyed by later books of the Old Testament was still more explicit. In the northern kingdom (itself brought into being by a denial of strict hereditary succession), dethronements and usurpations had been recurrent. But even in the Davidic monarchy, where dynasticism was certainly established as a Divinely sanctioned point of reference, neither the *keter kehunah* nor the *keter malkhut* had always adhered to its principles. Notwithstanding their respective pedigrees, Abiathar had been ruthlessly deposed from the high priesthood and replaced by Zadok; similarly, Solomon (I Kings 1), Abijah (II Chron. 11:22) and Jehoahaz (II Kings 23:31; TB *Horayot* 11b) were designated kings during the lifetimes of their older brothers.

Although sensitive to the influence of conventional power-struggles on each of those appointments, early rabbinic commentators focussed their remarks on a different facet of the relevant incidents. Such deviations from the norm of strict hereditary succession, they explained, were generally caused by the personal failings of the individual candidates. Each had in some, not always specified, way 'failed to match up to his father(s)', and had therefore disqualified himself from the position which he otherwise deserved to inherit. Replacements, on the other hand, had been selected precisely because they had promised – at least, initially – to fulfil the requirements of the office to which they were elevated. At the very inception of the *keter kehunah*, Aaron's eldest sons, Nadab and Abihu, had forfeited their right to succeed their father when anticipating with unbecoming relish the powers which they would wield as soon as he and Moses had died (Leviticus *Rabbah* 20:10; Elazar, on the other hand, had studied diligently; *Sifrei* Numbers 157 [p. 213]); Zadok was seen to be fit for the high priesthood when, unlike Abiathar, he received a response from the *'urim* and *tumim*

(TB *Soṭah* 48b). Similar considerations had influenced the transmission of royal crowns. Jeroboam deserved the kingship because he had rebuked Solomon for his misdemeanours (but was punished because he did so publicly; TB *Sanhedrin* 101b); and Ahab because he honoured the *torah* (idem., 102b).

More underlay these portraits than homiletical reflections on the standards of good behaviour expected from the incumbents of public office and their heirs-apparent. Set within a wider framework, they also comprise early rabbinic assessments of the nature of the institutions to which they were applied. Several texts suggest that there had always been something provisional about the restriction of the *keter kehunah* and the *keter malkhut* to specific segments of Israel. Like the *keter torah*, those franchises were originally intended to be the common property of all Israel. That, indeed, was the meaning of the Sinaitic declaration that 'You will be to me a kingdom of priests and a holy nation' (Exodus 19:6; see exegesis in *Mekhilta' de ba-Ḥodesh*; ed. Lauterbach, II, p. 205). Only at a secondary stage – *ex hypothesi* a retrogressive one – had God considered it necessary to institutionalise the priesthood and the monarchy, initially through the medium of first-born sons (TB *Bekhorot* 4b–5a; *Zevaḥim* 112b and TJ *Megilah* 1:11), and then by delegating their privileges exclusively to the sons of Aaron and of David (*Mekhilta' de-Pisha'*; ed. Lauterbach, I, p. 5, commentary on Numbers 18:19, 25:13 and II Chron. 13:5). It followed, however, that what had thus been progressively removed from the congregation could also be restored to the public domain. At a future moment of messianic glory, R. Yishma'el b. R. 'El'azar was eventually reported to have taught, every Jew would indeed reclaim the crowns (*ketarim*) with which he had once rightfully been adorned. (*Seder 'Eliyahu Zuṭa'*, chap. 4).

Thus perceived, the *keter kehunah* and the *keter malkhut* constituted interim trusteeships, not everlasting fiefdoms. The original charters granted to their senior officers were not understood to be open-ended licences for untrammelled behaviour on the part of their successors. In making provisions for the punishment of transgressing priests and *nesi'im*, *Mishnah* (*Horayot* 3:1) had shown that they – like the false prophet and *zaqen mamrei* ('rebellious elder', both referred to in *Mishnah, Sanhedrin* 11:2–6) – would always be accountable for their actions. Dynastic election did not preclude deposition, still less individual punishment.[17] Even at its inception, the covenant with David and his dynasty had been conditional on their correct behaviour, and although the same was not strictly true of the covenant with Aaron (or, for that matter, of the *torah* itself),[18] the thrust of the message remained the same. Priests – even high priests – had been made to suffer displacement and/or demotion because of their failure to live up to the demands of their office. Perhaps the most outstanding example was provided by Phineas – the grandson of Aaron, the recipient of God's covenant of priesthood and (in subsequent mythology) a figure of messianic properties and significance. According to one later tradition, none of these attributes guaranteed his life-long possession of the privileges associated with the station to which he had been elevated. As soon as he sacrificed Jephtach's unfortunate daughter on the altar of his own official vanity, Phineas was summarily deprived of 'the holy spirit' (*ruaḥ ha-qodesh*; Genesis *Rabbah* 60:3).

Beer has traced the origins of the last particular teaching to the parish pumps of third-century Galilee, where it served a useful purpose in the factional fights between priestly and non-priestly contenders for local influence.[19] But the attitude to which it conformed was not necessarily so restricted. Other, quite unrelated, rabbinic analyses of appointments to office in the *keter kehunah* similarly modified the absolute sufficiency of genetic criteria, stressing that succession had normatively to depend upon certified fitness as well as attested pedigree. In order to make that point, rabbis also drew on several of the features which had discredited the history of the *keter kehunah* during the latter stages of the second Commonwealth. Their traditions long retained bitter memories of the nepotism which the priesthood's embedded caste-system had facilitated during that period (*Tosefta', Menaḥot* 13:21 and TB *Pesaḥim* 57a); they also preserved relatively detailed records of the fissiparous – indeed fratricidal – consequences to which, in the case of the two sons of Simeon the Just, the insistence on straightforward primogeniture had given rise.[20] One of the many lessons to be drawn from such experiences was that all high priests, no matter how impeccable their pedigree, had to conform to certain standards. Some of the requirements were catalogued in the teaching that incumbents of the office ought (the term used is '*miṣwah*', not the more compulsory '*ḥayyav*') to be superior to all their brother-priests in 'beauty, strength, wealth, wisdom and appearance'.[21]

As Alon stressed, no rabbinic text ever went to the lengths of advocating that the hereditary transmission of the *keter kehunah* be replaced by procedures of open election. Although *halakhah* did imply that high priests were less sure of dynastic succession than were kings (*Tosefta'*, *Sanhedrin* 4:11; TB *Horayot* 11b and parallels, see also below, p. 252), the basic relevance of the dynastic principle to sacerdotal appointments remained secure. Consequently, and notwithstanding their criticisms of the inequities to which it could give rise, the relevant talmudic texts faithfully reproduce the Scriptural norm that the high-priestly office should pass in hereditary sequence from father to son. (Indeed, in rabbinic eyes not the least of Herod's faults was his violation of that rule by the sale of the high-priestly office, which was remembered to have changed hands with unseemly frequency.)[22] What can be discerned, however, is a recognition of the need to impose definite safeguards, designed to ensure that the nation would indeed receive the high priests it deserved. Thus, within the parameters laid down by hereditary prescriptions, certain regulatory devices would have to be applied. At the very end of the second Temple period, in the admittedly singular circumstances occasioned by the Great Revolt, *kohanim* had themselves apparently come close to that notion when injecting an element of random election into their appointment procedures. Pinḥas of Ḥavta', the very last High Priest, had been chosen by lot.[23] As codified in *Tosefta'* (*Sanhedrin* 3:4) early rabbinic *halakhah* was to regulate the need for an equally impartial – and considerably less risky – mechanism. Specifically, it was to ordain that no high priests – and no kings – were to be appointed (*'ein ma'amidim*) other than by 'the *beit din* of seventy-one'.

It is tempting to interpret that ruling as an expression of the republican perspective which often informs rabbinic disquisitions on all appointment procedures. As such, it is apparently consistent with several other aphorisms, many of which proclaim that authority – including that exercised by rabbis in the capacity of *parnasim* – is ultimately dependent upon the consent of the governed; all appointees, they consequently declare, have to be approved of by the public or, more formally, to be selected through a process of popular consultation.[24] But the *Tosefta'* text, because it specifically refers to participation of a *beit din* in the elevation to power of kings and high priests, also carries a deeper significance. What it mandates is not simply some form of democratic choice across the board of communal office, but the normative superiority of one particular component of a designated selection committee. Precisely how the verification process thus prescribed would run its due course is nowhere specified.[25] Unmistakable, nevertheless, are the constitutional inferences. In neither the *kehunah* nor the *malkhut* can appointments be automatic. According to some traditions, even candidates to comparatively minor sacerdotal office had been required to submit their genealogical credentials to inspection by the 'great *sanhedrin*' of second Temple times (*Mishnah, Midot* 5:4).[26] In the case of more senior functionaries, requirements would have been (or should have been) necessarily more stringent. All candidates would have to be screened by a synod which, whatever its precise composition, would be bound by the dictates of rabbinic *halakhah*. In each instance, the right of ultimate approval would thus become the prerogative of the *keter torah*.

The force of that claim was considerably strengthened by the contrasting nature of the provisions which the early rabbis prescribed for the selection of candidates to senior positions in their own domain. Rabbinic appointees, it was acknowledged, did have to win the approval of their prospective publics; as even so distinguished a scholar as R. Levi ben Sisi was to discover, failure to do so could lead to petitions for dismissal (TJ *Yevamot* 12:7). Nevertheless, the procedure of their selection ought to be entirely their own affair. Thus, the close control which Patriarchs and Exilarchs exercised over *minuyim* during the second and third centuries was unconstitutional as well as high-handed. It certainly contradicted previous practice. During the period of the second Commonwealth, tanna'itic traditions recalled, the sages had never been subject to the same type of multi-lateral and inter-*keter* vetting procedures which *Tosefta'* prescribed for monarchs and priests. Rather, their appointments had been the exclusive prerogative of their own franchise. Candidates for elevation to the High Court had been selected by their own principals, often from an approved roster ('the three rows' of *talmidei ḥakhamim*; *Mishnah, Sanhedrin* 4:4; cf. TJ *Sanhedrin* 1:3). Likewise, each prospective local magistrate had been investigated by his peers and thereafter promoted in steady sequence (*Tosefta', Ḥagigah* 2:9 and *Sheqalim* 3:27).

Authentic or not,[27] those memories undoubtedly suited contemporary rabbinic purposes. For one thing, they furnished historical precedents for the notional independence of the *keter torah* indicated by the prescription that no student might give instruction unless he had received prior authority (*reshut*) from his master (TB *Sanhedrin* 5b). What is more, when contrasted with appointment procedures specified for the *malkhut* and the *kehunah*, they also provided testimonies to the hierarchical position of their domain in the traditional framework of Jewish government. By thus making the past a prelude to present experience, early rabbinic authors emphasised their corporate status as representatives of a sovereign jurisdiction. It was in that capacity that they sought public confirmation of the communal supremacy which they believed to be their contemporary due.

Ceremonies of installation

As described in early rabbinic sources, ceremonies of induction into public office constitute mandatory stages in the process whereby the functional links between a particular person and a specific public position are consummated and made sacred. In none of the three *ketarim* is an appointed officer considered to have come into full constitutional possession of the prerogatives and duties of his office until the relevant ceremonies of induction have run their prescribed and public course. Moreover only with installation, and not before, is the designated incumbent deemed to have attained partnership with God in the covenant which brought his office into being. Pomp, in other words, expresses and reflects power; it ascertains that the acquisition of authority or its passage from one mortal to another has been confirmed and thereby constitutionalised. That is why, quite apart from its importance in the history of society as a whole, the moment of installation also marks a watershed in the life of the ordinand. As well as transforming his status, it can also transform his nature and – where necessary – even his physique.[28]

One consequence of the significance thus attached to the theatre of ritual is that every detail of installation ceremonies requires precise choreography and meticulous pageantry. In that respect, early rabbinic Judaism was only marginally less assiduous than other 'pre-modern' societies.[29] Unlike some peoples of the ancient Middle East, talmudic society did not schedule formal inductions into the highest offices to coincide with a particularly propitious moment in the solar cycle (although it did, for legal purposes, designate a 'New Year for Kings'; *Mishnah, R'osh ha-Shanah* 1:1). But, like them, it did specify all other aspects of the procedures whereby public rites of passage were to be enacted. Indeed, the texts lavish almost as much quantitative attention on the investiture of kings and high priests as on the ordination of rabbis themselves. That fact alone precludes the possibility that such stipulations were sustained by nothing more substantial than a nostalgic desire to preserve the memory of quaint customs which, unhappily, were now defunct. The juxtaposition of the sources suggests that – in addition – rabbinic interest was nourished by more practical concerns. Through the extended analysis of installation rites in each of the three *ketarim*, rabbis invited comparisons of the three domains. In so doing, they also transmitted their own view of their hierarchy, and thereby further illustrated the intrinsic superiority of the 'crown' which they claimed to own.

If the magnitude of that achievement is to be fully appreciated, due note must be taken of the unfavourable literary and historical contexts with which early rabbis had to contend. By any reading, it was to the *keter kehunah* and *keter malkhut* that Israel's past had bequeathed the most majestic traditions of Jewish public ceremonial. Biblical precedents were especially clear on that score. Chapters 29 of Exodus and 8 of Leviticus, for example, provide graphic literary portraits of the ceremonies whereby, at God's command, Moses initiated Aaron and his sons into the priesthood. Equally vivid, albeit less gory and elaborate, are the depictions of the enthronements of Solomon (I Kings 1:33–40) and of Joash (II Kings 11:10–20). Admittedly, none of those passages truly fulfil the conditions necessary for their consideration as paradigmatic texts. The ceremonies which they describe were performed under circumstances of an obviously extraordinary political nature (the formal creation of the Israelite priesthood and the resolution of disputed royal successions); hence there exist no *prima facie* grounds for regarding them as in any way prototypes. But rabbinical exegetes, although sensitive to that consideration, invariably minimised its importance. Their preferred tendency was to cite such sources as prooftexts for the extrapolation of normative models, all authenticated by historical continuity as well as original sanctity.

Thus, to read early rabbinic depictions of the installation rites prescribed for both priests and kings is to gain an impression of somewhat static ceremonial patterns. It is also to review broadly similar procedures. Drawing on the experience of the second Commonwealth, with its rich history of sacerdotal pageant, rabbinic authors were far more explicit than their attested Biblical sources in tracing analogies between inductions into the *keter kehunah* and the *keter malkhut*. (e.g. *Safra', Ṣav* 18:1 [40a]). Often transposing elements of one case to the other, they constructed consolidated prescriptions which in many essentials attributed identical characteristics to them both. Differences constituted no more than discreet variations on a shared theme.

All male members of priestly families, once they had reached the required age for ministration (twenty years old, according to TB *Ḥulin* 24b), were individually called upon to undergo public ceremonies of investiture in prescribed sacral garments: four in the case of 'ordinary' priests (*hedyoṭot*) and eight in that of the *kohen gadol* (who was hence also referred to as the *merubeh begadim*).[30] Unction, the application of holy oil to the appointee in a particular form, was also required for the *mashuaḥ milkhamah* (second only to the High Priest and his deputy in the ecclesiastical hierarchy; TB *Ta'anit* 31a, cf. TJ *Horayot* 3:9), and – even in cases of direct dynastic descent – for all high priests too.[31] Monarchical inductions, although necessarily less stratified, had normatively to follow a similar pattern, the only significant difference being that the need for anointment was waived where a crown prince succeeded his deceased father unopposed. Otherwise, the requirements imposed for the rites of monarchical installations were equally stringent. Early rabbinic texts lay down strict provisions for the exact location of the rite, its publication and – if unction was deemed appropriate – the precise composition of the oil, the manner whereby it was to be applied and the nature of the container from which it was to be poured.[32]

Whether or not each and every detail of the ceremonies thus reconstructed had always been implemented was a moot question.[33] Early rabbinic tradents were far too intimately acquainted with the gyrations of Israel's turbulent past to overlook the fact that in this aspect of public life, as in so many others, Jewish history was riddled with ritual discontinuities, some of which they considered to be symptomatic of the degree to which second Commonwealth monarchs and priests were inferior to their Biblical precursors.[34] But even that circumstance left little room for polemic manoeuvre. Whichever construction was placed on the memories of priestly and royal installation ceremonies, their sheer quantity was awesome. The *keter torah*, by contrast, was in this respect something of a poor relation.

In addition, the Biblical sources also presented the rabbis with two other problems. One was their apparent failure to provide instruments of the *keter torah* with an *ex officio* role in the production and direction of all induction proceedings. Not even prophets, the attested precursors of the rabbis' own domain, had always been the *metteurs-en-scène* in each of the installation pageants which the Bible describes. True, Aaron had been anointed by Moses, Saul and David by Samuel, and Jehu by the unnamed prophet of II Kings 9:1–6; it nevertheless remained awkward that in the case of Solomon the rite had been performed by Zadok, not Nathan (I Kings 1:39) and in that of Joash by Jehoidah (II Chron. 23:11). Secondly, the Biblical texts afforded very little evidence that the *keter torah*, in its institutional form, had ever possessed installation ceremonies of its own which could in any way match the solemnity and pageantry stage-managed at the inductions of Israel's ancient kings and priests.

Exegetical intrusion provided a solution to the first difficulty. The complexities generated by the walk-on parts attributed to individual prophets in some of the installation ceremonies described in the Bible were deftly avoided.[35] Instead, rabbinic tradents focussed their attentions on those texts which provided for some degree of popular participation in the proceedings. Particularly relevant in this context were the available accounts of royal inductions which, in the Scriptural accounts, were often said to have reached their climax when the new king was publicly acclaimed by groups whom the Bible variously describes as *''ish yisra'el'*; *''ish yehudah'*; *''am ha'areṣ'* or *''edah'*. By positing that these were representative bodies, whose functional prerogatives had altogether been inherited by the *keter torah*'s own *sanhedrin*,[36] early rabbinic authors were able to assign to their own domain precisely the sort of validating role in the proceedings which it otherwise seemed to lack. Still more remarkably, they could also imply that the same synod also possessed the final word in the case of the *keter kehunah*. Indeed, it had always done so. Admittedly, talmudic texts nowhere suggest that the '*sanhedrin*' of their own description was to be identified with the 'great assembly' which, according to I Maccabees 14:25–49, had in 145/6 B.C.E. formally confirmed Simon's possession of supreme sacerdotal and civil office. (In fact, they overlook the entire episode.) But they do cite earlier, and presumably less ambiguous precedents. Aaron's induction, they taught, had itself been witnessed – and thereby sanctioned – by the *sanhedrin*. As much was thought to be apparent from Leviticus 8:3, with its record that Moses had been instructed to invite the congregation (*'edah*) to the entrance of the tent of meeting in order to view the ceremony. By replacing what might have been a ritual acclamation and elevation by the people with a constitutive act of sanction performed by persons like themselves, the rabbis in effect transported the sacerdotal and civil rule of society to the rabbinic precincts.[37]

By their own admission, early rabbinic authors were somewhat less rigorous in their attention to scriptural detail when prescribing installation rites in their own domain. They were also less unanimous in their descriptions of the specifics which such ceremonies were thought to require. All concurred in the belief that the grant of authority in the *keter torah* was normatively contingent upon a formal process of *semikhah* (lit. 'laying [of hands]'). Even when manual ordination was replaced by an oral formula (*ba-peh*),[38] it remained true to say that without the rite there would be no rabbinate. That, it was remembered, was why the Romans had expressly outlawed its practice during the first century persecutions associated with the name of Hadrian; that too was why, despite the ban, R. Judah ben Bava' had risked his life by thus inducting some of his pupils in the no-man's land between 'Usha' and Shefar'am (TB *Sanhedrin* 14a). It was also generally agreed (idem., 13b) that only after *semikhah* could designated rabbis adjudicate cases involving the imposition of fines. Otherwise, however, the specifics of the mechanism were a matter of dispute. Was the validity of rabbinic appointment in any way lessened by the cessation of manual ordination? who could perform the rite? where exactly did it have to take place?

Such uncertainties project a somewhat confused appearance on early rabbinic induction procedures into the *keter torah*. From a literary point of view, talmudic portraits of the ceremony are thus inferior to those prescribed for kings and high priests. Descriptions of royal and sacerdotal elevations, although scattered in several rabbinic sources and obviously dependent on separate traditions, are for the most part internally consistent; built on a solid foundation of Biblical references and allusions, they leave remarkably few loose ends. *Semikhah*, on the other hand, is a portmanteau term; as unpacked in early rabbinic sources, it covers a ramified network of jurisdictional categories and vests authority in a variety of (sometimes competing) instruments. Despite the heroic labours undertaken by subsequent generations of rabbinic scholars, the ceremonial framework thus engineered cannot neatly be compartmentalised. Even the nomenclature employed to describe ordination itself remains riddled with anomalies.[39] Hardly less successful have been efforts to define strict categories of the process. The ordination of rabbis, especially when granted by the *nasi'* Judah I, exhibited a bewildering range of nuances. Talmudic sources cite instances of some which were confined to limited periods of time, others which were restricted to the treatment of specified subjects, and yet a third category which were effective only in named locations.[40]

Much of the confusion surrounding the precise form of ordinations into the *keter torah* seems to have resulted from the comparative novelty of such ceremonies. Faithful to the methodology applied with respect to both kings and priests, early rabbinic exegetes would clearly have preferred to assign the origins of their own rites to explicit Biblical sources. But suitable texts, it transpired, were difficult to locate. Of all the Old Testament dignitaries from whom the rabbis traced their own constitutional descent, only Moses was reported to have employed the procedure of manual ordination when transmitting his majesty (*hod*; Numbers 27:20; more precisely some of his majesty) to his designated successor. The instance was certainly sufficiently significant to merit portrayal in terms which immediately called to mind rabbinic inductions (e.g. *Sifrei* Numbers 140 [p. 186]). Nevertheless, and as is often pointed out, the instance was neither straightforward nor typical; consequently, the preferred scriptural sources for the details of manual ordination were more often derived from the verbal associations aroused by the ritual designation of sacrifices (*semikhah u-semikhut zeqeinim*; e.g. *Tosefta'*, *Sanhedrin* 1:1). It was equally difficult to prove that ceremonial ordination had established an unbroken chain of *torah* authorisation throughout post-Biblical history. Even if *semikhah* did constitute an integral facet of some Pharisaic inductions during the second Commonwealth,[41] the interim periods of apparent abeyance remained uncomfortably conspicuous. Manual ordination is not a feature of the Biblical depictions of either the appointment of the seventy elders in the wilderness (Numbers 11:16) nor, for instance, of the succession of Elisha to Elijah (I Kings 19:16; where, in fact, the pouring of oil is cited as the means of transmission).

Besides, not only were the installation procedures of the *keter torah* – in their rabbinic form – more recent than those remembered to have been deployed by the *kehunah* and the *malkhut*; they were also more susceptible to contemporary pressures. In this respect, the very vigour of their domain worked to the rabbis' disadvantage. If they had found it possible to unify – perhaps even to fossilise – their prescriptions of induction rites for high priests and kings, that was primarily because both offices were now defunct (or, at best, matters of purely eschatological aspiration).

Rabbinic ordinations, however, raised issues of contemporary and on-going relevance; how they were conducted would necessarily reflect and affect the relative standings of persons and groups who still had much to thereby gain. Awareness of that fact perhaps explains why Babylonian *'amora'im* were particularly anxious to develop elaborate induction ceremonies which were distinctly their own; to some extent, they thus hoped to compensate for the sense of regional inferiority implied by R. Joshua b. Levi's categorical ruling that the rite of *semikhah* was not valid unless performed in *'Ereṣ Yisra'el* (TB *Sanhedrin* 14a).[42] Further layers of ceremonial heterogeneity were created by the development of intra-communal competition for prestige between local representatives of the *keter torah* and the *keter malkhut*. However called and wherever performed, the rite of rabbinic ordination was far too serious a matter to be left to exclusive rabbinic influence. Patriarchs and Exilarchs insisted that the identity and composition of the ordinating body, and the mandates conferred on the ordinands, had also to be commensurate with their own authority. It will be recalled that procedures in *'Ereṣ Yisra'el* were particularly affected by such pressures. Indeed, they were explicitly remembered (TJ *Sanhedrin* 1:2; see above pp. 202–3), to have coincided with periodic shifts in the relative prestige of individual *nesi'im* on the one hand and of the college of local rabbis on the other.

It was within that jagged context of manifest political conflict that between the third and fifth centuries early rabbinic instruments of the *keter torah* fashioned, and in some cases re-formulated, rites of induction into their own domain. The brevity and rarity of available descriptions does not permit an entirely satisfactory reconstruction of such ceremonies, especially as practised in *'Ereṣ Yisra'el*. Even as they stand, however, the materials do reflect the extent to which the rabbis were anxious to invest their ceremonials with pronounced public significance. To that end, they employed two principal methods. One, particularly prominent in *Bavel*, was to envelop the ritual of rabbinic elevation in as much festivity and flamboyance as circumstances would allow. With the substitution of oral induction for manual ordination, *semikhah* in effect assumed several of the characteristics adopted by other academic societies when conferring recognition of scholastic attainment. Ordinations were pronounced by an alliterative litany (*'yoreh yoreh, yadin yadin, yatir yatir'*: 'May he decide? he may decide; May he judge? he may judge; May he permit? he may permit'); ordinands received distinguishing robes (the *gulta'* of TB *Bava' Meṣi'a* 85a or *ṭalit* of TJ *Bikurim* 3:3); and some are reported to have been praised by their peers in rhythmic verse (TB *Ketubot* 17a). In order to symbolise both the antiquity and sovereignty of their offices, *dayanim* (community judges) were also later to be seated in pews specifically designated the '*katedra*'' of Moses.[43]

A second device – and one even more indicative of rabbinic purposes – was deliberately to apply to the highest appointments in the *keter torah* practices and terms which were transferred for that purpose from the domains of *kehunah* and the *malkhut*. The pageantry of *semikhah*, thus, did not simply reflect the rabbis' propensity for ceremonial; it also illustrated the extent of their determination to demonstrate that the corporate framework of the *torah* now encompassed the prestige of the priesthood and the authority of the monarchy. In isolated instances, some of the details of rabbinic inductions were explicitly derived from procedures associated with parallel processes in the *keter kehunah*.[44] More frequently, literary portraits of the process – and particularly at its senior levels – employed verbal symbols deliberately divorced from the connotations which they had acquired through application to the *keter malkhut*. The roots *yashav* and *malakh* provide the most prominent examples. In the scriptural canon both words are conventionally reserved to describe the initiation and duration of royal office. It is Biblical kings who are 'enthroned' on a designated chair (*kis'ei*) and who thereafter reign. In the Babylonian Talmud, however, the terminology is transferred to an entirely different institutional context. *R'ashei metivta'ot* and *r'ashei yeshivot* are now the public figures who are elevated to office through being 'seated' in their academies; by Gafni's count, ten such individuals are also said to have 'reigned' during their incumbency.[45]

Changes in linguistic fashion cannot be the sole explanation for the incremental manner in which early rabbinic authors progressively resorted to these two terms, both resonant with monarchical associations. (Gafni calculates that only two of the ten academic principals to whom TB applies the root *malakh* lived in the third century; all others are dated to the fourth and fifth centuries.)[46] In transporting their application to the most authoritative precincts of the *keter torah*, the texts suggested and made concrete a notion of hierarchy which extended throughout Jewry. At the same time, they also reflected the extent to which office within the domain, especially in *Bavel*, had become a mark of bureaucratic status rather than of personal charisma.[47] Now that the rabbinic estate commanded the resources of permanent and institutionally articulate 'seats' of learning, its senior members deserved to be treated in every way as Israel's true monarchs. The 'crown' of the *torah*, was the implication, had at last been bestowed on its rightful owners.

NOTES

1. J.R. Goody, *Succession to High Office* (Cambridge Papers in Social Anthropology, 4 [1966]), pp. 2–8.
2. At any one time, there can be only one High Priest and one King. Multiple appointments would lead to strife; TJ *Yoma'* 1:1 and TB *Sanhedrin* 8a.
3. E.g., TB *Bava' Batra'* 109b; cf., however, the sources cited in Finkelstein's notes to *Sifrei* Deut. 157 (p. 209). For the exceptional case of the *mashuaḥ milkhamah*, whose office could not be inherited, see TB *Yoma'* 72b–73a.
4. On the various locations at which the *torah* was said to have been covenanted, see *Sifrei* Deut. 104 (p. 163); *Mekhilta'*, *Mishpaṭim* 20 (ed. Lauterbach, III, p. 187); and TB *Berakhot* 48b (s.v. Rashi '*torah*'). See also the sources cited in M. M. Kasher, *Torah Shelemah* [hereafter TS vol.], 20 (N.Y., 1961), p. 25 notes to no. 94.
5. Separate reasons for the comparison of the *torah* to water are supplied in *Sifrei* Deut. 48 (pp. 110–11); and TB *Ta'anit* 7a.
6. I Kings 20:35 and II Kings 2:3–16; and 6:1–6; rabbinic commentaries traditionally rendered the translations as 'disciples'. Note, however, 'Ula's tradition that, where the father's name of an individual prophet is mentioned, he too had been one. TB *Megilah* 15a.
7. Several do not; for what follows see: M. Beer, 'Banav Shel Mosheh be-'Agadot Ḥazal', *Bar-Ilan Annual*, 13 (1976), pp. 150–2.
8. TJ *Berakhot* 4:1 and *Ta'aniyot* 4:1. These sources, together with the later account in TB *Berakhot* 27b–28a and *Bekhorot* 36a, are analysed and compared in R. Goldenberg, 'The Deposition of Rabban Gamaliel II: An Examination of the Sources', *JJS*, 23 (1972), pp. 167–90. Following Alon, Goldenberg emphasises the fact that R. 'Ela'zar was a *kohen*, and may therefore have personified priestly aspirations for power. Perhaps; but the story shows that other rabbis also resorted to genealogical criteria, whose force was (eventually) also accepted by R. 'Aqiva'.
9. Y. Gafni, 'Shevet u-Meḥoqeq: 'Al Defusie Manhigut Ḥadashim Bitqufat ha-Talmud be-'Ereṣ Yisra'el u-ve-Bavel', *Kehunah u-Melukhah* (eds. Gafni and G. Motzkin; Jerusalem, 1983), p. 85 and n. 37; noting – but dismissing – the exceptions suggested by the cases of Rav 'Ashi and Mar bar 'Ashi; TB *Bava' Batra'* 12b.

10. 'The Sons of Sages', *Jews, Judaism* [...], pp. 436–57; see also the sources cited in M. Beer, 'Meridat Qoraḥ u-Meni'ehah be-'Agadot Ḥazal', *Sefer* [...] *Heinemann* (ed. E. Fleischer & J. Petuchowski; Jerusalem, 1981), pp. 14–18.
11. Some of the instances in *'Ereṣ Yisra'el* are noted in Goodman, *State and Society*, pp. 225, 227–9. On the father–son teaching relationship, see Gerhardsson, *Memory and Manuscript*, p. 75.
12. TB *Bava' Meṣi'a* 85a. In fact, the interest of that particular story goes even deeper. R. 'El'azar's son was promised the various trappings of rabbinical distinction ('they'll make you a *ḥakham*, dress you in a robe of gold, and call you "rabbi"') even before he had embarked upon his (ultimately successful) course of study.
13. *Jews, Judaism*, pp. 451–2; rejecting the theory proposed by Funk in 1911. But cf. Hoenig, *Sanhedrin*, pp. 57–8.
14. M. Beer, 'Banav Shel 'Eli be-'Agadot Ḥazal', *Bar-Ilan Annual*, 14 (1977), pp. 79–93 and 'Banav Shel Shemu'el be-'Agadot Ḥazal', *Sefer Yiṣḥaq 'Aryeh Seligman* (eds. J. Zakovitch, A. Rofeh; Jerusalem, 1983), Vol. 2, pp. 427–39.
15. Thus, in reply to Beit Shamm'ai's dictum, cited above, Beit Hillel is reported to have replied: 'Every man deserves to be taught. For many of Israel's sinners were brought close to the *torah* and produced righteous persons, saints, and worthy men.' Compare TB *Nedarim* 81a, which states as fact that scholars do not produce offspring of their own rank, (a) 'lest they claim the *torah* as their own inheritance'; (b) 'lest they make themselves more important than the public'. On the extent to which dynasticism became rife in rabbinic circles in the post-talmudic periods, see A. Grossman, 'Yerushat 'Avot be-Hanhagah ha-Ruḥanit Shel Qehilot Yisra'el Bimei ha-Beinayim ha-Muqdamim', *Zion*, 50 (1985), pp. 189–220.
16. *Tosefta', Sheqalim* 2:15. Note, however, the absence of this caveat in *Sifrei* Deut. 162 (p. 212) and in the statement attributed to R. 'El'azar ben 'Azariah (himself a priest) in *Safra', Shemini* 1:2. Other sources in Kasher, TS, vol. 26 (N.Y., 1974), pp. 187–9 and vol. 36 (Jerusalem, 1982), p. 56 no. 37.
17. TJ *Horayot* 3:1; nevertheless, on the complexities of the issue see S. Lieberman, *Tosefta' Kifshutah* [hereafter TK, vol.] 4 (*Mo'ed*; N.Y., 1962), p. 722 and (on the difficulties aroused by a regency) Kasher, TS, vol. 26, p. 189 n. 145.
18. *Mekhilta', Yitro* 2 (Lauterbach, vol. 2, p. 187ff): 'Three things were given conditionally (*'al ten'ai*): the land of Israel, and the Temple and the Davidic monarchy. But the Law (*sefer torah*) and the covenant with Aaron were not given conditionally.' See, however, the alternative versions cited in Ginzberg, *Legends*, Vol. 6, p. 29 n. 173.

19. M. Beer, ''Al Manhigim Shel Yehudei Ṣiporie ba-Me'ah ha-Shelishit', *Sinai*, 74 (1974), pp. 133–8.
20. TB *Menaḥot* 109b. Compare, however, the reconstructions in *tosafot*'s comments on the passage and in Maimonides' commentary to *Mishnah*, *Menaḥot* 13:10.
21. *Tosefta'*, *Kipurim* 1:6; parallels and variants in Lieberman, idem., p. 727.
22. Above chapter 2, p. 40 and E. M. Smallwood, 'High Priests and Politics in Roman Palestine', *Journal of Theological Studies*, 13 (1962), esp. p. 15 and appendix pp. 31–4.
23. *Tosefta'*, idem. 1:6 (and Lieberman, TK, idem., p. 728); Josephus – who takes a far dimmer view of the incident (and the choice) records that 'The excuse given for this arrangement was ancient custom'. BJ 4:155. This may not be as far fetched as Josephus would like us to believe. The tradition that all high priests had to serve an apprenticeship as deputies (TJ *Yoma'* 3:8) suggests an elective procedure. Even more explicit is the ruling pronounced at Qumran (*The Scroll of the Sons of Light*, 15:4ff; ed. Yadin, p. 210) that 'the priest anointed for war' be appointed 'by the agreement of his brother-priests'.
24. The injunction is especially pronounced in, e.g., *Sifrei* Deut. 13 (p. 22); the exegesis on Deut. 17:5 quoted at the end of TJ *Sanhedrin* 2:6, and the rule laid down by R. Isaac (in some MS versions, R. Yoḥanan) in TB *Berakhot* 55a, which also uses the term *'ein ma'amidim*.
25. Even more confusing is the absence of explicit talmudic provisions for the participation of the *beit din* in procedures of high priestly displacement. Compare *tosafot* on TB *Yoma'* 12b [s.v. *kohen*] with *tosafot* to TB *Megilah* 9b [*we-lo'*] and the discussion in Lieberman, TK, idem., p. 722.
26. Cf., however, the more vague recollection in *Sifrei* Numb. 116 (p. 133): 'There was a place behind the veil [*beit la-parokhet*] where they investigate the genealogies of the priesthood'. See: Lieberman, *Hellenism in Jewish Palestine*, p. 172.
27. The issue is discussed in Hoenig, *Sanhedrin*, pp. 54–5. For an analysis of the materials which purport to describe procedures after the Destruction (especially TB *Sanhedrin* 17a–b), see: R. Margoliot, 'Tena'ei ha-Minui ke-Ḥaver ha-Sanhedrin', *Sinai*, 20 (1947), pp. 16–26.
28. See, e.g. the various citations in S. Leiter, 'Worthiness, Acclamation and Appointment: Some Rabbinic Terms', *PAAJR*, 41–2 (1974), pp. 155, 157–8. Particularly picturesque is one commentary on Psalm 45:3 (quoted idem., p. 155 citing *Yalquṭ Shim'oni*): 'If [the High Priest] were short, he became tall; if he was black, he became white; if his countenance was troubled, he became cheerful.'
29. Several examples are examined in D. Cannadine and S. Price (eds.), *Rituals of Royalty: Power and Ceremonial in Traditional Societies*

(Cambridge, 1987). Far less informative, in every respect, is R. Patai, 'Hebrew Installation Rituals', *HUCA*, 20 (1947), pp. 143–225.

30. Thereafter, such uniforms were mandatory. With regards to *hedyoṭot*, TB *Zevaḥim* 17b–18a was to rule: 'When their priestly garments are on them, so is their priestly sanctity; if their garments are not on them, neither is their priestly sanctity.' For the atoning power of the High Priest's eight vestments; TB *Zevaḥim* 88b and Kasher, TS, 28 (Jerusalem, 1978), p. 290, n. 46.
31. *Tosefta'*, *Sanhedrin* 4:11; and parallels. For other sources relating to high priestly investiture and anointment see: Kasher, TS, 21 (N.Y., 1964), p. 33, nos. 148–51; and – on the *mashuaḥ milkhamah* – idem., 26, p. 187 n. 142.
 The single normative exception to unction seems to have been allowed in the case of a *kohen* called upon to substitute for the High Priest who had suddenly become incapacitated immediately prior to the Day of Atonement. Even then, however, enrobement in eight garments remained necessary. On unction as a generic symbol of elevation (*gedulah*); *Sifrei* Numb. 117 (p. 135).
32. TJ *Horayot* 3:4 and also Kasher, TS, 21, p. 39 no. 176.
33. And must remain so, since neither Philo nor Josephus describe the installation rites practised during the second Commonwealth and with respect to earlier periods add nothing to the Biblical text. However, a brief description of high priestly elevation is provided in I Macc, 10:20–1 (which speaks of investiture and crowning, but not of anointment). Unfortunately – but perhaps significantly – talmudic sources do not provide literary accounts of the investiture of either Patriarchs or Exilarchs (although it is hard to believe that no such ceremonies took place). For descriptions of the pageant involved we have to wait until the report compiled by R. Natan ha-Bavli, reprinted in B. Dinur, *Yisra'el ba-Golah: Meqorot we-Te'udot*, Vol. 5 (2nd edtn.; Tel Aviv, 1961), pp. 91–4.
34. E.g., 'when the ark was hidden so was the container of the oil of anointment' (alternatively, 'from the days of Josiah [...]'); compare *Tosefta'*, *Soṭah* 13:1 with *Yoma'* 3:7; TB *Horayot* 11b [which notes the miraculous properties of the liquid]; and *Yoma'* 52b and parallels.
35. E.g. in *Sifrei* Deut. 157 (p. 208), which blandly rules that all kings must be appointed by [*'al pi*] a prophet. Compare, however, *Sifrei Zuṭa'* no. 19.
36. The transcription of *'edah* by ('great' or 'lesser') *sanhedrin* is a common motif in early rabbinic literature. E.g. the exegesis of Numbers 35:24–5 in TB *R'osh ha-Shanah* 26a and sources in Hoenig, *Sanhedrin*, pp. 50 and 246 (notes 20 and 20a).
37. See the sources cited in Kasher, TS, 20 (N.Y., 1961), p. 152 no. 2, and 27 (Jerusalem, 1975), p. 117 no. 13.
 Midrash ha-Gadol (*Wayiqra'*; ed. Rabinowicz, p. 198), adds: 'And

similarly all public appointments must be in the presence of the entire congregation.'

38. Compare the analyses of the present text of TB *Sanhedrin* 13b in Newman, *Semikhah*, pp. 103–6 with S. Lieberman, 'Raymond Martini's Alleged Forgeries', *Historica Judaica*, 5 (1945), pp. 99–100. The various theories adduced to explain the change are summarised in Waharftig, 'Ha-Semikhah Bizman ha-Talmud', p. 146.
39. In general, ordination in *'Ereṣ Yisra'el* was by the second century, at the latest, designated *minui*; in *Bavel*, however, the term *semikhah* was retained. Possible explanations – and exceptions – are discussed in H. Albeck, 'Semikhah, u-Minui u-Veit Din', *Zion*, 8 (1943), pp. 85–7 and Waharftig, p. 145.
40. Specific instances are cited in Waharftig, pp. 154–9, 170–3; and Newman, *Semikhah*, pp. 78–80, 97–8, 102–4.
41. As is argued with intricate ingenuity in H. Mantel, 'Ordination and Appointment in the Period of the Temple', *HThR*, 57 (1964), pp. 325–46. On comparisons with the rite as described in the NT (e.g. Acts 6:5–6), D. Daube, *The New Testament and Rabbinic Judaism* (London, 1956), pp. 209 and 224–46.
42. Newman, *Semikhah*, pp. 131, 137. This also explains the fact that Babylonian 'rabbis' were entitled '*rav*' or '*mar*' rather than, as was the case in *'Ereṣ Yisra'el*, '*rabi*'. Moreover, in recognition of the inferiority thus indicated, they also tended to defer to their Palestinian colleagues (TB *Pesaḥim* 51a).
43. M. Bar-Ilan, ''Even, Kis'ei, we-Katedra' she-Yashav 'Aleihem Mosheh', *Sidra*, 2 (1986), pp. 15–24; on the ceremonial of rabbinic ordinations, especially in *Bavel*, Waharftig, pp. 146–50 and Newman, pp. 121–3. Festive inductions of rabbis 'Ami and 'Asi (both Babylonians) in *'Ereṣ Yisra'el* are mentioned in TB *Sanhedrin* 14a and *Ketubot* 17a.
44. Significantly, it was from the provisions reportedly mandated for the High Priest that R. 'Abbahu of Caesarea deduced the need to ensure the financial independence of R. 'Abba' of 'Akko, his preferred candidate for the presidency of the academy of Caesarea (TB *Soṭah* 40a and Rashi s.v. '*'amar R. 'Abbahu*'). Similarly, it was by reference to the manner whereby the *kohen gadol*'s deputy had been installed in office on the Day of Atonement that explanations (or justifications) were found for the replacement of manual rabbinic ordination by an oral process (TJ *Yoma'* 1:1 and *Megilah* 1:10).
45. Y. Gafni, '"Yeshivah" u-"Metivta"', *Zion*, 43 (1978), pp. 32–3, analyses uses of both terms in the Babylonian context. Ceremonial transpositions of the root *yashav* are also discussed in Albeck, 'Semikhah u-Minui', pp. 85–7; Hoenig, *Sanhedrin*, p. 160, and – less rigorously – in S. Leiter, 'Worthiness, Acclamation', p. 160. Further sources in H. J. Kasowski, *Thesaurus Talmudis*, vol. 17 (Jerusalem, 1966), pp. 648–9.

46. Equally important is the geographical spread of the names named: only three headed the acaḍemy of Pumbediṭa' ('Abbayei; Rabah and R. Joseph). Of the others, two (R. Yoḥanan and R. Ḥanina' bar Ḥama') officiated in *'Ereṣ Yisra'el*; Rava' was principal at Maḥoza' (although of course he had spent many of his formative years in Pumbediṭa'); and Sura' is represented by R. Ḥuna', Ḥisda' and 'Ashi (whose son, Mar bar Rav 'Ashi, is also said to have 'reigned' in Mata' Meḥasya'). As is often pointed out, the use of monarchical terms (*melekh* and *keter*) with reference to rabbinic offices and appointments became increasingly common in the Geonic and medieval periods. See: M. Breuer, 'Ha-Semikhah ha-'Ashkenazit', *Zion*, 33 (1968), pp. 15–46.
47. A facet which has been said to explain the differences between Babylonian and Palestinian traditions in this regard. J. Katz, 'Rabbinical Authority and Authorization in the Middle Ages', *Studies in Jewish History and Literature* (ed. I. Twersky; Cambridge, Mass., 1979), p. 49.

Afterword: a symbol and its resonance

In the introduction to his *History of the Crusades*, Sir Steven Runciman noted the historian's professional preference for small fortresses of learning. Although comparatively easy to defend from the slings and arrows of critical assault, such castles of scholasticism (Runciman complained) command too narrow a field of fire to support exploratory excursions further afield. Deliberately – perhaps rashly – this book has attempted to avoid that particular charge. It covers a large slice of Jewish history during one of its most convulsive ages. Moreover, it has attempted to trace in manageable compass what are in retrospect two of the period's crucial themes: first, the incubation and institutionalisation of the 'official' rabbinic version of Israel's ordained constitutional chronology; second, and consequently, the propulsion of the rabbis and their disciples to positions from which they could claim (and sometimes attain) commanding communal authority.

Early rabbinic renditions and manipulations of the paradigm of the three *ketarim* mirror those developments. Approached as both a construct of power-sharing and as an implicit design for the examination of its operation, the model became a prominent article of constitutional polemic. Still more coherently, the intellectual architecture of the crown *motif* also articulated latent rabbinic notions about the very texture of ordained Jewish society. The way in which the symbols of *torah*, *kehunah* and *malkhut* were arranged and re-arranged conveyed how deeply the proponents of rabbinic Judaism were imbued with a sense of the distinctiveness of their mission in life, and how determined they were to embark upon a course which might translate their convictions into the realities of power. By projecting a hierarchy of the *ketarim* and identifying their respective agents (past and present), proponents of rabbinic supremacy paraded their own *keter torah* as the multi-generational repository of authentic Jewish government. Rabbis, thus portrayed, comprised a timeless elite. Their eminence, because founded on the bedrock of their understanding of God's own word, transcended that of even the most aristocratic of other earthly instruments of rule.

As the rabbis themselves testify, their road to authority during the period of late antiquity was often hazardous and never straightforward. *En route* to power, they encountered severe resistance – even from co-religionists who otherwise accepted rabbinic interpretations of Judaism. Nevertheless, so conspicuous was the ultimate success of their enterprise that there has traditionally existed a tendency to depict the rabbis' projection of communal government as the only one then in vogue; the alternatives possibly proposed by their domestic opponents are conventionally consigned to oblivion. Irremediable gaps in the source material relating to the authority still claimed in post-Destruction Jewry by contemporary agencies of the *keter malkhut* and *keter kehunah* provide one possible explanation. Vividly articulate though hierocrats and monarchists had been prior to 70 C.E. their defeat thereafter left a legacy of subsequent silence. Whatever ambitions they continued to nurture must now be culled primarily from texts composed and edited by the rabbis themselves.

Equally salient, however, seems to be a conscious or unconscious brand of tunnel vision. Rabbinic perspectives on communal government, when studied at all, are invariably approached in isolation; how they might have interacted with, and been influenced by, alternative Jewish projections is hardly explored. This situation is to be regretted, not only because it induces a lopsided picture, but principally because it does violence to the cultural ecology of the period as a whole. Constitutional conflicts of an ideological nature, after all, are rarely conducted through the medium of insulated doctrinal monologues. Invariably, the respective positions are worked out through the process of dialogue, in which the contending parties – although proposing adversarial programmes – employ shared and mutually understood conventions of debate. It is the task of political scientists to propose a framework of analysis which might identify those conventions and measure their consistency.

The concept of the three *ketarim* offers just such a framework. Apparently rooted in pre-rabbinic Jewish political traditions, its resonance during the period of late antiquity illuminates the political world which the rabbis (at least) then imagined themselves to inhabit. More substantively, the resilience of the triangular paradigm also provides a sharp focus for their understanding of the parameters of permissible constitutional action. As a vehicle of political mobilisation, their image of the inherent superiority and continuity of the *keter torah* was unabashedly hegemonic. It was not, however, either innovative or destructive. For one thing, spokesmen for the other two domains had at various junctures during the second Commonwealth already posited equally far-reaching claims, on occasion employing precisely the same polemical tools of scriptural exegesis and historical allusion to which the rabbis had resort. Secondly, and still more strikingly, proponents of the authority said to reside in the *keter torah* were to abide by what appear to have been deliberately self-denying ordinances. None of the early rabbinic texts to hand advocate the utter elimination of either the *kehunah* or the *malkhut*; neither do they intimate that the circumstances of post-Destruction Jewish life had rendered those franchises of Jewish self-government entirely redundant. What they advocate, rather, is a more subtle process of co-option: the virtues of scholastic piety epitomised by the sages are said to have empowered them to straddle the other two domains and enjoy their prerogatives. *Kehunah* and *malkhut* were thus to be regulated, not rejected. Only the advent of the Messiah would re-incarnate those franchises. Thereto, they could not find proper constitutional expression unless amalgamated within the overarching span of the *keter torah*.

Precisely how that doctrine fared during the intermittent constitutional convulsions which subsequently punctuated Jewish political life must await further examination.[1] Impossible to overlook even at this stage, however, is the manner in which it was characteristically buttressed in later Jewish depictions of the *keter* motif. One example is provided by the responsa literature, the massive collection of rabbinic writings which constituted medieval and early modern Jewry's primary network of world-wide halakhic communications and discourse. A preliminary search through the thousands of such texts now stored on computer at Bar-Ilan University in Israel reveals their inherent bias. Over ninety percent of *keter* references, the vast majority of which are themselves to be found in the acclamations which the individual respondent addresses to his enquirer, denote possession of the *keter torah* as the supreme accolade of Jewish life. Only in scattered cases (all similarly honorific) is any reference whatsoever made to the prerogatives inherent in the *ketarim* of the *malkhut and kehunah*. Moreover, in this entire storehouse, there is just one sustained analysis of the independent roles which formative Jewish texts assign to all three domains.[2]

Graphic sources convey that message even more forcefully. The *keter* motif, they reveal, did certainly become a standard item of synagogue decoration. As far as the ravages of Nazism permit us now to tell, it was especially favoured by the late medieval and early modern Jewish communities of northern Africa, Italy, Germany and Poland. There, crowns of various local design were regularly portrayed above the synagogue ark which housed the *torah* scrolls or on the curtains which covered the ark doors. Alternatively (where communal budgets permitted, in addition), they decorated the scrolls' own velvet mantel (*me'il*), breastplate (*ṭas*), finials (*rimmonim*) and – most prominently of all – the silver headpiece (itself termed *keter*) with which the scrolls were ultimately crested. Few of the surviving examples of such items pre-date the early eighteenth century. However, it has been noted that:

> The custom of placing a crown over the Torah scrolls is evidenced from archival documents as early as the twelfth century. Such crowns are mentioned in an inventory of 1186–7, and were among the textual fragments that were discovered in the Fostat Genizah. In 1439, a contract was drawn up commissioning the Avignon goldsmith Robin Tissard to fashion a crown for fifty florins for 'le rouleau des Juifs'.[3]

What is most striking about such depictions is that the *keter* thus given prominence is unquestionably that of the *torah* itself. True, the other franchises are not always allowed to drop from view. In many cases, graphic references to the *malkhut* and *kehunah* are squeezed in by the supplementary depictions of the rampant lion of Judah (representing the former) and the priestly breastplate or seven-branched candelabra (signifying the latter). Some constructions – as in the case of the late medieval Italian scroll-headpiece noted by Roth[4] – are still more elaborate, accommodating three crown devices in one single feat of metallurgy. Even so, the supremacy of the *keter torah* is nowhere questioned. Almost always[5] it stands at the very apex of the triangular design, thus symbolising the majesty which is its due.

Whether or not such portraits comprise authentic representations of the framework of government universally desired by all Jews in all ages must for the moment be left an open question. What they do undoubtedly reflect, however, is the extent to which the concept of the three *ketarim* – in its early rabbinic guise and early rabbinic interpretation – had come to exercise a singularly powerful hold on articulate segments of the Jewish public.

NOTES

1. A preliminary sketch was essayed in D. J. Elazar and S. A. Cohen, *The Jewish Polity: Jewish Political Organization from Biblical Times to the Present* (Bloomington, Indiana, 1985).
2. The (admittedly massive) exception is to be found in *Shut Ḥatam Sofer* (Pressburg [i.e. Bratislava], 1896). *'Oraḥ Ḥayyim*, pt. 1 no. 12, composed by R. Moses Sofer (the '*Ḥatam Sofer*', 1762–1839), a recognised leader of contemporary Jewish orthodoxy in central Europe. For translation and annotation see my: 'La succession à un office publique dans la Halakhah', *Pardes*, 1 (1985), pp. 150–68.
3. G. Sed-Rajna, *Ancient Jewish Art* (Paris, 1985), p. 150. References to the notion of the three *ketarim* cited in *'Avot* have become standard in catalogues of such items. Amongst recent examples, see, e.g.: S.L. Braunstein, *Personal Vision: The Jacobo and Asea Furman Collection of Jewish Ceremonial Art* (N.Y., 1985), esp. pp. 7–9 and C. Benjamin, *The Stieglitz Collection: Masterpieces of Jewish Art* (Jerusalem, 1987), esp. pp. 30–2, 52.
4. C. Roth, *Jewish Art: An Illustrated History* (2nd ed., Jerusalem, 1971), p. 317. Another example in S. S. Kayser (ed.), *Jewish Ceremonial Art* (Phila., 1959), p. 28, n. 8.
5. The only exception which I have personally encountered is located in the Touro Synagogue, constructed in Newport, Rhode Island, during the colonial period of American history. There, above the ark, three crowns (modelled on the contemporary British royal diadem) are arranged in triangular design, with the *keter malkhut* (designated by the Hebrew letters *kaf* and *mem*) being placed **above** those of the *torah* (*kaf* and *taf*) and *kehunah* (here designated *keter lewiyah*, hence *kaf* and *lamed*). Artistic error cannot be discounted. But one is intrigued by the thought that the arrangement may have been a deliberate, if somewhat arcane, expression of Empire loyalism in a community known for its fidelity to the British government. (See: A.F. Losben, 'Newport Jews in the American Revolution', *Rhode Island Jewish Historical Notes*, 7 [1976], pp. 258–76.)

BIBLIOGRAPHY

1. PRIMARY SOURCES

(a) Texts and translations

THE BIBLE

Torah, Nevi'im u-Ketuvim (The Old Testament; [Koren edition] Jerusalem, 1980).
The New English Bible (Old and New Testaments; Cambridge, 1970).

APOCRYPHA & PSEUDOEPIGRAPHICA

The Apocrypha and Pseudoepigraphica of the Old Testament (ed. R.H. Charles; 2 vols., Oxford, 1913).
Sefer Ben Sira' ha-Shalem (ed. M.S. Segal; Jerusalem, 1959).
I Maccabees [The Anchor Bible, vol. 41] (trans. and ed. J.A. Goldstein; N.Y., 1976).

QUMRAN TEXTS

Megilot Midbar Yehudah (ed. A.M. Haberman; Jerusalem, 1959).
The Essene Writings from Qumran (ed. A. Dupont-Sommer; English trans. by G. Vermes; Oxford, 1962).
The Dead Sea Scrolls in English (intro. & trans. G. Vermes; Harmondsworth, 1962).
The Rule of Qumran and its Meaning [The 'Manual of Discipline'] (ed. A.R.C. Leaney; London, 1966).
The Thanksgiving Hymns (ed., M. Mansoor; Grand Rapids, 1961).
The Scroll of the War of the Sons of Light Against the Sons of Darkness (ed. Y. Yadin; English trans. by B. & C. Rabin; Oxford, 1962).
Megilat ha-Miqdash [The Temple Scroll] (ed. Y. Yadin; 3 vols., Jerusalem, 1977).

PHILO

Philo: Complete Works (Loeb Classical Library ed., 10 vols.; trans. and eds., R. Marcus, F.H. Colson & G.H. Whittaker; London, 1953–63).

JOSEPHUS

Josephus: Complete Works (Loeb Classical Library ed., 9 vols.; trans. and eds. H. St. John Thackeray, R. Marcus, & L.H. Feldman; London, 1926–1935).

RABBINIC LITERATURE

Mishnayot (ed. P. Kahati; 12 vols.; Jerusalem, 1970).
The Mishnah (trans. H. Danby; Oxford, 1933).
Tosefta' (ed. M.S. Zuckermandel with additions by S. Lieberman; Jerusalem, 1975).
Tosefta' Kifshutah ['A Comprehensive Commentary on the Tosefta'] (ed. S. Lieberman; 8 parts [covering the orders *Zera'im, Mo'ed* and *Nashim*], New York, 1955–73).
Sifra' de-Bei Rav. Hu Sefer Torat Kohanim (reprint; Jerusalem, 1959).
Sifrei 'Al Sefer Bamidbar [Numbers] (also incorporating *Sifrei Zuṭa'*; ed. H.S. Horovitz; Leipzig, 1917).
Sifrei 'Al Sefer Devarim [Deuteronomy] (ed. L. Finkelstein & H.S. Horovitz; New York, 1939).
Sifre: A Tannaitic Commentary on the Book of Deuteronomy (ed. and trans. R. Hammer; New Haven, Conn., 1986).
Mekhilta de-Rabbi Ishmael (ed. & trans. J.Z. Lauterbach; 3 vols., Phila., 1933–35).
'Avot de Rabi Natan (ed. S. Schechter; corrected ed., N.Y., 1967).
The Fathers According to Rabbi Nathan (trans. J. Goldin; New Haven, Conn., 1955).
Talmud Bavli [The Babylonian Talmud] (reprint; 20 vols., Jerusalem, 1972).
Talmud Bavli (ed. & trans. into Hebrew, A. Steinzaltz; 17 vols., so far, Jerusalem, 1976–88).
The Babylonian Talmud (translated under the general editorship of I. Epstein; 18 vols., London, 1961).
Talmud Yerushalmi [The Jerusalem Talmud] (reprint, 5 vols.; Jerusalem, 1976).
Talmud Yerushalmi (ed. and trans. into Hebrew; A. Steinzaltz; vol. 1 [tractate *Pe'ah*], Jerusalem, 1987).
Midrash Rabbah (ed. M.A. Mirkin; 11 vols., Tel Aviv, 1977).
Midrash Rabbah (translated under the general editorship of H. Freedman & M. Simon; 10 vols., London, 1939).
Midrash Tanhuma' [on the Pentateuch] (reprint; Jerusalem, 1965).

(b) Collections and aids

Ginzberg, L. *The Legends of the Jews* (6 vols. reprint; Phila., 1965).
Halprin, R. *'Atlas 'Eiṣ-Ḥayim* [chronological map of rabbinic authorities], vols. 3 & 4 (*'Tana'im we-'Amora'im'*; Tel Aviv, 1980).
Hyman, A. *Torah ha-Ketuvah we-ha-Mesurah* ['A Reference Book of the Scriptural Passages quoted in Talmudic, Midrashic and Early Rabbinic Literature'] (2nd., ed., 3 vols., Tel-Aviv, 1979).
Kanowitz, Y. *R. Shim'on bar Yoḥ'ai. 'Osef Shalem Shel Devaraw u-Ma'amaraw ba-Sifrut ha-Talmudit we-ha-Midrashit* [Concordance of sayings attributed to R. Simeon bar Yoḥ'ai in early rabbinic texts] (Jerusalem, 1965).
Kasher, M. M. *Torah Shelemah* [Concordance of early rabbinic commentaries on the Pentateuch] (39 vols. so far; N.Y., and Jerusalem, 1949–85).
Rabbinovicz, R. N. N. *Sefer Diqduqei Soferim* [Catalogue of Variant Readings on the Babylonian Talmud] (reprint, N.Y., 1976).

2. SECONDARY SOURCES

Aberbach, M. *Ha-Ḥinukh ha-Yehudi Bitqufat ha-Mishnah we-ha-Talmud* (Tel Aviv, 1983).
Aberbach, M. & Smolar, L. 'Aaron, Jeroboam, and the Golden Calves', *JBL*, 86 (1967), pp. 129–10.
'Jeroboam and Solomon: Rabbinic Interpretations', *JQR*, 59 (1969), pp. 118–32.
Adler, A. 'Une image controversée d'Alexander Jannée', *REJ*, 138 (1979), pp. 337–49.
Albeck, C. *Mavo' la-Talmudim* (Tel Aviv, 1969).
Albeck, H. 'Semikhah u-Minui u-Veit Din', *Zion*, 8 (1943), pp. 85–93.
Albeck, S. *Batei ha-Din Bimei ha-Talmud* (Ramat Gan, 1980).
Albright, W. F. 'The Judicial Reforms of Jehoshafat', *Alexander Mark Jubilee Volume* (Eng. section; N.Y., 1970), pp. 61–82.
Aleksandrov, G. S. 'The Role of 'Aqiba in the Bar Kokhba Rebellion', in J. Neusner, *Eliezer Ben Hyrcanus: The Tradition and the Man*, vol. 2 (Leiden, 1973), pp. 422–36.
Allan, N. 'The Identity of the Jerusalem Priesthood during the Exile', *Heythrop Journal*, 23 (1982), pp. 254–69.
Alon, G. *Jews, Judaism and the Classical World* (trans. I. Abrahams; Jerusalem, 1977).
The Jews in their Land in the Talmudic Age (70–640 C. E.) (translated and edited by G. Levi; 2 vols., Jerusalem, 1980 and 1984).
Aptovitzer, A. 'Politiqah Ḥashmona'it we-Neged Ḥashmona'it ba-Halakhah u-va-'Agadah', *Sefer Zikaron Likhvod ha-Doqtor Shemu'el 'Avraham Poznanski* (reprint., Jerusalem, 1969), pp. 145–69.

Avi-Yonah, M. *The Jews Under Roman and Byzantine Rule: A Political History of Palestine from the Bar Kokhba War to the Arab Conquest* (Jerusalem, 1984).

Hellenism and the East: Contacts and Interrelations from Alexander to the Roman Conquest (Univ. microfilms; Ann Arbor, 1978).

Babelin, J. *Le Portrait dans l'Antiquité* (Paris, 1942).

Baer, Y. 'Ha-Yesodot ha-Historiyim Shel ha-Halakhah', *Zion*, 17 (1952), pp. 1–35.

Bamberger, B. J. 'The Dating of Aggadic Materials', *JBL*, 68 (1949), pp. 115–23.

'Revelations of Torah after Sinai', *HUCA*, 16 (1941), pp. 97–113.

Baron, S. W. *A Social and Religious History of the Jewish People*, vol. 2 (Phila., 1952).

Bar-Ilan, M. *Ha-Pulmus Bein ha-Ḥakhamim la-Kohanim be-Shelhei Yemei Bayit Sheini* (Unpub. Ph. D. Thesis; Bar-Ilan University, 1982).

''Ofyah u-Meqorah Shel Megilat Ta'anit', *Sinai*, 98 (1985), pp. 114–37.

''Even, Kis'ei, we-Qatedrah she-Yashav 'Aleihem Mosheh', *Sidra*, 2 (1986), pp. 15–24.

Barraclough, R. 'Philo's Politics. Roman Rule and Hellenistic Judaism', *ANRW*, 4:21 (1984), pp. 417–553.

Bartlett, J. R. 'Zadok and his Successors at Jerusalem', *JTS*, 19 (1968), pp. 1–18.

Baumgarten, A. I. 'The Akiban Opposition', *HUCA*, 50 (1974), pp. 179–97.

'The Politics of Reconciliation: The Education of R. Judah the Prince', *Jewish and Christian Self-Definition* (ed. E. P. Sanders, et al.; Phila., 1981), vol. 2, pp. 213–25.

'Rabbi Judah I and his Opponents', *JSJ*, 12 (1982), pp. 135–72.

'The Name of the Pharisees', *JBL*, 102/3 (1983), pp. 411–28.

'The Torah as a Public Document in Judaism', *Studies in Religion*, 14 (1985), pp. 17–24.

'The Pharisaic *Paradosis*', *HThR*, 50 (1987), pp. 63–77.

Baumgarten, J. M. 'Art in the Synagogue: Some Talmudic Views', *Judaism*, 19 (1970), pp. 196–206.

'The Unwritten Law in the pre-Rabbinic Period', *JSJ*, 3 (1972), pp. 7–29.

'The Duodecimal Courts of Qumran, Revelation and the Sanhedrin', *JBL*, 95 (1976), pp. 59–78.

'The Essenes and the Temple: A Reappraisal', *Studies in Qumran Law* (Leiden, 1978), pp. 57–74.

Beckwith, R. T. 'The Pre-History and Relations of the Pharisees, Sadducees and Essenes', *Revue de Qûmran*, 41 (1982), pp. 3–46.

Beer, M. 'Rivo Shel Geniva' be-Mar 'Uqba'', *Tarbitz*, 31 (1962), pp. 281–6.

'Talmud Torah we-Derekh 'Ereṣ', *Bar-Ilan Annual*, 2 (1964), pp. 134–62.

'Mi-Ba'ayot Hithawutah Shel ha-Metivta' be-Bavel', *WCJS*, 4 (1), (1967), pp. 99–101.

'Yissakhar u-Zevulun', *Bar-Ilan Annual*, 6 (1968), pp. 167–80.
'Kavod u-Biqoret', *PAAJR*, 38–39 (1972), Hebrew section, pp. 47–57.
''Al Manhigim Shel Yehudei Ṣiporie ba-Me'ah ha-Shelishist', *Sinai*, 74 (1974), pp. 133–8.
R'eshut ha-Golah be-Bavel Bimei ha-Mishnah we-ha-Talmud (Tel Aviv, 1976).
'Banav Shel Mosheh be-'Agadot Ḥazal', *Bar-Ilan Annual*, 13 (1976), pp. 149–57.
'Banav Shel 'Eli be-'Agadot Ḥazal', *Bar-Ilan Annual*, 14 (1977), pp. 79–93.
''Edut 'Aḥat li-She'eilat 'i-Ḥidush 'Avodat ha-Qorbanot be-Yamav Shel Bar-Kokhba'', *Nezir 'Eḥav: Sefer Zikaron le-R. David Kohen, ha-Nazir* (Jerusalem, 1978), pp. 196–206.
'Har ha-Bayit u-Veit ha-Miqdash be-Mishnato Shel Rashb'i', *Peraqim be-Toledot Yerushalayim Bimei Bayit Sheini* (eds. A. Oppenheimer, et al.; Jerusalem, 1981), pp. 361–85.
'Meridat Qoraḥ u-Meni'ehah be-'Agadot Ḥazal', *Meḥqarim ba-'Agadah, Tirgumim u-Tefilot be-Yisra'el le-Zekher Yosef Heinemann* (eds. E. Fleischer & S. J. Petuchowski; Jerusalem, 1981), Hebrew sectn., pp. 9–33.
''Al ha-Ḥavurah be-'Ereṣ Yisra'el Bimei ha-'Amora'im', *Zion*, 43 (1982), pp. 178–85.
'Amor'ai Bavel: Peraqim Beḥayei ha-Kalkalah (2nd. ed.; Ramat Gan, 1982).
''Al ha-Ḥevraya': mei-'Olaman Shel ha-Yeshivot be-'Ereṣ-Yisra'el ba-Mei'ot ha-3 we-ha-4', *Bar-Ilan Annual*, 20/21 (1983), pp. 76–95.
'Ha-Reqa' ha-Medini u-Fe'iluto Shel Rav be-Bavel', *Zion*, 50 (1985), pp. 155–72.
'Banav Shel Shemu'el be-'Agadot Ḥazal', *Sefer Yiṣḥaq 'Aryeh Seligman* (eds. J. Zakovitch & A. Rofeh; Jerusalem, 1983), vol. 2, pp. 427–39.
Belkin, S. *Philo and the Oral Law* (Cambridge, Mass., 1940).
Bickerman, E. *Institutions des Seleucids* (Paris, 1938).
'La chaine de la tradition Pharisienne', *Revue Biblique*, 59 (1952), pp. 44–54.
From Ezra to the Last of the Maccabees: Foundations of Post-Biblical Judaism (N.Y., 1962).
Blenkinskopp, J. 'Prophecy and Priesthood in Josephus', *JJS*, 25 (1974), pp. 239–62.
Blidstein, G. (Y). 'The Monarchic Imperative in Rabbinic Perspective', *AJS review*, 7–8 (1983), pp. 15–40.
'Le-Qorot ha-Munaḥ Torah she-be-'Al Peh', *Tarbitz*, 42 (1973), pp. 496–8.
'Kafah 'Aleihem Har ka-Gigit; Midrash u-Metaḥim', *Bar-Ilan Covenant Workshop Papers*, no. 28 (1988).
Bloch, R. 'Quelques aspects de la figure de Moïse dans la tradition rabbinique', *Cahiers Sioniens*, vol. 8 (1954), pp. 211–85.
Bowker, J. *Jesus and the Pharisees* (Cambridge, 1973).

Bowman, J. W. 'Prophets and Prophecy in Talmud and Midrash', *Evangelical Quarterly*, 22 (1950), pp. 107–14, 205–20, 255–75.

Breuer, M. 'Ha-Semikhah ha-'Ashkenazit', *Zion*, 33 (1968), pp. 15–46.

Brown, J. R. *Temple and Sacrifice in Rabbinic Judaism* (N.Y., 1963).

Brown, P. *The Making of Late Antiquity* (Cambridge, 1978).

Brownlee, W. H. 'The Wicked Priest, the Man of Lies and the Righteous Teacher – the Problem of Identity', *JQR*, 73 (1982), pp. 1–37.

Bruner, Z. *Malkhei Yehudah be-Midrashei Ḥazal* (unpub. M.A. thesis, Bar-Ilan University, 1970).

Buchanan, G. W. *The Consequences of the Covenant* (Leiden, 1970).

'The Priestly Teacher of Righteousness', *Revue de Qûmran*, 6 (1969), pp. 553–8.

Büchler, A. *Studies in Jewish History* (eds. I. Brodie and J. Rabbinowitz; Oxford, 1956).

Ha-Kohanim we-'Avodatam be-Miqdash Yerushalayim ba-'Asor ha-Shanim ha-'Aḥaron she-Lifnei Ḥurban Bayit Sheini (trans. N. Ginton; Jerusalem, 1966).

Studies in Sin and Atonement in the Rabbinic Literature of the First Century (reprint; N.Y., 1967).

Types of Jewish-Palestinian Piety from 70 B. C. E. to 70 C. E. (reprint; N.Y., 1968).

Buehler, W. W. *The Pre-Herodian Civil War and Social Debate: Jewish Society in the Period 76–40 B.C. and the Social Factors Contributing to the Rise of the Pharisees and the Sadducees* (Basel, 1974).

Cannadine, D. & Price, S. (eds.), *Rituals of Royalty: Power and Ceremonial in Traditional Societies* (Cambridge, 1987).

Carroll, R. T. 'The Elijah-Elisha Sagas: Some Remarks on Prophetic Succession in Ancient Israel', *VT*, 19 (1969), pp. 400–15.

Clark, K. W. 'Worship in the Jerusalem Temple after A.D. 70', *New Testament Studies*, 6 (1960), pp. 269–80.

Cohen, M. A. 'The Hasmonean Revolt Politically Considered', *S. W. Baron Jubilee Volume* (ed. S. Lieberman; Jerusalem, 1974), vol. 2, pp. 263–85.

Cohen, S. J. D. *Josephus in Galilee and Rome: His Vita and Development as a Historian* (Leiden, 1979).

'Patriarchs and Scholarchs', *PAAJR*, 48 (1981), pp. 57–95.

'Epigraphical Rabbis', *JQR*, 72 (1981), pp. 1–17.

'Yavneh Revisited: Pharisees, Rabbis and the End of Jewish Sectarianism', *SBL Seminar Papers*, 21 (1982), pp. 45–61.

'The Destruction: From Scripture to Midrash', *Prooftexts*, 2 (1982), pp. 18–39.

'The Temple and the Synagogue', *The Temple in Late Antiquity* (ed. T. G. Madsen; Provo, Utah, 1984), pp. 151–74.

Daube, D. *Studies in Biblical Law* (Cambridge, 1947).

The New Testament and Rabbinic Judaism (London, 1956).

'Three Notes Having to Do with Johanan ben Zaccai', *JTS*, 11 (1960), pp. 53–62.

Davies, P.R. 'The Ideology of the Temple in the Damascus Document', *JJS*, 33 (1982), pp. 287–301.

Davies, W.D. 'Torah in the Messianic Age and/or the Age to Come', *JBL Monograph Series*, 7 (1952).

Delcor, M. 'Le temple d'Onias en Egypte', *Revue Biblique*, 75 (1968), pp. 188–203.

D'Entreves, A.P. *The Notion of the State* (Oxford, 1967).

Dinur, B. 'Le-Mashma'utah Shel Masekhet 'Avot ke-Maqor Hisṭorie', *Zion*, 35 (1970), pp. 1–18.

Doran, R. *Temple Propaganda: the Purpose and Character of 2 Maccabees* (Washington, D.C., 1981).

Duby, G. *The Three Orders: Feudal Society Imagined* (trans. A. Goldhammer; Chicago, 1980).

Dupont-Sommer, A. 'Observations sur le Commentaire de Nahum découvert près de la Mer Morte', *Journal des Savants*, Oct.–Dec. 1963, pp. 201–27.

Dvornick, F. *Early Christian and Byzantine Political Philosophy: Origins and Background*, 2 vols. (Washington, D.C., 1966).

Eastwood, C.C. *The Royal Priesthood of the Faithful* (London, 1963).

Eddy, S.K. *The Kind is Dead: Studies in Near Eastern Resistance to Hellenism, 334–31 B.C.* (Lincoln, Nebraska, 1961).

Efron, Y. *Ḥiqerei ha-Tequfah ha-Ḥashmona'it* (Tel Aviv, 1980).

Elazar, D.J. 'Government in Biblical Israel', *Tradition*, 8 (1968), pp. 103–12.

'Covenant as the Basis of the Jewish Political Tradition', *Kinship and Consent: The Jewish Political Tradition and its Contemporary Uses* (ed. Elazar; Ramat Gan, 1981), pp. 21–56.

Elazar, D.J. & S.A. Cohen, *The Jewish Polity: Jewish Political Organisation from Biblical Times to the Present* (Bloomington, Indiana, 1985).

Englard, Y. 'Tanur Shel 'Akhn'ai: Peirushehah Shel 'Agadah', *Shenaṭon ha-Mishpaṭ ha-'Ivri*, 1 (1975), pp. 45–56.

Eppstein, V. 'When and How the Sadducees were Excommunicated', *JBL*, 85 (1966), pp. 213–23.

Epstein, J.N. *Mevo'ot la-Sifrut ha-Tana'im: Mishnah, Tosefta', Midrashei Halakhah* (Jerusalem, 1957).

Mavo' la-Nusaḥ ha-Mishnah (2nd ed.; Tel Aviv, 1964).

Finkelstein, L. 'The Maxims of the Men of the Great Synagogue', *JBL*, 59 (1940), pp. 455–69.

'The Transmission of Early Rabbinic Tradition', *HUCA*, 16 (1941), pp. 115–35.

Mav'o le-Masekhtot 'Avot we-'Avot de-Rabi Natan (New York, 1950).

The Pharisees: The Sociological Background of Their Faith, 2 vols. (3rd ed.; N.Y., 1962).

Akiba: Scholar, Saint, Martyr (Cleveland, 1962).

Fitzmayer, J. A. 'Further Light on Melchizedek from Qumran Cave 11', *JBL*, 86 (1967), pp. 25–41.

Flanagan, J. W. 'Genealogy and Dynasty in the Early Monarchy of Israel and Judah', *WCJS*, 8 (1982), pp. 23–8.

Fluersheim, Y. 'Yesudon we-R'eishit Hitpatḥutan Shel Yeshivot Bavel Bimei ha-Mishnah we-ha-Talmud – Sura' u-Pumbediṭa'', *Zion*, 39 (1974), pp. 183–97.

Flusser, D. 'Kat Midbar Yehudah we-Hashqafotehah', *Zion*, 19 (1954), pp. 89–103.

'Two Notes on the Midrash in 2 Sam. vii', *IEJ*, 9 (1959), pp. 99–109.

'Hishtaqfutan Shel 'Emunot Meshiḥiyot Yehudiyot ba-Naṣrut ha-Qedumah', *Meshiḥiyut we-'Eskhatalogiah* (ed. Z. Baras; Jerusalem, 1984), pp. 103–34.

Fortes, M. 'Of Installation Ceremonies', *Proceedings of the Royal Anthropological Institute* 1967 (London, 1968), pp. 5–20.

Frankfort, H. *Kingship and the Gods* (Chicago, 1948).

Freeman, G. *The Heavenly Commonwealth; Aspects of Political Thought in the Talmud and Midrash* (London, 1986).

von Fritz, K. *The Theory of the Mixed Constitution in Antiquity* (N.Y., 1954).

Gafni, Y. '"Yeshivah" u-"Metivta"', *Zion*, 43 (1978), pp. 12–37.

'Le-Darkei Shimusho Shel Yusefus be-Sefer Maqabim I', *Zion*, 45 (1980), pp. 81–95.

'Ha-Yeshivah ha-Bavlit le'Or Sugyat Bava' Qama' 117a', *Tarbitz*, 49 (1980), pp. 292–301.

'He'arot le-Ma'amaro Shel D. Goodblatt', *Zion*, 46 (1981), pp. 52–6.

'Ma'asei Beit Din be-Talmud Bavli – Ṣurot Sifrutiyot we-Hashlakhot Hisṭoriyot', *PAAJR*, 49 (1982), pp. 31–6.

'Ḥiburim Nestorioniyim ke-Maqor le-Toledot Yeshivot Bavel', *Tarbitz*, 51 (1982), pp. 567–75.

'Public Sermons in Talmudic Babylonia: The Pirqa'', in *Yad la-Talmud: Selected Chapters* (ed. E. E. Urbach; n.d. [Jerusalem, 1984 ??]), pp. 39–42.

'Sheveṭ u-Meḥoqeq. 'Al Defusie Manhigut Ḥadashim Bitqufat ha-Talmud be-'Ereṣ Yisra'el u-ve-Bavel', *Kehunah u-Melukhah: Yaḥasei Dat u-Medinah be-Yisra'el u-ve-'Amim* (eds., Y. Gafni, G. Motzkin; Jerusalem, 1987), pp. 79–91.

Gartner, B. *The Temple and the Community in Qumran and the New Testament* (Cambridge, 1965).

Gerhardsson, B. 'Memory and Manuscript: Oral Tradition and Written Transmission in Rabbinic Judaism and Early Christianity' (trans. E. J. Sharpe), *Acta Seminarii Neotestamentici Upsaliensis*, no. 22 (Uppsala, 1961).

Gilat, Y. D. *R. Eliezer ben Hyrcanus. A Scholar Outcast* (Ramat Gan, 1984).

Ginzberg, L. *On Jewish Law and Lore* (Phila., 1955).
Glatzer, N. N. 'A Study of the Talmudic Interpretation of Prophecy', *Review of Religion*, 10 (1946), pp. 115–37.
Hillel the Elder: The Emergence of Classical Judaism (Washington, D.C., 1956).
Goldberg, A. 'Darko shel R. Yehudah ha-Nasi' be-Sidur ha-Mishnah', *Tarbitz*, 28 (1959), pp. 260–70.
Goldenberg, R. 'The Deposition of Rabban Gamaliel II: An Examination of the Sources', *JJS*, 23 (1972), pp. 167–90.
'Early Rabbinic Explanations of the Destruction of Jerusalem', *JJS*, 33 (1982), pp. 518–25.
Goldin, J. 'The Three Pillars of Simeon the Righteous', *PAAJR*, 27 (1958), pp. 43–58.
'Of Change and Adaptation in Judaism', *History of Religions*, 4 (1965), pp. 269–94.
'The First Pair (Yose ben Yoezer and Yose ben Yohanan) or the Home of a Pharisee', *AJS review*, 5 (1980), pp. 41–61.
Goldstein, N. *Meḥqarim ba-Hagutam Shel Ḥazal 'Al ha-'Avodah u-Veit ha-Miqdash we-Hashpa'atam 'Al 'Iṣuvah* (unpub. Ph.D.; Hebrew University, Jerusalem, 1977).
Goodblatt, D. *Rabbinic Instruction in Sasanian Babylon* (Leiden, 1975).
'R'eishitah Shel ha-Nesi'ut ha-'Arṣi-Yisra'elit ha-Mukeret', *Meḥqarim be-Toledot 'Am Yisra'el we-'Ereṣ Yisra'el*, 4 (1978), pp. 89–102.
'Temikhat ha-Tana'im 'O Hashpa'at ha-Kohanim', *Kathedra*, 29 (1983), pp. 6–12.
''Al Sipur ha-''Qesher'' Neged Raban Shim'on ben Gamli'el ha-Sheini', *Zion*, 49 (1984), pp. 349–74.
'Yehudei 'Ereṣ-Yisra'el ba-Shanim 70 – 132', *Historiyah Shel 'Am Yisra'el*, Vol. 11, 'Yehudah we-Roma''; (ed. U. Rappaport; Jerusalem, 1983), pp. 155–84.
'Ha-To'ar ''Nasi''' we-ha-Reka' ha-Dati 'Idei'ologie Shel ha-Mered ha-Sheini', *Mered Bar Kokhba': Meḥqarim Ḥadashim* (eds. A. Oppenheimer, U. Rappaport; Jerusalem, 1984), pp. 113–32.
'Agrippa I and Palestinian Judaism in the First Century', *Jewish History*, 2 (1987), pp. 7–32.
Goodenough, E. E. 'The Political Philosophy of Hellenistic Kingship', *Yale Classical Studies*, 1 (1928), pp. 65–78.
By Light, Light: The Mystic Gospel of Hellenistic Judaism (New Haven, Conn., 1935).
The Politics of Philo Judaeus: Practice and Theory (New Haven, Conn., 1938).
Jewish Symbols in the Greco-Roman Period (13 vols., Princeton, N.J., 1952–1968).
Goodman, M. 'The First Jewish Revolt: Social Conflict and the Problem

of Debt', *JJS*, 33 (1982), pp. 417–27.
State and Society in Roman Galilee, A.D. 132–212 (Totowa, N.J., 1983).
The Ruling Class of Judaea: The Origins of the Jewish Revolt Against Rome, A.D. 66–70 (Cambridge, 1987).
Goody, J. R. *Succession to High Office*, Cambridge Papers in Social Anthropology, 4 (1966), pp. 2–8.
Gordis, R. 'Democratic Origins in Ancient Israel – The Biblical Edah', *Alexander Marx Jubilee Volume* (ed. S. Lieberman; N.Y., 1950), pp. 369–88.
Grant, M. *The Jews in the Roman World* (N.Y., 1973).
Green, W. S. 'Palestinian Holy Men: Charismatic Leadership and Rabbinic Tradition', *ANRW*, 19:2 (1979), pp. 619–47.
Greenwald, Y. *Toledot ha-Kohanim ha-Gedolim* (N.Y., 1933).
Gruber, M.I. 'The Mishnah as Oral Torah: A Reconsideration', *JSJ*, 15 (1984), pp. 112–22.
Guttmann, A. ''Akiba: Rescuer of the Torah', *HUCA*, 17 (1943), pp. 395–421.
Rabbinic Judaism in the Making (Detroit, 1970).
Gwyn, W. B. *The Meaning of the Separation of Powers* (Tulane Studies in Political Science, no. 11; New Orleans, 1965).
Haran, M. *Temple and Temple Service in Ancient Israel* (Oxford, 1978).
'Ha-Kohen, ha-Miqdash, we-ha-'Avodah', *Tarbitz*, 48 (1979), pp. 175–85.
Hauret, C. 'Moïse était-il prêtre?', *Analecta Biblica*, 10 (1959), pp. 375–82.
Hengel, M. *Judaism and Hellenism: Studies in their Encounter in Palestine during the Early Hellenistic Period*, 2 vols., (trans. J. Bowden; London, 1974).
The Charismatic Leader and His Followers (Edinburgh, 1981).
with J. H. Charlesworth & D. Mendels, 'The Polemical Character of "On Kingship" in the Temple Scroll: An Attempt at Dating IIQ Temple', *JJS*, 37 (1986), pp. 28–38.
Herr, M. D. 'The Historical Significance of the Dialogues between Jewish Sages and Roman Dignitaries', *Scripta Hierosolymitana*, 22 (1971), pp. 123–50.
'Tefisat ha-Hisṭoriyah 'Eṣel Ḥazal', *WCJS*, 6 (3) (1977), pp. 129–42.
'Sibotav Shel Mered Bar Kokhba'', *Zion*, 43 (1978), pp. 2–11.
'Ha-Reṣef she-ba-Shalshelet Mesiratah Shel ha-Torah', *Zion*, 44 (1979), pp. 43–56.
'Yerushalayim, ha-Miqdash we-ha-'Avodah ba-Meṣi'ut u-va-Toda'ah Bimei ha-Bayit ha-Sheini', *Peraqim be-Toledot Yerushalayim Bimei Bayit Sheini* (eds. A. Oppenheimer, et al.; Jerusalem, 1981), pp. 166–77.
'Meshiḥiyut Medinit Re'alit u-Meshiḥiyut 'Eskhatologit Qosmit be-Divrei Ḥazal', *Tarbitz*, 54 (1985), pp. 331–46.
Heschel, A. J. *Torah Min ha-Shamayim be-'Aspaqlariyah Shel ha-Dorot* (2 vols.; Jerusalem, 1962–5).

Hittenmeister, G. 'Beit ha-Keneset u-veit ha-Midrash we-ha-Ziqah Beineihem', *Kathedra*, 18 (1981), pp. 37–44.

Hoehner, H. W. *Herod Antipas: A Contemporary of Jesus Christ* (Michigan, 1980).

Hoenig, S. B. *The Great Sanhedrin* (Phila., 1953).

Hoffmann, D. *The First Mishna and the Controversies of the Tannaim* (translated P. Forchheimer; N.Y., 1977).

The Highest Court in the City of the Sanctuary (translated by P. Forchheimer; N.Y., 1977).

Horton, F. L. *The Melchizedek Tradition: A Critical Examination of the Sources to the Fifth Century AD and in the Epistle to the Hebrews* (Cambridge, 1976).

Isaac, B. and Oppenheimer, A. 'The Revolt of Bar Kokhba: Ideology and Modern Scholarship', *JJS*, 36 (1985), pp. 33–60.

Ishida, T. *The Royal Dynasties in Ancient Israel* (N.Y., 1977).

Jackson, B. 'Ha-Hakarah ha-'Enoshit we-ha-Yedi'ah ha-'Eloqit ba-Mishpaṭ ha-Miqra'i we-ha-Tana'i', *Shenaṭon ha-Mishpaṭ ha-'Ivri*, 6–7 (1980), pp. 61–70.

'Jésus et Moïse: le statut du prophète a l'égard de la Loi', *Revue Historique de Droit Français et l'Etranger*, 59 (1981), pp. 341–60.

Jacobs, L. 'The Concept of the Ḥassid in Biblical and Rabbinic Literature', *JJS*, 8 (1957), pp. 143–54.

'The Economic Conditions of the Jews in Babylon in Talmudic Times Compared with Palestine', *Jewish Journal of Sociology*, 2 (1957), pp. 349–59.

Jeremias, J. *Jerusalem in the Time of Jesus* (trans. F.H. & C.H. Cave, London, 1969).

Johnson, A.R. *Sacral Kingship in Ancient Israel* (Cardiff, 1967).

Kadushin, M. *The Rabbinic Mind* (3rd ed.; N.Y., 1972).

Kantorowicz, E. H. *The King's Two Bodies: A Study in Medieval Political Theology* (Princeton, N.J., 1957).

Katzenstein, H. J. 'Some Remarks on the Lists of the Chief Priests of the Temple of Solomon', *JBL*, 81 (1962), pp. 371–84.

Kimelman, R. 'The Conflict between R. Yohanan and Resh Laqish on the Supremacy of the Patriarchate', *WCJS*, 7 (3), (1981), pp. 1–20.

'Ha-'Oligarkhiah ha-Kohanit we-Talmidei Ḥakhamim', *Zion*, 48 (1983), pp. 136–47.

'R. Yoḥanan u-Ma'amad ha-Rabanut Bitqufat ha-Talmud', *Shenaṭon ha-Mishpaṭ ha-'Ivri*, 9–10 (1983), pp. 329–58.

Kindler, A. 'The Elazar Coins of the Bar Kokhba War', *Numismatic Circular* (1962), pp. 27–9.

Klausner, Y. *Ha-Ra'ayon ha-Meshiḥi be-Yisra'el* (Jerusalem, 1926).

Krauss, S. 'Outdoor Teaching in Talmudic Times', *JJS*, 1 (1948–9), pp. 82–4.

Lauterbach, J. Z. 'The Names of the Rabbinical Schools and Assemblies in Babylon', *HUCA: Jubliee Volume* (1926), pp. 211–22.

Rabbinical Essays (Cincinnati, 1951).

Leibson, G. ''Al Mah Menadin', *Shenaṭon ha-Mishpaṭ ha-'Ivri*, 2 (1976), pp. 292–342.

Leiter, S. 'Worthiness, Acclamation and Appointment: Some Rabbinic Terms', *PAAJR*, 41–2 (1974), pp. 137–68.

Levine, L. I. (Y. L.) 'R. Abbahu of Caesarea', *Christianity, Judaism and Other Greco-Roman Cults: Studies for Morton Smith at Sixty*, Vol. 4 (ed. J. Neusner; Leiden, 1975), pp. 67–76.

Caesarea Under Roman Rule (Leiden, 1975).

'R. Simon bar Yoḥai and the Purification of Tiberias: History and Tradition', *HUCA*, 49 (1978), pp. 143–85.

''Al ha-Me'oravut ha-Poliṭit Shel ha-Perushim Bitqufat Hordus u-Vimei ha-Neṣivim', *Kathedra*, 8 (1978), pp. 12–28.

'The Jewish Patriarch (*Nasi*) in Third Century Palestine', *ANRW*, 19:2 (1979), pp. 649–88.

'Ha-Ma'avak ha-Poliṭie Bein ha-Perushim la-Ṣedukim bi-Tequfah ha-Ḥashmona'it', *Peraqim be-Toledot Yerushalayim Bimei Bayit Sheini* (eds. A. Oppenheimer, et al.; Jerusalem, 1981), pp. 61–83.

'Ma'amad ha-Ḥakhamim be-'Ereṣ Yisra'el ba-Me'ah ha-Shelishit', *WCJS*, 8 (2), (1982), pp. 5–8.

'Tequfato Shel Rabi Yehudah ha-Nasi'', *'Ereṣ Yisra'el, mei-Ḥurban Bayit Sheini we-'Ad ha-Kibush ha-Muslemi*, Vol. 1 (eds. Z. Baras, et al.; Jerusalem, 1982), pp. 93–118.

'Megamot Meshiḥiyot be-Sof Yemei ha-Bayit ha-Sheini', *Meshiḥiyut we-'Eskhatologiah* (ed. Z. Baras; Jerusalem, 1984), pp. 135–52.

Ma'amad ha-Ḥakhamim be-'Ereṣ-Yisra'el Bitqufat ha-Talmud (Jerusalem, 1986).

'The Second Temple Synagogue: The Formative Years', *The Synagogue in Late Antiquity* (ed. Levine; N.Y., 1987), pp. 7–32.

Lieberman, S. 'Raymond Martini's Alleged Forgeries', *Historica Judaica*, 5 (1945), pp. 99–100.

'Palestine in the Third and Fourth Centuries', *JQR*, 36 (1946), pp. 329–70.

Hellenism in Jewish Palestine (N.Y., 1950).

'The Discipline in the So-Called Dead Sea Manual of Discipline', *JBL*, 71 (1952), pp. 199–206.

'Jewish Life in *Eretz Yisrael* as Reflected in the Palestinian Talmud', *Israel: Its Role in Civilization* (ed. M. Davis; N.Y., 1956), pp. 82–91.

'How Much Greek in Jewish Palestine', *Biblical and Other Studies* (ed. A. Altman; Cambridge, Mass., 1963), pp. 123–41.

Lindars, B. 'Gideon and Kingship', *JTS*, 16 (1965), pp. 315–26.

Liver, Y. *Toledot Beit David* (Jerusalem, 1959).

'The Doctrine of the Two Messiahs in Sectarian Literature in the Time

of the Second Commonwealth', *HThR*, 52 (1959), pp. 149–85.
Loew, L. 'Kranz und Krone', *Gesamelte Schriften*, vol. 3 (Szegedin, 1893), pp. 407–37.
Luria, B. 'Ha-Kohanim ba-'Avodatam', *Sinai*, 68 (1971), pp. 1–17.
Mi-Yan'ai 'Ad Hordus (Jerusalem, 1974).
'Be-Sodam Shel ha-Kohanim', *Beit Miqra'*, 70 (1977), pp. 283–90.
McCarthy, D. J. *Old Testament Covenant* (Oxford, 1972).
McIlwain, C. H. *Constitutionalism: Ancient and Modern* (N.Y., 1940).
Mantel, H. 'Ordination and Appointment in the Period of the Temple', *HThR*, 57 (1964), pp. 325–46.
Studies in the History of the Sanhedrin (Cambridge, Mass., 1965).
'The Nature of the Great Synagogue', *HThR*, 60 (1967), pp. 69–91.
'The Causes of the Bar-Kokhba Revolt', *JQR*, 58 (1968), pp. 224–42, 274–96.
'The Development of the Oral Law', *The World History of the Jewish People*, 1st series, vol. 8 (ed. M. Avi-Yonah & Z. Baras; Jerusalem, 1977), pp. 57–61.
'The Sadducees and the Pharisees', idem., pp. 99–123.
'The Antiquity of the Oral Law', *Annual of the Swedish Theological Institute*, 12 (1982), pp. 93–112.
'Anshei Keneset ha-Gedolah (Tel Aviv, 1983).
Margoliot, R. 'Tena'ei ha-Minui ke-Ḥaver ha-Sanhedrin', *Sinai*, 20 (1947), pp. 16–26.
Marmorstein, A. 'L'Opposition contre le Patriarche Juda II', *REJ*, 64 (1912), pp. 59–66.
'Ma'alat Talmud Torah (be-Ma'amarei Rabi Shim'on bar Yoḥ'ai)', *Sefer ha-Yovel le-B. M. Levin* (Jerusalem, 1939), pp. 140–70.
Meshorer, Y. *Maṭbe'ot ha-Yehudim Bimei Bayit Sheini* (Tel Aviv, 1966).
'Jewish Symbols on Roman Coins Struck in Eretz Israel', *Israel Museum News*, 14 (1978), pp. 60–3.
Ancient Jewish Coinage, 2 vols. (N.Y., 1982).
Mildenberg, L. *The Coinage of the Bar-Kokhba War* (Salzburg, 1984).
'The Bar-Kokhba War in the Light of the Coins and Document Finds, 1947–1982', *Israel Numismatic Journal*, 8 (1985), pp. 27–33.
Mirsky, S. 'Le-Sidrei ha-Yeshivot be-Bavel Bitqufat ha-'Amora'im', *Ḥorev*, 3 (1936), pp. 109–24.
Moore, G. F. *Judaism in the First Centuries of the Christian Era: The Age of the Tannaim*, 3 vols., (Oxford, 1927–1930).
Morgenstern, J. 'A Chapter in the History of the High Priesthood', *American Journal of Semitic Languages and Literature*, 55 (1938), pp. 1–24, 183–97, 360–77.
Moyne, J. Le. *Les Sadducéens* (Paris, 1972).
Neusner, J. 'The Fellowship in the Second Jewish Commonwealth', *HThR*, 53 (1960), pp. 126–42.

'Rabi Tarfon', *Judaica*, 17 (1961), pp. 141–67.

A Life of Rabban Yohanan ben Zakkai, ca. 1–60 C.E. (Leiden, 1962).

A History of the Jews in Babylonia, 5 vols. (Leiden, 1966–1970).

'Rabbis and Community in Third Century Babylonia', *Religions in Antiquity. Essays in Memory of Erwin Ramsdell Goodenough* (ed. J. Neusner; Leiden, 1968), pp. 438–59.

Development of a Legend. Studies on the Traditions Concerning Yohanan ben Zakkai (Leiden, 1970).

The Idea of Purity in Ancient Judaism (Leiden, 1973).

'Pharisaism and Rabbinic Judaism. A Clarification', *History of Religions*, 12 (1973), pp. 250–70.

Eliezer Ben Hyrcanus: The Tradition and the Man, 2 vols. (Leiden, 1973).

From Politics to Piety. The Emergence of Rabbinic Judaism (Hoboken, N.J., 1973).

'Yohanan ben Zakkai Reconsidered', *JJS*, 24 (1973), pp. 65–73.

'From Exegesis to Fable in Rabbinic Traditions about the Pharisees', *JJS*, 25 (1974), pp. 263–9.

First Century Judaism in Crisis (N.Y., 1975).

'The Formation of Rabbinic Judaism: Yavneh (Jamnia) from A.D. 70 to 100', *ANRW*, 19:2 (1979), pp. 3–42.

'Scriptural, Essenic and Mishnaic approaches to civil law and government; some comparative remarks', *HThR*, 73 (1980), pp. 419–34.

'On the Use of the Mishnah for the History of Judaism Prior to the Time of the Mishnah; a Methodological Note', *JSJ*, 11 (1980), pp. 177–85.

Judaism: The Evidence of the Mishnah (Chicago, 1982).

Judaism in Society. The Evidence of the Yerushalmi (Chicago, 1983).

Torah: From Scroll to Symbol in Formative Judaism (Phila., 1985).

Wrong Ways and Right Ways in the Study of Formative Judaism (Atlanta, Georgia, 1988).

Newman, J. *Semikhah (Ordination), A Study of its Origins, History and Functions in Rabbinic Literature* (Manchester, 1950).

North, C.R. 'The Old Testament Estimate of the Monarchy', *American Journal of Semitic Languages and Literature*, 48 (1932), pp. 1–19.

'The Religious Aspect of Hebrew Kingship', *ZAW*, 50 (1932), pp. 6–38.

Oppenheimer, A. *The 'Am Ha-Aretz: A Study in the Social History of the Jewish People in the Hellenistic Period* (Leiden, 1977).

'Hafrashat Ma'aser Ri'shon ba-Meṣi'ut she-le-'Aḥar Ḥurban ha-Bayit ha-Sheini', *Sinai*, 83 (1978), pp. 267–87.

'Batei Midrashot be-'Ereṣ Yisra'el be-R'eishit Tequfat ha-'Amora'im', *Kathedra*, 8 (1978), pp. 80–9.

Babylonia Judaica in the Talmudic Period (Wiesbaden, 1983).

'Meshiḥiyuto Shel Bar Kokhba'', *Meshiḥiyut we-Eskhatologiah* (ed. Z. Baras; Jerusalem, 1985), pp. 153–65.

'Ḥavurot Shehayu Birushalayim', *Yerushalayim (Mivḥar Ma'amarim mi-Sifrei Yad Ben Ṣvi)* (Jerusalem, 1987), pp. 35–47.

Oppenheimer, B. 'Lishe'eilat Rikuz ha-Pulḥan be-Yisra'el', *Tarbitz*, 28 (1959), pp. 138–53.

Patai, R. *Man and Temple* (2nd ed., N.Y., 1967).

Phillips, C.R. 'Julian's Rebuilding of the Temple: A Sociological Study of Religious Competition', *SBL Seminar Papers*, 2 (1979), pp. 167–72.

Porter, J.R. *Moses and Monarchy. A Study in the Biblical Traditions of Moses* (Oxford, 1963).

'The Succession of Joshua', *Proclamation and Presence* (eds. J.L. Durham and J.R. Porter; London, 1970), pp. 102–32.

Rad, G. von 'The Royal Ritual in Judah', *The Problem of the Hextateuch and Other Essays* (trans. E.W.T. Dicken; N.Y., 1966), pp. 222–31.

Rajak, T. *Josephus: the Historian and His Society* (Phila., 1984).

Ramsay, P. 'Elements of Biblical Political Theory', *Journal of Religion*, 29 (1949), pp. 258–83.

Rappaport, U. 'Le-Mashma'ut "Ḥever ha-Yehudim"', *Meḥqarim be-Toledot 'Am-Yisra'el we-'Ereṣ Yisra'el*, 3 (1985), pp. 59–67.

Rhoads, D.M. *Israel in Revolution 6–74 C.E.* (Phila., 1976).

Rivkin, E. 'Ben Sira. The Bridge between the Aaronide and Pharisaic Revolutions', *Eretz Israel*, 12 (1975), English section, pp. 95–103.

'Beth Din, Boulé, Sanhedrin. A Tragedy of Errors', *HUCA*, 46 (1975), pp. 181–99.

A Hidden Revolution: The Pharisees' Search for the Kingdom Within (Nashville, Ten., 1978).

Rofé, A. 'R'eishit Ṣemihatan Shel ha-Kitot Bimei Bayit Sheini', *Kathedra*, 49 (1988), pp. 13–22.

Rosenfeld, B. 'Mashber ha-Nesi'ut be-'Ereṣ Yisra'el ba-Me'ah ha-4 la-Sefirah', *Zion*, 53 (1988), pp. 239–57.

Roth, C. 'The Constitution of the Jewish Republic of 66–70', *Jewish Social Studies*, 9 (1964), pp. 295–320.

Safrai, S. 'Miṣwat ha-Aliyah la-Regel we-Qiyumah Bimei ha-Bayit ha-Sheini', *Zion*, 25 (1960), pp. 67–84.

'Ha-Tafqidim ha-Qehilatiyim Shel Beit ha-Keneset be-'Ereṣ Yisra'el', *Beit ha-Keneset Bitqufat ha-Mishnah we-ha-Talmud* (Jerusalem, 1968), pp. 105–24.

'Tales of the Sages in the Palestinian Tradition and the Babylonian Talmud', *Scripta Hierosolymitana*, 22 (1971), pp. 209–32.

'Relations between the Diaspora and the Land of Israel', *Compendia Rerum Iudaicarum ad Novum Testamentum*, section I, vol. 1 (eds. S. Safrai and M. Stern; Assen, 1974), pp. 184–215.

'Jewish Self-Government', idem., pp. 377–419.

'The Temple', idem., vol. 2 (Amsterdam, 1976), pp. 865–907.

Beshelhei ha-Bayit ha-Sheini u-Vitqufat ha-Mishnah (Jerusalem, 1981).

'Ha-'Aliyah la-Regel Lirushalayim la-'Aḥar Ḥurban Bayit Sheini', *Peraqim be-Toledot Yerushalayim Bimei Bayit Sheini* (eds. A. Oppenheimer, et al., Jerusalem, 1981), pp. 376–93.

'Ereṣ Yisra'el we-Ḥakhamehah Bitqufat ha-Mishnah we-ha-Talmud (Jerusalem, 1983).

'Halakhah le-Mosheh Mi-Sinai: Hisṭoriyah 'O Te'ologiah?', *WCJS*, 9 (3), (Jerusalem, 1986), pp. 23–30.

Saldarini, A. J. 'The End of the Rabbinic Chain of Tradition', *JBL*, 93 (1974), pp. 97–106.

'Johanan ben Zakkai's Escape from Jerusalem. Origins and Development of a Rabbinic Story', *JSJ*, 6 (1975), pp. 189–204.

'Form Criticism of Rabbinic Literature', *JBL*, 96 (1977), pp. 257–74.

'Varieties of Rabbinic Response to the Destruction of the Temple', *SBL Seminar Papers*, 21 (1982), pp. 437–58.

Scholastic Rabbinism: A Literary Study of the Fathers According to Rabi Nathan (Chico, Cali., 1982).

Sanders, E. P. *Paul and Palestinian Judaism: A Comparison of Patterns of Religion* (Phila., 1977).

Jesus and Judaism (London, 1985).

Sandmel, S. *Philo of Alexandria. An Introduction* (N.Y., 1979).

Sanson, M. C. 'Laying on of Hands in the Old Testament', *Expository Times*, 94 (1983), pp. 323–6.

Sawyer, J. F. A. 'Was Jeshua ben Sira a Priest?', *WCJS*, 8 (1), (1982), pp. 65–71.

Schaefer, P. 'Rabbi Akiva and Bar Kokhba', *Approaches to Ancient Judaism*, vol. 2 (ed. W. S. Green; Ann Arbor, Michigan, 1980), pp. 117–19.

'Research into Rabbinic Literature: An Attempt to Define the Status Quaestionis', *JJS*, vol. 37 (1986), pp. 139–52.

Schalit, A. C. *Hordus ha-Melekh: Ha-'Ish u-Fo'alo* (Jerusalem, 1960).

Schiffer, I. J. 'The Men of the Great Assembly', *Persons and Institutions in Early Rabbinic Judaism* (ed. W. S. Green; Missoula, Montana, 1977), pp. 237–76.

Schurer, E. *The History of the Jewish People in the Age of Jesus Christ (175 B.C.–A.D. 135). A New English Version* (eds. G. Vermes, et al.), vols. 1–3(ii) (Edinburgh, 1973–87).

Schwartz, D. R. 'The Priests in EP. Arist. 30', *JBL*, 97 (1978), pp. 567–71.

'Mamlekhet Kohanim ke-Sismah Perushit', *Zion*, 45 (1980), pp. 117–96.

'Priesthood and Priestly Descent in Josephus' *Antiquities* 10:80', *JTS*, 32 (1981), pp. 129–35.

'Ha-'Im Hayah Raban Yoḥanan ben Zak'ai Kohen?', *Sinai*, 88 (1981), pp. 37–9.

'The Messianic Departure from Judah (4Q Patriarchal Blessings)', *Theologische Zeitschrift*, 37 (1982), pp. 257–66.

'Lishe'eilat Hitnagdut ha-Perushim la-Malkhut ha-Ḥashmona'im', *'Umah we-Toldotehah*, vol. 1 (ed. M. Stern, Jerusalem, 1983), pp. 39–50.

'Josephus on the Jewish Constitutions and Community', *Scripta Classica Israelica*, 7 (1984), pp. 30–52.

'Philo's Priestly Descent', *Nourished with Peace: Studies in Hellenistic Judaism in Memory of Samuel Sandmel* (eds. F.E. Greenspahn et al.; Chico, Cali., 1984), pp. 155–71.

'Soferim u-Ferushim Ḥanfanim: Mi Heim ha-Soferim bi-Vrit ha-Ḥadashah?', *Zion*, 50 (1985), pp. 121–32.

'Midbar u-Miqdash: 'Al Dat u-Medinah Bimei Bayit Sheini', *Kehunah u-Melukhah: Yaḥesei Dat u-Medinah be-Yisra'el u-ve-'Amim* (eds. Y. Gafni, G. Motzkin; Jerusalem, 1987), pp. 61–78.

'Agripas ha-R'ishon: Melekh Yehudah ha-'Aḥaron (Jerusalem, 1987).

Schwartz, J. 'Aliya from Babylonia during the Amoraic Period', *The Jerusalem Cathedra*, 3 (1983), pp. 58–69.

Ha-Yishuv ha-Yehudi bi-Yehudah mi-la'Aḥar Milkhemet Bar-Kokhba' we-'Ad la-Kibush ha-'Aravi, 135–640 C.E. (Jerusalem, 1986).

Sharvit, B. 'Ha-Kohen be-Kat Midbar Yehudah', *Beit Miqra'*, 70 (1977), pp. 313–20.

'Ha-Hanhagah shel Kat Midbar Yehudah', *Beit Miqra'*, 78 (1979), pp. 295–304.

Sievers, J. 'The High Priesthood of Simon Maccabaeus. An Analysis of I. Macc. 14:25–49', *SBL Seminar Papers*, (1981), pp. 309–18.

Smallwood, E.M. 'High Priests and Politics in Roman Palestine', *JTS*, 13 (1962), pp. 14–34.

Smith, M. 'Palestinian Judaism in the First Century', *Israel. Its Role in Civilization* (ed. M. Davis; N.Y., 1956), pp. 67–81.

'The Image of God', *Bulletin of the John Rylands Library*, 40 (1958), pp. 473–512.

'A Comparison of Early Christian and Early Rabbinic Traditions', *JBL*, 82 (1963), pp. 169–76.

'The Dead Sea Sect in its Relation to Ancient Judaism', *NTS*, 7 (1961), pp. 347–60.

'Goodenough's *Jewish Symbols* in Retrospect', *JBL*, 86 (1967), pp. 53–68.

Sonne, I. 'The Paintings of the Dura Synagogue', *HUCA*, 20 (1947), pp. 255–362.

'The Zodiac Theme in Ancient Synagogues and in Hebrew Printed Books', *Studies in Bibliography and Booklore*, 1 (1953), pp. 3–13.

Spiro, S.J. 'Who was the Ḥaber? A New Approach to an Ancient Institution', *JSJ*, 11 (1980), pp. 186–216.

Steinfeld, Z. 'Le-Dinam Shel Merubeh Begadim Meshamesh u- Merubeh Begadim she-'Avar', *Sinai*, 93 (1983), pp. 43–51.

'Mashiaḥ, Merubeh Begadim, Kohen Meshamesh, we-Kohen she-'Avar', *Tarbitz*, 52 (1983), pp. 411–34.

'Hora'at ha-Kohen ha-Mashiaḥ', *Sinai*, 95 (1984), pp. 135–56.

'Le-Sugei ha-Rov ba-Hora'ah', *Sidra*, 1 (1985), pp. 69–90.

Stern, M. 'The Reign of Herod and the Herodian Dynasty', *Compendia Rerum Iudaicarum ad Novum Testamentum*, section I, vol. 1 (eds. S. Safrai, M. Stern; Assen, 1974), pp. 216–307.

'Social and Political Realignments in Herodian Judaea', *The Jerusalem Cathedra*, 2 (1982), pp. 40–62.

'Ha-Manhigut Biqvuṣot Loḥamei ha-Ḥerut be-Sof Yemei Bayit Sheini', *Ha-Mered ha-Gadol: Ha-Sibot we-ha-Nesibot li-Periṣato* (ed. A. Kasher; Jerusalem, 1983), pp. 299–308.

Tannenblatt, M.A. *Peraqim Ḥadashim le-Toledot 'Ereṣ Yisra'el u-Bavel Bitqufat ha-Talmud* (Tel Aviv, 1966).

Tcherikover, V. *Hellenistic Civilization and the Jews* (trans. S. Applebaum; Phila., 1959).

Tchernowitz, H. *Toledot ha-Halakhah*, 4 vols. (N.Y., 1945).

Thiering, B.E. *Redating the Teacher of Righteousness* (Sydney, 1979).

Trifon, D. *Ha-Kohanim mi-Ḥurban Bayit Sheini we-'Ad 'Aliyat ha-Naṣrut* (unpub. Ph.D. thesis; Tel Aviv University, 1985).

'Ha-Reqa' ha-Politi ha-Penimi Shel Mered Bar Kokhba'', *Mered Bar Kokhba': Meḥqarim Ḥadashim* (eds. A. Oppenheimer, U. Rappaport; Jerusalem, 1984), pp. 13–26.

Tropper, D. 'Bet Din Shel Kohanim', *JQR*, 63 (1973), pp. 204–21.

Urbach, E.E. 'Matai Pasqah ha-Nevu'ah?', *Tarbitz*, 17 (1946), pp. 1–11.

'Halakhah u-Nevu'ah', *Tarbitz*, 18 (1947), pp. 1–27.

'Hilkhot 'Avodah Zarah we-ha-Meṣi'ut ha-'Arkhiologit we-ha-Hisṭorit ba-Me'ah ha-Sheniyah u-va-Me'ah he-Shelishit', *Eretz Israel*, 5 (1959), pp. 189–205.

'Ha-Derashah ke-Yesod ha-Halakhah u-Va'ayat ha-Soferim', *Tarbitz*, 27 (1958), pp. 166–82.

'Koresh we-Hakhrazato be-'Einei Ḥazal', *Molad*, 19 (1961), pp. 368–74.

'The Talmudic Sage: Character and Authority', *Journal of World History*, 11 (1968), pp. 116–42.

'Class Status and Leadership in the World of the Palestinian Sages', *Proceedings of the Israel Academy of Sciences and Humanities*, 2 (1968), pp. 38–74.

'Ha-Mesorot 'Al Torat ha-Sod Bitqufat ha-Tana'im', *Meḥkarim be-Qabalah u-ve-Toledot ha-Datot, Mugashim le-Gershom Scholem* (ed. Urbach; Jerusalem, 1968), Hebrew sectn., pp. 1–28.

'Mishmarot u-Ma'amadot', *Tarbitz*, 42 (1973), pp. 304–27.

The Sages: Their Concepts and Beliefs, 2 vols. (trans. I. Abrahams; Jerusalem, 1979).

Ha-Halakhah: Meqorotehah we-Hitpatḥutah (Jerusalem, 1984).

'Ha-Melukhah ha-Miqra'it be-'Einei Ḥakhamim', *Sefer Seligman* (ed. J. Zakovitz, et al.; Jerusalem, 1983), Vol. 1, pp. 439–51.

de Vaux, R. 'Le Sens de l'expression 'Peuple du Pays' dans l'Ancien testament et le rôle politique du peuple en Israel', *Revue d'Assyriologie*,

58 (1964), pp. 167–72.
Vermes, G. *Scripture and Tradition in Judaism: Haggadic Studies* (Leiden, 1961).
Jesus the Jew: A Historian's Reading of the Gospels (Phila., 1975).
'The Impact of the Dead Sea Scrolls on Jewish Studies during the last Twenty-Five Years', *JJS*, 26 (1975), pp. 1–14.
'The Essenes and History', *JJS*, 32 (1981), pp. 18–31.
'Methodology in the Study of Jewish Literature in the Greco-Roman Period', *JJS*, 36 (1985), pp. 145–58.
Vile, M. J. C. *Constitutionalism and the Separation of Powers* (Oxford, 1967).
Viviano, R. T. *Study as Worship. Aboth and the New Testament* (Leiden, 1978).
Waharftig, S. 'Ha-Semikhah Bizman ha-Talmud', *Sinai*, 45 (1959), pp. 140–76.
Wallach, L. 'The Colloquy of Marcus Aurelius with the Patriarch Judah I', *JQR*, 31 (1940–41), pp. 259–85.
Weingreen, J. *From Bible to Mishnah: The Continuity of Tradition* (Manchester, 1976).
Weiss Halivni, D. 'The Reception Accorded to Rabbi Judah's Mishnah', *Jewish and Christian Self-Definition* (eds. E. P. Sanders, et al.; Phila., 1981), vol. 2, pp. 204–12.
Widengren, G. 'The Status of the Jews in the Sassanian Empire', *Iranica Antiqua*, 1 (1966), pp. 117–61.
Wolfson, H. A. *Philo: Foundations of Religious Philosophy in Judaism, Christianity and Islam*, 2 vols. (Cambridge, Mass., 1948).
Wormuth, F. D. *The Origins of Modern Constitutionalism* (N.Y., 1949).
Yankelevitch, R. 'Mishqalo Shel ha-Yiḥus ha-Mishpaḥti ba-Ḥevrah ha-Yehudit be-'Ereṣ Yisra'el', *'Umah we-Toldotehah*, vol. 1 (ed. M. Stern; Jerusalem, 1983), pp. 151–62.
'Lishe'eilat Yiḥuso Shel Bar Kokhba'', *Mered Bar Kokhba': Meḥqarim Ḥadashim* (eds. A. Oppenheimer and U. Rappaport; Jerusalem, 1984), pp. 133–9.
Zeitlin, S. N. 'Ṣedukim u-Ferushim', *Ḥorev*, 3 (1936), pp. 57–89.
Zeitlin, S. *Religious and Secular Leadership* (Phila., 1943).
'Johanan the High Priest's Abrogations and Decrees', *Studies and Essays in Honor of A. Neuman* (Leiden, 1962), pp. 569–79.
The Rise and Fall of the Judean State, 3 vols. (Phila., 1968–9).

Index

Aaron: embodiment of *keter kehunah*, 23–4, 32, 238; challenged by Korach, 38; transmits *torah*, 61, 62; depicted in Ecclesiasticus, 102; Messiah of, 110; induction of, 246, 251; sons of, 245
'Abbahu of Caesarea, 173 n. 24, 192, 204, 233 n. 39
'Abbayei, 174 n. 27, 177 n. 57, 228, 263 n. 46
academic freedom: Judah I challenges, 199, 227; rabbis demand, 227–8
academies: choice of principals, 194 (*see also* Geniva'), 227–8; status of, 204; terms for, 215–16, 230–1, n. 9; titles of principals, 204; functions, 216, 219; origins, 216–17; principals of, 218–19; as permanent institutions, 219; growth in size, 222, 225; ranks within, 223; financial independence, 226–7; induction of principals, 257–8
Agrippa I, 46, 96; and sects, 121, 130
Ahab, 21, 246
'amora', *see*: rabbis, titles
'Aqiva', 15, 49, 161, 202; school of, 84 n. 16, 84 n. 19, 196, 198, 231 n. 17; and Bar Kokhba' rebellion, 161; and deposition of Rabban Gamli'el, 193, 241
Alexander Yannai, 22, 28 n. 26, 46, 78, 129. policies of, 91–3
'am ha-'arets, 151, 157, 240, 253
anointment: of kings and priests, 11, 252; of prophets, 255
Aristobulus I, 99–100
'asar'am'el, title, 92
'Ashi (*'amora'*), 204, 263 n. 46
'av beit din: office, 127, 163, 193, 199; David as, 83 n. 80
'Avot (tractate), political bias of, 58–62; compared with Ecclesiasticus, 101–2
'Avot de rabi Natan, 17

Bar Kokhba': revolt, 15, 43, 44, 155, 157, 161–3; rabbis and, 44, 161–3; and messianic expectations, 44; title of, 44, 161, 180, 182, 180, 206 n. 4; priests and, 161
bat qol 62, 115 n. 35
batei din: functions of, 47–8, 156, 231 n. 9; and rabbinic appointments, 202–3
Bavel: contribution to scholarship, 80, 150; rivalry with *'Ereṣ Yisra'el*, 152–3; definition, 171 n. 5; Exilarchate in, 180–9, 204–6
beit din shel kohanim, 124
beit Hillel, *see*: Hillel, students of
beit Shamm'ai, *see*: *Shamm'ai*, students of
Ben Sira', *see*: Ecclesiasticus
Bible, political doctrines in, 1, 7–11, 17–18; canonisation, 76; text guarded by priests, 101, 125; *see also*: exegesis

catacombs, 208 n. 23
Caesarea (academy), 219, 233 n. 39
Christianity, 68
covenant, 9–10, 25 n. 5, 31, 66;